Beyond Sugar and Spice

Beyond Sugar and Spice

How Women Grow, Learn, and Thrive

by

Caryl Rivers
Rosalind Barnett
and
Grace Baruch

G. P. Putnam's Sons
New York

The authors gratefully acknowledge permission from the following sources to quote material in the text:

Alfred A. Knopf, Inc., for material from *Menstruation and Menopause: The Physiology and Psychology, The Myth and the Reality* by Paula Weideger, copyright © 1976 by Paula Weideger.

Basic Books, Inc., for material from *The Quality of American Life: Perceptions, Evaluations and Satisfactions* by Angus Campbell et al., © 1976 by The Russell Sage Foundation; and for material from *Worlds of Pain: Life in the Working Class Family* by Lillian Breslow Rubin, © 1976 by Lillian Breslow Rubin.

Beacon Press for material from *Toward a New Psychology of Women* by Jean Baker Miller, copyright © 1976 by Jean Baker Miller.

Sandra Bem for material from "Beyond Androgyny: Some Presumptuous Prescriptions for a Liberated Sexual Identity," in *Beyond Sex-Role Stereotypes*, A. G. Kaplan and J. P. Bean, eds. (Boston: Little, Brown, 1976).

The Boston Globe for an Op-ed piece by Rosemarie Mitchell, which appeared March 16, 1977.

Beverly Fagot for material from "Sex Determined Parental Reinforcing Contingencies in Toddler Children,"

Martin Greenberg for material from "Engrossment: The Newborn's Impact Upon the Father," by Martin Greenberg and Norman Morris, in *American Journal of Orthopsychiatry* 44 (1974) 520–31.

Harper & Row for material from *Memoirs of a Dutiful Daughter* by Simone de Beauvoir, translated by James Kirkup, copyright © 1958 by Librairie Gallimard, translation copyright © 1959 by The World Publishing Company; and for material from "Reflections of a Seventeen-Year-Old" in *Letters Home* by Sylvia Plath, selected and edited by Aurelia Schober Plath, copyright © 1975 by Aurelia Schober Plath.

Hemisphere Publishing Corp. for article by Matina Horner in *Women and Achievement* by T. M. S. Mednick, S. S. Tangri and L. W. Hoffman, copyright 1975 by Hemisphere Books.

Lois W. Hoffman for material from her article "The Effects of Maternal Employment on the Child: A Review of the Research," in *Developmental Psychology* 10 (1974) 204–28.

McGraw-Hill Book Co. for material from articles by Arlie Russell Hochschild, Florence Howe and Adrienne Rich in *Women and the Power to Change* by the Carnegie Commission on Higher Education and Adrienne Rich, © 1975 by McGraw-Hill Book Co.

The Menninger Foundation for material from "The Taboo Against Female Anger," by Harriet Lerner (staff psychologist at the Menninger Foundation) from *Menninger Perspective*, Winter 1977.

William Morrow & Company for material from *Man's World, Woman's Place* by Elizabeth Janeway, copyright © 1971 by Elizabeth Janeway.

Ms. Magazine Corp. for letters from teenage girls © 1974 Ms. Magazine Corp.

Time Inc. for a poem from *Reminiscences* by General of the Army Douglas MacArthur, © 1964 by Time Inc., published by McGraw-Hill Book Co.

Lynn S. Walker, Barbara Strudler Wallston and Howard M. Sandler for material from their paper "Dual Career Couples: Job Seeking Strategies and Marital Satisfaction," George Peabody College, Nashville, TN.

Library of Congress Cataloging in Publication Data

Rivers, Caryl.
    Beyond sugar and spice.

    Includes bibliographical references.
    Index.
    1. Girls. 2. Children—Management. 3. Women—Socialization. I. Baruch, Grace K., joint author.
II. Barnett, Rosalind C., joint author. III. Title.
HQ777.R58   649'.133   79-12516
ISBN 0-399-12164-1

Printed in the United States of America

For Alan, Steven and Alyssa
C.R.

For Jonathan and Amy
R.C.B.

For Franklin and Susannah
G.K.B.

CONTENTS

Preface   9

Chapter One:
   Introduction: Growing Up Competent   15

Chapter Two:
   Fathers and Daughters: Out of the Shadow   28

Chapter Three:
   Fathers and Daughters: The Magic White Knight
   (and Others)   44

Chapter Four:
   Mothers and Daughters: How Will My Life Affect
   My Daughter's?   70

Chapter Five:
   Games: The Playing Fields of Childhood   97

Chapter Six:
   The Sporting Life: The Second Baseperson
   Is Here to Stay   109

Chapter Seven:
   Achievement: Stamping Out Smother Love   132

Chapter Eight:
   Adolescence: To Hear a Different Drummer   152

Chapter Nine:
    Adolescence: Prince Charming Revisited   173
Chapter Ten:
    Sexuality and Conflict   193
Chapter Eleven:
    School Days: The Pedagogical Harem   218
Chapter Twelve:
    Life Choices: The Traditional Role   244
Chapter Thirteen:
    Life Choices: Women at Work   268
Chapter Fourteen:
    Alternate Patterns: Staking Out New Territory   285
Notes   310
Index   325

PREFACE

This book is the joint effort of three women. By training, two of us, Rosalind Barnett and Grace Baruch, are social scientists, and one, Caryl Rivers is a journalist. In our personal lives, we are wives and mothers of daughters (and sons) and deal regularly with the issues raised in these pages. They are not simply academic questions to us!

There is an abundance of theories, research and opinions about how girls grow to be adult women and what kind of women they should be. In its raw form, this material is often inaccessible, contradictory and heavily laden with jargon. It's almost impossible for people to wade through this morass, no matter how concerned they might be. Our special mission was to analyze this material and create a new framework for understanding women's lives. Our goal is to share this information with women and men—mothers, fathers, sons, daughters—who are concerned with living full lives free from constraints inherited from the past and unexamined in the present.

Why us? Because not only are we struggling with these issues in our own lives, but a big part of our jobs has been to keep abreast of the exploding research about women. Grace Baruch, a developmental psychologist, wrote her Ph.D. thesis (while pregnant) on maternal influences on college women's attitudes toward women and work. It won the Susan B. Anthony prize at Bryn Mawr College. Her studies of college women led her to look into the ways girls at even younger ages are influenced by their families, particularly by their mothers. She received a postdoctoral fellowship from the National Institute of Child Health and Human Development to conduct a study of pre- and post-adolescent girls—their feelings about their competence and the relationship of these feelings to their career aspirations, sex-role stereotyping and to their mothers' own values and expectations. This research then led her to plan a study of the origin of these patterns in very young girls, those of preschool age. At this point her work dovetailed with that of Rosalind.

Rosalind Barnett, a clinical psychologist, did her Ph.D. thesis at Harvard University on the career planning of college women, analyzing the factors that contributed to strong career commitments in senior class women. Her work won the award for outstanding research from the American Personnel and Guidance Association.

As research fellow at the Harvard Business School, Rosalind next conducted studies of the career preferences of young people, ages nine to eighteen. She was also interested in how components of managerial behavior—such as the ability to organize and supervise and a talent for leadership—developed in children. To find the best answers, she then decided she would have to start looking at children at a very young age. This interest led to her collaboration with Grace on a study of preschoolers.

Together, Grace and Rosalind obtained a grant from the National Institute of Mental Health to study family and school influences on competence and sex-role attitudes in preschool girls. The three-year study was conducted at the Radcliffe Institute, Harvard University. Many of the findings from this and from their previous studies appear in this book. Their interest in mothers as well as daughters led to their current study of women in the middle and later years, funded by a grant from the National Science Foundation. They have also been exploring the impact of fathers' participation in child care on children's sex-role stereotyping and self-perceptions. In addition to the original research that Grace and Rosalind bring to this book, they have spent a combined total of over twenty-five woman-years working with the literature in these fields.

Caryl Rivers, a former Washington correspondent, developed a strong interest in the impact of society on women's lives, and dealt with some of these issues in her book, *Aphrodite at Mid-Century: Growing up Female and Catholic in Postwar America.* She is a contributor to the syndicated column "One Woman's Voice" and has written widely on such subjects as sex roles, marriage, women at work and other behavioral topics.

10

Among the three of us, we've drawn from current work in the fields of psychology, anthropology, sociology, biology—as well as history and literature. The common thread we followed in our selection and evaluation of material was the notion of competence. We've described this concept in detail in the first chapter. Why competence? We live in a time of accelerating social change, a time in which women's lives will be complex, more challenging than in the past. Equipping girls for this changing society is a big job, a necessary job, but too often a puzzling one—particularly for parents. The purpose of this book is to bring crucial information, not only to parents but to everyone, male and female, who is interested in the question of how girls and women learn, grow and thrive.

We are aware of the argument that the achievement-oriented society in which we live is a "rotten pie" and that no sane woman would want a piece of it. But that's asking women to reject something they've never even tasted. Though our society is seriously flawed and badly in need of humanizing, women belong in the mainstream of adult life.

The three of us consider ourselves feminists. So is this book a political rallying cry, an angry polemic? No. Anger has its uses, but what is needed now is an objective and reasoned analysis of the social mythology about what women ought to be and the realities of what they are. Today, innovative and exciting ideas about this subject come from both men and women. We want to look in new ways at these ideas and at the forces that impinge on women's lives.

In writing this book, we found that our experiences belied the old myth that women are inept team players. Each of us brought individual strengths to this joint effort. The close cooperation and interdependence resulted in a more stimulating venture than what we could have produced working alone. We met constantly for almost two years, generating ideas, reflecting on our own lives as well as on the data (ours and others), often debating until we arrived at a cohesive point of view. Perhaps the most important outcome of this collaboration was generating practical implications and suggestions from an overwhelming mass of material. Grace and Rosalind take final responsibility for the scientific accuracy of the material. Decisions about style, sequence and language are Caryl's province.

Although we shall be warning the reader about the dangers of "expert" advice, we want to mention the fact that we have come up with some practical suggestions growing out of our work. We offer them as a taking-off place for implementing change, hoping that parents, teachers and others who work with children will be creative in drawing out further practical implications from what we have learned about how girls thrive and grow. The particular changes one makes should be the result of adapting ideas to one's life-style and values. In the past, women in particular have been too ready to accept other people's "rules" without evaluating the fit between them and their own values. We think that if parents understand the forces that impinge on girls, and the kinds of experiences girls usually *don't* get that would help in the development of competence, they will be better able to come up with solutions of their own.

We've called our special sections "Nuts and Bolts"; they come at the end of chapters 3, 4, 6, 7, 9, 11 and 12. We've also included chapter notes at the end of the book for readers who want to pursue certain issues. They are not meant to be exhaustive, but rather to offer a starting point.

Beyond Sugar and Spice

1

INTRODUCTION

Growing Up Competent

I discovered something quite shocking about myself. I *want* to be supported. It's not simply a question of having someone else pay the bills. What I want is full time emotional protection, a buffer between me and the world. Over the past two years, events have conspired to bring home a peculiar truth. At base, I do not believe I should have to bear the full responsibility for my life. I want what I was born and bred to want, in Baltimore, in the fifties, which is that someone else should do the hard stuff, not me . . .

—Colette Dowling in "Confessions of a Dependent Woman"

As I walked by myself
And talked to myself
Myself said unto me
Look to thyself
Take care of thyself
　　　　　　Ask none to take care of thee.

　　　　　　　　　　　　—Old English rhyme

The ability to "take care of thyself" as a woman is what this book is all about. The world has never been an easy place for women—the truth is, it isn't an easy place for anyone. In the past women were often raised on a dream of prolonged childhood, a world where they were entitled to be taken care of, supported, wrapped in some kind of emotional swaddling clothes, protected from the chill winds of life. They dreamed of a prince who would come riding by someday, sang of someone to watch over them. And then at some point in their lives, often alone, in some cold corner of their psyche, they had to confront the truth: they would have to rely on themselves to make it through a crisis. Perhaps they were divorced, or widowed, or simply took a job where there was no one to hold their hand and say, "That's all right, dear." Too often they were ill-prepared for that moment of truth.

The mythical kingdom of a childhood that would not end was never more than an illusion. More and more women are coming to understand that a girl today has inherited a world which can be either fearful or challenging, depending upon your point of view. First of all, the female child who is born today can look forward to a life-span of nearly eighty years, according to demographic projections. The years she will spend bearing and raising children—if she chooses to do so—will account for no more than one-fourth of her life. For long periods of her life, she will be part of the labor force. Today, 90 percent of all American women work outside the home at some point in their lives. Over 50 percent of all mothers with school-age children are employed.[1] The most dramatic increase in the proportion of workers entering the labor force has occurred among mothers of preschool children (fully 37 percent in 1975 as compared to 19 percent in 1960). Today's "average" woman, according to demographers, is thirty-two when her youngest child is in school full time. American women are completing more years of education and having fewer children. They are marrying later and spending more of their early years in the work force. These patterns are not likely to change. Economists predict that we will be living with an annual inflation rate of at least 8 percent—a conservative estimate—and the two-income family will probably become the predominant pattern in American life. Today, the "normal" American family—the breadwinner father and the mother at home with children—accounts for only a minority of the population, according to recent surveys. The probability that a woman will be the sole support of herself—and perhaps her children—is increasing. Forty percent of American marriages are predicted to end in divorce. And, since women tend to outlive their husbands, a period of widowhood is highly probable. The American woman today who cannot support herself is either an actual or a potential victim.

Given these facts, which point to the shape of things to come, we believe that now is the time to take a hard look at the way women are socialized. How are they educated and trained to cope with tomorrow, to shoulder the burden of their own lives?

16

In the past, not very well. Colette Dowling, a talented writer, gives a vivid example of this in "Confessions of a Dependent Woman."[2] She awoke one night in a panic.

> What I felt was that I had no place to go, no niche into which I could climb in the hope of living comfortably with myself. I was furious with the man sleeping beside me because he'd grown tired of supporting me and had begun to insist that I do something about it. We had never planned that he support me, but for a number of reasons he'd ended up doing so, and with the surfacing of his discontent, I discovered something quite shocking about myself. I *want* to be supported. It's not simply a question of having someone else pay the bills. What I want is full time emotional protection, a buffer between me and the world. Over the past two years, events have conspired to bring home a peculiar truth. At base, I do not believe I should have to bear the full responsibility for my life. I want what I was born and bred to want, in Baltimore, in the fifties, which is that someone else should do the hard stuff, not me . . . No one had prepared or educated us for it, no one had taught us to manipulate the air currents so that we might stay airborne once we got off the ground.

Sooner or later, women discover that they have to do "the hard stuff." And the hard stuff is a lot easier to face if you are told early on that it is out there waiting for you. The free ride is a myth. The burden of a woman's life will, in the end, rest on her own shoulders. No one will carry it for her—at least not all the way.

Colette Dowling says that she—like most women—was never prepared for this inevitable task. In the jargon of social science, women weren't "socialized" for the job. We intend to look at the process of socialization through the lens of one core concept—that of competence.

What do we mean by competence? Dictionaries tell that to be competent is to be able, fit, adequate, qualified. But for what? The dictionaries don't tell us whether we should be competent at planting a garden, running a corporation, making a quilt, raising children or repairing a car.

This is where the idea of social value comes in. Different societies value different skills. Psychologists Kevin Connolly and Jerome Bruner say, "In any given society, there are a set of skills which are essential for coping with existing realities."[3] So the acquisition of competence involves looking at society and figuring out what skills will enable you to survive—and thrive—in that society.

If you live in a village culture, the ability to plant and grow crops on a small plot is indispensable. On the Upper East Side of Manhattan, it won't keep you in peanut butter and newspapers. In labor-scarce economies, where children are a highly valued resource, the ability to bear and rear a child may be highly valued. The identical ability in an overpopulated, underemployed society such as ours does not have much social value.

Yet, in our society, women have been encouraged to become competent in very limited activities centering around home and family, putting a woman in what might be called a no-win situation. She has become competent in a skill that is socially devalued. (The idea that any idiot can stay home and raise kids is patently untrue, but it comes close to what our achievement-oriented society *really* believes about being a wife and mother.) She is being programmed for planned obsolescence. By the time a woman is forty, her child-rearing skills will be of little use; her children will be grown, and she still has nearly forty years or so to live.

What we are saying, of course, is not that women shouldn't be competent in the areas of home and family, but that their range of skills must be broadened and extended. Women in our society have been educated and socialized away from achievement and independence. They have been told that to move in those directions is to move away from "femininity." We believe that competence is in no way opposed to womanliness. The old definitions of femininity—the clinging vine, the woman who is passive and dependent and needs a man to make her whole—are already passing from the scene.

Women are now moving in large numbers into areas that were once all-male preserves and broadening the base of what are considered "acceptable" skills for women. This is all to the good. Women are diverse creatures, as diverse as men, and are as different from one another in their talents and abilities as are men. To say that nature intended women to master only certain skills, in the limited arena of home and family, is like saying all men ought to be plumbers—or bank presidents or bricklayers. Many women have been kept from developing the full range of their human potential by social pressures which can cripple their own vision of who and what they might be, of how far they ought to venture. Those pressures start early in life and often gain intensity as the girl grows older.

There are deeply rooted social myths about women and their nature, their place in the world and their "appropriate" behavior that are still at

18

work. One of the things we do in this book is identify those forces and how they operate, and examine ways in which they can be countered. In the past decade there has been an explosion of new scientific research— new theories, new studies, new ideas. We want to try to pull as many of those threads together as we can for a broad-ranging look at how women can be socialized for competence.

We don't mean to suggest that all the elements in the socialization of women have been bad. We would give that label only to those which prevent a woman from making the most of her individual potential. We certainly don't mean to suggest that male socialization is wonderful and that if we raised girls just as we raised boys, everything would be fine. It wouldn't. Girls often come out of the growing-up process with invaluable interpersonal skills, concern for others and a capacity for intimacy that is crucial in a time when alienation seems to be a national disease. None of those traits is inconsistent with being competent, or more simply, "being the best you can be."

There are several themes that we want to emphasize right at the start. We urge the reader to share our skepticism toward the "experts" in the whole area of child development. All of us—parents in particular—are terribly vulnerable these days to the pronouncements of "expert opinion." This is partly due to the nature of our urban, rootless, mobile society. In days past, child-raising lore, advice and skills were passed from one generation to another. When a new baby was born, the mother's mother, sisters and assorted relatives were on hand to help out and give on-the-job training. Today, more often than not, new parents find themselves alone with a newborn who seems as alien to them as a small Martian might be. Frantically they dash out to buy the newest child-rearing guide. While those guides may indeed contain some useful information, they may also contain the latest fads and bad science. The fact that their authors have some kind of scientific title after their name can make each pronouncement carry the full weight of the history of science. If your grandmother gave you a piece of advice about child-raising that you regarded as silly, you could write it off because, after all, it's only grandma. It's not so easy to dismiss an equally silly statement from people who have a Ph.D. or an M.D. after their name. Parents ought to be aware that "scientific" child rearing has fads as ephemeral as the Hula-Hoop, and what they are reading in Dr. Somebody's new book is not Eternal Truth, but only what Dr. Somebody thinks today.

A dramatic example of the zigzag of child-rearing theories and advice can be seen in a review of forty years of "authoritative" information on how to bring up your baby from the official pamphlets of the U.S. Children's Bureau.[4] Just after the First World War, parents were told that thumb-sucking and masturbation were harmful and should be stopped, even if parents had to go so far as to bind the child's arms in the crib. By 1942, parents were being told that these practices were harmless, and it would be wrong for them to interfere. Early in the century, mothers were instructed to wean their children late—but severely. By 1942, weaning was supposed to be gradual and gentle. Between 1914 and 1921, the word on toilet training was: do it early and strictly; regular habits are important. By 1942, the virtues of regular habits were forgotten. Parents were told that "late and gentle" was the new motto.

One has to question not only what the experts say, but also look at where they are "coming from." For example, a clinician who spends all day working with "problem" families may not really know a lot about healthy families. With some experts, one finds "the case of illogical deduction." For example, a psychologist who works with families where the children have problems and the mothers are working might conclude that in all families with working mothers, children have problems. This isn't true, but that kind of judgment is often made—not on the basis of data, but of faulty generalizations.

Our society's deification of science and the scientific process can easily blind the layperson to one fact: there is good science and bad science, and particularly where women are concerned, there is plenty of the latter around. A great deal of social myth masquerades as science. A good example is the issue of "maternal deprivation"—which we deal with at some length later in the book. Briefly, this is what happened. In the thirties and forties, studies were done of infants in dismal orphanages, where they had minimal human contact and little sensory stimuli. In these deprived environments children, not surprisingly, showed serious emotional and developmental problems. These studies were cited for years as proof that mothers shouldn't work—despite the fact that the situations in the orphanages had nothing at all to do with loving homes and working mothers.

The parent who relies heavily on the experts is at the end of a yo-yo. Slavish dependency on expert opinion can be dangerous to your health and happiness—as the case of a woman who had an abortion because otherwise her children would not be spaced at the precise time span suggested by one child development expert.

20

Another problem with expert advice is that it often exclusively focuses on the child, with the welfare of the mother given little attention. The mother who feels depressed or isolated because she is alone so much with a young child is often told to go out and buy a new hat, or see a movie, as if her problem were a totally frivolous one. This intense concentration on what is good for the child—and only the child—can make a mother feel constant anxiety and guilt over whether she is being a "good enough" mother for her child. This in turn can lead women to neglect their own lives and needs in a sometimes frantic attempt to be the perfect mother. In the long run, this isn't good for the child. For one thing, it certainly interferes with the ability of a young girl to identify with her mother. Many young women today complain that they don't want their lives to be like their mothers'. "She was always a doormat for everybody else" is the theme that echoes through their comments.

Women who follow the advice of the experts and invest so heavily in their children's lives then face the problem of getting uninvested. Nobody explains how a woman who has spent fifteen years of her life raising the perfect child can suddenly turn off all that emotional investment like a light switch. Human nature doesn't work that way.

Sometimes it seems that mothers can't win. Today, some child development authorities say that "alienation" in young people is caused by the fact that their mothers were not available enough. Twenty years ago, the women who expended all their energies on their children suddenly found themselves attacked as "overprotective" moms. In the fifties, the author Philip Wylie said "momism" was destroying the sons of America. Studies done on American prisoners of war who were brainwashed in Korea suggest that they hadn't resisted because they were sons of overprotective mothers. So the woman who followed the experts' advice when her children were young found herself being attacked by other "experts" when her children got older.

In addition to viewing experts with healthy skepticism, we have another theme we want to stress in this book: the idea of plasticity.

That word may sound a bit formidable, but what it refers to is one of the most important new concepts in psychology, that human nature may not be as fixed and rigid as we once thought. When it was first realized that the early years of life are of tremendous importance, scientific attention focused almost exclusively on that period of life. The idea evolved that what happened in that time was not only crucial, but irrevocable and unchanging, that character and destiny hardened in the very early years, and that significant change did not really occur in later years.

When you read some of today's child-rearing manuals, they are a bit like the sex manuals—they present an awesome amount of technical material that has to be mastered. They give the idea that parenting—like sex—can be turned into an exact science, suggesting that the parents can, in effect, turn the baby into a wonder child by rigid adherence to each detailed instruction in the child's early years.

For example, one authority says in the preface to a 260-page manual, "I will try to explain what you can do during those very important first thirty-six months to *ensure* [italics ours] that your child will develop the full range of social and intellectual skills that now appear to be necessary for good subsequent development."[5]

Do specific techniques really determine the way children turn out? In the 1950s, one group of researchers studied 379 mothers of kindergarteners in two towns near Boston and charted 150 techniques in child rearing[6]: Was the mother permissive or severe in dealing with sex play? Did she control the child by spanking or by withdrawing love? The study gave a detailed picture of varied child-rearing practices. What could not be answered was the question of whether any one of these techniques— as opposed to another—had any ultimate impact on the child's personality.

Recently, another group of scientists returned to look at these children—now in their early thirties—to try to get some answers to that question.[7] A Harvard team wanted to find out, "Did it really matter, years later, whether the mother had breast fed the child, punished it, rejected it or smothered it with love? Were the Freudians right in assuming that, for better or worse, what the parents did in the first five years was crucial?"

The team, David McClelland and his colleagues, interviewed the now-grown children and gave them psychological tests. They found that the techniques used by the parents did not seem to make much difference: "We concluded that most of what people do and think and believe as adults is not determined by specific techniques of child rearing in the first five years . . . we believe that parents should rest assured that what they do is not all that important in how their children turn out. Many other influences in later life serve to shape what adults think and do."

The important thing, these psychologists found, was how the parents felt about their children. When parents loved the children, and the children felt that love, the children seemed to achieve the highest levels of social and moral maturity. The only specific child-rearing practice that seemed to have a real impact was parental rigidity. When parents tolerated no noise, no mess or roughhousing, when the children were to be "seen but not heard," the child was not as likely to become an emotionally sensitive and independent adult.

This understanding of a child's plasticity should lead to the relaxation of the all-too-frequent obsession with the details of raising the very young child. It should also release mothers from the terrible guilt that stems from thinking they are doing something "wrong" in taking care of their own life and needs when a child is young. After all, life is an ongoing process of change. While the early years are very important, they may not be as utterly crucial as we once thought. The human psyche may be less like cement that hardens early than like modeling clay which can continually be shaped by forces around it.

In the past, this whole debate about what parents should or shouldn't do with their children assumed that the child was a *tabula rasa*, an unmarked slate. Today, we know that the infant starts life with its own temperament and personality.

Not only is the young child *not* a blank slate, but the nature of its thinking processes undergoes drastic changes at fairly predictable ages. People used to assume that mental growth was a fairly straight-line process, that children were simply pint-sized versions of the adults they were to be. We know now that the child's cognitive development is more like a three-stage rocket than a ladder; sometimes, great leaps are made.[8] For example, a baby assumes that when something is out of sight, it has ceased to exist. So you won't see any babies searching for the rattle that dropped under the sofa cushion. Soon, the child's brain matures, and she can understand that an object still exists even if it's temporarily out of her vision. This is an enormous leap in cognitive growth which requires no deliberate training by parents.

In a way, the child is not the same person at each "stage" of its development. In cognitive growth, there are orderly, predictable steps, each a platform for an increasingly complex view of oneself and the world. The practical implications of this view of the child are enormous. The four-year-old who thinks boys are dreadful may be the boy-crazy teenager at thirteen—and the accomplished physicist at thirty-five. The mother who sees her four-year-old daughter insisting on frilly pink skirts and turning her nose up at toy trucks doesn't have to think she has produced the superfeminine "Total Woman." As the saying goes—it's only a stage.

We've been talking a lot in this chapter about children, but this book isn't just about the early years in the life of a girl—it's about her entire life. One thing absent from ideas about women is a focus on the long haul. Young men tend to take a serious look at their futures because they have to face the fact of earning a living. Women's goals have been more short term. Often they have concentrated their energies on the immediate future—finding a man to marry, for example. Most young women have not had the faintest notion about what their lives would really be like at forty, at fifty or at sixty. Somehow, they imagined that the choice of a mate would automatically take care of all that. They often felt cheated when it didn't. Women have acted as if the only crucial years of their lives would be the ones in which they were raising children. It did not occur to them to plan for what might happen afterward. Not planning for a lifetime which will span many years often leaves women in the position of floundering in mid-life. Sometimes they wait for some sort of "magical" solution—instead of taking action on their own, they wait for things to happen to them. That passivity can in turn lead to feelings of powerlessness and lack of control. Young girls have to be encouraged to make decisions that will take into account not just the immediate future, but the years far ahead.

From our own experience and studies, we've been impressed by the many different ways women can lead gratifying lives. We are convinced that there are no "right" or "wrong" life patterns for all women. There has been too much acrimony and guilt attached to women's different life-styles. The working mother is told she is damaging her child and abandoning her womanly role. The mother at home is told she is an economic parasite or a dullard. The single woman is pitied because she "can't get a man." All this emotional baggage ought to be thrown overboard. Each woman needs to choose for herself—but the notion of choice is meaningless unless she understands the costs and benefits of different options. Too often a woman's life choices are motivated by factors that are not helpful to the development of competence and self-esteem. If because of social pressure, sex-role stereotypes or peer pressure, she chooses a role that doesn't mesh with her own talents and personality, she will probably spend years trying to wriggle into a life that is simply a bad fit.

24

In the past, because too many women's lives *have* been a bad fit, studies of women have repeatedly shown disturbing patterns: lack of self-esteem, an inability to feel powerful or in control of one's own life, a vulnerability to depression, a tendency to see oneself as less talented, less able than one really is. The myriad of studies that have been done over the years give the distinct impression of constriction, a crippling, a sense of being somehow not quite as good, not quite as able, not quite as bright, not quite as valuable as men. Women seem to see themselves as "The Second Sex," as Simone de Beauvoir put it, second in the sense of being second-class. Certainly there are many women who escaped that blight, who have lived full and happy lives, but when you leaf through the studies you can sense, floating in the air, ghosts of unborn dreams, unrealized hopes, undiscovered talents. The tragedies are the "might have beens," and they are the most poignant.

In this book, we want to focus on the hopes, not the regrets. There is an encouraging new trend in the behavioral sciences today, a critical examination by women of the myths and distortions of the past views of the nature of woman. Many of the classic theories of female development were created by men, who accepted the male as the norm and looked at the female as some mysterious "other." Sigmund Freud, for example, began his speculations about the female psyche after observations of hysterics in his clinic—not exactly the optimum situation for gaining an understanding of the dynamics of the healthy female. Psychoanalysis had its origins in the nineteenth century, and it is no accident that the model of woman that emerged was similar to the ideal of the upper-class bourgeois woman of that era—passive, dependent, sexually inhibited, rather childlike, content in her doll's house. But that sort of woman was hardly typical of women throughout history or women in other cultures. Throughout most of history, women have been economic providers, engaged in vital and often strenuous work, not allowed the luxury of passivity and usually vitally involved in the life and commerce of society. In some cultures women are aggressive and independent, in others more docile and dependent. The market women of Kenya[9] probably wouldn't have the faintest notion of what the characters in Ibsen's play A *Doll's House* were talking about.

A major problem with theory about feminine development is that theory turns into iron law—which one shouldn't expect in a scientific field. Psychologist Naomi Weisstein[10] points out that many of her colleagues are too ready to accept "theory without evidence." She notes

25

about psychological literature, "It is immediately obvious that the bulk of it is written by clinicians and psychiatrists whose major support for their theories is 'years of intensive clinical experience.'"

This is a perfectly valid way to come up with theories; as Weisstein points out, "a person is free to make up theories with any inspiration that works: divine revelation, intensive clinical practice, a random numbers table. However, he is not free to claim any validity for his theory until it has been tested and confirmed."

Sigmund Freud never said he *knew* about feminine development. He once said that he did not know whether what he saw in woman was innate or a product of culture. But his theories—and he never claimed they were more than that—were turned, in later years, into something approaching Sacred Writ. In addition, the complex and sometimes contradictory body of his work was reduced to rather simpleminded dicta in the popular media, such as, "A woman can't be happy unless she's married," or "A woman's place is in the home." Freud himself, an innovative thinker who challenged many of society's conventional notions, would probably have been dismayed to see how his hypotheses were rigidified into law by the people who came after him.

We don't present any Sacred Writ here: we have no magic formulas, no step-by-step guide to raising daughters. What we do have is information and ideas about some of the forces that act upon girls and young women in this society, what the results of those forces can be and some ideas for change.

It is an exciting time to be a woman, there is no doubt about that. Woman's new freedom can be intoxicating. On the other hand, an unsung Chinese sage expressed well the uncertainties of life in a period of transition: For the Chinese, the phrase, "May you live in interesting times," is a curse.

These are "interesting times," especially for parents of female children. The changes seem dizzying. Little more than a decade ago, the word "sexist" didn't exist, girls enrolled in secretarial school instead of courses in karate, the Pig family had not yet been blessed with the arrival of a new species (Male Chauvinist) and there was no such thing as a pig-tailed moppet in Little League called a second baseperson.

Those of us who have daughters are aware of the fact that the world they will inherit will be different from ours, and that awareness can produce more than a dash of anxiety. Those of us who are anxious for our daughters to escape the stereotypes of the past grit our teeth when our

26

daughters dote on Ballerina Barbie, love long dresses and would rather play house than shortstop. Those of us who have known satisfaction in the role of caring for a home and family wonder if our daughters are going to be pushed blindly out into a harsh, competitive world which has little time for nurture.

There is no way, it seems, to avoid the uncertainties and the conflict of interesting times, and pretending they don't exist won't help. What can help is an understanding of the realities of the society we live in, and the ways in which parents, teachers, husbands and social institutions can promote the development of feminine competence. Women themselves, at all stages of life, can learn to:

> Look to thyself
> Take care of thyself
> Ask none to take care of thee.

2

FATHERS AND DAUGHTERS
Out of the Shadow

> If such an aggressive and inflexible creature as the Rhesus monkey
> male is capable of such positive interaction with infants, there is reason
> to suspect at least comparable potential in less sexually dimorphous,
> relatively monogamous, more flexible creatures such as Homo sapiens.
> —Biologist William Redican

For too many years now, the father has been the Lamont Cranston of
the American Family. (Fans of the old radio show may remember
Cranston as the alter ego of The Shadow, who had the ability to make
himself invisible whenever he chose.)

In the post-Freudian era, the tendency of "Dad" to fade away into a
peripheral figure in family dynamics has been pronounced. If the
ancient images of Fatherhood—stern lawmaker, source of authority and
wisdom—had more to do with power than with tenderness, the new ones
make the male parent even more remote from his children. Social
scientists, looking at the obvious physical involvement between mother
and child, have until recently assumed that relationship to be the only
one fraught with significance and have pored over it exhaustively. Like
gilded madonnas of medieval art, the psychological case study of mother
and child has only two characters; the father does not appear.

The father's invisibility has had important consequences for his
daughter, for his wife and not least of all, for himself. Often when he is
needed most he has just "faded away." Unsure of how he can help his

daughter thrive and grow, feeling inept around babies and children, he often unwillingly retreats to a safe distance. His retreat is a sad and unnecessary withdrawal. His daughter senses his aloofness, keenly, but his son may also suffer from it. For many men, the first step may be to realize that men can be parents in the true sense, they can care for and nurture their children from infancy on. This first step may be the big one. The old stereotypes about the father have roots that go very deep.

The central fact about the father in the family as we have come to understand it is that he is not there much. Mother is all-nurturing, feeding, protecting, loving. The father is supposed to be The Breadwinner, marching out to do battle each day with the world to make existence possible for his wife and children. Even in this, his expression of love, he is The Shadow, because his work is unseen and mysterious to his family. The more bread he wins, the more approval he gains. Until fairly recently, the workaholic who spent his weekends at the office was not considered an inadequate father; quite the contrary, he was a "good provider." In fact, the eminent pediatrician T. Berry Brazelton[1] once argued that a man's work life should not be seen as competitive with his family life but as "the very core of his position in the family."

His absence should be regarded, Brazelton said, as a sign of love for his family and should be described as such to the children. Children will feel cheated by the shortness of their time with their fathers "only if the mother feels sorry for the child because daddy comes home late."

Somehow this image has been fixed in our heads as Eternal Truth—Beatific Mom at home tending to all the children's needs and Daddy venturing forth. We are so used to it that we assume it has been thus since Adam and Eve were booted out of Eden. But the family structure that we seem to think of as "natural" is in fact not very old. The concept of "home" as the dwelling place of the single family dates back to the eighteenth century and the rise of the cities and the middle class. Before that time, the "home" was a large conglomeration of people, often part factory, part workshop, part subsistence farm. In many cases, the care of children was shared by several women, and "women's work" included working on the farm or managing the laborers and apprentices who lived in the house that was also a shop. The work of men as well as that of women was familiar to children because it was done in close proximity to them.

Elizabeth Janeway notes in *Man's World, Woman's Place*[2] that the eighteenth century saw the rise of a new style of architecture, of the house that had small, separate rooms designed for privacy rather than the open living areas of older buildings. "Until quite recently," Janeway says, "when women were at home, men were too, and both sexes were working there. Home, then, was a workshop for artisans, apprentices, journeymen and many wives; or a trading center, or both; or it was a minimal shelter for farm labor or a Great House which was both a center of economic activity and of general sociability that extended far beyond the family."

The world of the child in those years included many adults, male and female; it was not the cocoon of mother and child that we assume to be universal. If it comes as a jolt to think that our idea of the "natural" family is scarcely older than our own "young" country, it will probably be even more unsettling to think about the idea that the special and mystic mother-child bond may also be a myth—one that has very neatly fit the economic and cultural status quo.

The behavioral scientists have also been victims of the myth. In their concentration on mother and child, they were not only assuming the existence of a special relationship, but also assuming the *absence* of any comparable relationship between father and child. Arguments have been made that a minor role for fathers is in fact anchored in biology, and that the ties of paternity are very fragile compared to that mother-child silver cord. Biologist Robert L. Trivers[3] suggests that if the evolutionary survival of the species dictates having the maximum number of offspring, nature's best plan would be for the male to have more than one sexual partner and remain relatively uninvolved in child care—leaving him free to beget more children. Psychologist David Gutmann[4] has argued that male concern for children is very fragile and that men only direct their violent aggression away from children in a social structure where they are the economic providers and feel themselves to be the dominant sex. Popular anthropological studies such as *The Imperial Animal*[5] by Lionel Tiger and Robin Fox picture males as hunters who tolerate their offspring because of the sexual bond with the mother. The general argument goes like this: Males are not biologically programmed to have much to do with offspring, unlike females, whose biological mechanisms are all geared to their young. Studies of primates are often used to illustrate the "fact" of the mother-infant bond and the father's detachment.

The problem with this is that you cannot make a simple one-to-one correlation between monkeys and people. And, of course, there are primates and primates—they are not all the same. The results of a study will depend on which species you look at and for how long. In the past, primate studies were flawed because they jumped to conclusions about behavior after looking at too few animals for too short a period of time.[6]

But primates are our ancestors, and carefully done studies can shed some light on the behavior of this biological group to which Homo sapiens belongs. A good example is the new research on primates that is calling into question many of the old assumptions about fathering behavior in the primate world. These studies also support an idea that is one of the themes of this book: "plasticity"—the notion that behavior, in humans and in their fellow primates, is less rigid than we have supposed it to be in the past.

Most primate studies have been done with animals that were readily accessible—easy to find and often observed in captivity. These were the rhesus monkeys, baboons and chimpanzees, which also happen to be species in which the male is relatively uninvolved with the young. These studies have given us a skewed picture of the way things really are in the primate world. In a wide-ranging survey of primate behavior, William K. Redican,[7] of the Department of Psychobiology and Physiology at Stanford University, found the same tendency among scientists studying animals as among the ones studying people—a focus on the mother. Paternal behavior, he says, is much harder to observe and record, but that behavior does exist, in varying degrees and styles throughout the primate world, a world which is more diverse than we once believed.

Some primates live in "family" situations not unlike our own. Male marmosets, for example, live in monogamous family units, assist during the birth of infants and chew up food for the infants to eat. They carry the infants throughout the day, except for periods when the infant is returned to the mother to nurse. Siaming ape infants are dependent on their mothers for the first twelve months of life, but from then on they are carried by their fathers until they are old enough to survive on their own. Siaming mothers groom and sleep with babies, while the fathers groom and sleep with the "juveniles." In Nairobi National Park, male adult baboons have on occasion "adopted" infants. The second-ranking male baboon in one troop was seen constantly with a year-old infant whose mother had died. A male macaque was observed patiently teaching an infant to walk, chattering encouragement to the baby.

In *Father Power*,[8] Dennis Meredith and Henry Biller report a dramatic instance of "fathering behavior": Adrian Deschryver, a game warden in

31

Zaire National Park, had spent four years studying the mountain gorilla. The warden, having gained the trust of the gorilla families, could crouch within a few yards of them to observe their behavior. His main focus was on a family headed by a 450-pound gorilla he called Kasimir, who, like the others, was a peaceable, shy creature.

One day the warden decided to carry an orphan baby gorilla he had been caring for into the forest to prepare it for the day it would be set free. As they neared the area where Kasimir's family lived, the baby began to cry.

Suddenly, "peaceable" Kasimir came charging out of the bush, "his huge white teeth parted in a raging snarl as he charged Deschryver. Thinking himself a dead man, Deschryver dropped the squalling infant and backed away. Stopping but a few feet from the game warden and still at the peak of his rage, the towering gorilla reached down, gently scooped up the baby gorilla and withdrew back into the bush, covering his retreat with terrifying roars. The scene is perhaps the most vivid example of the fathering instinct in animals ever observed."

Not only does the capacity for fathering exist in primates, but it has been observed in species where it was thought not to exist at all. Male rhesus monkeys, for example, are generally indifferent to infants, rarely approach the young, and when infants approach them, their general attitude is to back off or to swat the offender. In certain situations, however, they display a very different sort of behavior. William Redican took rhesus monkeys and put them in cages in pairs—some mother-infant pairs and some pairs of adult males and infants. In this situation, the adult males were not indifferent to the young. In fact, the behavior of the adult males with the infants was not so different from the females' behavior. Adult males were observed to groom the infant as much as the mothers did. Mothers had more physical contact, but the males played more with the infants. Both mothers and adult males were powerful attachment figures for the infants. These studies showed that the adult males had a significant potential for fathering behavior, but whether or not it surfaced depended on the opportunities offered to the individual monkey. In the absence of the mother, who would preempt the male from many caretaking functions, the male rhesus monkey was a father to the infant in a way rarely seen in the wild. Redican concludes: "If such an aggressive and inflexible creature as the Rhesus monkey male is capable of such positive interaction with infants, there is reason to suspect at least comparable potential in less sexually dimorphous, relatively monogamous, more flexible creatures such as Homo sapiens."

The studies with the rhesus monkeys certainly suggest that fathering behavior, like mothering behavior, is an innate capacity in primates, but one that is not always used. The male has to be given the opportunity to interact with the infant before that capacity shows up. The situation may not be so different with humans.

Human males in different cultures display a wide range of fathering behavior—from remoteness to intimate involvement. Harvard anthropologists Mary Maxwell West and Melvin J. Konner found this great variety in a study of the role of the father in a "cross-cultural" perspective.[9] Among the Bushmen of Northern Botswana, children are indulged and pampered. The women collect and grow 60 percent of the food, the men hunt for the rest. Each sex works about half the week, allowing a great deal of leisure time. The families are generally monogamous, and while mothers provide routine care for the infants, the fathers hold and fondle even the youngest babies. Young children often approach them, ask for food or ask questions and are never rebuffed. Preparation for fighting does not occupy the men and boys at all; wars are rare, and learning to fight is not considered an important skill for boys.

In contrast, the Rwala Bedouin of the north Arabian desert live in a society of herders where the men are warriors and the women work hard at domestic chores. In this strongly patriarchal society, with strong emphasis on male authority, cultivation of fierceness for boys is important for the frequent warfare with other groups. The father is distant from the young child; the child lives with its mother in the women's tent, approaching the father only for an occasional talk or for punishment. Older boys are punished for disobedience "with a sabre or dagger."

Halfway across the world, in Lesu Village in New Ireland, Melanesia, the population survives by fishing and small-scale gardening. The men fish, the women tend the plants—both important chores—and the household is usually a monogamous, nuclear family. The husband frequently cares for the baby while the wife is cooking or gardening. He will often sit in front of his house fondling and petting the infant. The men will often sit and talk "baby talk" to the infant, and when there are groups of men sitting together on the sand, they may pass an infant around, playing, fondling or crooning a dance song to the infant. Warfare is almost nonexistent; fighting between villages has occurred in the past, but on a small scale.

Among the Thonga, a tribal people on the east coast of South Africa,

33

the women grow grain and vegetables and the men herd animals. The society is polygamous and patriarchal and the men do not relate to infants or young children. Though the men have a substantial amount of leisure, strong taboos prevent them from any contact with infants under three months. The father demands absolute obedience from his children, and he is the one who thrashes and punishes them. The tribe has an army numbering about two thousand and an elaborate structure of war costumes and weapons.

These and other examples of human cultures illustrate that there is no one "natural" way for fathers to behave. In their survey of the role of the father in eighty societies, West and Konner try to sort out those conditions in which close relations between fathers and children can occur. This relationship seems to be closer in gathering than in hunting societies. Popular anthropological studies make much of man the hunter, and trace many elements of "male" behavior back to hunting instincts. In fact, throughout most of human history, most human groups have been gatherers.

Another factor is marital structure. The father-child relationship is closer in societies where polygamy is not practiced. In cultures where men have a number of wives, the male spends much of his time accumulating the resources to maintain the wives. There is a strong association between aggression and polygamy. But is the aggressive male the "natural" male? West and Konner say that the greater physical strength and higher metabolic rate of the male "can be used for aggressive purposes when necessary, but this does not mean that they evolved for that purpose, nor does it dictate aggression as part of the future." They say that most of human evolution was probably characterized by a fairly high amount of paternal behavior and a low amount of aggression and violence. The fierce, male-dominated Bedouin are less typical of human society than the gentler Bushmen and islanders.

Women's contribution to society can also have an effect on the father-child relationship. West and Konner's survey makes the crucial point that where women's work other than child care is considered essential and important, male investment in parenting increases. It is interesting to note that in cultures where men are closely involved with young children, there is little warfare. In societies where warfare is important, fathers tend to be distant. And, in societies where war is an important occupation for men, women's role is generally not considered to be of high importance.

So paternal involvement, West and Konner show us, is plastic; it is not

34

a fixed and unwavering biological reality but can vary when cultures and conditions vary. "There is no evidence that fathers cannot be very nurturant and fully adequate caretakers, but whether they will do so depends on sociological conditions—conditions that in modern cultures are largely economic."

The highest degree of male parental investment can be expected when relationships are monogamous, when local warfare is absent, when the division of labor allows fathers access to their children and when women's contributions are important. In our culture, the last two items pose a problem. West and Konner point out that the American middle-class mother and her child are extremely isolated compared to other cultures, and the work she does at home is "frivolous"—it is not essential for subsistence. Despite Mother's Day editorials and "Mom of the Year" contests, the woman at home has a low status in our society; very little of what she does is seen as essential for survival. The division of labor which requires males to be away from home so much means that women assume the total burden of child care. It is unclear, say West and Konner, whether the economic conditions that would make possible the maximum amount of parental investment by fathers will develop in our Western society. "Short of this, there is still an opportunity for close relationships between father and child that is as great or greater than in any other type of previous subsistence [society] and that can be increased, depending on the situation of individual families."

The idea of the role of the father as plastic—and as of critical importance to the young child—is a new one. Because of the assumption that mother and child formed a special, hermetically sealed unit, the data on fathering tend to be conspicuous by their absence. Studies done in World War II on children without parents are referred to as studies of "maternal deprivation" even though the father was also absent. He hardly seemed worth mentioning. Studies of father absence done in the United States during the war focused mainly on what that absence meant to boys.[10] Researchers assumed that the major impact of an absent father would be on his son, not his daughter. It is interesting to note that the researchers did not look at the development of girls' skills. The major concern about father absence as far as girls were concerned was its effect on her sex-role development and her ability to form a heterosexual relationship in later life. The very choice of what was studied speaks of society's values. It is important for a boy to develop skills; what matters for a girl is her ability to marry successfully.

In the 1950s and 1960s studies of fathers were few and far between.

While the behavioral sciences exploded—at times it seemed we were obsessed with examining everything about the way we live, die, eat, dress, make love, go to school and marry—fathers stayed back there in the shadows.

Today, those old assumptions that consigned father to the psychological dustbin are being challenged. Is there, in fact, a special relationship between father and infant that is as important in its own way as the one between mother and child? The newest research suggests there is. Much of this new research[11] is being done by young men—men who have experienced the upheavals of the last decade that have altered so many of the ways we used to look at things, particularly at the situation of women and the traditional male role.

Michael Lamb of Yale is one of these young psychologists. He edited a recent comprehensive collection of new research on the role of the father in child development.[12] He believes that by focusing so intently on the mother and overlooking the father, "we may have ignored a relationship which is of great consequence."

In his own research, Lamb decided to look at the "attachment behaviors" of infants to find out more about that relationship. Attachment behaviors are the ways in which infants demonstrate they have a special relationship with someone; they coo, smile, touch and show great distress when the object of their affection disappears. Lamb notes that according to previous theories of attachment, infants should be forming their first and primary attachment with the mother when they are between seven and eight months old. The preference for the mother at this stage should be clearly evident, if this theory were to hold true, and "attachments to fathers, if they existed at all, should be vastly inferior in quality."

Lamb designed his study so that infants would be visited in their homes, not seen in laboratories, allowing him to observe behavior that was typical of the infant. Attachment behaviors—smiling, reaching, touching—were recorded and measured. Lamb found that the infants showed no preference for the mother over the father. In fact, they showed a definite preference for the fathers when it came to playing. The fathers, Lamb found, indulged in more physically stimulating and unpredictable games. "What this suggests," he says, "is that neither mothers or fathers are superior attachment figures in this situation but that fathers are just more fun." One reason could be that the mother is usually the prime caretaker, and the father in his time with the infant may be fresher and consequently more playful.

Lamb became convinced that behavioral scientists had been wrong in overlooking the father. He is convinced that the father *is* important—the question is, in what ways? He thinks that play between father and infant may be a special component of that relationship and may help determine the attitude with which that child will approach the world. He is also convinced that further research on fathering will "substantiate my belief that the infant's social world is far more complex and multidimensional than we are accustomed to portraying it."

Another scientist who is questioning the "unique" mother-child bond is psychologist Milton Kotelchuck[13] of the University of Massachusetts. He asks, "What hard evidence is there to support the notion that children relate uniquely to their mothers? Here, psychologists have a definitive answer. There is *no* hard evidence whatsoever."

To assess the father-infant relationship is not a difficult task, Kotelchuck argues. "It merely requires that one ignore the cultural assumptions of the father's unimportance and bring him into an experimental situation and watch his behavior."

In his experiments, Kotelchuck brought infants into an unfamiliar playroom and observed the infant's reactions to its mother, its father and a stranger. In the past, studies had not included fathers, and the infants had shown attachments only to their mothers. "These results very logically, but incorrectly, led to the conclusion that children have a special relationship to their mothers," Kotelchuck observes. As so often happens, no one thought of asking Dad to join the party. He was assumed to be unimportant.

Kotelchuck found that the infants he studied interacted with both mother and father, and not with the stranger. The infants showed equal dismay when either parent left the room.

Most of the families Kotelchuck studied were middle class, and the mother was the primary caretaker; 75 percent of the fathers did not physically care for their infants from day to day. Kotelchuck found, as did Lamb, that fathers spent a greater percentage of time in play behavior than did the mothers.

The infants displayed a clear attachment to their fathers, despite the fact that the fathers were rarely available on the same full-time basis that the mothers were. Kotelchuck concluded that "the crude amount of caretaking or playing is not the critical variable in determining whom the child is comfortable with or to whom the child relates."

There is, however, a link between the amount of care a father gives his infant and the infant's attachment to him. Kotelchuck found that apparently a minimum level of "fathering" has to take place before the child can relate. The few children in his studies who did not relate to their fathers came from families where the father's involvement in caretaking was in the lowest ranking of the group. Fathers who are distant from their infants do not form a bond with them. When the study that Kotelchuck concluded in this country was duplicated in Guatemala, where fathers have almost nothing to do with young children, the infants related more strongly to their mothers. These cross-cultural comparisons[14] indicate that something other than unalterable biology was at work. Kotelchuck concludes unequivocally, "Children do not innately and instinctively relate to their mothers. The presumed uniqueness of the mother-child relationship is ephemeral."

The Kotelchuck studies indicate how important it is for the father to be involved in the care of the infant. Just how much involvement is enough, we do not know exactly, but we do know that fathers spend little time with their young children. Studies show that the average time a father is directly involved with his kids ranges from less than a minute to slightly more than an hour each day. Kotelchuck suspects that there are benefits to the child when both parents are actively involved with caretaking. He found that children with two parents who took care of them tended to find the experiment an enjoyable play session and not a period of distress, even when left alone with strangers.

One of the factors that has kept fathers out of the picture where infants are concerned has been the mystification of motherhood. The mother is seen as a possessor of magical biological powers, a creature with "inner space" too arcane for a mere male to understand, forming a mystic bond with her baby that has been enshrined in a million saccharine Mother's Day cards. But what of the mechanisms in the father that link him to his newborn? There is no umbilical cord to give witness to the connection. Does the connection exist? Or is he simply the onlooker, whose job is to give aid and comfort to his wife? In his classic 1940s text, *Maternal Care and Mental Health*, the British psychiatrist John Bowlby wrote, "Fathers have their uses in infancy. Not only do they provide for their wives and enable them to devote themselves unrestrictedly to the care of the infant and toddler, but by providing love and companionship, they support her emotionally and help maintain that harmonious, contented mood in the aura of which the infant thrives."

That scenario gives the father a minor supporting part in the drama of having a baby. He is passive, and his relation to the infant is seen as indirect at best, crucial to the child only through the mother. But there is evidence today of a direct and powerful relationship between father and child that occurs at birth and may have a strong biological component. Physicians Martin Greenberg at the Langly Porter Neuro-psychiatric Institute in San Francisco and Norman Norris of Charing Cross Hospital in London, in a 1975 study, report a phenomenon they called "engrossment"—the newborn's impact on the father.[15]

When they started their work, the two physicians found a scarcity of research on fathers and newborns. They looked at animal studies, which showed that newborns have a strong impact on males of many species, and found evidence of male caretaking of infants throughout the vertebrate world. In looking at cross-cultural studies, they found that primitive cultures often stressed the father's role in childbirth, sometimes requiring that the father remain in bed during the birth and mimic the motions of birth with his own body. They found that "In many primitive cultures men hold and caress infants and show considerable interest in and enjoyment of babies."

Greenberg and Norris studied fathers at three London hospitals and observed the powerful impact their babies had on them. "Their attraction to the newborn is very powerful, and it appears to be something over which they have no control. They do not will it to happen; it just does."

Fathers caught up in the engrossment phenomenon often described the strength of the infant's effect on them as if it were a magnet from which they could not pull away. They felt extreme emotion, often described as a "high," and took a special visual and tactile delight in their babies. The fathers described it in their own words:

> "I just took a look at it and I took a look at the face and I left the ground. I thought, 'Oh Jesus Christ, this is marvelous!'"

> "When I come up to see my wife I say, 'Hi. How's things? Everything all right? You need anything?' And then I go and look at the kid and then I pick her up and then I put her down and I say [to my wife] 'Everything all right'? and then go back to the kid. I keep going back to that kid. It's like a magnet. That's what I can't get over, the fact that I feel like that."

> "I feel great, just great! Can't stop picking her up. It's really a strong feeling of pleasure. She wriggles in your hands, she wriggles when she's against your chest and in your arms."

"I thought it was going to be a boy and everything was going to be great, we could go out and jump around together. I was thinking about eighteen months, two years, that's when we'd start to have a relationship. I thought for the first eighteen months it would just be the wife and everything would be fine for her and I'd just take it easy. But it wasn't like that at all. It was completely different. The kid was born—and I was there—and I really did have a strong feeling towards her."

"He was sleeping peacefully and his eyes were closed and as I looked over he opened his eyes and I moved away and he closed them and I moved back again and he opened them. Now, I don't know what that is, some kind of telepathy or something, but I think he knew I was standing over him and opened his eyes. It felt wonderful!"

Greenberg and Norris conclude that fathers begin by developing a bond to their newborn by the first three days of its life. The "engrossment" is not only a fascination with the newborn, but a heightened sense of self-esteem on the part of the father. The sensation is a powerful one. "It is as if he had been 'hooked' by something that has transpired in the father-infant relationship."

This engrossment—getting "hooked"—that occurs after birth may be a strong factor in the developing relationship between father and child. But, as Greenberg and Norris note, certain factors in American culture—and traditional hospital practices—may interfere with this process.

Some men think it is unmanly to express tender feelings towards small babies. They may feel the baby is just for the wife, a notion mentioned by one of the fathers in this study. Hospital procedures may also be important in hindering or enhancing the father's engrossment in its newborn. Frequently, after the baby is born it is given to its mother and then returned to the nursery without the father having an opportunity to hold it. As a non-medical person he may be afraid to assert himself, thinking that the staff have medical reasons for not inviting him to hold the baby. It is our impression that the infant should be offered to the father as well as to the mother.

The phenomenon of engrossment needs more study. What is the time interval during which it can develop? What is its significance for later years? Greenberg and Norris say that a father who is engrossed in his newborn is likely to maintain his contact with the developing child. And, they suggest, since the father who is enraptured by his child has a heightened sense of self-worth, the fathering experience could be a powerful source of feelings of success in a society that too often measures a man's success by his financial worth.

Even if the father is engrossed in his newborn, even if he has just as much potential as his wife to become a tender caretaker of his infant, what encouragement is there for him to do so? He probably feels awkward in the nursery, all thumbs with a diaper pin, terrified that he will drop the baby or do something wrong. He probably assumes that his wife, guided by some unswerving maternal instinct, glides into these tasks with ease. He probably doesn't know that she is as panicky as he is. If she is a typical American woman having her first baby, she probably came from a family with few siblings and has little experience with child care. She is more familiar with a textbook or an IBM typewriter than she is with a baby. She, too, stabs herself with the diaper pin, prays she won't drown the baby when she gives it a bath and anxiously leafs through Dr. Spock when the baby won't stop screeching. The job of mothering is learned behavior. Instinct has nothing to do with getting the Pampers on right. The mother learns on the job because she has to.

The father may need encouragement not to defer to her "superior" ability. Like the rhesus monkey, his fathering abilities may not surface if the mother is there to answer every need, do every job. After Boston psychologist Robert Fein studied fathers and their newborns,[16] he suggested that fathers needed a "mentor" to help them feel comfortable in the tasks of fathering. A woman often has the help of relatives or friends, and she has society's approval—insistence, in fact—that she get on with the job. The wife can often be the mentor to her husband in child care, stepping aside to give him opportunities, encouraging and supporting his efforts. One woman, for example, knowing her husband's ability with anything mechanical, suggested to her husband that he think of the baby as a little machine. If he could handle complicated machines with lots of moving parts, a baby would be a snap. Sometimes a father just has to be given time and space to manage on his own with the baby without the mother constantly hovering. That will mean that women will have to give up some of the territory that was once all theirs, to share that "special" relationship. That may be difficult, especially to women who have prepared to invest their whole lives in the baby. Greenberg and Norris noted that a wife often felt threatened by her husband's involvement with the baby, an area she had considered her own "staked-out territory." The wife who puts up this kind of wall around herself and her child may be keeping her husband from learning how to care for his child, an experience that can be rewarding both for him and the child. She needn't worry that the child will somehow love her less or that she will be less of a mother. Even in day-care centers, where children have multiple caretakers, the child's attachment to the mother is in no way diminished. A child's love is more like an underground spring than a keg of beer that runs dry after it is tapped. The more people a child learns to love, the greater will be his or her capacity to love.

The father may need his wife's permission to get involved. The father who doesn't get this permission may react by withdrawing. One man told Robert Fein:

> "I feel in a bind. When I was little my father never really took care of me. He was the breadwinner and, I guess, demanded respect more than he gave affection. But now the norms seem to have changed. Men are expected to take care of children. I feel like I want to care for our baby and I feel that I ought to care for the child, but frankly, I don't really know how. I'm afraid that I won't be a good father."

How often is the father's retreat from the baby a result of this fear? Without encouragement, he may retreat not because he wants to, but because he sees no other options.

If fathers too often receive little encouragement at home for interacting with their infants, they generally receive even less at work. One Air Force captain told Robert Fein that he asked his commanding officer for paternity leave. "Captain," he was told, "why don't you come back for that when *you* can have a baby?" Society still operates as if the world is composed of men who are always free to be at work and women who are at home with the children. But attitudes are changing, if slowly. More men are beginning to feel it is legitimate to rearrange work schedules to meet their children's needs, nor is a man considered unmanly to want to be with his infant child. Robert Fein found in his studies that while women are thinking about their life-styles, men are, too. He found that "a wide range of feelings and forms are available to men. Beyond the biological realities that only men can impregnate and only women can be pregnant lie possibilities for androgynous experience, areas where men and women need not be restricted by the arbitrary limitations imposed by traditional sex roles."

Fathers can play a crucial role in dismantling those "arbitrary" limits by getting involved early with their daughters. In a study Grace and Rosalind did with preschool girls, they found that the more a father took over child-care tasks, the less stereotyped were his daughter's views of men and women. It seems that when a father takes on some of the responsibility of his child's care, not just "helping mom," his daughter sees men as more caring and less aggressive. She also sees women as more independent, more capable of being "in charge."

These girls, with their father's help, are seeing a world in which boys and girls aren't cast early on in molds marked "his" and "hers." "Perhaps," says Robert Fein, "we are moving towards that androgynous world, a place where women are free to love and to work, and men are free to work and to love."

3

FATHERS AND DAUGHTERS

The Magic White Knight (and Others)

> He was the one great love of my life as a child, and in fact, like many children I have lived a dream life with him. So his memory is still a vivid, living thing to me.
> —Eleanor Roosevelt, writing of her father forty years after his death

Let me mention some of the general things that a father may spend time doing on a one-to-one basis with a middle-childhood boy. First, he can take him along when he needs to buy something at a hardware store or nursery or sporting goods store. He can invite him for a walk to the library or to an ice cream or a grocery store. He can teach him some of the basic skills such as catching or throwing a football or baseball, batting, or shooting a basketball. He can take him to spectator sports such as baseball, football, soccer, basketball or hockey games. He can take him hiking, camping or fishing. . . .

With a middle-childhood girl, you can take her to lunch, which will be a special treat and a valued experience.

—Fitzhugh Dodson, *How to Father*

When a father hears the words, "It's a girl!" he may be delighted, but also puzzled. What, he may wonder, does one *do* with a girl? With a boy, things seem much more clear-cut.

A girl child can be a bit worrisome for a new father. Used to working—and often playing—mainly with men, he can be unsure of how he will act with a daughter. With a boy, he knows, he can get involved in sports and introduce his son to the world of men. He knows about men. They are direct, straightforward, easy to comprehend. Women, he may think, are different creatures. He has been told it's impossible for a man to understand them.

Now he is the father of a girl. How does a man behave with a daughter? He wonders. He is probably unsure, but thinks that whatever he does, it will be something different from what he would do with a boy. His baby daughter even looks different to him. She seems so tiny, so delicate, so vulnerable. He has already begun to think of her as a *girl*, and if so, he is probably typical of most parents. When they look at their newborns, parents often see not just a healthy baby, but a *boy* baby or a *girl* baby. They bring to their view of a newborn child a whole universe of cultural stereotypes. Fathers may easily draw conclusions about their newborn children based on all the ideas they have inherited from the culture about women.

Three researchers at Tufts University, Jeffrey Rubin, Frank J. Provenzano and Zella Luria, set up a study in 1974 to examine parents' sex-role stereotyping of newborns.[1] "If it can be demonstrated," they said, "that parental sex typing has already begun its course at the earliest moment in the life of the child, it may be possible to understand better one of the important antecedents of the complex process by which the growing child comes to view itself as boy-ish or girl-ish." In previous studies,[2] fathers were found to have different expectations for daughters than for sons. Daughters were expected to be pretty, sweet, fragile and delicate, while sons were expected to be aggressive and athletic. One study found that fathers of infant daughters showed more behavior labeled as apprehension over the well-being of their babies than did fathers of sons. Mothers of kindergarten children were more tolerant of aggression from boys than from girls. In another study, adults were shown videotapes of two seventeen-month-old children—each of whom was sometimes described as a boy, and sometimes as a girl. Male subjects were more likely to rate the children in a stereotypical fashion— attributing male qualities such as independence, activity and alertness to the boy—even when the "boy" was really a girl. If the baby was presented as a girl, it was said to be cuddly and delicate. The responses had much more to do with the subjects' preconceived ideas about boys and girls than with reality.

The Tufts researchers studied thirty pairs of parents of first babies, half of whom had girls, the other half, boys. The parents were asked to rate

45

their infants on a scale of qualities, such as firm-soft, strong-weak, hardy-delicate, large-featured–fine-featured, and so on. In advance, the infants were weighed and tested, and were found to have no significant differences in birth weight, length, muscle tone, heart or respiratory rate. Fathers, it turned out, were more extreme in their rating of both sons and daughters than the mothers were. Sons were rated as firmer, larger-featured, better-coordinated and hardier, and daughters as softer, finer-featured and more delicate by the fathers. "The results are particularly striking," said the researchers, "in the light of the fact that our sample of male and female infants did not differ in birth length, weight or Apgar scores [health at birth]. Thus, the results appear to be a pure case of parental labeling."

Not only do parents perceive their newborn sons or daughters in different ways, but they may also have a strikingly different reaction to the birth of a girl than to that of a boy.

Almost all surveys[3] of which sex parents prefer in an infant reveal that most men and women prefer a boy—especially for the first or only child. One researcher[4] looking into patterns of interaction between mothers, fathers and newborns detected a period of distress and disequilibrium in the family after the birth of a daughter that didn't seem to exist after the birth of a son. Often a man whose wife has just given birth to a baby girl may, for reasons he can't fully identify, feel disappointed, deprived or even ashamed. The mother may feel the same way. One woman recently wrote into a "Chat" section of a metropolitan newspaper, "I just had our third daughter. Yes, I had my jealous feelings towards anyone who had a son, but I have overcome them. It was after the birth of our second daughter that I felt so miserable. I felt I had disappointed my husband. I was forever saying to myself, 'Why couldn't you have a boy? Why couldn't things work out the way they are supposed to?' It took me three years to look at our second girl and accept her for what she was and not what I wanted her to be, a boy." One wonders what messages this little girl has picked up. Children understand very acutely when they are not what their parents want them to be. If what the parents want is something they can't possibly be—like the opposite sex—the damage to their egos is likely to be considerable.

Richard Burton, the actor, recently supplied a dramatic illustration of the relative value of girls and boys in today's society. *Time* magazine reported that in 1974, just before he proposed to Princess Elizabeth of Yugoslavia, he gave an English magazine a handwritten advertisement for a woman under thirty-eight to bear him a son for a fee. "Explained the actor: 'The sound of a little son running around again would be the saving of me.' The price offered . . . was $50,000 for a boy, $25,000 for a girl."

This universal preference for male babies cannot help but give girl children a diminished sense of their own value. In many families where there are several daughters, it is no secret that the parents were "trying for a boy." A daughter is, then, another "failure." The preference for boy babies might also have profound consequences for the future of society. "Sex selection" of babies may become routine in the near future. Several clinics already offer clients an ironclad guarantee of a male baby, thanks to improvements in the technique of collecting sperm and then separating out the Y-bearing (male) sperm.

Today, a process called amniocentesis can detect the sex of an unborn fetus. But should physicians inform the parents of the sex of the child? That's a controversial question. A physician wrote an angry letter to the *Journal of the American Medical Association* several years ago about a case in which he was involved. A thirty-eight-year-old woman had requested amniocentesis for Down's syndrome, and was informed that the fetus was female, with no evidence of Down's syndrome. The woman and her husband wanted a boy, and aborted the female fetus.

The case of parents who want a child and yet would abort a healthy female fetus because they wanted a boy may be not the norm. But what would happen if simple sex-selection techniques were readily available? Demographers predict a rash of boy babies. What would that do to the stability of our society? Some demographers predict the situation would soon level off with a batch of girl babies, but some scientists believe the damage would not be that easy to undo. By artifically selecting one sperm type over another, we may be selecting sperm that would produce offspring whose own gametes (sperm or egg) would again have a predilection for the same sex. In other words, we might be producing not just a generation of male children, but a whole dynasty of males.

What are the reasons for the overwhelming preference for boy babies that all the studies show to exist? When fathers were asked in one study[5] why they wanted a boy, some said they wanted to perpetuate the family name, and that they could identify with a boy more easily. Mothers interviewed also preferred a boy as the firstborn, but the only reason frequently expressed was that their husbands wanted a son.

No doubt, the underlying reason for a preference for male children is the universally higher status of the male in our society. This desire is particularly strong in patrilineal societies—those in which ancestry is traced through the father and property is handed down through male heirs. In the Old Testament, the section often referred to as "the Begats" is a good example of this. It is a long list of precisely which father "begat" which male child. Somebody somewhere along the way must have "begat" a Ruth or a Rachel, but that didn't get mentioned.

In the culture of the Old Testament, property was handed down only from father to son. When a man had no son, women were permitted to inherit property but had to pass it on to their own sons. Much of this patrilineal tradition still lingers in our own society; men see a male heir as the main vehicle of their own desire for continuity. In Jewish culture, the birth of a son confers special status on the father. A ceremonial circumcision marks the boy's entrance into the community. The birth of a female child is not the occasion for any ritual ceremony.

Despite the near universality of the wish for boy babies, some men do prefer daughters. When Robert Fein interviewed fathers before and after the birth of their first child, he found that of thirty-seven men interviewed, eight expressed a desire for a girl. (The men interviewed were all middle class and probably atypical because all attended childbirth classes with their wives.) Four men gave answers that clearly expressed their concern about an ability to raise a son; for example, one man could not relate well to his own father. The others gave positive reasons for wanting girls—an interest in feminism, a belief that their wife would be a good role model for a girl and the notion that a good relationship with their own mother meant they would relate well to a daughter. It was intriguing that the wives of these men were more likely than the other wives to be deeply interested in careers and planned an early return to work. So it may be that a man's participation in a relationship in which his wife has a career commitment goes along with his desire for a firstborn daughter.

Not all men who want female children have such positive reasons. In another study of men who wanted daughters, one couple wanted a girl because there would not be so much fuss and family involvement as there would be with the birth of a boy. They were Jewish and felt they would be pressured to have a ritual circumcision. One man pictured his daughter as daddy's girl, constantly adoring him. Another, who wanted a boy but had a girl, adapted to the situation by similar fantasies of a worshipful daughter running to him after work.

48

We've seen that sex-role stereotyping begins at birth and follows us all through our lives, but it has only been recently that social scientists have taken a critical look at this process. In the past, it was assumed that little girls and little boys ought to be quite different, and a main job of the father in the family was to help them to fit into society's expectations for male or female behavior. The father's role with his son was to teach him to be manly and to initiate him into the mores of the outside world. The girl child was presumed to have little need for such knowledge. Her father's job was to facilitate her heterosexual development so she would grow up to marry happily.

All this concentration on a girl's erotic development gave a lopsided picture of the role of the father in the life of his daughter. There is no question that a warm and loving father is important for a girl's erotic life as she matures, but theories made this the *only* vital role the father performed. Talcott Parsons,[6] whose studies of family structure done in the 1940s and 1950s have been influential among behavioral scientists, thought that a major role of the father in the family was to teach sex-role differentiation—in other words, to teach his son to be a man and his daughter to be a woman.

The problem, of course, was the question of what a woman *ought* to be. As Michael Lamb points out, "Most social theorists believe that the father facilitates her femininity by rewarding dependent, flirtatious and similarly 'feminine' behavior and discouraging 'masculine' behavior." But what was a father doing who was teaching his daughter to be this kind of woman? He was teaching her not to be like a man. Unfortunately, the qualities most identified with good mental health—like self-reliance, independence, the ability to control one's destiny—were seen as "male attributes." So if the male virtues were the normal, healthy ones, what was it he was supposed to be teaching his daughter? If he was indeed teaching her to be dependent, to find fulfillment only through something outside her own self—a husband, children—then he was unknowingly giving her a course in How to Be a Victim.

A good many fathers, of course, ignored the experts, used their common sense and tried to raise daughters—as well as sons—who were self-reliant, self-trusting individuals. By insisting that dad's job is to help mold a marriageable woman, the behavioral scientists have been operating in a fairy tale—the idea that women will always be protected from the outside world by some beneficent male. The fairy tale assumed that women would never be divorced or widowed or unmarried, or that

49

their husbands would never be sick, unemployed or otherwise unavailable for the job of twenty-four-hour knight errant.

Many of the traditional modes of fathering were based on the division of power in society. Men have almost always held economic and legal power; women had access to it only through men, which led to the "feminine behavior" of manipulation and seduction. As Elizabeth Janeway writes, "Where men are seen as the only powerful actors and agents, a woman who cannot charm them has lost every chance of happiness and sees every road to fulfillment closed. Since, in this mythic world, she can do nothing for herself, her inability to persuade the dominant to take her part will doom her to being an old maid, a drudge, a beggar or a hanger on, an alien outside the feast of life."[7] Such manipulative behavior patterns are in opposition to a woman's sense of her own competence. If she must entice others to act for her, this means she does not think herself capable of independent action. If the world she sees around her tells a girl she is powerless, that she must use charm as her only weapon to achieve her goals, the pattern for her later life will be set. It is her father who will represent to the girl most dynamically the outside world, but many of the traditional behaviors identified with "Daddy" have been designed to enhance the passivity and manipulative behavior of the girl child. Some of those styles are evident in the lives of women, past and present, and in the roles their fathers chose to adopt:

The White Knight: To many a girl, there is something magical about her father. He is the visitor from the Outside, someone special, whose attentions and affections make the girl herself seem special—a little princess. Writer Barbara Grizzuti Harrison[8] interviewed a number of women about their fathers and found that "almost without exception, the grown women who talked to me about their fathers spoke as if a kind of magic aura surrounded their male parents when they were little girls." One woman, whose father deserted her when she was seventeen, remembers the way he danced with her at weddings and told her she was prettier than Grace Kelly. In contrast, she remembers her mother as "ironing all the time for me."

This woman reserves all her admiration for her father, in spite of the fact that her mother worked long and hard for her, while her father deserted her. "Laura sees the injustice of this—yet the hours her father spent with her she invests with special fairy tale quality. Laura's mother was ordinary—'like bread, good and plain,' and Laura was grateful to her. Laura's father was magic." Since it is usually the father who controls the economic resources in the family, he is the one with the power to be "magic"—to bring presents, to plan special outings. A woman, particularly one who is "ironing all the time" can hardly compete.

Eleanor Roosevelt[9] wrote of her father, forty years after his death, "He was the one great love of my life as a child, and in fact, like many children I have lived a dream life with him. So his memory is still a vivid, living thing to me."

Eleanor, plain and shy as a child, suffered from the mockery of her beautiful socialite mother who used to call her "Granny" and make the child feel ugly and clumsy. Her father, Elliott Roosevelt, a handsome, promising man whose life fell into disjointed shards under worsening alcoholism, was rarely with her, but he wrote to her often of how he loved her, of what they would do together in the future. The times she spent with him were magical to her, even though more often than not he would disappoint her. He would send a message that he was coming to take her for a drive and then he would not appear. One time, Mrs. Roosevelt remembered, "My father had several fox terriers that he seemed to carry everywhere with him. One day he took me and three of his fox terriers and left us with the doorman at the Knickerbocker club. When he failed to return after six hours, the doorman took me home." Elliott Roosevelt died after a fall he suffered while he was drunk, but his daughter was to write, years later, "He lived in my dreams and he does to this day."

The father often has a compelling aura for a daughter. "The life of the father," Simone de Beauvoir writes, "has a mysterious prestige. The hours he spends at home, the room where he works, the things around him, his pursuits . . . his hobbies, have a sacred character. He is God."[10]

The White Knight is an easy role for a father to play. To a girl child prepared to invest in him magic qualities, it requires little effort for him to turn his daughter into a princess. It is a convenient role for busy men—the corporate executive dashing from city to city, the high-powered lawyer spending all his time on his cases. The White Knight is rarely involved with his daughter's day-to-day problems, and he makes no effort to present his world—the world of men—as anything but magical. He is not there to help her as she comes to womanhood and prepares to enter the real world. Or if he is there, he isn't accessible. Often he can see no real connection between his world and any life he

51

can envision for his daughter. He can't see her as any kind of an actor in the world he knows—the world outside home and family.

The mythical power of the White Knight echoes through the lives of the daughters of such men—even those who were deserted or sorely disappointed by their fathers. Some of them go through life expecting their hopes to be dashed—and that becomes a self-fulfilling prophecy. Eleanor Roosevelt's biographer, Joseph Lash, writes that Elliott Roosevelt's death made it possible for his daughter to maintain her dream picture of him. But, he says, somewhere inside her lurked the image of the other side of her father—the man who took her to his club and forgot about her, who always promised to come to her but often failed to arrive. When he disappointed her, she withdrew into herself and closed herself off from others. She would continue to do that throughout her life when someone she trusted or cared about disappointed her.

Unlike many fathers who play the White Knight, who are content to be magical and adored, Elliott Roosevelt invested a great deal of energy in writing long letters to his daughter, telling her just the sort of girl she ought to be—intelligent, noble, loyal and brave. It is a testament to the power of a father's influence that the woman she finally became was almost an exact portrait of the woman he wished her to be.

In many homes where the life and schedule of the family are built around the work of a largely absent father, the daughter gets a clear picture of a woman's role in life as being an appendage and support of male activity. The father becomes a novelty, almost an honored guest. Susan Ford recalls that when her father was a busy member of Congress, "He really wasn't home a lot, so when he was there, it was so special we did everything we could to make him happy—and he did everything he could to make us happy."

Big Daddy: It is tempting—more tempting to fathers of cute little girls than of sturdy little boys—to be the one who solves all the problems. Fathers realize that little boys will grow up to be men who are going to be facing a tough world out there—and so they will have to learn to pick themselves up when they fall and hit back when somebody gives them a right to the jaw. Women, on the other hand, are presumed to be helpless creatures who will always have a man around to protect them, so they don't have to learn those lessons about self-reliance. The protective instincts that a father has toward his small son are tempered by the knowledge that, painful as it might be, a few hard knocks are necessary for his growth. Too often, fathers do let those instincts get in the way of hard knocks for their daughters. They are too eager to help her climb to a higher step, to forgive her for doing poorly in math when she could do better, to allow themselves to be cajoled into letting her have her own way when what she wants isn't good for her. While sons usually have to stand up and take punishment, daughters often charm their way out of it, and thus they learn not to expect to take the consequences of their own behavior. Unfortunately, the world is not as benign as Daddy. A woman who did not learn as a child that she must be responsible for her actions is in for painful adult experiences. Many girls find they can "seduce" their fathers into acquiescence.

Barbara Grizzuti Harrison remembers: "When I was a little girl I was obligated, by ritual, to tease and cajole my father for my weekly allowance. My brother had to do chores to get his. The clear message was that while I could always wheedle what I wanted with charm, my brother would have to work for what he got. Given the fact that most women find, at one time or another, that they have to work for survival, I think my brother got a realistic message, and I got a fairy tale."

In trying to be protective, Big Daddy does indeed give his daughter a fairy tale. She may grow up believing that there will always be some big, strong and loving man to make things come out right. The happy ending is not seen as anything she can do, but as something that is done for her. How will she then cope with failure, with disappointments, with divorce or with the everyday problems of being alive? Unable to see that she can change her life by her own actions, she may keep up a lifelong search for another Daddy, to make things come out right. It is a search doomed to failure, a failure she has been set up for by a loving father who wanted nothing but the best for her.

The Big Daddy style of fathering can produce a pattern of passivity and expectation in a woman that has been defined as the Jewish American Princess syndrome. The CAP (Catholic American Princess) and the WASP (White Anglo-Saxon Princess) are other strains of the type. Such girls have been lavished with "the best of everything" by indulgent fathers. They grow to young womanhood believing that they are entitled to the best, which is to be handed to them. They do not have the skills, the training or the motivation to get the best by their own actions. Life may be a series of rude awakenings, for what man will be as good, as generous, as oblivious to any flaws as "Daddy"? There are few sights sadder than the middle-aged princess disgruntled with her lot in life, blaming her husband, her children or fate, because she has never outgrown the belief that life owes her something special.

Pygmalion: The Pygmalion myth is one that can prove to be irresistible to some men. If you remember the Greek legend, the sculptor Pygmalion created his ideal woman in stone and fell in love with her. His love transformed the stone to flesh. Men have been trying to create "ideal" women for a long time, from the opulent fertility goddesses of ancient people to Rubens's plump ladies and Modigliani's skinny ones, to the movie moguls who told Marilyn Monroe to get a nose job. The birth of a daughter can bring out the Pygmalion instincts in a father. What a perfect opportunity to sculpt a life, what more malleable object than a tiny, perfect little baby girl? Fathers have done the Pygmalion bit with their sons, too—certainly Joseph Kennedy, Sr., raised his sons as presidential timber. But there is a difference. Fathers recognize that sons will—must—replace the father as the controlling force in their own lives. Most fathers do not expect to have a little boy forever, but it is different with a girl. Daughters are not expected to challenge paternal authority in such a direct way.

This pattern is different from that of the father who teaches his daughter about the outside world, who helps her gain a sense of her own competence and demystifies that world for her. A Pygmalion wants somebody sitting at his feet. The relationship is to be ever that of the teacher with his pupil, not that of equals.

Sally Kempton,[11] in a powerful essay on her encounter with feminism, "Cutting Loose," discusses her relationship with her own father:

> Like many men who are uncomfortable with adult women, my father saw his daughter as a potential antidote to his disappointment in her sex. I was someone who could be moulded into someone compatible with his needs, and also, unlike my mother, I was too impressionable to talk back. So I became the vessel into which he fed his opinions about novels and politics and sex; he fed me also his most hopeful self image. It reached a point where I later suspected him of nourishing a sort of eighteenth-century fantasy about our relationship—the one in which the count teaches his daughter to read Virgil and ride like a man, and she grows up to be the perfect feminine companion, parroting him with so much subtlety that it is impossible to tell that her thoughts and feelings, so perfectly coincident with his, are not original.

Kempton has three brothers, and she says that her father did not choose one of them to mold because he had too great a respect for masculine power. "Boys grow up and have to kill their fathers. Girls can be made to understand their place."

Kempton watched as her father outfenced her mother in intellectual sparring matches, and she believed that he preferred his daughter to his wife. She came to see male power—especially intellectual power—as too formidable to be confronted directly. Women could only control it by seduction, and the most natural relationship between man and woman, she came to believe, was that of teacher and pupil.

Through adolescence and young adulthood, Kempton found herself attracted only to men who were smarter than she, with whom she could re-enact the teacher-pupil relationship she had with her father. She could not really believe in her own work as a writer: "The strongest belief I had retained from my childhood was that nothing I could achieve was worth taking seriously."

Her marriage echoed her relationship with her father. She saw her husband as a father figure, and he, she says, wanted an intelligent child. It worked for a while, and then he began to tire of being a father and she began to resent being a child. They fought continually. She accused him of keeping her dependent and he said she was making it difficult for him to do his work, spending too much and not keeping the house in order. "I was living in a place I didn't want to be and seeing people I didn't like because that was where my man was. I was living my husband's life and I hated him for it."

The Patriarch: For a man uncomfortable about getting involved with his own feelings about his children, whose ambivalence or uncertainty about having a girl could make him uneasy, the role of the Patriarch is a comfortable one to slip into. He can thus view the goings-on of the rest of the family from an Olympian height, stepping in only to settle a dispute, discharging his duty by bringing home the paycheck. He might feel at times a sense of isolation, of being used by his family. The Patriarch uses distance to avoid his emotions, and his need for authority may in reality be withdrawal. Barbara Howar writes in *Laughing All the Way*[12] of her genteel Southern family.

> I grew up in Raleigh, the middle child of mismatched parents acting out a Strindbergian marriage that was kept together by a fear of God

and social censure and made tolerable by alcohol and a peculiar need for one another that I am neither equipped nor disposed to explain. We pussyfooted around my father, never using his fountain pen or fingernail scissors or touching his newspaper until he had finished. We ate when he was hungry, took accurate telephone messages, and learned rather early that he would stand by us in the face of financial or criminal disaster, but could be a tyrant if we failed to return his car keys to the proper bowl on the table in the hall. Rather than defy Daddy, we worked around him, gave lip service to his idiosyncrasies and soft-pedalled our political differences. . . . He was a basically dear and likeable man surrounded by a pack of female Uncle Toms who pandered to his masculinity and allowed him to rule unchallenged, to assert himself right out of the picture.

The Invisible Man: There are some men who, faced with uncertainty or inability to relate to a daughter, simply dematerialize. They may be physically present, but emotionally, they are simply not there. Unlike the White Knight, they do not fall into the roles of prince and princess. They abdicate any role at all, except the most minimal one. One psychoanalyst reports that most women who come to see her feel they are victims of paternal deprivation. As one woman described it: "He worked all day and commuted and then he came home and retreated behind a newspaper. He wasn't harsh or scary. He just wasn't there for me."

The daughters of such men may feel that they, too, are invisible. They may fantasize about a father who is more imagined than real. One of singer Liza Minnelli's friends said in an interview: "Liza forced herself to believe that Vincente [her father Vincente Minnelli] was always there for her. In fact, he was an absentee father. But she can't accept that. She denies it to herself. When you interview her, you'll hear her say, 'Daddy always took the hurt away.' She won't be lying to you; she'll be lying to herself."[13]

But if the father can stunt his daughter's growth, turn her into an enchanted princess or a protected darling or leave her with nothing but fantasies or fury, he can also be the midwife to her growth, an agent through which his daughter—like his son—can be helped to walk with strength and dignity toward the world at childhood's end. It is high time we took a look at the way the father's behavior affects not only his daughter's erotic future, but her ability to live in the outside world as a fully developed human.

That this aspect of the father's role has been so long ignored is unfortunate. It may be more crucial in our modern, industrial society than in the past or in other nonindustrial cultures. For in other cultures, it is less common than in ours for the father to represent The Outside World and the mother to represent The Home. Anthropologists Mary Maxwell West and Melvin Konner say that the role of the father in representing the outside world to children is peculiar to Western culture. "In many non-Western societies, the amount of time spent by father, mother and children 'around the house' varies, and so does the nature of their work; it is possible that a child may not associate mother with home and father with outside of home so strongly. In many non-Western cultures the most likely source of introduction to the outside world is actually the juvenile play group, which also introduces the child to adult skills and values."

There may indeed be a time in our own culture, as women move into more public arenas, that the mother as well as the father can serve to open a gateway to the world beyond the home; it is happening today in many families. But by and large, it is still a "man's world," so the father's role remains crucial. In traditional families, psychiatrist Marjorie R. Leonard points out,[14] the father's occupation "determines the social and economic status of the family; his ethical and spiritual values set the moral climate in which the children will be brought up. Thus, while the mother is the one who deals with the day-to-day problems and conflicts, she is to a large extent serving as a surrogate for the father's authority. Since the children are aware of this, it is probable that the father, more than the mother, serves as a superego model for the girls as well as the boys."

There is a credibility gap between much of developmental theory and real life as far as fathers and daughters are concerned, one that ought to be corrected. A person will be healthy and sound, so the theory goes, if he or she grows up identifying with the parent of the same sex. This has proved to be true for men—but *not* for women.

There is a great deal of scientific evidence that women who identify with their fathers—or with the male role as society presents it—turn out to be high in self-esteem and autonomy, the ability to act independently.[15] In one study, junior-high-school girls who preferred their fathers as a model were found to be better adjusted than those who chose mothers. A four-year study by Marjorie Lozoff of the Wright Institute at Berkeley looked at autonomy in the lives of college girls. She found that highly autonomous college girls tended to identify primarily with their fathers, but were also able to relate to their mothers. These girls were the ones who showed the greatest eagerness for growing and developing as independent human beings. Lozoff concluded that women are more likely to be self-determining individuals when their fathers treat them as interesting people, worthy and deserving of respect and encouragement.

On the other hand, students identifying with the traditional female role were low in self-esteem and they tended to feel "constricted" in their development; they tended to be "oversocialized," for example, not just polite but too polite, too conforming.

It seems, in fact, that for a woman to be a healthy, self-confident individual, she must identify with virtues that have been associated with the male role in our society. While there is plenty of evidence that this will be healthy for her, there is no evidence that it will be harmful. Clearly by identifying with privilege and power, she does not have to forgo a healthy erotic life. Nor does she have to reject her mother. In fact, girls will usually find traits to admire and emulate in both parents.

It is time to broaden our understanding of the father's role in his daughter's life. Certainly we want to remember that he can promote her erotic development by being a warm, loving, available man, one who can give her a positive model of the opposite sex. That is in no way inconsistent with efforts to try to develop in his daughter the same qualities he would respect in a son, teaching her to be competent and independent, to take her accomplishments seriously and introducing her to the outside world—the one in which he lives and works and in which she will also one day live and work.

There is evidence that many fathers are doing just that. A look at two studies—both done in the same geographic area, one in the fifties and the other in the seventies—gives an idea of the change.

In the fifties, American fathers had different and distinct ambitions for their sons and for their daughters. In a 1952 study[16] of middle-class families in the Boston area, researchers David F. Aberle of Johns Hopkins University and Kaspar D. Naegele of the Harvard School of Public Health, said at the outset: "We would assume that fathers in this group would be oriented towards their sons in terms of an expectation that they will ultimately occupy positions in the middle-class occupational structure and towards their daughters with the expectation that they will not. The data confirm this assumption."

In this study, half of the fathers interviewed would accept the possibility of a career for their daughters—but only as a *possibility*. They

58

preferred that their daughters would marry. The other fathers rejected the career possibility out of hand. "Only two fathers want their daughters to know how to earn a living, and both of them have wives who are working or did work during married life."

Fifty-six children were involved in the study, twenty-nine boys and twenty-seven girls. In discussing the behavior of their children, the fathers were clearly more concerned about the boys and "the emotional strength of those concerns is considerably greater with respect to boys than to girls."

The fathers were worried if their sons weren't doing well in school, if they were acting "childish," or if they were too fearful or too docile. The fathers were just not as worried about what their daughters did, and their satisfactions with them "seem to focus strongly on the girls being 'nice,' 'sweet,' pretty, affectionate and well liked . . . Occupational career is not taken seriously, marriage is the primary hope and expectation. The same sorts of demands (as on sons) are not made and the father does not seem to fuss too much as to whether his daughter will ultimately be a good mate. If she is a sweet little girl, that is enough."

The fathers were not concerned when their daughters were less athletic or aggressive than others, but some of the fathers were troubled if their daughters were "bossy."

"Though we know that some of the boys were holy terrors in their play groups, no father shows any concern that his son be a bully, and some proudly mention that they guess the boy is a bit of a devil. It might be noted that though the 'bad boy' is a stereotype of American life, ambivalent but never wholly negative, there is no corresponding stereotype for a girl, the phrase 'bad girl' having quite different connotations."

The picture of American society that emerges from this study is clear-cut: it is a society firmly in the grip of traditional sex-role stereotypes, with the "Feminine Mystique" and male authority in full sway. However, a study Grace and Rosalind conducted in 1976 suggests that American reality today is quite different from the sex-stereotyped world of the fifties. The seventy-nine fathers of preschool girls who (along with the mothers) took part in the study were, like those of the 1950s study, residents of the Boston area and largely middle class. Unlike the fathers of the fifties, worried about their sons' careers and wishing some vague sort of marital bliss for their daughters, the fathers in our study were concerned with their daughter's full human potential. In brief essays these fathers wrote about their relationship with their young daughters, the theme of self-realization comes up again and again.

One father writes:

> With regard to the future, I hope school [he was a medical student] will allow Amy and me more time together. It's important to me to be a part of her formative years. Looking even further beyond, I hope she will do well enough in school so that opportunities won't be limited in that respect. . . . Basically I want her to grow up with the idea that she can do anything she wants with regard to career, job etc. I want her to set her goals high and not be inhibited by sex-role stereotyping. I don't want her to feel that she can't do, or even try to do, something just because she's a girl. . . . I guess you can say my greatest fear is that she might be afraid *to explore her potential and in that sense never know satisfaction.*

A second man says:

> I am anxious to have her feel that there are no particularly sex-linked limitations of her ability—that she can fix things around the house or carry heavy things or play football, just like everyone else. Socialization from outside the home environment and unconscious behavior and speech in a traditional vein from Jennifer and me have combined to give her a pretty good idea of male and female roles anyway, and that's not particularly bad *if* we can successfully teach her that being feminine (and that's hard to define) doesn't necessarily mean being limited or taking a back seat.

Another father comments:

> I feel a great responsibility to our children and will try to raise them to be thinking, feeling humans. My only real aspiration for Tracy (aside from the trivial ones such as wanting her to be a concert pianist or a Madame Curie) is that she be given the opportunity to choose what she wants to do and have pride in doing it.

And another admits:

> One must understand that I am from the old school and it's hard for me to change; but, I am changing, adjusting, understanding, and hopefully, when my daughter grows into womanhood, I will be "with it."

Unlike the fathers of the fifties, who figured everything was going to turn out all right and were happy with their sweet little girls, the fathers we saw tended to worry about their fathering.

Another father describes his relationship with his daughter as:

> . . . warm and loving on both sides . . . although we both wish we had more time together, which the pressures of my job seem to prevent. Her mother is very conscious of trying to foster a good relationship between Kim and me. My attempt to provide time for the two of us alone seems to mean a lot to her. I am also aware it would be easy for me to become the "seductive father" with its attendant problems.

Another man writes:

> Because of my employment I am not able to spend as much time with either of my children as I would like. I am very close to my daughter and unfortunately show her more affection than I do my son. My greatest frustration is that it is very difficult for me to punish her and she often uses her femininity to avoid same. For the future, I hope she has the opportunity and desire to use her talents for whatever she considers fulfillment.

These fathers obviously have different sorts of concerns for their daughters than did the fathers of the fifties. One man, in his essay, talked about his identification with his daughter in a way that is reminiscent of the manner in which fathers talk about their sons.

> She is the most important person in my life. She is extremely important to my sense of purpose in my own life. I tend to be demanding and extremely sensitive to her happiness, her progress and behavior and style. She obviously is the barometer of my fathering since she's my only child. I want her to like me, but I also expect a lot in terms of behavior and performance. She is not exactly a project, but if she doesn't meet my expectations I'm disappointed and sometimes angry and quite severe. I want her to look to me as a guide, but I make mistakes often in modeling and have concern about the impact of that.

It's heartening to see this father so concerned about being an "identification figure" for his daughter. Why is that so important? The answer is that when you look at successful women of past eras, a clear pattern emerges. Almost without exception, women who defied conventional notions about female frailty had strong encouragement from their fathers. A glance through a book published in 1866 called *Girls Who Became Famous* is instructive. It is a pious text by Sarah K. Bolton, a woman who wrote other such uplifting tracts as *Poor Boys Who Became Famous*. Despite the Horatio Alger tone, it contains some intriguing facts about the women it depicts. Margaret Fuller, essayist and feminist, was the daughter of a man determined that his eldest daughter should have an education. Since no colleges admitted women in those days, Timothy Fuller, a lawyer, gave lessons to his daughter in the evenings when he came home from work. He taught her to read Latin at six. At fifteen, she was pursuing studies in Greek, French and Italian. Astronomer Maria Mitchell had two older brothers, but her father, who had built his own observatory, taught her the same lessons as the boys, including celestial navigation. The author comments, "Perhaps it is not strange that after such teaching, his daughter could have no taste for making worsted work or Kensington stitches."

Sculptor Harriet Hosmer was the daughter of a physician, who, after losing his wife and another child to illness, determined that his daughter would grow up healthy and strong. He taught her to hunt and ride and let her roam the countryside. When her early interest in playing with clay developed into a serious profession, her father built a studio for her. Florence Nightingale's father taught her classics and higher mathematics. Rosa Bonheur, the renowned painter of animals, was the daughter of a painter who gave her her early training in art.

The experiences of famous women of the past dovetail with studies of women who have achieved a modern version of success: corporate executive status. Margaret Hennig, director of the management program for women at Simmons College in Boston, studied twenty-five women executives of high-powered corporations for her doctoral thesis at Harvard Business School.[17] Hennig found that all these women executives reported unusually strong relationships in early childhood with their fathers. (All were eldest or only children.) They shared many "male" activities with their fathers, not only sports but taking part in their fathers' work life. At the same time, they had affectionate relationships with their mothers. They viewed their mothers as "warm, fluffy pillows," Hennig said, while their fathers were dynamic, charismatic personalities.

One executive remembered wanting to climb a very tall tree when she was about five years old. Her mother was afraid that she would fall but, "My dad said that if I fell, I would learn a good lesson about what my limits were, but if I made it, I'd learn not to always let others set limitations for me. I climbed that tall tree right to the top and I never forgot that lesson."

The daughter of a railroad executive used to go with her father while he supervised the building of a line in Pennsylvania. "I am probably the only woman alive who walked the railroad track construction at the age of five. I loved those times, and all the men knew us and talked to us. My dad was very proud of me and he often joked with the men about my becoming the first woman train engineer."

The fathers behaved with these firstborn girls as they might have with sons. "I think my father never stopped hoping for a son, but in the meantime I think he singled me out for that role," one woman remembers.

The girls ran into sex-role conflicts not inside the home, but outside. They had developed a drive for success, a task orientation, a desire to be respected for their abilities and a love of competition, and these values were encouraged by their fathers. It was the outside world that said, "Don't do, don't dare." The young girls developed these "masculine" traits without ever questioning their identity as females. "Rather," says Hennig, "they found their girlhood confining and fought the role for more freedoms. Their reaction to boys was not overtly wishing for male sexuality, but rather one of jealousy at the perceived lack of role constraints on boys."

For a daughter, it seems, a father's encouragement to achieve has an impact that is felt long after she leaves childhood behind. Caryl was looking through one of her old scrapbooks not long ago and came upon a picture of herself at five, all done up in her favorite cowboy outfit—chaps and plaid shirt and a huge six-gun. She was nestled happily in her father's lap. The picture made her think of the stories he used to make up for her—night after night he would patiently spin yarns of which she never tired. They were cowboy stories, to fit her obsession with anything Western—an obsession that gleamed even more brightly because she lived in a suburban neighborhood on the East Coast where the sound of galloping hooves had never echoed. Caryl was the heroine of her father's stories—Cowboy Caryl, to be exact. Night after night they thwarted the blackest plans of evildoers, whether they were rustling cattle or robbing the town bank. She could ride, shoot, lasso and subdue bad guys with a single punch. The thought of those stories always brings back happy memories of her father—a warm, gentle and witty man who died not long ago. But it wasn't until she began to gather material on fathers and daughters, and to talk with Grace and Rosalind about the meaning of the data, that she began to understand what those stories meant to her. How many fathers, she wondered, told that special type of story to their daughters? Cowboy Caryl was neither a beautiful princess nor a good sweet little girl. Her father created for his daughter a role in which she was both active and competent. She was the boss of her troop—the best rider, roper, shooter, always the rescuer, never the rescued.

Her father built for her a world in which she was a doer, a master of her own destiny—and that world has stayed alive inside of her.

Some fathers, as Barbara Grizzuti Harrison has noted, make their daughters charm and manipulate them to get their way. Caryl realizes now that it wouldn't have occurred to her to wheedle her father into doing something for her. She could please him by doing, not being.

Caryl was the older child—her brother is seven years younger—and her father chose to share his passion for sports with her. He was delighted when she went out for the basketball team in seventh grade, because he had once played semipro basketball himself. He taught her all sorts of things that proved useful—how to knee, how to elbow and how to fall down when you bumped somebody else so it would look as though it was *you* who had been fouled. When she would hang back and not go after the ball aggressively enough he would holler, "Go after it! Don't be so damned ladylike!" He wanted her to be "ladylike" in other areas, but the basketball court was no place for ladies. He was delighted with the silver trophies she won, and he set them up on the television set proudly for all to see. Once she wanted to pack the trophies away, but he wouldn't hear of it. "You worked hard to earn those," he said. "Be proud of them."

Nuts and Bolts

There aren't, of course, any Ten Commandments for being a father, no easy step-by-step guidelines to raising daughters. But fathers can take pains to understand some of the social pressures and stereotypes that impinge on girls. If they are aware of some of the patterns that fathers can fall into that impair the development of a sense of competence in their daughters, they can devise their own ways of coping with these forces. The following are a few suggestions that grow out of the major themes in these chapters on fathering.

First of all, we've seen that the father-infant bond is an important one,

64

despite the fact that it has been given scant attention in the past. This bond ought to be taken into consideration by couples who are just starting to think about having a family. The mother has to do this; if she is working, she thinks about whether she will plan to continue and how her work can fit in with the demands of having a baby. She probably doesn't decide to take on a demanding new challenge at work that requires long hours at the same time that she's thinking of starting a family. Rarely is such thought given to the father's life. Part of this has been because the father viewed himself and was viewed by his wife only as peripheral to the whole drama of having a child. He would be there for aid and comfort, but the spotlight would stay on the woman and baby. We have seen how important it is that the infant be able to develop an attachment to its father, and how powerful the sensation of engrossment can be to the father of an infant. Fathers should therefore do some serious thinking and planning before couples decide when and if to have a baby.

This process could affect the timing of a pregnancy. Is it a good idea for a couple to start a family when the husband is in the middle of a surgical residency, for instance, or trying to get a degree at night while working during the day, or starting out in a new job in which he will have to work long hours to prove himself? If a father finds himself trying to cope with a new baby in such a situation, he may feel he has no choice but to leave the home front to his wife. He can find himself overworked, exhausted and with little patience to really get to know his infant—a real loss which can lead to feelings of frustration and resentment.

The father of an infant may find he has to assert himself in stepping into a nurturing role with his newborn, especially if it is a daughter. Some people are horrified when they see a father carrying a newborn around. They assume the father is a clumsy oaf who will no doubt drop the baby on its head. One new father, whose house was full of helpful female relatives, complained that every time he picked up the baby, one grandmother or another would dash up and snatch it away. "I am perfectly capable of feeding the baby," he complained, but had to fight to hang onto his own child. Fathers shouldn't be ashamed or retreat if they are clumsy at first with infants. Most men haven't had any experience with babies, but they can learn quickly. We've talked about the role of the mentor, the wife encouraging the husband to get involved with the physical job of caring for the baby. At times, the father should be alone with the infant so he won't always feel there's somebody hovering to see that he does it "right."

It's important for the father to spend time alone with his daughter, caring for her, not just during infancy. We've talked about the study which Grace and Rosalind did with preschool girls, showing that the more the father took over child-care tasks, the less stereotyped were his daughter's views of adults. The important factor was not the specific things the father did, but the fact that he was the sole parent in charge, the one who was caring for the girl, not just functioning as "Mommy's helper." Fathers can devise ways to be the primary caretaker often enough so that they can make an impact on their daughters.

One of the major traps that fathers can fall into with their daughters is encouraging the "Princess" fantasy—or variations thereof—some of which we've looked at in these chapters. It's very easy to let a pretty little girl charm you into a reward—or out of a deserved punishment—by flirtatious behavior. There is a natural instinct among fathers to want to protect their little girls who seem so small, so vulnerable, so helpless. A little boy may also seem defenseless, but the father often hears a stern voice inside his head warning him that the boy will grow up to be a man, and it's a tough world out there, and he has to start growing some protective covering early on. The girl needs that same covering. She especially has to know that she had better count on her own actions, and not on charm, to get along in the world. Girls need to see that there is a direct connection between what they do and some concrete result. A girl can be praised for things that she does, which she can control, rather than just for how pretty she is—which she can't control at all. (Not that fathers can't praise their daughters or sons for looking attractive, just that it shouldn't be the only—or the major—praise they get.)

Fathers should think about the jobs they assign to their daughters—a subject that often doesn't get much thought. It's a good idea to get girls involved in jobs where they can see a lasting result. For example, washing the dishes gives only a temporary result. The dishes are dirty a few hours later and have to be washed again. One father asked his daughter to help him paint a fence. Every time she looks in the yard, she can see the permanent result of the work she did. Fathers (and mothers) can think up any number of jobs that can have this kind of result. Girls below the age of puberty are just as strong physically as boys—often stronger, because they mature earlier—and can do any of the tasks boys do. It's easy to forget that. Rosalind remembers that when her eleven-year-old son broke his hand, she wondered whom she could get to take over his job of cutting the grass. She had already called a neighbor's son when she realized that it hadn't even occurred to her to ask her nine-year-old daughter, who was perfectly willing and capable of pushing a mower across the lawn. Girls can easily be overlooked for jobs that not only would be helpful to them but that they may very well enjoy doing.

Fathers often have more trouble punishing daughters than they do disciplining sons. Daughters can often do a good imitation of the wounded fawn—the quivering lip, the tear sliding out of the eye, the look of woe on the angelic little face. But if little girls consistently get away with that act, they receive a dangerous message—that they don't have to take the consequences of their actions. A father may, on occasion, feel like Attila the Hun, but he may feel better if he keeps in mind that his daughter has to learn that a certain standard of behavior is expected of her. If she chooses to violate the rules, she pays the piper like everyone else.

A father can help his daughter to feel she is a person of consequence by taking her seriously, by not automatically turning over decisions about her life to the mother. For example, a daughter who sees her father going to a conference with her teacher is more likely to feel that what she does is important to him. Sometimes society doesn't make this easy for him; it assumes that only mothers have this job. Schools, for example, often schedule parent meetings and conferences in midday, rather than in the evening, assuming that fathers won't be coming. Fathers are often not made particularly welcome at girls' activities, and they feel alien and out of place. When Caryl's husband went to his daughter's Brownie fly-up, he felt like an idiot standing in line to let her pin a gardenia corsage on him. Nobody expected a *father* to be there. Fathers may find they have to take the initiative in pointing out to the school or group that flexibility is necessary in order to allow fathers to participate.

The nature of girls' activities can make it harder for fathers to get involved. When a girl takes ballet lessons, or skating lessons, the father is usually asked to attend once a year, for recital. But with a son's activities, Little League, hockey, and so forth, the father can be on hand every week, watching the games, cheering his son on. Although it may be hard, fathers can find some activity that they can share in this same way with their daughters—tennis, jogging, crafts.

The tendency for a father to be seen as "magical" and "special"—and thus for men to be seen in the same way—can be a problem for fathers and daughters. It's tempting for a father to play "The White Knight" role with his daughter—who wouldn't want to be seen as somebody very special, magical? But it's not helpful for girls to grow up thinking that men are the special people and women are ordinary. One way for a father to get around this trap is to let his daughter accompany him doing ordinary things—getting the car filled with gas, stopping at the supermarket, going to the hardware store. Every excursion with Daddy shouldn't be a treat, or a party, something out of the ordinary, even (especially) if he's home only rarely.

One thing we have seen is that although fathers often represent the outside world to their daughters, they may not try to demystify that world. Fathers should take their daughters along with them to the place where they work, and explain what they do. It is helpful to show them that the world of work is not only a place for men, and to point out to them women who have responsibility and do important jobs. Fathers can devise their own ways to introduce their daughters to the workplace and help them to understand that there is nothing inaccessible or mysterious about it, and that they could find a place in it for themselves one day.

The theme that runs through the comments of many adult women about their fathers is that they were more or less invisible—emotionally or in fact. Many fathers seem to relinquish the whole job of raising a daughter to the mother—perhaps out of a fear that it's a subject they know nothing about. But, as we have seen, it is important for a girl that her father be accessible to her. Fathers can find their own ways of being attentive to their daughters. Many men come home from work exhausted and feel they have very little patience for a child at that time. But there are other ways a father can be available. He could give his daughter his phone number at work and let her call him. He could call his daughter during the afternoon and ask about her day. He could set aside a special time later in the evening just for her. (Mothers and fathers who work do need some time to unwind when they get home from work. It's not unreasonable for adults to ask for some set time for themselves when they get home, if the children know that later on, feeling a bit rested, they will take a real interest in their children's activities.)

Not only daughters will benefit from a good relationship between father and child. There are some real bonuses in it for the father, too. Often, in the past, fathers felt alienated from their daughters, didn't understand their lives and were never able to understand them as people. Daughters saw their fathers as people they could manipulate, or the

68

remote figures who were rarely there. Fathers often were left out of the pleasures of caring for an infant, seeing a special relationship bloom and grow. A father could feel even more alienated as the girl child grew to womanhood, watching her share her activities and her hopes and dreams with her mother. Father and daughter were strangers in the same house. The father may have been the "head" of the family, but never really a part of it. Loneliness and alienation were often the price he paid for letting his wife be the "heart" of the home.

In fact, recent studies have shown that men may be more vulnerable than women to the "empty nest" syndrome—feelings of loss and depression when the children leave home. Unlike most mothers, when the children were small the men didn't make the time to get deeply involved with their children. Now they feel a sense of irrevocable loss. Their grown children no longer need them in the special way they did when they were young. Now the father has time for the children—but they no longer have time for him.

4

MOTHERS AND DAUGHTERS

How Will My Life Affect My Daughter's?

> My words were cutting right through to her heart. . . . She understood only too well. It was something she had wanted to do herself once, a long time ago when her spirit was independent, before she had succumbed to being what she thought she should be. . . . I wondered what had happened, and I guess I didn't want it to happen to me.
> —Shirley MacLaine in *Don't Fall Off the Mountain*

> Sir, a woman's preaching is like a dog's walking on his hind legs. It is not done well; but you are surprised to find it done at all."
> —Dr. Samuel Johnson, 1709–1784

> The souls of women are so small
> That some believe they've none at all.
> —Samuel Butler, 1612–1680

Leaf through any book of "wise and famous" sayings, and you'll find many quotations similar to the ones above, testifying to the "differences" between men and women. Men usually come off a good deal better in these utterances, probably because it's the men who are doing the talking. The idea that men and women are different sorts of people, with women being the second sex, the sex with more limited talents, options and abilities, is firmly rooted in our social mores. Sex stereotypes are not hard to find in our culture, and children learn them very early. From the mouths of babes often come ideas about the world that reflect very rigid notions about who men and women are, and what they do.

How, in fact, do children see men and women? Quite differently, according to tests and studies done over the years. In a classic 1957 study,[1] researchers Charles Osgood, George Suci and Percy Tannenbaum found that young adults, in trying to sort out the world around them, used three "conceptual dimensions" to look at reality. That is, they tended to set up three separate categories in evaluating people or ideas. They saw things in terms of whether they were good or bad (evaluative), strong or weak (potency), and active or passive (activity). In the "good or bad" category, there was no discernible link to sex—the students did not tend to see things regarded as male as good or female as bad, or vice versa. But it was a different story in the categories of potency and activity. The adjectives that described strength and activity were generally applied to males, while their polar opposites were ascribed to females.

In another study,[2] college-age students were asked to describe a variety of concepts, including "father" and "mother." They rated father, in relation to mother, higher on these concepts: cruel, successful, strong and bad.

It was clear that these students applied labels—and highly stereotyped ones—to men and women. When does this pattern of labeling begin? Jerome Kagan and Judith Lemkin of Harvard set out to find some answers.[3] Do young children see men and women as being very different sorts of people? And do their perceptions of their own parents shape a world view that will remain with them throughout life?

"If the typical child perceives the father as stronger and more active than the mother," Kagan and Lemkin write, "then one might expect the child's perception of maleness and femaleness to be colored by these earlier perceptions."

Kagan had done other work in this area. In earlier studies, he had found that children six to ten perceived fathers as more dominant and less friendly than mothers, and other studies confirmed these findings. Kagan and Lemkin set out to do an in-depth study of even younger children, thirty-two boys and thirty-five girls, ages three to eight. The children were first asked indirect questions about "mommies and daddies," such as, "Someone is yelling at the child. Who is it? Someone is picking up the child. Who is it, the mommy or the daddy? Who is the strongest? Who is the smartest?" They were also questioned directly about their own parents. The first question was, "Who gives you the most presents? Your mommy or your daddy?" The questions covered a wide range of parental behaviors—hugging, spanking, protecting, playing on the seesaw, taking a walk.

The children's answers dovetailed with findings from earlier studies. Young children saw mothers as more nurturing, less punitive and less competent than fathers. Children's images of parents, as reflected in these studies, show parents as being less than whole individuals. Dad is strong and competent, but also the punisher, the authority, someone to be feared. Mom is nice, the one who hugs, but not the one who is the smartest or equal to Dad in being able to manage things. Stereotypes are voiced by the youngest of children. But why? Is it due to some innate, bipolar difference between men and women, the opposites yin and yang? Is it the children's perceptions of the reality they see in their own families? Or does it arise in part from strongly held myths about men and women that permeate our culture? Kagan and Lemkin give a nod to the latter view.

"The authors do not believe that the child's perception of the parents is solely a function of each parent's behavior towards the child. The mass media, peer communications and the content of children's books all paint the adult male as competent, aggressive and powerful. These sources of communication describe the mother as weak, loving and subordinate. It is likely that the child's answers to our questions were influenced by these stereotyped conceptions of the mother and father role. At a more speculative level, it is suggested that these extrafamilial communications also influence the child's perceptions of his parents."

It is clear that *something* other than what they see at home is getting to the kids. What that something is, argues Harvard psychologist Lawrence Kohlberg,[4] is largely the structure of the child's own mind. Some of these stereotypes could come from the way four-year-olds think. To a four-year-old, it may be logical that someone who is physically larger must be stronger, somebody who has a bigger head—Daddy—must therefore be smarter. (It's hard to convince a four-year-old, for example, that somebody who is tall could be *younger* than somebody who is short.) In our study of preschool girls, four-year-olds had equally stereotyped ideas about men and women regardless of whether they came from traditional homes or from those in which their mothers were employed.

Too often, at a very young age, children translate these stereotyped notions of men and women into one ominous idea: both men and women are people, but women are *limited* people. Compared to men, there are fewer things that are okay for women to do. One study pointed up this fact dramatically.

In the late fifties and early sixties, Ruth Hartley of the City College of New York set up tests for groups of boys and girls five, eight and eleven years old.[5] She asked the children to talk to an imaginary visitor from the planet Mars, who knew nothing about our society. They were supposed to tell the Martian what boys need to know and do to get along in our world, and what girls need to know and do. The same questions were asked about mothers and fathers.

The message came through loud and clear. The "turf" that belongs to women and girls is very small, the things they need to know and do are concentrated in a narrow corridor of activity. Of a total of 640 items mentioned for women, 60 percent of them had to do with housework, child care and relations with a husband. Hartley found that "the comparative concentration of women's role activities within the home and family is striking, particularly since half our subjects came from 'working mother' families. There is no area in male activities which approaches it."

The social myths about men and women are so powerful that they can at times eradicate reality. We personally know of children of women physicians who say that only men can be doctors. If children see the world in terms of these stereotypes, they can't help seeing their own parents in the same limited way.

Kagan and Lemkin say, "If a five-year-old views men as generally more hostile and aggressive than women there is reason to believe that he will generalize this expectation to his own father and view the latter as potentially more aggressive than he is in reality. By the same token, he or she could see the mother as less competitive, less strong than she really is."

So the picture that children evolve in their own heads is a complicated tangle of what they see, immature thinking, and what society tells them they should see. Whatever the mixture of reality and myth that nestles in each child's head, there is little question about the result. Too many children in our society grow up with a highly stereotyped view of men and women, in which women are seen as weak and constricted in comparison to men.

The pervasive acceptance of a limited view of women is a fact, one that is fraught with danger for children, especially those who happen to be female. It is particularly alarming when you are looking—as we are—at the question of developing competence in girls.

At this point we run up against the notion of identification, an important process in growing up. A child needs someone to observe, to relate to, to feel a special closeness to, to be like, in order to grow up to be a healthy adult. We know the process is a critical and complicated one. There are a number of theories about how identification works in human beings, but we don't know enough to label each of them "right" or "wrong."

The theory which has probably had the greatest social impact is the one that derives from psychoanalysis. Perhaps because Freud was the first to probe the mysteries of sexuality and its relation to personality, psychoanalytic theory has focused on erotic development. Healthy identification, so this theory goes, is identification with the parent of the same sex. This is probably an oversimplified view of the world. As we have seen, the women executives in Margaret Hennig's study that we dealt with in the chapter on fathers seemed able to identify with both parents—and their fathers in particular—without suffering psychic damage. A broader view of identification is probably necessary, for something more than a parent's sex is involved. Power, for example. Some newer theories of identification—emerging out of such disciplines as anthropology and psychology—center on the idea that the parent the child wants to be like is the one who controls the resources.[6] From studies of the identification process in children, many theorists conclude that the model a child would most likely choose for identification is the one viewed as competent, powerful and in control of the sources of gratification.

Here is the problem for female children. As Jerome Kagan explains: "The present data suggest that girls view the father as a more competent and powerful figure than the mother. However, to the question, 'Who do you want to be like when you grow up?' the girls answered mother. Thus, the role model that the girls have chosen is not the one whom they view as the most competent."

What does this mean to the young girl? She has a natural tendency to want to be like her mother, but this identification may bring with it a sense of inadequacy, even incompetence. In Kagan's words, "girls have a more anxiety-arousing identification and a less positive self-image than boys."

74

If young girls see their mother as a person of diminished competence and power, they may incorporate this notion into their own self-image. Perhaps for this reason the young girl's self-esteem diminishes with age. When one researcher asked two hundred children from eight to fifteen about whether boys or girls possessed more desirable traits, an intriguing pattern emerged.[7] As the girls grew older, boys seemed to get better in their eyes, and the value of their own sex declined. The boys' answers showed that they, too, thought that the number of desirable traits that girls possessed diminished as they grew older. The nearer the children got to the state of adulthood, the more diminished the image of the female seemed.

So, here is the girl child, with a desire to identify with the parent of the same sex, but with an equally strong urge to identify with the powerful parent. She wants to identify with her mother, but she looks around her and what does she see? A society in which women are said to be less than competent and restricted in what they can do. For some girls, a close look at the lives their mothers lead makes them want to run as fast as they can in the opposite direction—a painful experience for both mothers and daughters.

Actress-author Shirley MacLaine writes in her autobiography, *Don't Fall Off the Mountain*,[8] that she had to leave her safe middle-class existence as the daughter of a suburban Virginia family and strike out on her own. Telling her mother this was painful.

> Mother paused in front of the door. With a glance toward the backyard where my father sat, she entered the room and sat down beside me on the bed.
>
> "What's wrong?" she asked, bracing herself as though anticipating disaster.
>
> "I guess I want to be too many things, too many people," I began, gesturing at the walls covered with the symbols of my restlessness. She looked at the maps, the photographs of famous ballerinas, at the books filled with other people and other places, and at the high-powered telescope I hoped would take me to the moon. The familiar sad sparkle filled her eyes.
>
> "But I have to go away from here—away from the schedule, the rigid discipline, the conformity. Perhaps it's been good, and useful, and necessary, but there's so much out there I have to see, and have to do, and have to be a part of."
>
> My words were cutting right through to her heart. I could see that,

and her expression was more than I could bear. She understood only too well. It was something she had wanted to do herself once, a long time ago when her spirit was independent, before she had succumbed to being what she thought she should be. Her friends told me she had been "delightfully carefree" and that her gaiety had infected everyone she met. I never remembered her that way. I wondered what had happened, and I guess I didn't want it to happen to me.

I didn't want it to happen to me. That is a phrase one hears all too often from women who are talking about their mothers. The irony in this is that *it* is domesticity, the sort of life women are supposed to glory in.

One woman who was part of a consciousness-raising group in New York (recorded by Claudia Dreifus in *Woman's Fate*[9]) says:

> "I think I became a feminist at a very young age. Growing up in a poor neighborhood in Akron, Ohio, naturally I felt unhappy with the female role I saw all around me. Girls got married and did nothing with their lives. Even when I was a kid, I thought I'd do something very special, very different. I couldn't conceive of dying without setting the world on its end.
>
> "My father owned a dry goods store. He worked all the time there. People would come in and talk to him about politics and the world, and it seemed very exciting. My mother hid in the house. She was afraid of meeting people, of going out, of confronting life. I thought of my mother as extremely incompetent, so I was ashamed of her . . . I liked my father and would often wonder how he could marry anyone as beneath him as my mother . . . Not that my father's life was so great; he worked twelve hours a day, but I knew the life my mother was leading was definitely something I didn't want. I certainly was not going to end up stuck in the house, taking care of children, having no fun, the way she was."

Girls growing up not only see that their mothers have abdicated power and lead restricted lives, but girls also get messages about their self-image. Society values women less than men, and in time, women accept that verdict; sometimes it seems they value themselves not at all. The adolescent heroine of Joan Marans Dim's novel, *Recollections of a Rotten Kid*,[10] is puzzled by her mother's behavior:

> My mother always played the martyr. She always gave up her good times, her few pleasures, her privacy, her food, for others. She never

took for herself. Even when my grandmother baked liver knishes or fried potato pancakes and offered them to my mother, my mother always said, "Give everybody else first; if there's any left, I'll take later."

My mother never asked my grandmother to make liver knishes or potato pancakes. Yet I knew she loved liver knishes and potato pancakes as much as I did. It was as if my mother didn't consider herself worthwhile enough to enjoy liver knishes or potato pancakes.

Another problem girls often have is that their mothers are overinvested in their lives. Jane Howard writes in A *Different Woman*[11]: "I know of one mother who wept to see her daughter marry because there would be no more intrigue over girlish romances." The daughter told Howard, "Since I got my first Valentine from a boy in third grade those intrigues were all that kept my mother going." Another woman remembers the intense competition for popularity in the neighborhood where she grew up; each girl's triumph—a date for a prom, an invitation for a college weekend—was a triumph for her mother, and the mothers were very good at keeping score. Barbara Howar, writing of her doting mother, said,

> When I look back at the two years since my mother died, I am enormously saddened to understand that I would not be on my way to real peace if my mother were still alive. I feel guilty that this is so. I also feel anger and frustration that a complex woman like my mother was forced to seek her fulfillment through me and that only through her needless death could I be free to arrange my life to bring me happiness. I waste no time regretting, but sometimes I wish Mama and I had channeled all the energy we spent making me noticed and publicized into something meaningful and lasting, something from which we both would have derived contentment. Such is her grip on me, even from the grave, that I wonder if Mama would approve of my life right now, if she would have gone along with my changing needs, encouraged my efforts for privacy, understood that I needed more for myself than my picture on a television screen, my name in print—and that she did too.

The mothers of all these women were not *bad* mothers—quite the contrary. They were, in fact, doing the sorts of things society told them that mothering was all about—putting their children first, denying their own wants and needs, investing their energies and talents in their families. As a result, their daughters found it impossible to want to identify with them.

Since identification is in part an unconscious process, however, a daughter can't simply *will* herself to be unlike her mother. On some levels, she is going to identify with her mother anyhow. The struggle to deny that can be a lifelong one, producing guilt, anxiety and an inexplicable need to hold back from doing things her mother didn't do. This is the core theme of Nancy Friday's book *My Mother/My Self*, a theme that resonated with enough readers to create a best seller.

There is a message for us here. It is time we started to redefine our concept of what makes a good mother. If it is important for a girl's development that she be able to identify with her mother, then we had better start thinking about the "ideal" mom as something other than a sacrificial creature a child can't want to emulate. "Mother" must be a strong, competent person in her own right. Mothers today who are concerned about their daughters have to start very close to home by looking at the quality of their own lives.

That is easy to say, but a lot harder to do. Women have been conditioned to the sacrificial virtues. One high-school paper produced an editorial for Mother's Day that was supposed to celebrate mothers. It said that we should be grateful for all the little services performed only by slaves, servants—and mothers. Where children are concerned, women feel guilty in putting their own needs first. How many of us feel we have a right to say to a young child who is asking for lunch, "Make yourself a peanut butter sandwich" even if the child is perfectly capable of smearing peanut butter on bread? How many of us jump to clear the table when we are coming down with the flu and other family members could do it perfectly well? One woman says she has to stop herself from jumping out of the chair when her children ask for something they could do perfectly well for themselves. She knows that she will do them no favor by waiting on them—that they will be in for a rude awakening if they think the world will jump at their command. Still, she feels guilty about it. All the logic in the world can't completely still those chords of guilt.

The guilt factor is such a serious one that the three of us ran into a dilemma when we were talking about the issue among ourselves. We could say to mothers—and the data make it clear we are right—that a mother ought to be concerned about herself *for her daughter's sake*. But wouldn't that be falling back into the same old trap of making women eternally obligated for their actions to someone else? Women have always said things like, "It's okay for me to work because I'm doing it so we can send the kids to college." Doing something for someone else makes that action legitimate, in the eyes of the world and in the eyes of the woman herself. It's much harder to say, "I am working because I want to work." Shouldn't women be concerned with their own well-being just because they are human beings, not because they are mothers of daughters? Yes. Of course. But it doesn't hurt to point out that a woman's concern for her own happiness and fulfillment has a positive fallout as far as her daughter is concerned.

The mother who would be a suitable object of identification for her daughter needs a solid sense of self-esteem. Again, that's easy to say, but for women, the road to self-esteem can be an uphill battle. As we've seen, the male role in society is viewed as decidedly more prestigious than the female role. In a number of studies in which men and women have been asked to evaluate which activities they consider worthwhile, male activities are usually ranked higher, and female activities are devalued.

Not only that, but studies also show that the more women there are in any occupation, the less prestige it has. Generally, when women get involved in formerly all-male activities, the "rating" of that activity goes down. One private school decided to stop giving out letters when the women's varsity teams were formed, on the basis that the letters would no longer have the meaning they used to.

It's hard to say to yourself "I am terrific" and believe it when society is saying that you—and the things you do—are not really all that great. There is a widespread and mistaken assumption that it is the advent of the women's movement that has devalued the traditional role of women. While some early movement rhetoric about the housewife was unfortunate, it was only an echo of the persistent convictions of a male-dominated society. Anyone who believes that the traditional role was really valued in—let's say—the fifties, may be looking back through rose-colored glasses. Studies conducted in those years show at least as great devaluation of women's role as do studies today. Papered over by tons of verbiage about "the joys of femininity," the reality festered underneath. Many of the articles from those days about how wonderful it is to be a housewife have a defensive ring, as if in answer to some unspoken statement that housewives aren't all that bright, or useful or interesting. When *Redbook* magazine asked young mothers in 1960 to write about "Why Young Mothers Feel Trapped" they were flooded with twenty-four thousand replies. Betty Friedan remembers that when a woman editor at one of the big women's magazines tried to convince her male colleagues to run articles about something outside the home, the men vetoed the idea.

One of the male editors said, "We decided against it. Women are so completely divorced from the world of ideas in their lives now, they couldn't take it."

The idea of all normal women as sublimely happy housewives, completely secure and content in a limited world, was at base a fraud. It was patronizing to women, and reflected society's contempt rather than its approval. Betty Friedan admitted in *The Feminine Mystique*,[12] "I helped create this image. I have watched American women for fifteen years try to conform to it. But I can no longer deny my own knowledge of its terrible implications."

The contortions many women went through to try to comply with the myths of femininity ate away at their self-esteem. They were in a no-win position. They were told that they were intended by nature to be content with activities centering on home and family. Whatever their individual talents and drives, all women were supposed to be happy in their own small space. At the same time, most men and many women perceived that space and its inhabitants as of lesser social value. To develop and maintain high self-esteem under those conditions is about as easy as running the 440 with someone standing on your back. The women who out of duty accepted the female space, and elected to stay within its bounds, could be expected to suffer in terms of their own self-esteem, and indeed, this has turned out to be the case.

In several studies the women taking part were asked to describe themselves in terms of traits commonly associated with "femininity" and "masculinity."[13] The feminine characteristics included "timid," "kind" and "dependent." The masculine traits were such things as "logical," "independent" and "aggressive." Not surprisingly, the women who saw themselves as the most feminine, and as lacking in most masculine traits, were also the lowest in self-esteem.

Which brings us back to the subject of competence—since women and men both associate competence with masculine traits more than with feminine ones, feminine traits aren't linked up with competence. However a woman's perception of herself as not very "masculine" need not be damaging to her self-esteem. A woman, for example, who saw herself as not very logical, independent or aggressive but as very kind and nurturant ought to be able to feel good about herself. The reality of our culture, though, is that you don't get many Brownie points for "warmth."

The masculine traits are the ones which are seen as crucial to a sense of competence, and this kind of competence is highly valued and rewarded in our culture. Over and over again in our studies, we find that women who describe themselves as high on masculine traits are also high in self-esteem. But what about those women who take on "masculine" activities as well—like venturing into the world of work beyond the home? Traditionally only poor women and unmarried women were expected to have to find a way to support themselves. Married women were expected to retreat to home and hearth to be cared for by a good-provider husband. For women with children, holding a job was thought to lead to disaster via the "domino theory." The children would suffer, the marriage would fall apart—a chain reaction of ill effects.

The question of "mommy at home" versus "mommy at work" is still a very touchy subject, one with tap roots that go down to deep feelings about woman's role, the sanctity of Motherhood and a reservoir of female guilt larger than Lake Erie. The whole subject is fraught with intimations of guilt, from the guilt of the mother who works and thinks she is damaging her children to the guilt of the woman at home who feels her life is newly under attack as being of little value.

We need a clear-eyed look at the subject, free from the hysteria, mythology and general wrongheaded notions that have surrounded the issue in the past. What exactly do we know about the working mother and the mother at home? What influences do women in each of these roles have on their daughters?

We will start with the working mother, because that role has been most often condemned, appraised, editorialized about and studied. For the last two decades American society has accepted, almost as an article of faith, that the working mother was in some way damaging her child. It is probably safe to say that no woman who ever held a job in the past twenty years while her children were still at home was entirely free of guilt. Among the people relaying this message about "damage" were behavioral scientists, whose warnings of "maternal deprivation" sounded ominous and weighty with scientific knowledge.

In fact those "scientific" warnings were the result of some very unscientific thinking. To understand why that is so, we have to look at the origin of the frightening term "maternal deprivation."

The term grew out of investigations by researchers on the importance to infants of forming attachments with adults early in life.[14] As we saw in our look at fathering, the unexamined assumption of the researchers led them to focus on the mother-child relationship exclusively.

To test the importance of "attachment" to the infant, researchers in the forties and fifties began to look at children in institutions—hospitals, orphanages. What they found was indeed frightening. As these parentless infants grew, they suffered from emotional problems and the development of many of their skills was found to be impaired. Because of the assumption that these problems were caused solely by damage to the mother-child relationship, "maternal deprivation" became the popular shorthand for this condition.

But was "maternal deprivation" really the reason for what happened to these children? A better term might be "Everything Deprivation." For these studies were carried out in institutions so bleak and barren they make one shudder to think of them. In many cases, babies were kept in cribs where they lay all day with no one to touch them, play with them or cuddle them, except in the most perfunctory way. The institutions were grossly understaffed and the infants had little in the way of sensory stimulation.

From this base the notion of a scientific rationale for mothers to avoid work outside the home seems to have sprung. The situations of these children, however, had nothing at all to do with a family where the mother was warm, loving—and working. The research compared apples and oranges. In fact, the British researcher, John Bowlby, who did some of the institutional studies, also studied children between two and four who were cared for in day nurseries. While the institutionalized children of that age were below average in "development quotient"—the growth of skills and perceptions—the children from the nurseries were normal. So it was clear very early on that the "maternal deprivation" studies did not apply to the case of the working mother. Why, then, have they been used as arguments against both day care and the employment of women? The arguments are another example of social mythology at work. Those elements of the studies that seemed to support the idea that a woman's place is in the home were filtered out and became part of "scientific" arguments to support the myth.

Out of the tangle of myth and misapplied social science came the notion that motherhood was a full-time occupation, and that this was the natural way of things. In "The Myth of the Working Mother,"[15] psychologists Barbara Wallston and Michelle Citron point out, "This full-time motherism is unprecedented in history. Never before has a mother been expected to spend so much time on her children. The farmer's wife couldn't worry about continuously entertaining her offspring; she was too busy helping run the farm. Cross-cultural studies, as well as historical evidence, suggest that full-time companionship between mother and child is unnecessary. Margaret Mead has condemned the over-emphasis on the importance of the tie between a child and her biological mother and the unfounded insistence that any separation is damaging. Mead suggests that on the contrary, the child will adjust better to the world around her if she is cared for by many friendly people."

The idea of "damage" to the child from maternal separation of any degree persists. The cross-cultural information seems to refute it, since children do grow up healthy in other societies where there are many caretakers. But what about the behavioral scientists who have been studying the working mother in our culture? What have they come up with?

First of all, there's the question of the infant-mother relationship. As we've seen, infancy has been regarded as the most crucial period for mother and child, a time when attachments are formed which will help the child develop and grow. If there is any time when maternal separation would be harmful to the child, this would seem to be it. In this country, the idea of day care for infants has been abhorrent to many—perhaps most—people. A baby separated during the day from its mother would invariably suffer greatly, or so most of us have believed. Is it true?

According to the Department of Health, Education, and Welfare, it is not. A review of the experience of the pilot programs on infant day-care across the United States says this: "With regard to the possibility of adverse effects, there appears to be little or no persuasive empirical research evidence thus far indicating that infant day care experience is likely to have unfavorable developmental consequences. This is a valid generalization whether one considers the child's intellectual development, affectional relationships between child and mother, or subsequent peer relationships and responsiveness to adult socialization influences."[16]

The HEW report points out that most of the research that has been done has focused on children in facilities set up to demonstrate high-quality infant care. Clearly, infants might not do so well in centers where the care was less adequate. But in the good infant-care centers, not only is no harm done, but there could be benefits that the child at home might not receive.

Could a day-care center do better than *Mom*? This is a touchy question that could be threatening to a great many women. The HEW report is cautiously worded on that point, suggesting that day-care experience does *not* enhance intellectual development of children from stable homes that are "supportive of normal development." But for children judged to be "at risk," rich day-care programs "hold some promise of preventing the decline in intellectual functioning." If the report seems to be walking on eggs at that point, it is. No one knows if long-term gains could be made by providing infant day care for children "at risk"—which often means those from low-income, disadvantaged families.

The experience of one day-care center, an experimental one at Syracuse University, does in fact suggest infant day care can be beneficial.[17] In this center, which serves children between the ages of six months and four years, children who took part in the program showed gains in developmental quotient that a control group outside the center did not show.

What we do know, because of the experience with infant care, is that separation of mother and infant during working hours is not intrinsically harmful to the infant's growth and development nor to its attachment to its mother. But the belief that it is will probably linger in people's minds.

Another aspect of the mythology concerning mothers and children that held particular sway in the 1950s was the idea that the children of working mothers would grow up to be juvenile delinquents. One woman remembers her mother turned down a good job offer because of her husband's comment that if she did go to work, they could drive out together on Sundays to visit their son at the reformatory. A number of studies were set up to investigate the working-mother delinquency link.[18]

What did the researchers find? In studies of middle-class families, a relationship did at first glance seem to exist. When one looked below the surface statistics of those studies, however, a different picture emerged. The link between maternal employment and delinquency showed up *only* in families that were unstable and troubled. In these families,

84

researchers thought, the mother's employment may have been another factor of stress in a family situation already under too much stress. In middle-class families that were stable there was no tendency at all for the children of working mothers to be delinquent.

The position of behavioral scientists on the question of the working mother has, in fact, changed considerably in the past twenty years. Psychologist Lois Hoffman[19] of the University of Michigan, author of a major review of the scientific literature on the subject, says in the past it was believed that maternal employment had many effects on the child— all of them bad. This old myth has been replaced by a new one, that maternal employment has no effects at all. Hoffman finds that if the old ideas were misguided, the new outlook is too simplistic.

Much of the research uses what she terms the "sniper" approach. A researcher will simply pick some quality in the child—IQ, adjustment, whatever—and compare it with whether or not the mother is working. So the typical study involves only two elements—the mother's employment and a characteristic of the child. Such studies do not take into account such other important factors as whether the mother likes her job and whether her child-care arrangements are suitable.

Hoffman tried to reduce a mass of data into some questions which could then be explored. One of the critical questions was this: If a mother is employed, does she, and possibly her husband, provide a different model of behavior for the children in the family? If she does, then one could expect that the child of a working mother would have a different idea of what a woman's role should be than would the child of the mother who does not work. A girl's concept of herself would also be similarly affected.

This is a most important question for women who have daughters— particularly because the female role has been so devalued in our society. Do girls whose mothers work see the world through a different prism than do daughters of nonworking mothers? There is considerable evidence that they do.

Ruth Hartley's studies—the ones where she asked what sorts of things men needed to know and do and women needed to know and do— provided some interesting data. She found that daughters of working mothers, compared to daughters of nonworking mothers, are more likely to say that women *and* men engage in a wide variety of adult activities— from using a gun or a sewing machine to climbing a mountain or buying furniture. In other words, daughters of working mothers see the world in a less sex-stereotyped fashion. There is an impressive array of data to support this idea.

Studies done with college women, elementary-school children and working professional women reveal that daughters of working women see work as something they will want to do when they are mothers.[20] Daughters of working mothers do not see the working mother as a threat to family happiness. If daughters of working women see the world as less stereotyped than girls of mothers at home, and view the idea of work for women as nonthreatening, are their personality traits also affected by maternal employment? There is evidence that they are. Daughters of working mothers have been found to score lower on indices of traditional femininity.[21] Maternal employment may also raise a girl's estimation of her own sex. Interestingly enough, the children of working mothers see each sex as less limited than do children of nonworking mothers. They tend to "add on" traits to each sex. For example, in one study daughters of working mothers saw their mothers both as warm and affectionate and as strong and competent. Sons of working mothers saw men both as competent and as warm and expressive. This may be due to the greater participation by fathers in child care in families where the mother is employed.

Daughters of working mothers, studies show, have a higher regard for their own sex, which helps generate a sense of their own competence. To have a sense of her own competence, a girl must not have a feeling of inferiority as a female. A study that Grace did in 1968 demonstrated again the link between maternal employment and self-esteem. In the past, researchers found, college women tended to value academic articles more highly if they thought the articles had been written by men. In such tests, for example, articles are given to two groups of young women. For one group, the articles are signed by a man. For the other, the same articles are signed by a woman. The male "authors" receive higher ratings for their insight, logic, presentation, and so forth. The principle that seems to be operating in the heads of the college women is: anything produced by a woman can't be all that good.

When Grace did her version of the study, she found that the daughters of employed women were significantly different from the daughters of full-time housewives in that they did not downgrade the articles attributed to women.

If the daughters of working women seem to regard their own sex more highly, do they tend to see their mothers as attractive role models more

86

readily than girls whose mothers are at home—full time? It seems that they do. In a 1963 paper on "Employment and the Adolescent,"[22] Elizabeth Douvan of the University of Michigan noted that adolescent daughters of working mothers were more likely to name their mothers as the person they most admire. Grace found in her study that college women with working mothers were more likely to name their mothers as the parent they wanted to be like.

In her overview of the scientific literature on working mothers and the self-esteem of their daughters, Lois Hoffman says that although more research is needed, "for girls, maternal employment seems to contribute to a greater admiration of the mother, a concept of the female role which includes less restriction and a wider range of activities, and a self-concept which incorporates these aspects of the female role."

If the daughters of working mothers see the world and themselves in less limited terms, does it follow that these girls will have greater ambition and achievement? There are some indications that this is so, although the research seems to be a hodgepodge. In some of these studies no distinction is made between affluent families and lower-income families, and that can be a key factor. The daughter of a waitress and the daughter of a college professor are too often lumped together under the statistical heading "daughters of working mothers," but their views of what it means to be a working mother and their own aspirations may be vastly different.

On the whole, however, daughters of working mothers seem to fare better in the areas relating to the development of competence than do daughters of nonworking mothers. So, should a woman take a look at the results of these studies and rush right out and get a job? It isn't quite that simple. Women who are thinking about going to work have at least three key issues to consider: What level of guilt and harassment would she have to contend with if she is to combine motherhood and work? Does she like what she is doing on the job? Would she be happier staying at home? (Not all women, of course, have that option.)

In 1962 a team of psychological researchers did a study of mothers of elementary-school children.[23] Instead of just dividing the mothers into employed and nonemployed, they took an additional step. The working mothers were split into two groups—those who wanted to work and those who didn't. The at-home mothers were divided in the same way. The mothers were scored on an index of adequacy of mothering, and the results were most interesting: The lowest scores were those of the dis-

87

satisfied homemakers. In contrast, the best scores were those of the women who were satisfied with their role, whether they were at home or at work. Of the lowest-ranking group, the very lowest scores showed up in the housewives who reported they were at home because they felt it was their "duty" to be there.

There is a message here that ought to be repeated loud and clear: The woman who is home with the kids solely out of a sense of duty is in trouble. When a woman bends her own needs and desires out of shape to accommodate the needs of others, the strain of that sacrifice shows up in the quality of her mothering. So for the woman with children who is on the verge of deciding whether she will work or stay home, the core issue for herself and her children is—"What do I *want* to do?" Lois Hoffman says, "The woman who gives up work out of a sense of duty to her children may, ironically, be doing the worst possible thing for herself and her children." Logically, the reverse must also be true. The woman who is happy at home, whose talents and temperament can best be exercised in a family setting rather than in the job market, could feel that she must get a job because everybody else is, or because she is afraid of being called a "blob" by staying home. But she will be a better role model for her daughter as a happy at-home mother than a miserable nine-to-fiver.

The "duty" theme echoes through one important study done at the University of Michigan in 1971 by psychologist Judith Birnbaum.[24] Birnbaum selected a group of college-educated middle-class women who had graduated with honors; some of them were employed as professionals, others were full-time homemakers. It wasn't clear that a sense of duty led the homemakers to forgo achievement outside the home, but it *was* clear that they had outstanding talents that could probably best be used in a job situation. How did these two groups compare?

The professional women had a higher sense of self-esteem and were more satisfied with their lives than the women at home, who, ironically, had a lower sense of their own competence, even at child-care skills. They felt less attractive, expressed more concern about their identity and felt lonelier than did the professional women.

The women were also compared with respect to their orientation toward their children. The differences here were striking. The full-time homemakers stressed the sacrifices involved in having children. The professional women stressed the enrichment and fulfillment that children brought to their lives. The homemakers expressed more anxiety about their own achievements and stressed their inadequacies as mothers. In response to a picture showing a little boy and his parents with a crutch in the background, the homemakers told more dramatic, depressed and anxious stories. There were also different responses between the groups to the growing independence of their children. The professional women responded positively while the homemakers expressed ambivalence, regret and concern. They felt less important to their children and feared the loss of familiar patterns.

Lois Hoffman, commenting on Birnbaum's study, says "The pattern of the able, educated full-time homemakers suggests that they would have shortcomings as mothers—particularly as their children approach adolescence. At that time, when the child needs a parent who can encourage independence and instill self-confidence, the anxieties and concerns of these women and their own frustrations would seem to operate as a handicap."

In our own study of mothers of young girls, we found evidence to support Hoffman's speculation. Women who saw themselves as relatively lacking in competence-related traits—like Birnbaum's homemakers—were unable to imagine their daughters as independent at an early age. The message of the Birnbaum study seems clear: Compliance with the time-honored expectation that all women must and should put others first results in anxious, self-critical women, who feel like less-than-adequate mothers. A slogan that would be helpful to all of today's mothers is, "Don't overdose on duty."

The mother-daughter relationship is clearly a crucial one for both parties involved—whether the mother is in the home or in the work force. It's a relationship that is receiving renewed attention today; much of the emphasis has been on the great conflict inherent in that relationship. The women in Nancy Friday's study of mothers and daughters are clearly under considerable stress, and invest a great deal of energy trying to deal with their differences. The current emphasis on problems is not surprising; in times of social change the relationship between the generations can be difficult. But it would be a mistake to assume that angst is an inevitable part of all mother-daughter relationships. We've seen that fathers can act as mentors for their daughters, can help them to grow and can introduce them to the world beyond the home. The mother-as-mentor has been a rarity in our society simply because few women have been admitted to positions of importance. That is changing now, and the "mentor" model of motherhood may no longer be so difficult to find. Such models do exist. Caryl believes that her relationship with her mother, one that grew in affection, respect and trust, that matured rather than soured when Caryl reached adulthood, was just such a one.

Caryl has two favorite photographs of her mother. They were taken more than thirty years apart. In one, she is a young woman, just entering her working life in the heady atmosphere of Washington in the New Deal. She is walking down one of the city's main streets dressed in the height of fashion—a coat with a fox collar and a large cartwheel hat. Her head is up, her back is straight and the jauntiness of her stride is unmistakable. She seems delighted with the world and with herself, and she seems to be walking toward the future as if she could hardly wait to feel its embrace.

In the second picture, much of that future has already happened. She is in her mid-sixties, and though she does not know it, near the end of her life. A stranger looking at the two pictures would know it was the same woman. The figure is still slim, the body erect. The face shows signs of age, but the eyes do not. They are as bright and as intelligent as they were in that other picture so long ago. She is standing by the desk of the governor of Maryland, reaching out as he hands her the pen with which he has just signed a bill creating a commission on aging in the state. Her smile is both mischievous and triumphant. A community activist, she has been the prime force in pushing the reluctant governor into signing the bill.

To her daughter, Helen Rivers was the main reason that there seemed to be no discrepancy between such ideas as competence, achievement and the condition of being female. Caryl remembers her as being at once the smartest and the most feminine person she ever knew. It seemed to her daughter that she could do anything—throw a baseball, edge a car around a curve while driving a bit too fast, swim with wonderful grace and style. Helen kept her letters from the high-school rifle and swim teams, proudly, and she was a lawyer as well. She was the first woman to practice at Covington Burling, one of Washington's most prestigious law firms. When Caryl was small, the two of them used to have a special time together when Helen came home from work. They would take a walk and her mother would tell her stories about the outside world into which she journeyed each day. Caryl can't remember what the stories were, exactly, but it seemed to her that the world was a magical place which she, too, would enter one day.

When World War II broke out, Helen left the firm to join her husband who was in the Navy and was stationed in Alabama. By the end of the war her second child, a son, was only a baby. With great regret, she decided not to return to legal practice. She poured her energies into the suburban rounds of PTA, school volunteering and selling real estate part-time. It was not a large enough world for her formidable talents, but she staved off frustration by sheer energy. Sometimes, however, it would overtake her. There were times when she would burst into tears and say, quietly, that the walls were closing in on her. Her daughter didn't know what she meant, then; she does now. But even then, Caryl was growing restive with the security of her small suburban world. As a teenager, the last thing she wanted was peace and security. She wanted to see and feel and taste every exotic thing in the universe. She saw no reason why she shouldn't. Her mother had done it, so why couldn't she? When Helen talked of the world out there, Caryl listened intently. Helen talked of how some men used power with ease, of how they simply lifted a phone and financial empires rose and fell. She told of the arrogance of those men, of how they believed they were destined by God and by genes to rule over others. Perhaps most important of all, she said that maybe a woman had to be twice as good as a man to succeed, but being better than a lot of men wasn't that hard. She had discovered that she was quicker, brighter, bolder than many men. They weren't God, or heroes. The world of men was not filled with Da Vincis and Einsteins. It was filled with mediocre men who seemed to be giants to only one group of people: women. Her daughter need not be afraid of them. She could do anything she wanted—anything she had the wit and the nerve and the skill to do.

For Caryl, her mother was her guide to the world of ideas, of power and public affairs, and in a very real sense, gave her daughter the key to that world. Her daughter grew up with no fear of men or the world they ran, and thus could never be a mirror to reflect back a man's image twice his size. And yet, Caryl saw her mother as a woman who genuinely liked men, who seemed to be able to deal with them as they dealt with one another. This was so, perhaps, because she saw them as they were, life-sized. It is only recently that Caryl has been able to link this quality that she and her mother shared to her own inability to feel rage against men. She understands, in an abstract way, that men run the world, but she has never had any sense that men control her individual destiny. Rage comes from the personal understanding that one is a victim, and Helen Rivers did not see herself as a victim, and neither does her daughter.

Caryl remembers that her mother seemed to combine an intense competitiveness, a love of a challenge or a good fight, with an earth-mother sort of maternalism. As a political activist, a career on which she embarked when she was nearly sixty, Helen found a job she loved that suited her talents perfectly. Once, involved in a fight against a group of doctors who wanted to build a profit-making hospital instead of a public one that would have benefited more people, she stood beside a woman who was an ally in the fight. The woman was literally shaking at the idea of confronting *doctors*. Helen took her in hand. "Come on, Dotty, you can do it. They're not so great. Stand up to them. And remember, don't be so damn *ladylike*."

When Helen died, Caryl lost not only her mother, but in the truest sense, a friend. Helen gave her daughter freedom, let her grow up and be what she would, took joy in her daughter's accomplishments with no touch of envy; after all, she had her own life as well. As Caryl sees it, "She gave me permission to be strong, because she was strong, free because she was free. I cannot imagine a finer gift."

Nuts and Bolts

Probably the most disturbing fact that emerges from studies of children's perceptions of men and women is that they see women as "limited" people, able to perform capably in only a small area of activity. Parents wondering about how their children see adults might find it interesting to repeat Ruth Hartley's "Martian" experiment, to ask their children what they would say if they had to explain to a visitor from Mars what men had to do and know to get along in our society, and what women had to do and know. The chances are good that the children would reflect society's stereotypes.

What can parents do about this? Perhaps the first answers lie close to home. As we've said, a young girl may see her mother as the less competent parent, as the person who does not control the resources, thus setting up some inner conflict over identifying with her mother. Women at home may face this problem most acutely, because they are not seen as breaking out of the traditional female role as readily as working women. Does this mean that all women ought to dash out and get a job? Not at all, because the woman who is happy with her life—whether she's employed or at home—makes a good model for her daughter. The mother at home is surely concerned with her daughter's competence and self-esteem. How does she deal with this problem? First of all, she doesn't have to buy the whole package of the traditional role—especially the devaluation of that role by society in general. The woman at home ought to see herself as a person who is doing a job which is important, and to think of herself as a competent, self-reliant individual. If she has any doubts about her competence, she ought to make sure to venture outward into activities that will enhance her sense of self-reliance, not withdraw into inactivity.

Since children have a need to identify with a parent who is powerful, who controls resources, the money-power situation ought to be given some thought in the family. The mother should not be treated in a childlike fashion, having to ask her husband for money or having it doled out to her like a kid's allowance. One woman who left work to be at home with her children full time found this aspect of her new life demeaning. She said she felt like a kid again, begging her father for fifty cents to go to the movies. Perhaps the best situation is the one in which the mother has her own checking account and a sum of money over which she has complete control. Whatever financial arrangement is made, the crucial point is that the daughter not perceive her mother as the supplicant, the one who has to behave manipulatively or furtively in order to have access to the family's funds.

It is also important for the mother at home to behave like a person who is entitled to respect and consideration. She is not everybody's maid. But it is easy for women to fall into the "servant" trap—running and fetching for everyone else in the family. Daughters have sensitive antennae—all children do—and if they see their mother acting like a local version of "Hazel," it is not going to be easy for them to identify with that particular role. One woman, now divorced, remembers that when she was married her family regarded her as "just another plug-in appliance." Everybody wants to have a plug-in appliance—but who would want to *be* one?

Since many studies show that daughters of nonworking mothers tend to have a more sex-stereotyped view of the world than do daughters of working mothers, the woman at home probably has to take special care in this area. It's important that she and her husband make an effort to cross rigid sex-role divisions, that he take an active role in the care of the house and children and that she cultivate some role outside of the strictly domestic one. When she does, she has to be careful that that role is taken seriously by the family. If the work is nonpaid, and often it is, it can be easily dismissed. One woman who worked with a volunteer

93

agency directed a chain of day-care centers all across the state, a demanding managerial task. But her husband always spoke of her volunteer work as "going out with the girls." If the work she does outside of the domestic sphere is dismissed as a hobby or light recreation, the children will also tend to devalue that work and to follow the sex-stereotyped way of thinking that only men's work is important work.

Mothers can take their daughters along sometimes when they are doing their nondomestic work. A woman who is chairing a League of Women Voters meeting on a political issue, or directing the PTA fund drive, or trying to get neighborhood people involved in a crucial local issue may not recognize the benefits of letting her daughter see her in this role. But doing so could give the daughter a whole new image of her mother, and of the role of women in society as well. Too often, children see their mothers only in the role of domestic servant—cooking, cleaning, doing housework—the other parts of their mothers' adult life are less visible.

Unfortunately, social mythology makes a heroine of the woman who lives for her young children (and at the same time attacks that woman when she is older as the interfering, meddlesome "Jewish" mother). People nod approval at the woman who says, "I won't let anything interfere with my obligations to my family." This puts the woman in the position of placing her own needs and priorities last on the list. Some women feel they have to put every "need" of a child before their own. If a child says she needs a ride to a ballet lesson because it's cold out, a mother often will cancel an activity she has scheduled to chauffeur the child. She will not feel she has a right to tell the child to put on an extra sweater and walk. Working mothers may be equally or even more prone to this tendency as women at home. Feeling guilty because of time away from the children, the working mother can often rush to do things for children that they could just as well do for themselves. Children—daughters in particular—should not be allowed to see mothers as people whose needs, desires and comfort come last on everybody's list.

Guilt may be the great scourge of the life of the working mother—along with the day-to-day hassles of keeping a busy life on track. She should remember that in few cultures throughout history have mothers spent so much of their time with their children. It would also be helpful for them to remember that they do, in fact, spend quite a lot of time with their children. People have always been able to send a dart straight to the heart of a working mother by saying, "She's letting somebody else raise her children." That just isn't so. Let's look at some of the mathematics of the situation of the woman who holds down a full-time job. Let's say she is away from home nine hours a day, five days a week. If her child sleeps twelve hours a day, that means that she spends something like thirty-nine hours a week at home during her child's approximately eighty-four waking hours. So for almost half of these waking hours, she is a major figure in her child's life. That is in no way "turning the child over" to someone else to raise. Clearly, the mother spends enough time with the child to have a great impact, and that impact is cumulative over the years.

Working mothers often suffer great anxiety over the quality of care they can arrange for their children. Certainly this is a crucial question, but some mothers get obsessive about it. They believe the saying that "nobody can give your child what you can," and make their demands for a mother substitute so impossible that they can't find anyone. An infant doesn't need someone with a college degree for a caretaker, just someone kind and patient. Caryl remembers that when her son was a baby, she decided she was going to "enrich" his life. She soon found out that her ability to write an analysis of a political issue or to paint a watercolor didn't have much to do with her relationship with her infant son. All he wanted was somebody who would play peekaboo for hours on end—a game which drove his mother slightly bananas. The nice, grandmotherly lady who baby-sat for him was much better at games. If Caryl had stayed home trying to produce an Einstein, she would have produced two neurotics—the baby and herself.

A working mother should remember that her daily absences do not interfere with the ability of her baby to form an attachment to her. The baby may also develop an attachment to the mother substitutes and that's all to the good. A working mother can feel a stab of pain near the heart when a child turns to a sitter to kiss a hurt instead of to her. It can be hard to remember at a time like this that you are not a bad mother, but in fact it is healthy that your child loves someone else as well. A child's love is boundless—when she gives love to someone else, she doesn't take any away from you.

Working mothers who read child development manuals with endless details about "helping your baby develop" often get the idea that it's a twelve-hour-a-day job—that you have to be there constantly, shoving colored blocks and balls of just the right size at the child. It's good for parents to be aware of materials that can be stimulating for the infant.

Working mothers can be sure to have these items on hand and can instruct sitters in how to use them—in addition, of course, to what they do themselves during those hours they are with the baby. Much of the infant's growth and development, however, occurs according to an internal time clock. Given a reasonably stimulating environment, parents only help this process along. In later years, the parents' values, interests and ideas will have a much stronger impact on the kind of person the child turns out to be.

5

GAMES

The Playing Fields of Childhood

Girls' soccer is pretty bad because most of the girls don't show up every time. We have to keep changing our teams to make them even. Then pretty soon we start arguing over whether something was fair or not. And then some girls quit and go home if they don't get their own way. Sometimes calling them "babies" helps to get them to stay and play a little longer.

—Janet Lever, in "Sex Differences in the Games Children Play"

What are little boys made of, made of?
What are little boys made of?
Snips and snails and puppy-dogs' tails;
that's what little boys are made of, made of.

What are little girls made of, made of?
What are little girls made of?
Sugar and spice and everything nice;
And that's what little girls are made of, made of.

—Mother Goose

We all grew up with this nursery rhyme, a bit of doggerel that may seem insignificant, but that gets to the heart of a widely held popular assumption—that males and females are such opposites that the "stuff" of which they are composed is vastly different. Since in our society the social roles which men and women play have been generally separated into "spheres" belonging to each, a whole rationale has developed to explain this fact. Woman, so this theory goes, being biologically different from man, is therefore emotionally and intellectually different. Femaleness or maleness colors the entire psychological life of a person and accounts for the social roles of men and women. Fixed, inborn biological differences are the reason that men are airline pilots or executives and women raise babies.

Such "biological" arguments are often not without political overtones: The institution of slavery was buoyed up by the argument that blacks occupied the social status of slave because they were biologically inferior and destined by nature for field labor. The "biological" arguments often are based more on wishful thinking or unconscious acceptance of the status quo than on any objective analysis of data.

A great deal of data exists on psychological sex differences, and wading through studies and statistics to make some sense out of the whole is a monumental job. That job was tackled by psychologists Eleanor Emmons Maccoby and Carol Nagy Jacklin,[1] both of whom had done their own previous research on the subject. They surveyed some two thousand studies published mainly between 1966 and 1973. To give you some idea of the scope of the task, their book, *The Psychology of Sex Differences*, includes a 233-page annotated bibliography.

Out of this massive pile of evidence, Maccoby and Jacklin come up with some intriguing but controversial conclusions. There are, they say, certain sex differences that show up; girls excel in verbal ability, boys in spatial ability. Boys are superior in mathematical ability and males are more aggressive than females. Keep in mind that the authors do not say whether these are inborn traits or acquired ones—we don't know—but just that these are things that show up in experiments, observations and tests. Data about other traits, say the scientists, are equivocal—that is, there is no clear evidence that boys and girls differ significantly in such things as fear, timidity, tactile sensitivity, competitiveness, dominance, compliance, nurturance or "maternal behavior." Sometimes different studies report mixed—or opposite—results.

Perhaps their most surprising conclusion is that they call most of the generally accepted notions about sex differences sheer "myth." In their reading of the evidence, there is no proof that girls are more "social" than boys, or more "suggestible" than boys, that girls have lower self-esteem or that they lack motivation to achieve. Nor is there evidence that boys are more analytic, that girls are better at rote learning while boys

98

are better at high level tasks that require them to inhibit previously learned responses.

"We must conclude from our survey of all the data that many popular beliefs about the psychological characteristics of the two sexes have little or no basis in fact. Yet people continue to believe, for example, that girls are more "social" than boys, or more suggestible than boys, ignoring the fact that careful observation and measurements show no sex differences."

They explain what they call the mythology of sex differences by the strong attachment people have to their stereotypes.

"It is well documented," they say, "that whenever a member of a group behaves the way an observer expects him to, the observer notes the fact and his prior belief is confirmed and strengthened. But when a member of the group behaves in a way that is not consistent with the observer's expectations, the behavior is likely to go unnoticed, so the observer's prior belief remains intact. This probably happens continually with those entrenched ideas about sex differences."

The most provocative statement the two psychologists make—one that stirred up a heated, ongoing debate—is that their survey revealed surprisingly little difference in parental behavior according to the sex of the child, other than in narrowly defined areas such as toy selection. The messages boys and girls get from their parents, Maccoby and Jacklin say, are "remarkably similar."

This finding seems to conflict with what many of us believe—that boys and girls do indeed get very different messages from parents, and from society, and as a result grow up to behave in markedly different ways. The psychologists' assessment of the data, particularly their presentation of all those "myths," raises questions for people interested in how young girls grow. Should we stop being concerned that girls are too dependent, lacking in self-esteem, that parents don't encourage them to be assertive or motivated to achieve? Are we worrying about illusions? Do any of these things we think we see in female behavior in our culture really exist?

Like many critics, we think that Maccoby and Jacklin have come up with an assessment of sex differences that is too optimistic in its implications for adult women. In her therapeutic work, Rosalind is all too familiar with women who, in spite of extensive evidence to the contrary and outstanding credentials, think themselves incapable of applying for positions they could easily handle, completing a professional degree or making a decision to change from one field to another.

Psychologist Jeanne H. Block, in an important critique of Maccoby and Jacklin's conclusions, finds them seriously flawed.[2] Block, of the University of California at Berkeley, says that the basic problem may be that Maccoby and Jacklin were forced to wrestle with such a huge mass of data, some carefully balanced, some hit-or-miss. Their task was like that of the blind men and the elephant, the old folk parable in which the blind men try to deduce the nature of the elephant from the part they grab on to. The man who gets the tail thinks the elephant is like a snake, while the one in the middle thinks the elephant is like a whale. As Block points out, Maccoby and Jacklin decided to include—and give equal weight to—any study they could find because there wasn't any reasonable basis for deciding which ones to leave out. Since the two psychologists could not evaluate two thousand-odd studies; the good ones got tossed into the pot with the bad, making for a "box score" tally of all the results.

A built-in problem with the studies that Maccoby and Jacklin analyzed was that, where the question of socialization was concerned, very young children were overrepresented. Seventy-five percent of all the studies cited used as subjects boys or girls five years old or younger. At this age, the effect of patterns of socialization aren't yet clear. When Jeanne Block sorted the studies—lumped together by Maccoby and Jacklin—according to the age of the subjects, she found that clear and significant sex differences, increased with age. Fewer sex differences are found among infants and very young children, suggesting that cultural factors, not inborn biological mechanisms, are at work.

So, while the debate on psychological sex differences goes on, some things are clear. When you look at the evidence, you tend to be more impressed by the similarities between the sexes than by the differences. Psychologically, we are more alike than different, and most of us possess traits described as "male" or "female" but which in fact may be simply human. Certainly, the data do not reveal the sort of quantum difference that makes the rigid sex-role divisions we know either inevitable or logical. But we do see significant differences in areas related to the development and exercise of competence: shaky self-esteem and unrealistically low aspirations in women. The search for the roots of these differences leads us back to parents—what they say, what they do and the messages they transmit.

A lot of "modern" parents would be surprised at what those messages are. The kinds of behavior parents say they accept in their children, the qualities they think they are promoting, may in fact be quite different from what really happens between parent and child. Psychologist Beverly Fagot, of the University of Oregon, recently completed an important study of parents' reactions to two-year-old children.[3]

When Fagot asked parents what kinds of behavior would be appropriate for girls and boys, the parents responded in a nonstereotyped fashion: "These parents would not restrict playmates to one sex, nor would they avoid buying an opposite-sex toy if the child wanted it. They planned to encourage their child to follow up interests, regardless of the sex-appropriateness of the interests as the child grew older. Eighty percent planned to actively encourage a viewpoint of sex equity . . ."

Fagot spent a great deal of time observing each child with its parents. She found that the parents' behavior was often at odds with what they said. For example, she asked parents if "asking for help" was a more appropriate behavior for either sex, and the parents did not think it was. In fact, she observed, parents were more likely to react positively when daughters asked for help, and more likely to react negatively when sons asked for help.

"Why this occurs is a critical question that cannot be answered from the data in this study. Do the girls ask for help in a more appealing fashion, or do they ask on tasks that parents feel are more appropriate for help-giving? Or perhaps, do boys ask for help as a way of annoying their parents? The difference in responding to requests for help is apparently not the result of attribution by parents that girls need or should receive more help . . . In fact, parents of girls in the interviews would often spontaneously mention that their daughters appear more competent than the sons of their friends."

The data suggest, Fagot says, "that parents are not fully aware of the methods they use to socialize their young children. Few parents would think of such a mundane behavior as 'manipulating objects' as a behavior important to sex-role socialization, yet girls are given more negative feedback when they engage in such behaviors. In effect, then, boys are allowed to explore objects, to learn about the physical world with less chance of criticism than are girls." There were not a great number of areas in which parents treated girls and boys differently. The important thing was that there were significant differences in a few key areas. Fagot agrees with Maccoby and Jacklin that the similarities in treatment of boys and girls at this young age are greater than the differences. "But the few areas where we do find significant differences have great consequences for the developmental process."

101

Beverly Fagot raises an important question when she speculates that some quality in girls may account for the parents' response.

In recent years it has been fashionable to blame parents for everything from psychosis to tooth decay. The general idea has been that the baby is a little blank slate, a *tabula rasa*, on which the parents make the markings, but the whole process, we now know, is more complicated than that. Some new research views the parenting process as a two-way street, in which the characteristics of the child have a profound impact on the actions of the parents. Richard Bell, a researcher at the National Institute of Mental Health, says that parents respond in different ways to different children.[4] Certain babies are high in "person orientation." They love being held, stroked, tickled, and their obvious delight in such behavior reinforces the parents' interaction with them. Other babies are more restless, more interested in physical activity than in being held, more interested in objects than in people.

When psychologist Howard Moss studied infants between three and twelve weeks in their homes, he found that the male infants were more irritable—cried and fussed more and slept less than the female infants. Mothers of male babies spent more time in caretaking—soothing, feeding, getting them to settle down. The mothers were more sociable with their less irritable girl babies and spent more time cooing and playing with them. Perhaps as a result, male babies seem to develop awareness of and sensitivity to other people at a slower rate than girls. A study of infants between ten and thirty-six months showed male babies markedly lower in responsiveness to other people than girl babies. So differences in the socialization of infants begin when they are only hours old.

The parents of a child are its first environment—the first universe that a child knows. Very quickly, though, the child's physical environment begins to have its own impact. In one intriguing study, two researchers, Harriet L. Rheingold and Kaye V. Cook of the University of North Carolina at Chapel Hill, decided to look at what parents put in boys' and girls' rooms to find out which objects and activities parents thought were appropriate for each sex.[5] They decided to look at children under six, because "children so young may indeed express their preferences and wishes, but it is their parents—now the mother, now the father—who decide what to buy or to place in the child's room." The children were all white, the majority lived in private homes and most of the fathers held academic positions.

They found that boys' rooms had more educational and art materials, more spatial toys (blocks), more sports equipment, and the girls' rooms had more dolls, more domestic objects and more ruffles. The "dolls" the boys had were usually toy soldiers or cowboys or other "action" figures. The range of types of toys found in the boys' rooms was much broader—and there were usually more of them. The researchers noted an almost complete absence in girls' rooms of such toys as wagons, boats and buses, while such toys were often found in boys' rooms. Is this because little girls just aren't interested in playing with them? According to the researchers, who observed children in play situations, eighteen-month-old girls spent as much time as boys playing with a large plastic truck. It is interesting to note that one of the differences between boys and girls that shows up consistently in tests is that boys are better in visual-spatial ability, which involves estimating distances and size of figures. Does what shows up on the tests reflect the absence of vehicles and other time-and-movement toys in girls' rooms, rather than any inborn psychological difference? Apparently so. Psychologists Lisa Serbin, Jane Connor and their colleagues at State University of New York, Binghamton, gave young girls and boys practice on visual-spatial tasks—making designs with blocks.[6] The girls' ability improved, but the boys' ability stayed the same. This seems to indicate that the reason the girls had not done as well as the boys was that they hadn't had as much practice. These sorts of skills are crucial to any field in which mathematics and mechanics play a part—architecture, stage design, physics, engineering, economics, among others.

So the fact that girls usually don't have trucks, erector sets, Tinker Toys and the like in their rooms reflects more than just their parents' decorating skills.

Interestingly, the study of children's rooms was done on children from families in a high socioeconomic class, children whose parents lived and worked in a university atmosphere—the sort of families where one would expect to find consciousness about sex-role stereotypes. But, the researchers say, the contents of these kids' rooms were similar to an illustration you might see of boys' or girls' rooms in a mail-order catalog.

Some people might ask why two scientists spent so much time rifling through children's rooms. Are the rooms that important?

Rheingold and Cook say they are. Rooms are a large part of the young children's environment. It's where they go to bed and wake up, and where they spend a fair amount of their time in play. "It's safe to assume

103

those rooms do have an impact on their behavior." One thing that stands out clearly in their findings, they say, is the extent to which the boys were provided with objects that encouraged activities directed away from the home—sports, cars, animals and the military—and the girls were given objects that directed them toward the home—keeping house and caring for children.

So very early, the boys and girls who live in these rooms are given a message about the competence they are supposed to develop—and the range of action for the boys is far wider.

Action is an important word in talking about how boys and girls grow. Consider the games children play in the streets and schoolyards.

An old British maxim holds that the Battle of Waterloo was won on the playing fields of Eton; that assessment of gamesmanship is probably not far from wrong. For children, games are often a preview—adult life in miniature. One ten-year-old boy—decked out in his football regalia—was heading off to Pop Warner football practice and his mother called out to him, "Have fun!"

He stared at her incredulously. "FUN!" he said. He already knew that football wasn't fun, it was the struggle of life, and it was serious business. The well-known sociologist George Herbert Mead looked at boys playing baseball and discovered that they learned a number of complex skills useful in later life—learning how to win and lose, how to handle aggression, how to play within the rules and the consequences of violating the rules. When the noted Swiss psychologist Jean Piaget wanted to examine how children learn moral values through games where there are set rules, he watched boys playing marbles. He said that he did not find a single girls' game that had as elaborate and organized a set of rules as the boys' game of marbles. So we're left with the question, "What happens to girls?"

Janet Lever of Northwestern University did her Ph.D. thesis on sex differences in the games children play.[7] She wanted to find out if there were in fact marked differences in the games of boys and girls, and if so, what those differences might mean. She set out to study 181 fifth-grade children, predominantly white and middle class—"a choice made deliberately because I believe that race and class distinctions would only confound the picture at this stage of exploratory research."

Using observation, interviews, written questionnaires and diaries kept by the children, she came away with a great deal of data on how boys and girls play.

The first thing she found was that boys play outdoors far more than girls. Many of the preferred games of girls, like playing with dolls or board games, are most easily played indoors. The boys preferred team sports or fantasy games like war, which have to be played outside. Forty percent of the girls spent less than a quarter of their playtime outdoors; only 15 percent of the boys spent that little time outside. This means, says Lever, that the girls playing inside are restricted in their physical movements and the noise they are allowed to make. Boys move in larger, more open spaces and go farther away from the home, which is undoubtedly part of their training in independence. The girls' indoor games, often played in their rooms behind closed doors, are private in nature, while the boys' games are public, open to scrutiny.

Both boys and girls spent about the same amount of time in solitary play, Lever found, but when they were involved in playing with other kids, boys played in larger groups. Even when the girls played outdoors, they played in smaller groups than did the boys. One reason for this was the nature of the boys' games. A baseball game needs a fair number of players before it's any fun. "Girls' games like jump rope or hopscotch can be played with very few."

Boys, Janet Lever discovered, play in age-heterogeneous groups more than girls do. That means that you might find a game of touch football that included six- and seven-year-old boys as well as older kids.

> The implicit understanding is that you're better off with a little kid in the outfield than no one at all. I witnessed numerous ice hockey games where ages ranged from 9 to 15 or 16. The youngest children tried their best to keep up with the older ones or dropped out. They learned to accept their bruises, stifle their frustrations, or not be invited to play again. The very few times I observed girls in age-mixed play was at summer camp when the 10-12 year olds used much younger children of five and six as "live dolls," leading them in circle songs of ring-around-the-rosy or versions of tag, like duck, duck goose. Here the oldest girls had to play on the level of the young instead of vice versa. The implications of this female play pattern for learning child care and nurturance are so obvious they require little comment.

Boys, Janet Lever found, play competitive games more than girls. Sixty-five percent of the boys' games had rules, goals and winners. Only 35 percent of the girls' activities fit this description. And the boys' games lasted longer. Watching the children at play during recess, she saw many boys' games that took up the whole twenty-five-minute period, but didn't observe a single girls' activity that lasted longer than fifteen minutes. There are several possible reasons for this. First of all, the level of skills needed to play the boys' games was much higher. Boys who start playing baseball at six find it much more fun at twelve because they are still learning the complex skills involved and it's still a challenge. But the girls who started playing jump rope in the first grade reached the peak of the skills needed for that simple game a long time ago. They are still playing jump rope at age eleven or twelve but get quickly bored with it. "Moreover, girls' games have less structured potential for surprise, such as stealing bases or bunting as in the game of baseball. It's likely that the boys find their games more challenging and therefore have a longer span of attention."

Even when girls do play games requiring a high degree of skill, they often find them frustrating because they haven't developed the motor skills necessary to play the game well. "Some girls I watched could not catch or throw a volleyball," Lever says. "The one spontaneous girls' sports game I observed—a game of kickball—ended after fifteen minutes because the fielders had not succeeded in getting a single player out, and they were both frustrated and bored."

In fact, most girls have dropped out of games—schoolyard or organized—by the time they are twelve or thirteen. Psychologists have noted that and attributed it to the fact that girls mature earlier and develop superior verbal skills, so they exchange games for conversation earlier than boys do. Janet Lever suggests that the opposite is true. "Our culture is deficient in games that are sufficiently sophisticated and challenging for older girls, thereby forcing them to drop out of playground activity. Development of verbal skills may be seen as a consequence, rather than as a cause, of this pattern."

One advantage of the more complicated games that boys play is that they learn to settle disputes more effectively. Lever saw the boys quarreling frequently, but no game was ended because of a quarrel and no argument continued for more than a few minutes. When a debate could not be settled—was he out or safe?—the play would be repeated. Even the youngest, least skillful players took an active part in the arguments. Were these boys learning how to deal with the disputes they will meet later on in life? Piaget argues that indeed they are. Lawrence Kohlberg, who studied children's moral development, suggests that

106

lessons are best learned when games involve some ambiguity—in other words, where there are areas of the game open to dispute.

"If Kohlberg is right," says Lever, "the moral lessons inherent in girls' play are fewer since there are almost no areas of ambiguity comparable to a player sliding into first base. Traditional girls' games are turn-taking games like jumprope and hopscotch where the nature of the competition is indirect." There are no fouls in jump rope and no "hogging" in hopscotch. So the nature of girls' games is such that disputes are less likely to arise than in boys' games. Thus, girls don't get much experience in the techniques of settling disputes. The typical pattern with girls, Lever says, is that when the quarrel begins, the game breaks up, and little effort is made to solve the problem. The captain of a girls' after-school soccer team explains what often happens:

"Girls' soccer is pretty bad because most of the girls don't show up every time. We have to keep changing our teams to make them even. Then pretty soon we start arguing over whether something was fair or not. And then some girls quit and go home if they don't get their own way. Sometimes calling them 'babies' helps to get them to stay and play a little longer." Another girl said that it was often hard to get the girls to decide on choosing up the sides, deciding who is to be captain and which team will start the play.

Taking an overall look at the striking differences between girls' and boys' play, Lever concludes that these patterns lead to the development of particular social skills, which in turn lead to the different roles of adult males and females in our society. "Specifically, I suggest that boys' games may help prepare their players for successful performance in a wide range of work settings in modern society. In contrast, girls' games may help prepare their players for the private sphere of the home and their future roles as wives and mothers."

The boys' games foster independence, they encourage the development of the skills necessary to organize activities involving many people. They also offer experience in resolving the disputes that arise when so many people are involved in an activity. They have to learn how to play on a team, and how to relate in a competitive situation to a number of people. Girls, on the other hand, take part most often in games that may help them develop a fine-tuned sensitivity to the moods and emotions of others. Girls' play usually occurs in small, intimate groups, especially the "dyad"—the group of two. Girls often said they had a single best friend, with whom they played almost every day. "They learn to know that person and her moods so well," says Lever, "that through non-verbal clues alone, a girl understands whether her playmate is hurt, happy, sad, bored and so on . . ." There is usually an open show of affection between the girls—with handholding, writing notes back and forth and sharing of secrets. "These girls experience the heartbreak of serial monogamy long before heterosexual dating begins, some three to six years later. These relationships resemble nothing so much as miniature marriages, in which the girls learn the kind of empathy they will use in later life as the peacemaker, mediator and 'glue' of the nuclear family. But they do not learn the organizational skills that make for success in a work-oriented society."

In their organized games, boys learn ways to resolve disputes so that friendships aren't ruptured in the process. They learn to do what Lever called "de-personalizing the attack," competing against good friends and not taking it personally. If you slide into the second baseman and knock him over, he sees it not as an attack but as the way the game is played. Boys learn to restrain their energy, temper and frustration for the good of the group. "Boys must develop skills of gregariousness and amiability—social skills which sociologist David Riesman says are linked closely to success in modern organizational life."

These ideas are supported by observations about the way adults often behave. Male managers often complain that women employees respond emotionally to criticism, and don't know how to read the unspoken "signals" of the organization "game." That may well be true, since boys have played that game since they were small and women have not.

Does this mean that the way boys grow up prepares them well for adult life, while girls don't learn any of the skills they need?

Not at all. Life is more than a team sport. Increasingly, men are complaining that their friendships with other men are only on the level of business associations, pleasant, useful, but lacking in any sense of intimacy or commitment. In relationships where intimacy is crucial, as with children and wives, men have tremendous difficulties expressing and understanding feelings. The games boys play do not prepare them for intimacy as men.

108

6

THE SPORTING LIFE

The Second Baseperson Is Here to Stay

> Girls are supposed to be all feminine and act Miss Prissy. They're not supposed to sweat when they get hot. I like to sweat. It makes me feel good.
>
> —A sixteen-year-old tomboy

Webster's Dictionary defines a tomboy simply as "a girl of boyish behavior," but there is an entire universe of assumptions behind those words. The term itself implies the existence of boundaries, of occupied "turf." It says that a male territory exists and that a young female who enters that turf loses the name girl and becomes something else: a *tomboy*. She is a sort of mutant, different from others of her species. The word can be an insult or a badge worn proudly, and this fact has to do with the whole maze of contradictions wrapped up in the rigid sex roles most of us grew up with. Women who crossed that line when they were children still remember the mixed emotions of pride and punishment.

Novelist Eve Babitz[1]:

> The very idea of the word tomboy enraged me when I found out about it. It was such a stupid trap. Either you were a girl—sugar and spice—or you were a "tomboy"—puppy dog tails. The idea that they

only had two categories and those were they turned me white-hot . . .
It was insulting enough that they expected you to be a cute little girl. It
was an outrage that the ones who wanted to play baseball until dark
were "tomboys" and would "grow out of it." I hid. I was neither a cute
little girl nor someone who'd grow out of my present indifference and
become a cute little girl. I could understand the pride of the ones who
were cute little girls, though. They were behaving well and able to
stand it. Who wouldn't be proud? But I didn't trust the stoic, grim
dignity that I sensed from the girls who allowed themselves to be called
tomboys—who basked in the word and proudly wore a sort of distant
"loner" mantle. They were buying a crummier product, yet they
seemed to feel they'd outsmarted us. They were traitors. They hated
girls. They became boys and hated girls the same as boys. They were
just as good as boys. That made them proud.

And novelist Alix Shulman says:

Everybody has to pay a price, tomboys and non-tomboys. Either
way, you must give up precious possibilities. To play a role means to
sacrifice other ways of behaving, whether you play the tomboy role or
the feminine role. The other side of you simply goes underground. It's
really naive to think of tomboy as an uncomplex category that people
we like fall into and people we don't like are out of. If we just say,
"Whoopee for tomboys" and drop it at that, we give up the chance to
understand something very important.

Caryl remembers:

Being a tomboy was a sensual experience, really; I remember, for
example, the texture of the wood on the top bar of my swing set pressed
against the flesh of my thighs as I hung upside down until my face
turned red. I remember the delicious, cool feel of a brand-new
American League baseball, smooth, white and unblemished except for
the ridges that you could grasp with three fingers. I used to love to
cartwheel off the five-foot wall of the driveway of my house and wait
precisely seven seconds until the door of my grandmother's house
across the street opened, and she cried out, "Don't do that, child!" I
savored her terror. I didn't worry. I knew I could cartwheel off that wall
blindfolded and know exactly where I would land, because I spent half
my life with my feet in the air.

To be a tomboy on a hot summer day is to live on a plane of

existence sweeter than any known to the adult world. The universe exists solely for you. The tree with the rippled bark and the stepladder branches to climb was installed in the firmament by a beneficent God simply for your pleasure. But I'm sure I understood the territorial notions of the word tomboy when I was quite young; at any rate I remember having a big argument with the kid next door when I couldn't have been more than seven years old. I was clad in my chaps, spurs and six-shooter, and proclaimed to the world that I was a cowboy. He said I had to be a cowgirl. I'd seen enough Western movies to know that all girls did was stand in the corner and cower while the heroes beat up the bad guys. By arguing that I could *too* be a cowboy if I wanted to, I was staking a claim to all the action and adventure in the great world that only boys seemed to have a claim to. "Penis envy" the shrinks would have said, but that wasn't it at all. The only time I remember real penis envy was when the kid up the street could hit a skinny dogwood with a stream of pee at fifteen feet. That was impressive. But none of the boys could cartwheel off a five-foot wall, and I figured that was a lot neater than watering a tree.

But in the days when I was pretending to be the James boys or the Daltons, I had no sense that the boundaries of male and female behavior weren't as fixed as the stars in the firmament. I had the notion that there were little cracks I could slide through—and I did—but neither I nor the rest of society challenged the territorial assumptions on which the rules are based. That is no longer true.

Even the word "tomboy" with its implications of "turf" has come under fire. When *WomenSports* magazine did a survey of young women around the country, it discovered that they were rejecting the word. An eighteen-year-old student in Hastings, Nebraska, said, "I don't think there are any tomboys anymore. Everyone is an individual. It's gotten to the point where you see guys and girls play alike. That word will soon be obsolete. I couldn't understand why there was a name for me and not for my brothers when we played games the same way. Right now I'd really hate to be called a tomboy. I'm into the idea of women as equal and that's not what I'd call an equal word."

In Alaska, a *WomenSports* correspondent reported, "All the young women I had conversations with are athletes by their own definition. These days many of the girls don't use or understand the word tomboy, but they do use 'jock.'"

It's clear that the areas staked out as "boyish behavior" are narrowing.

"There are more areas that are being labeled as appropriate for girls today," says syndicated columnist Ellen Goodman. "Girls have a lot more leeway in behavior now. I don't hear Katie [her eleven-year-old] describing a kid in her class as a tomboy. We always used to hear, 'Oh she's just like a boy!'" But what defines a tomboy today? "Most girls wear jeans and most are into organized sports," she says. "You practically have to be a wrestler, a hyperaggressive type wearing a football shirt to be a tomboy."

Ellen plays squash three times a week, sometimes with her daughter. "It wouldn't occur to her that squash isn't a girl's sport. Her mother plays it all the time."

If the area of women's activities is getting larger, it should be remembered that it used to be very small indeed. Many of our ideas about female weakness and physical ineptitude are hangovers from a Victorian upper-class society that idealized and romanticized "the Lady." The image had little to do with the reality of women's lives throughout history, which has involved performing hard physical labor. The behavioral sciences were born in the nineteenth century, when the Victorian woman—an atypical figure given the experience of most of the world's women—became the model, the female norm. The behavioral sciences built upon a mistaken idea of female passivity and physical weakness. They came to regard the very active female child, the "tomboy," as abnormal in female development. The little research that was done on tomboys focused on the supposed link between tomboyism and lesbianism. Some researchers said it was dangerous to a girl's erotic development for her to be a tomboy. One went so far as to say that tomboyism was "rare" in heterosexual female development.

In 1974, psychologists Janet S. Hyde, Benjamin G. Rosenberg and J. Behrman set out to test that theory.[2] Is the tomboy the atypical female? Their research suggests exactly the opposite. They studied three groups of females: college students, junior-high-school students and adult women. The women were identified as tomboys or nontomboys by their own assessment, and by scoring their activities and interests.

Seventy-eight percent of the college women were identified as tomboys, as were 63 percent of the junior-high girls and 51 percent of the adult women. Furthermore, there did not seem to be striking differences in other areas between tomboys and nontomboys. Among the adult women, for example, there were no differences in sexual attitudes or adjustment between those who reported they were tomboys in childhood and those who did not.

These data indicate, say Hyde, Rosenberg and Behrman, that tomboys are neither a minority among women nor are they abnormal: "One is tempted to speculate that tomboyism is not so much abnormal as typical for girls . . . the stereotype of the sweet little girl staying sweetly indoors and embroidering while sitting at her mother's knee which behavioral scientists have tried so diligently to document may well have to fall in favor of the empirical data. Motor activity and expressive acting out are characteristic of *children*, whether male or female."

What seems to have happened is that small differences in children's play behavior have been overemphasized in the past. For example, studies consistently find that little boys very often engage in roughhouse behavior of the sort that could be called mock fighting while girls generally do not. It appears that this is an inherent male behavior which some scientists feel is linked to male hormones. But this is a very specific type of behavior, and has little to do with other play activities staked-out as male: climbing a tree, running a race or hitting a double. It has even less to do with the complex skills one needs to be a university professor, manage an office or try a legal case. A small difference in the behavior of young boys and girls was used to support the status quo in sex roles: unlimited opportunities for boys and the back of the bus for girls.

The role of hormones in influencing what has been called "male" and "female" behavior is an area of scientific examination that is just opening up. The new research does seem to indicate that hormones are an important ingredient in predisposing males and females to act somewhat differently in certain similar situations. But the human temperament is varied, with traits and characteristics scattered between the sexes.

Eleanor Maccoby and Carol Jacklin, whose work we discussed earlier, took up the question of hormones in their review of studies on sex differences in aggression.[3] They believe this sex difference is not totally due to cultural factors, that there is a biological contribution. But their final assessment is a balanced one: "We have been emphasizing male aggression to the point of allowing females to be thought of, by implication, as either angelic or weak. Women share with men the human capacity to heap all sorts of injury upon their fellows. And, in almost every group that has been observed, there are some women who are fully as aggressive as the men. Furthermore, an individual's

113

aggressive behavior is strengthened, weakened, redirected, or altered in form by his or her unique pattern of experiences. All we mean to argue is that there is a sex-linked differential readiness to respond in aggressive ways to the relevant experiences."

In the past, it was often said that hormones were the reason why men played sports and women were cheerleaders. As we have seen, a lot more women did get involved in vigorous physical activity than anyone realized. Today, with what might be called a revolution in women's participation in sports, the old arguments seem even less credible. As *Time* magazine reports: Eight years ago, 294,000 high-school girls participated in interscholastic sports. During the 1976-77 academic year, the number was 1.6 million, nearly a sixfold increase . . . The Association for Intercollegiate Athletics for Women estimates that more than 100,000 women now take part in intercollegiate sports, compared with 170,000 men. In 1972, the first all-women minimarathon in New York's Central Park drew 78 entries. In 1978, 4360 competitors entered the 6.2-mile race. One of the world's largest manufacturers of athletic shoes, Adidas, reports a one-year sales increase of 63 percent in its women's shoes. Sales in equipment especially designed for women have soared as females are finally getting gear that fits, from catcher's masks to hockey skates.

Despite the increasing numbers of women moving into organized sports, the new women athletes often run into resistance along the way. A big turning point came with the "Great Little League War." The pig-tailed moppet tossing a baseball in the backyard may have been looked on as "cute," but when she wanted to put on a Little League uniform, all hell broke loose.

Grown men and women made fools of themselves, coaches gave a good imitation of King Kong, doctors gave testimony that made walking onto a Little League field sound as hazardous as marching off to the Battle of the Bulge. Girls, it was said, would develop cancer from being hit with baseballs. One physician based his claims that eight- to twelve-year-old girls' skeletal structures were weaker than those of boys on studies done on diseased, postmenopausal Japanese cadavers. High-paid lawyers marched into court to protect the men of America from eleven-year-old second basepersons. A favorite piece of insanity, however, came from the Little League coach who declared that if girls were going to play on his team, they'd have to wear jockstraps.

What was this bizarre behavior all about? What could supposedly sensible men and women possibly have been afraid of?

"Fear of change," says Boston psychoanalyst Joan Zilbach, "is a very strong and powerful motive." When she attended a panel on women in sports at Wellesley College in 1977, Dr. Zilbach found that the questions from coaches and teachers tended to be negative ones: "What kind of damage will it do? What about cancer of the breast from playing ice hockey?"

She says, "People are more comfortable with things that are familiar. When I said if a ball hit a wrist it wouldn't cause cancer I got a hostile reaction because I said it was okay to change."

The same hostility greeted Phyllis Boring, dean for affirmative action at Rutgers University in New Jersey, at similar meetings she attended. One man summed up the emotions of an audience when he came up to her afterward. "You have to understand," he said, "that I was raised to believe in God, Country and Motherhood. Religion is crumbling. Then we had the Vietnam War and we started to question patriotism. Motherhood and women's role are the last things I have to cling to of the values I was raised with."

Many people worry about behavior in their children that crosses traditional sex boundaries because they think rigid boundaries ensure that a boy will grow up to be a "real man" and a girl a "real woman." The notion that a solid sex-role identity must be based on definite and different characteristics and behaviors for each sex has been promulgated by behavioral scientists who should know better. As the research of John Money of Johns Hopkins University (and many others) has shown, a child at a very early age forms a firm and irreversible gender identity— awareness of the self as male or female. This occurs by age three, as soon as the child can learn to label itself as *boy* or *girl*—much earlier than Freudian theorists realized.

It's also important to note that a healthy sense of self, including of femaleness or maleness, develops at least as easily and firmly in a family where the father does child care and the mother is a breadwinner. As is true for so many of the issues we are dealing with, mythology in the absence of evidence has also held sway on this point. Too many child-rearing books still argue that parents must make a gargantuan effort not to let their roles overlap too much lest their children not be able to tell them apart and become genderless little psychiatric cases. Nonsense! So,

115

gender identity is established very early in life, well before a child is old enough to play baseball. Once established, it is not going to change. The girl who plays tackle football or the boy who takes ballet lessons are not going to lose pieces of their sexual identity.

Beneath the "protective" rhetoric of the people who want to keep girls out of Little League, out of marathons and the 100-yard dash lie fiercer emotions. Dean Phyllis Boring went to the opening ceremonies of her son's Little League last year. "The speeches were all about these fine young boys, go, boys, go! The handful of girls who were playing were being told, 'You don't belong—and if you choose to play, we will ignore you.'" What tends to happen is that the girls who get support for their tomboyish activities at home can disregard the slights and play anyhow. "But what happens to the girl who gets no such support? If my friends were telling me, and my parents were telling me, and the league was telling me that I didn't belong, what would I do?" asks Dr. Boring. "I'd turn right around and go home."

Too many girls are turning around and going home—most others never even get to the ball field in the first place. If you look at the average Little League team, you'll often find that the girls who are playing are the best female athletes, while the boys range from all-star to awful. While the opening up of Little League was a major symbolic victory, it hasn't had much impact on the lives of most girls. Nobody teaches little girls how to throw a ball, swing a bat or field a pop fly. Understandably, they feel foolish and inept at Little League tryouts, and drop out very quickly. The girls who do persist in "boys' sports" can find the level of harassment still fairly high. Dean Boring cites one instance in which a coach told a girl who went out for the track team that he had to take her, but she would have to wear the team shirt to run. The shirt was a low-cut tank top, totally inappropriate for a teenage girl. At another school, 125 girls and 95 boys turned out for tryouts for the track team. The coach cut 34 of the boys and all of the girls. The school board subsequently fired the coach.

Time magazine reported in 1978 that Springfield (Massachusetts) College, a school that has specialized in training coaches and physical education instructors since 1885, has long had a substantial program for women. Yet even there the men's swimming team has access to the pool for three hours each day; the women are allowed into the water for only one. So Deborah Kinney, a seven-time all-American distance swimmer, goes to the pool at 6:00 A.M. for an extra workout before beginning her day's studies. Says she: "An hour of practice isn't much use to a long-distance swimmer." But the real crunch for women athletes—particularly in high school and college—comes over the issue of money. Male athletes have had the sports budgets almost totally to themselves for decades, and they're reluctant to give their monopoly up.

For example, under the prodding of HEW, the University of Georgia has started to make amends for a program that spent about $1000 on women's athletics in 1973. The figure is now up to $120,000 (versus the men's $2.5 million), but the indignities remain. Item: male golfers receive an unlimited supply of balls, while the women are given one per competitive round.

The sports picture for girls is changing, however, thanks to Title IX of the Education Amendment Act of 1972, which guarantees both sexes equal opportunity for participation in programs in all schools receiving federal funds. Title IX is making a difference, according to Carol Parr of the Women's Equity Action League, a group which has actively lobbied in Congress for equal treatment of women and girls in sports. Athletic programs for women are better funded than they were in the past, though they are not yet on the level of men's programs.

Another battle in the drive for equality for women in athletics is the attempt to integrate physical education classes, starting in the primary grades. On the surface, this seems like a logical step forward. But what is actually happening in these integrated classes?

Helen Harris Solomons, a psychologist who specializes in vocational counseling for women, studied fifth-grade integrated gym classes in Pennsylvania schools.[4] She not only observed the children in their classes, but she tested them for strength with a specially designed electronic device and enlisted the aid of a computer for the assessment of their level of skill. She then set up teams composed of boys and girls whose ability she had tested. She found that the girls tended to get cut out of the action by the boys—even when the girls played better than the boys.

Both the boys and the girls in the class regarded boys as better players than girls even in cases where the girls were better. The boys actually preferred to pass the ball to an unskilled boy player rather than to a skilled girl. In one game, the rules were that the best player was to try to score, and the others were to pass off to the best players. The girls at the highest level of skill and strength passed the ball away twice as many times as boys at the same level—and these girls received only half as many passes as boys who were at their level. Girls tended to give away chances to score to the boys—even when they were better players than their male teammates. The unskilled girls tended to get left out of most of the activity. The result was that both skilled and unskilled girls got fewer passes than boys, and thus received less opportunity to develop their skills.

"It's the girls who suffer throughout," says Cyril Solomons, who worked with his wife on designing the electronic equipment for the studies. "They don't think they can do it, and so they don't try—and eventually they can't. It becomes a self-fulfilling prophecy."

Most crucial of all, Helen Solomons found that teachers had different expectations for girls than for boys. For example, a girl was often overpraised for catching a ball, while a boy was simply expected to catch it. Girls were often given "permission" to fail. In a game that resembles volleyball, girls were permitted to serve from the halfway line. Boys were not permitted to do so, even though some of the boys were less skilled than the girls.

Solomons saw a number of instances in which the girls feigned weakness, and they were not urged to perform up to the level of their ability. Unless the level of the demands made on girls in co-ed gym classes is raised, such classes can hinder rather than improve girls' athletic ability. The key to the success of integrated gym classes is clearly the teacher's awareness of these sex-related dynamics and his or her willingness to intervene. Simply mixing the sexes won't change the status quo.

Some gym teachers may have seen these things happening in their classes but hesitated to interfere because of a concern about physical damage to the girls. Parents may also share this concern. According to several sports medicine specialists, their worries are exaggerated.

It is evident by now that there is no reason that preadolescent girls cannot keep up with boys in sports. "The erroneous and illfounded misconception that girls from eight to ten years old are physically inferior to boys of this age group should be dispelled," says Dr. Joseph S. Torg,[5] director of Temple University's Center for Sports Medicine and Science in Philadelphia. In fact, since girls tend to get their growth spurts earlier, girls might turn out to be better players than boys at this age, if they received adequate conditioning.

The specter of serious and special harm to girls has been raised unnecessarily, say physicians and trainers. A woman's body is not

118

especially prone to injury. "A woman's ovaries sit inside a great big sac of fluid," says John Marshall,[6] director of sports medicine at Manhattan's Hospital for Special Surgery, "beautifully protected." A woman's breasts are not especially vulnerable. "There's no evidence that trauma to the breasts is a precursor to cancer." A girl's training does not have to be less vigorous than a boy's. Barbara Drinkwater, a research physiologist at the University of California's Institute of Environmental Stress, says that prepuberty girls are precisely the same as boys in the endurance capacity of their hearts and lungs.

With the onset of menstruation, girls—and their parents—often worry about activity "at certain times of the month." But women have set world and Olympic records during their periods. For most women, exertion doesn't disrupt the menstrual cycle. Nor do women who train seriously for sports have to worry about becoming muscle bound. Jack H. Wilmore,[7] a physiologist at the University of California, says that women, because they have low levels of the muscle-building hormones, can increase their strength 50 to 75 percent with no increase in muscle bulk. Even pregnant women can often engage in competitive sports without worry. One former Olympic champion swimmer competed in a national AAU freestyle meet when she was five months pregnant.

As the "revolution" in women's sports continues, we may expect that more women will enjoy greater physical capacity. If a tomboy is a girl who is athletic, then all girls ought to be tomboys. Dr. Wilmore says the idealization of the dainty female has resulted in the average American woman's beginning a physical decline between the ages of ten and twelve. A similar decline in men does not begin until the ages of twenty-two to twenty-five. Training can turn this around. Maximum work capacity of female distance runners and that of male competitors compare very favorably: "This indicates that the decrease we see in female activity at ten or twelve years is more of a social and cultural phenomenon than a biological necessity. They stop running around and start becoming young ladies."

Being a "young lady" may be a health hazard for a young girl. A 1978 study of sixth graders in a Chicago suburb found that, among these children, nearly a third of the girls had poor heart recovery rates after strenuous exercise, compared with under 7 percent of the boys. The executive director of the group that sponsored the study called the sedentary life-style of American girls "a blind spot in preventive medicine."

119

Girls who are athletic are not only more physically fit, but they usually feel better about themselves. As one sixteen-year-old girl puts it, "Girls are supposed to be all feminine and act Miss Prissy. They're not supposed to sweat when they get hot. I like to sweat. It makes me feel good."

Being athletic is seen by some girls as a way to shake off oppressive female stereotypes. There's a good chance that the girl who breaks out of the mold at nine or ten has a better chance than other girls to break out of a rigid stereotype in later years. The studies done by Margaret Hennig and Anne Jardim[8] at Simmons College that we discussed earlier offer evidence for this. The women who became top managers were often involved at a younger age in sports activities with their fathers.

One executive said, "By the time I went to elementary school, I was a good junior tennis player and was quite proficient at baseball—hardball, not sissy softball. I found little girls playing at softball were very dull and always tried to wander over where the boys were playing."

Another woman remembers, "Dad cultivated me as his sports partner. I went to my first boxing match before I went to school."

Hennig also interviewed 125 women planning business careers for her book *The Managerial Woman* (coauthored by Anne Jardim) and analyzed why so few women become top corporation executives. One major reason, they believe, is that women don't play football or other team sports. Corporate men start to learn about gamesmanship on the playing fields of their childhood. Women, say Hennig and Jardim, don't learn how to plan ahead, take risks and deal with victory or defeat.

Women in business, they find, underestimate their own achievements, often attribute their success to luck and doubt their ability even when they are highly competent. Men assume they are competent and set out to prove it.

The behavior of men and women in business, as they picture it, is so similar to the boys and girls in the gym classes Helen Solomons studied that it is uncanny. The talented little girls pass the ball away instead of trying to score and don't see themselves as good players. In a metaphorical sense, women in the workplace do the same.

From the segregated gym class to the female "ghetto" in the job world, an underlying assumption about the nature and role of the sexes has been the ruling principle: Men and women are very different from one another. That's the reason why there was so much anger about little girls playing shortstop—it was a violation of *nature*.

But today, women are starting to occupy places that were off limits to

120

them before, from third base to the corporate boardroom. The behavioral sciences have had a hard time keeping up with reality. They, too, accepted the theorem that men and women were very different creatures, and spent considerable effort codifying those differences. But what if it turns out that, in fact, we are more alike than different? Can the theorists deal with that reality? Only recently have they begun to try. The old notions die hard.

Traditionally, the behavioral sciences have tried to grapple with the relationship of sex and gender to behavior by setting up mutually exclusive categories—little boxes labeled "masculine" and "feminine"— and trying to figure out what characteristics belonged to each sex. Men and women were expected to act in different ways, to have different interests and goals, to possess different and complementary traits. But how were those traits to be divided up?

Theorists have held a number of ideas on how to conceptualize masculinity and femininity. Talcott Parsons,[9] for example, saw masculinity as being associated with an "instrumental" orientation—the man is the person who solves problems at hand, gets the job done, who is concerned with action. Femininity is associated, on the other hand, with an "expressive" orientation—the woman feels, nurtures, loves and heals.

Erik Erikson said that men are concerned with outer space—with things that can be built and destroyed—while women are focused on inner space, on their capacity to bear children, and are more concerned with nurture and healing.

The problem with these theories, of course, was that in trying to grapple with the complexities of behavior, in looking for a handle with which to come to terms with how humans behave, they set up a series of pigeonholes that had to bear one label or another. The theories weren't really designed to deal with the possibility that certain behaviors might be simply "human" acts, appropriate to both sexes. By stamping such behavior "masculine" or "feminine" the theorists were also making a judgment about what actions were proper for each sex. The way one labels behavior can have a very strong social impact on the way people view that behavior. For example, if you told a man he was a sensitive and caring person he would probably be flattered. But if you told him he was high in "feminine" behavior, he would hardly be overjoyed. In the same way, if you told a woman she was bright and did her job very well, she would take it as a compliment. The reverse would be true if you said she was high in "masculine" traits.

Most people who have lived awhile know that human beings are more complex than most theories would allow; we know men and women who are both caring and strong, who can nurture and create, solve a problem and comfort a child. Common sense may have been well ahead of theory in this area, but now a new theoretical approach to the whole question of sex roles is developing, one which may be better able to create a more workable conceptual framework than those of the past. This is the idea of "androgyny," which is increasingly drawing attention and research efforts.

"Androgyny" is a peculiar-sounding word. What it means, in the words of psychologist Sandra Bem, now at Cornell University, is that it is possible for an individual to be both "masculine" and "feminine," both instrumental and expressive.[10] In fact, she argues that "for fully effective and healthy human functioning, masculinity and femininity must be tempered by the other and the two must be integrated into a more balanced, a more fully human personality."

In the past, however, it was difficult to study androgynous behavior, since "masculine" and "feminine" qualities were seen as polar opposites. To score high in one automatically meant scoring low on the other. Even worse, "feminine" behavior was often seen simply as the absence of masculine behavior. For example, if a masculine trait was identified as being "logical," a feminine characteristic was labeled "illogical." Bem calls this "A practice that may itself be partially responsible for the negative picture of the feminine woman which emerges in the psychological literature." She adds, "For once, I wanted to give the feminine woman a chance to be no sicker than anyone else."

In her research, Bem designed a measure that treated traditional concepts of masculinity and femininity as two separate scales, so that a person could receive high scores on both, thus making it possible to identify subjects who were, in fact, androgynous. She then used her measure to find out whether traditional sex roles really do cause people to restrict their behavior.

First the subjects—male and female—were asked to rate themselves separately on masculine and feminine qualities. Those giving themselves high scores on both were considered androgynous. The men who saw themselves largely in masculine terms, and the women who pictured themselves as mostly feminine, were the "sex-typed" subjects. There were also men who claimed more feminine traits and women who described themselves highest on masculine traits. These were the "sex-reversed" subjects.

122

The subjects were first asked to choose (but not perform) certain activities, some of them stereotypically masculine (nailing two boards together), feminine (ironing a cloth napkin) or neutral (playing with a yo-yo.) The subjects were offered varying rates of payment for each activity. The test was designed so that the payment was higher for each subject for the less sex-appropriate activity. In other words, a male subject could earn more by ironing a napkin than by nailing a board.

As expected, the "sex-typed" subjects—the masculine males and the feminine women—were more likely to reject the opposite-sex activities than were the androgynous subjects—even though these choices cost them money.

So the sex-typed subjects were less likely to opt for activities that seem to require moving across sex-role boundaries. Would they also be less comfortable than the androgynous subjects after they actually performed these activities? To test this proposition, Bem had each subject perform three masculine, three feminine and three neutral activities and be photographed while doing so. Afterward, they were asked how they felt performing the activities—for example, how masculine, feminine, nervous, attractive, likable or peculiar they felt while performing each activity. The sex-typed individuals felt significantly worse than the androgynous subjects. "It was the masculine men and the feminine women who experienced the most discomfort and who felt the worst about themselves after performing cross-sex activities. Thus, it would appear that cross-sex activity is problematic for sex-typed individuals and that traditional sex roles do produce an unnecessary and perhaps even dysfunctional pattern of avoidance for many people."

After demonstrating that sex-role stereotyping can restrict people's simple, everyday activities, Bem then asked whether stereotyping also constricts an individual's ability to function in "even more profound ways . . . Is the masculine male deficient in the domains of expressiveness and communion? Does the feminine female have but limited access to the domains of instrumentality and agency? Are men, in other words, suffering from what might be called a constipation of feelings, while women are blocked in their efforts to 'do'?" To test this theory, Bem designed a pair of studies on independence and nurturance.

In the first, subjects were asked to judge whether cartoons were funny or not. The subjects were seated alone in a room, and they thought they were hearing comments over a loudspeaker from other members of the test group. In fact they were hearing tape-recorded voices, which

123

intentionally said that some of the unfunny cartoons were very funny. The subjects had to give their own opinions in the face of contradictory views.

What were the results? The masculine and androgynous subjects were significantly more independent in their opinions than the feminine subjects—and this was true for both males and females.

The second study of nurturance was done in two parts. In one, the subjects were put in an experimental room with a tiny kitten; in the second, with a baby. With the kitten, both the androgynous and the feminine men were more responsive and playful than the masculine men. The androgynous women were quite responsive to the kitten, but the feminine women were, surprisingly, significantly less responsive. The masculine women fell someplace in between.

With the baby, both androgynous and feminine men were more responsive than masculine men, but there seemed to be little difference among the women. The feminine women did say on a questionnaire that they were more interested in having an affectionate relationship with the baby than did any of the other women, but they did not behave any more affectionately.

Looking at the results of those two experiments, Bem wondered why the feminine women weren't more affectionate and nurturant than the other women. Then, she writes, "It occurred to me that both the kitten and the baby can be thought of as relatively passive stimuli, stimuli that required the subject to initiate and sustain the interaction. It therefore seemed possible that feminine women might simply be insufficiently assertive to act out their nurturant feelings in a situation where they must take responsibility for initiating and sustaining the interaction, and that they might display much more nurturance if they were permitted to play a more passive or responsive role in the interaction."

So Bem designed another study in which the subjects were exposed to a "lonely student" (actually an experimenter) who talked about missing old friends and being unable to make new ones. The conversation was observed from behind a one-way mirror, and subjects were asked afterward about their concern for this "poor unhappy student."

The result, Bem says, was that "for the first time in our entire research program, the feminine females apparently found a situation tailored for their talents, for they were the most responsive listeners of all." They were significantly more responsive than anyone else, while the masculine males were the least responsive; the other groups responded similarly and somewhere between the other two.

Summing up her research, Bem focused first on the androgynous male. She reports: "He performs spectacularly. He shuns no behavior just because our culture happens to label it as female, and his competence crosses both the instrumental and the expressive domains. Thus, he stands firm in his opinions, he cuddles kittens and bounces babies, and he has a sympathetic ear for someone in distress. Clearly, he is a liberated companion for the most feminist among us."

In contrast, the masculine male does well only in the realm of doing and the feminine male seems to succeed only in the realm of emotions. Bem says she is not sure whether the laboratory situations just weren't powerful enough to tap the tender feelings of the masculine men, but she says that it does seem that their threshold for tender feeling—the level at which they can respond with loving concern to others—was higher than for all the other men and women in the study. "And that, I believe, is cause for concern."

Interestingly enough, both the androgynous women and the masculine women did well in both expressive and instrumental areas. They were both able to perform competently in areas that society has labeled "male," and both groups also responded positively to the baby and the kitten. Based on her findings, Bem concludes that the emphasis on the importance of nurturance in women in our society is so strong that most women do in fact develop that capacity.

Bem's analysis of the behavior of the feminine woman is an intriguing one. She points out that these women did well only in one test, that with the lonely student, in which the socially approved behavior was completely obvious.

The women knew that they "ought" to be responsive to the student. "In contrast, all of our other studies have left the subjects much more to their own devices with regard to the particular behavior they were 'supposed' to initiate."

The feminine woman, Bem notes, does not willingly perform cross-sex behaviors and is uncomfortable when asked to do so; she yields to pressures for conformity and does not distinguish herself in the "most traditional of female behaviors, the nurturance of a human infant." But she *does* do well in a situation in which the things required of her are crystal clear.

"What this pattern suggests to me is that the major effect of femininity in women—untempered by a sufficient level of masculinity—may not be to inhibit instrumental or masculine behaviors per se, but to inhibit any behavior at all in a situation where the 'appropriate' behavior is left ambiguous or unspecified."

In other words, "feminine" women can be paralyzed in any situation which requires a fair amount of independent decision-making or initiative.

Bem says that her research leads her to the notion that the feminine woman may be so concerned about the negative consequences of her actions that she tends to withdraw from situations that offer the risk of doing something "wrong."

"Either they withdraw from the situation, or if withdrawal is not feasible, they engage in the 'safest' behavior or as little behavior as possible. Their goal in such a situation is to avoid doing anything that might get them into trouble, embarrass them or bring any kind of negative evaluation upon themselves. In other words, they take no risks—they play it safe."

But most of us find out, sooner or later, that you can't always get away with playing it safe. You must make decisions, take action. At the same time, if human life is to mean anything, you have to be able to love, to feel, to nurture, to give to other human beings. It's disturbing to think that sex-role stereotypes have kept people from developing their full human potential in all of these areas, fenced men off from their feelings and women from competence. And, it's distressing to know that the behavioral sciences have not helped much. For, as psychologists Alexandra Kaplan and Joan P. Bean point out in Beyond Sex-Role Stereotypes: "Although androgynous people have always existed, they have remained invisible to social scientists."

We think it's high time for them to start materializing.

Nuts and Bolts

Since sex stereotyping is so pervasive, and begins so early, it's necessary to be alert for ways of combating it in the everyday lives of children. The studies done by Beverly Fagot show that parents often send messages to their children different from the ones they intend—even those parents who voice the most "liberal" ideology. It's helpful to be aware of this gap between ideology and behavior. We are not mentioning this to induce vibrations of guilt. After all, we have all grown up in a society that is very sex stereotyped, and have all picked up ways of behaving we would prefer not to have. We are not suggesting that parents start tracking down their behavioral "sins" with the zeal of the Red Guard. It does help to know that, although translating some of the things you believe into practice is sometimes hard, it's easier if you are aware of the difficulty.

The study of children's rooms raises some especially interesting questions. Environments do send messages to children, and as we've seen, the contents of girls' rooms may be sending them the message that their range of activities should be limited. The popular decorating magazines are not always helpful in this regard. They often feature little girls' rooms that are miniature palaces of dainty pink froth, filled with fabrics that show dirt and tear easily. Which is not to say, of course, that girls' rooms should be austere as monks' cells, or that a little girl's craving for a pink canopy bed must be harshly denied. But a girl can be reminded that a pink shag rug is confining, if lovely. You can't wipe paint spills easily, Play-Doh gets stuck in it, it's hard to make a decent block tower on a shag rug and all the dirt tracked in spoils the effect. The toys in girls' rooms should offer a wide range of behavior and activities, not just those stamped by society as "female."

Much of the discussion about "nonsexist" toys for children centers on the issue of stereotyping, which is indeed important. But there are equally crucial issues involved. Toys, after all, are more than playthings. They are just as much instruments of learning as are algebra books or globes. Children at play are hard at work learning skills, so it's a good idea to examine what toys and activities teach what skills. For girls, there are at least two areas of major concern—spatial abilities and a sense of mastery over the environment.

As we've seen, girls consistently do less well than boys in tests involving spatial abilities. This may be due not to inborn differences but to the fact that girls are rarely encouraged to use toys or to play games that develop these abilities. Since these skills are crucial to the mastery of math, which in turn is essential to so many adult skills and occupations, girls need special attention in this area. There are many toys that develop spatial abilities—blocks, put-together toys like Leggos and the like, erector sets, most kinds of puzzles, checkers, chess, the more complicated board games that involve some strategy. The kind of play that seems to involve almost no learning of spatial skills is doll play and the traditional "like mommy" play—sweeping, play cooking, dusting. These are perfectly fine activities but we must be aware of what they don't do.

Some toys can be a problem to parents because they send out conflicting messages. For example, Caryl's daughter was enchanted with *Charlie's Angels*, and wanted a doll and accessories for her birthday. Caryl hated the message implicit in the doll about how important it is to be beautiful. On the other hand, the accessories were action-oriented toys—scuba gear, a boat, skis. Caryl's daughter and her friends played with dolls in an active rather than in a passive way—letting them scuba in the sink and perform heroic rescues. Parents may run into the dual message problem with a whole range of toys.

There are many toys that can give girls a sense of mastery of the environment—toys that exist to be built with, such as blocks, models and train sets. (But electric trains in particular can be difficult and complicated. Too often, a child receives these when she is too young and winds up being frustrated, feeling anything but a sense of mastery.) A tool kit is fine for a girl when she's old enough to use tools safely. But you don't need anything elaborate. Some wood, hammer and nails can enchant her. Parents will probably be more inventive than we are in this area. One note of warning—"overhelp" can be deadly to the sense of mastery. Don't jump in and help a child with something until she asks. And even then, don't help when it's something she can do for herself— suggest a first step rather than the whole solution. The message a child gets from the overeager parent is that she can't do things for herself. Since people do seem more eager to help girls than boys, this may be an area of special concern.

The urge to dash out and help a vulnerable child is a natural one, but stop to think about where that impulse comes from. Maybe what's really showing up is the parent's anxieties stemming from his or her own remembered childhood. It's easy to project your own concerns onto a child in a situation where she doesn't really need help. For instance, Rosalind says that she had always been anxious for her daughter in situations that involved social relations skills—going to a new place, meeting new people. Rosalind knows that this was because she was shy as a child—but her daughter Amy is not, and gets along just fine when in those situations.

We've thought a lot about the parents' role in helping children develop the skills we have stressed here. It's obviously good for a parent to get involved with a child in a skill-building activity, but there is also the danger of taking on the burden of being "superteacher" as well as parent. Mothers may have some special problems with this. Many women are lacking in skills they might want to see their daughters develop—do you really want to sit down and try to put an electric train together and have your daughter dismiss you as a hopeless dummy when you can't? Do you have to take a course in electrical engineering to help her out? Of course not. Parents can pick the areas where they do have some skills, or possibly they can set out on a joint learning venture with the child—if the parent really is interested.

The studies that Janet Lever did of differences between the games boys and girls play bring up some other concerns. One of these is that girls play inside more, and thus usually get less strenuous physical activity. As a result, girls begin a decline in physical fitness much earlier than boys do. Schools traditionally direct more attention to boys' sports and physical education programs when in fact girls may need them more. Girls should be introduced early to some form of strenuous activity which offers them exercise and an opportunity to develop increasingly higher levels of skill.

But the games and sports in which boys usually get involved offer more than mere physical exercise. As Janet Lever points out, they offer boys experience in settling disputes, working together as a team and dealing with the hard realities of winning and losing. While the analogy between the playing field and real life can sometimes be overdrawn—football will not automatically make you a good corporate manager—it does exist. Girls do need to learn to deal with the issues that team sports present. They particularly need to be exposed to competition, to "the thrill of victory and the agony of defeat" as the cliché puts it. Competition is a fact of life, and when not pushed to the "winning is everything" extreme, it can be a healthy part of life. Sports are not the only vehicle for competition—a girl can compete in the scholastic area, in musicianship, in any skill she possesses. But girls have to learn that there are standards, discipline and levels of performance involved in doing anything well. There is perhaps nothing quite so helpful to building confidence, self-esteem and a sense of mastery as competing successfully.

This doesn't mean that parents have to rush right out and sign their daughters up for Little League. There is a whole range of activities in which girls can learn about discipline, competition and standards of excellence. Too often, however, the athletic activities in which girls are

129

involved are taken lightly and do not offer the girls any incentive to work really hard and improve their skills. Gymnastics, for example, is very popular with girls, and it can be a rigorous, exacting sport. But many gymnastics programs are more like dancing classes, where the girls learn to do a few cartwheels for a yearly recital, and that's about it. Figure skating is often the same; the emphasis is not really on honing skills, but learning enough to look pretty doing a simple routine in a recital. If there has been too much pressure on boys to excel in their sports activities, there has been too little for girls. Girls' sports activities were seen in some vague sense as "good" for them, but they rarely result in prestige or status for the school or family, or in athletic scholarships. Girls' games have traditionally been poorly attended. In most schools, the cheerleader is still a more important person than the captain of any of the girls' teams.

This theme of lack of competition and absence of standards has been a hallmark of all kinds of organized activities for girls. Boys' activities tend to be more structured, with more "tests" of ability. Girls' activities sometimes seem to be designed mainly for passing the time.

Girls may also receive too lavish praise for less-than-noteworthy accomplishments in their activities. It's always tempting for parents to tell their children that everything they do is wonderful, even when it isn't so. But parents of boys know that the world outside will not offer rewards for a level of performance that isn't very high. Girls may not get that message until they are nearly grown. In her work with college students, for example, Caryl finds that many bright young female students have real difficulty dealing with stiff competition and with harsh criticisms from instructors. Having heard little but praise, they overreact to critical comments, taking them not as helpful advice, but as personal attacks.

If girls need standards to live up to, they also need instruction in the skills they will need, especially in the area of sports. Simply opening up programs to girls is not always enough. Little League is a good example. If you look at Little Leagues in most towns, there are usually only a handful of girls on the teams, and these girls are usually the gifted natural athletes. The usual pattern is for the older girls to be playing on the B teams with the younger boys. The younger boys' fathers often take them out for private coaching, but that's not usual with girls. Mothers don't often know how to field a grounder or hit a line drive. The girls start out eagerly, but perform poorly because they get no special attention and soon lose interest. In some towns, the league holds clinics for the younger boys and girls, so they can get intensive coaching in the

130

fundamentals the year before they start to play in competition. This gives the girls a better chance to start playing on an even footing.

The studies Helen Harris Solomons conducted on integrated gym classes spell out one message loud and clear—simply mixing the sexes in physical education won't be helpful to girls if that's as far as it goes. Integration may simply set up a situation where girls get even less chance to learn skills than in the old segregated classes. School administrators and physical education teachers have got to pay careful attention to the dynamics in those classes, to see that girls are not being cut out of the action or being given permission to fail at feats they can actually perform.

7

ACHIEVEMENT

Stamping Out Smother Love

The idea of the twenty-four-hour-on-call mother was so ingrained that the absence of this kind of mothering was seen as abnormal. In one study, social scientists observed mothers who weren't always ready to drop what they were doing to respond to a child's demands, who didn't hesitate to criticize a child when her behavior warranted it, perhaps insisting, at times, that their activities as adults took priority. What did the scientists call these mothers? Hostile.

Mother, may I go out to swim?
Yes, my darling daughter
Hang your clothes on a hickory limb
And don't go near the water.

—Anonymous

"Don't go near the water" is the message many young girls have been getting, with the emphasis on the word *don't*. Stay away from the water, stick close to home, don't take risks.

Risk, after all, is an uncertain business. Why get involved with it at all? Why not play it safe, if you can get away with it?

The answer is that venture involves risk, and it is only by striking out on its own that a child learns and grows. Parents may look at their sturdy little boys and see the future. As men, they will have to be tough enough to survive in a difficult world, and if a few hard knocks are painful, they are also necessary.

132

How many parents think about the benefits of hard knocks for daughters? The fondest wish many parents have had for their little girl was that she would be carried off by a tall, strong, handsome man who would support her and shield her from the harder blows of life. These kinds of attitudes lay the solid foundation for a disturbing pattern we see in adult women: underachievement. Time and time again we see individual women with talents, skills and brainpower that have been allowed to atrophy—like muscles that are not used. We can see why psychologist Lois Hoffman[1] says, in an influential essay on feminine development, that "the precursors of the underachieving woman can be seen in the female child."

Hoffman's theory is that the female child is given inadequate encouragement by her parents in her early strivings for independence. She also believes that it is more difficult for the little girl to separate herself from her mother than for the little boy, because the young girl is of the same sex. As a result, the girl does not develop confidence in her ability to cope on her own in the environment. She retains her infantile fear of abandonment, believing that safety lies in her relationships with and her dependence on other people.

All babies are totally dependent, and the process of growing up involves breaking away from that dependence to become people who can function on their own in the world. Very early the child learns to deal with the world around her—by grabbing, touching, throwing (Who hasn't seen the unalloyed delight of a kid who has just found she can dump her oatmeal on the floor?). As the young child learns what he or she can do, the adventures get more and more daring, and take the child farther away from the parent. These first risks often take place with the parent looking on. Mom or Dad are a sort of emotional safety net, and their attitudes are quickly picked up by the child. This period—which falls roughly between the ages of one and four—is critical to the sense of independence. The mother has traditionally been the parent who oversees the child at this age, and her reaction to her child's adventures is important. "The mother's delight is part of her independence training," says Hoffman. "Her apprehension is training in dependence." Of course, common sense has to enter here; any parent would be crazy not to display apprehension if a child was about to take a swan dive off the sofa. But the parent who is overconcerned for her child's safety can cripple the growth of independence.

For complex reasons, the mother-daughter relationship can be a seedbed of girls' problems with achievement and independence, says Nancy Chodorow. Chodorow, a sociologist whose work reflects a strong psychoanalytic background, emphasizes that little girls are very much like the parent who gives them their primary care—their mother.[2] As we've seen, though, the ability of the child to "separate" from the parent is crucial to growth and development. Boys can see that they are different from their mothers and very early on learn to identify with the male role. Girls, who see that they are *not* different from their mothers, can have a harder time moving away.

Mothers may have a hard time helping them to go, making the separation process even more difficult. Mothers, says Nancy Chodorow, experience a "double identification" with their daughters. They identified with their own mothers, and when they become mothers themselves, they relive that relationship—the experience of being a cared-for child—through the identification with their daughters. The strength of these ties can deter a mother from encouraging her daughter to develop a separate self.

An extreme example of this occurs in certain psychotic women, Chodorow says. These women seem to focus their pathologies on their daughters. They do not allow their daughters to perceive themselves as separate beings, but act as if the children are simply extensions of themselves, who feel what they feel and can be used for their own gratification.

"These mothers, then, perpetuate a mutual relationship with their daughters of both primary identification and infantile dependence."

This is admittedly an extreme and abnormal process. In a more normal situation, a mother would not see herself and her child as one being. However, she may still identify more strongly with a daughter than with a son. With a daughter, "the processes of separation and individuation are much more difficult."

Mothers may not encourage their daughters to break their dependency and develop a firm sense of self, Chodorow argues. This is a particular problem for Western, middle-class women, because they are often isolated and forced to spend so much of their energy on their children. They may tend to hang on to their children because once their active mothering is ended, much of their sense of status and usefulness is ended, too.

In other non-Western societies, Chodorow says, women have a valued "kin" role in the extended family. These women gain more status and

134

prestige as they get older rather than in early motherhood. They may also have strong ties with other women, making them less dependent on their daughters.

But the life situation of the Western woman is one that leads to overinvolvement with her children, Chodorow says. She may try to perpetuate both her son's and her daughter's dependence, but in the case of the son, "society and his father are more likely to interfere in order to assure that, behaviorally at least, he doesn't *act* dependent."

The best mothering, Chodorow says, the kind that doesn't reproduce psychological problems in boys and girls "comes from a person with a firm sense of self and her own value, whose care is a freely chosen activity rather than a reflection of a conscious and unconscious sense of inescapable connection to and responsibility for her children."

So both Hoffman and Chodorow are concerned about the ways that the mother-daughter relationship could interfere with the growing girl's independence. Do empirical studies show that mothers—and fathers— treat their girl children differently than their sons in this area?

We've seen that parents behave differently toward male and female babies as soon as they are born. The same baby—dressed in blue—was called "sturdy" and "hardy," but dressed in pink was called "pretty" and "fragile." We also saw in Beverly Fagot's work that two-year-old girls asked for help more often than boys of the same age, and that parents reacted more positively to girls' requests for help than to boys'. Lois Hoffman, after reviewing the relevant studies in this area, says, "there is more encouragement by parents of boys for independent exploration of the environment."

One study asked mothers of four-year-olds to indicate the ages they thought children should be allowed to do such things as use sharp scissors, play away from home for a long time with no adult supervision and other independent—and slightly risky—activities.[3] Mothers of girls responded with later ages than did mothers of boys, and the difference was particularly strong in the middle class.

(That study was done in 1964. In our study, in 1976, we found that parents did *not* show a difference in the ages they would grant independence to girls and boys. In addition, many parents were concerned with undoing sex-role stereotypes and not transmitting to their daughters messages that they should be dependent. So parental attitudes may be undergoing some changes.)

But what about parents' *behavior?* That question is being studied in

135

some detail right now. Remember, Beverly Fagot found that what parents said about treating boys and girls the same wasn't always reflected in what they did. But parents don't have to wait for studies of what other people do in order to be aware of the problem.

One of the most interesting things that emerged from our study was that women who described themselves as independent, capable people were the most likely to value those traits in their daughters and to grant them independence at an early age. These findings confirm Chodorow's arguments about the importance of a mother's firm sense of self.

What happens to girls who experience too much maternal involvement and protection during their early years? According to Hoffman, "Because of this, they find themselves as adults unwilling (or unable) to face stress and with inadequate motivation for autonomous achievement."

If the little girl has experienced less encouragement for independence, too much protectiveness and not enough conflict, she is likely to engage less in independent exploration of her environment. "As a result she does not develop skills in coping with her environment nor confidence in her ability to do so. She continues to be dependent on adults for solving her problems, and because of this, she needs her affective ties to adults." Unsure of her abilities to cope on her own, the girl is fearful of abandonment by parents or others on whom she depends, and that fear often persists into adulthood. "The anticipation of being alone and unloved, then, may have a particularly desperate quality in women."

There is a sad irony in all this. Mothers, wanting only good things for their girls, can deprive them of the armor they need for an independent life. Wanting to protect their daughters, they end up by making them vulnerable.

If this sounds like an attack on mothers, it isn't. These mothers were only doing their job as it was portrayed by child-care experts of all sorts, including the social scientists. The idea of the twenty-four-hour-on-call mother was so ingrained that the absence of this kind of mothering was seen as abnormal. In one study,[4] social scientists saw mothers who weren't always ready to drop what they were doing to respond to a child's demands, who didn't hesitate to criticize a child when her behavior warranted it, perhaps insisting, at times, that their activities as adults took priority. What did the scientists call these mothers? Hostile.

To most people, this term "maternal hostility" sounds chilling. It makes one think of a tearful child being locked in a closet or being beaten by her mother. That was decidedly *not* the sort of thing the scientists were talking about. Probably because the "normal" mother was seen as the one who was always available, always approving, even sacrificial, any mother who wasn't like this was called "hostile." In this context, hostility is really the absence of what Lois Hoffman calls "smother love."

Because the study covered a span of more than twenty-five years, the researchers had a chance not only to examine the relationships between parents and their children, but to follow the children as they moved into adulthood. To their great surprise, they found out that the daughters of these very same "hostile" mothers turned out to be high achievers. Not only did they achieve as adults, but they were also less likely than daughters of less "hostile" mothers to pull back from stressful situations.

Trying to make some sense of what they saw as puzzling results, the researchers said that the ability to confront stress head on "may reflect the mother's early pressure for independence and autonomy."

Today, social scientists are beginning to look askance at "smother love." Girls, it seems, need a certain amount of what used to be called "hostility" or "rejection" to grow into self-reliant adults.

Diana Baumrind,[5] a Berkeley psychologist, in detailed studies of the interactions of children and parents, found that girls who were achievement-oriented, independent and competent had mothers and fathers who demanded mature behavior. They set standards for their daughters and were firm in enforcing their demands. In these households there was some conflict, some tension, between parents and children—everything wasn't always peaceful and serene. A reasonable amount of conflict and tension is inevitable and appears to help children grow into "separate" people. Parents of boys have expected conflict—boys will be boys—but find conflict with daughters more distressing. Yet girls whose parents take every opportunity to avoid it are cheating girls out of something they very much need.

Encouraging independence—and being careful not to reward dependent behavior—is the first key step in helping girls become self-reliant and free to develop to their full potential. There is another part to this process that is just as vital, but more subtle and easier to miss. Girls have to learn to take credit for their own accomplishments. Too many girls and women do something good and then write it off to luck.

A young woman, a college senior, applies to graduate school in the field of her choice. She has maintained an A average throughout four years of college. When she is admitted to a good graduate school, she breathes a sigh of relief and says to her friends, "I guess they needed women, that's why I got in."

One of her classmates, a young man whose grades have been consistently lower than the young woman's, also applies to graduate school. When he is admitted he says to his friends that it's going to be "no sweat," he has the brains to do the work.

Both these students have succeeded in reaching a goal, but are seeing their success in dramatically different ways, ways that may be more important than they know in predicting how they will act in the future.

The way we explain our behavior to ourselves can sometimes be more important than the behavior itself. Take the case of the two students we just mentioned. The young woman got into graduate school but wrote that success off to luck and to the fact that the school probably needed women. She attributed her success to sources outside herself—things she couldn't control, such as good luck. The male student, on the other hand, saw his success as due to something he could and did control—his own ability and effort. What does this difference mean? The chances are that the young man will gain in confidence and will meet without hesitation the next challenge that comes along. If his brainpower worked for him the last time, why shouldn't it work as well the next time? The young woman, however, doesn't see any such guarantees. Luck is something she can't control; it's a random throw of the dice. She has no assurance that the dice will fall her way the next time, so her success isn't going to build her confidence or make her eager to accept new challenges. The ironic thing is that the young man will probably achieve more with lesser skills and talent than the young woman, because he *expects* to. Expectations often turn into reality if they have a reasonable base to begin with.

These examples are a good introduction to an area of the study of cognitive behavior called attribution theory—a way of looking at how people interpret their behavior to themselves, and how that in turn influences what they do in the future.[6]

According to the research in this area, people tend to have stable tendencies—habits, if you will—to make either internal or external "attributions." The young woman was demonstrating an external attribution—deciding her success was due to luck. Many people write off their success to external factors—the man who thinks he was promoted because the boss liked him, the student who says she won an art award

138

because the competition wasn't very stiff, the boy who thinks he passed the math test because it wasn't very hard. Sometimes it's realistic to give credit to luck or circumstance for a success. But *all* successes can't be flukes, and the person who gets into the habit of writing them off as such can run into trouble—usually in the form of underrating his or her own ability and refusing to take reasonable risks for major gain.

The person with a stable pattern of internal attributions is a different case. If you think that your success is due to your intelligence, your hard work or your talent, presumably you won't shy from challenges or opportunities in the future, since brains, hard work and talent are not likely to desert you suddenly, as luck might.

Similarly, the ways people explain failure to themselves can also be internal or external. If you lose a tennis match, you can decide that your serve was off that day, you weren't used to the surface or you had a hangover. Or you may decide you just weren't as good a player as the other person. If it's the latter, then the next time you play that particular opponent, you will probably expect to lose. If it's one of the others, all you have to do is get your serve working, or play on a different court or stay away from martinis the night before, and you've got a chance of winning. If you're a writer who sends off an article to a journal and it gets rejected, you could decide that it was because the article (and you) just weren't good enough, or you might decide the editor was an idiot, or your timing was bad or the market wasn't right. In the first instance, you'd probably be tempted to throw the article in the drawer and leave it there. But if your reasons for failure have nothing to do with your ability—then why not try again?

In general, attributing success to internal factors leads to feelings of pride and self-esteem; attributing failure to internal factors leads to feelings of inferiority or shame. It's a lot easier on the ego to think that you flunked a test because the test was unfair or because you didn't study the right thing than to think it was because you're stupid. Since attribution is so crucial to what a person will—or will not—accomplish in life, it's important to look at the differences between men and women and boys and girls, in the way they "code" their behavior.

There is a considerable body of research that shows that from a very early age, girls expect to do less well at a variety of tasks than do boys. This difference shows up at least as early as kindergarten. In one study, first-grade girls and boys both estimated that the girls would perform less well on a ball-throwing task, even though the girls actually did as well.

Even in areas where the girls outperformed the boys, the girls believed they would do worse than the boys. An overview of such research shows that males tend to overestimate their future success relative to ability, while females tend to underestimate their future performance.

A dramatic demonstration of this sex difference and of the way expectancies shape behavior comes from a major follow-up study of 7700 college seniors one year after graduation.[7] The researchers had available to them the grade point averages of their subjects when they were seniors, their anticipated plans with respect to graduate school and their actual attendance at graduate or professional schools. The major findings were that women less often than men planned advanced study, and when they did plan to go on, they less often actually did so, and when they went on, less often entered the field they had planned. Perhaps the most startling finding was while men with C+ averages felt confident they could successfully complete a Ph.D. program, women with B+ averages did not. The power of this kind of thinking turns expectation into reality. Women who had A to A+ grades attended graduate school only about as often as men with B grades.

Women not only expect to do less well than men from an early age, but research shows that they are more likely than men to attribute success to external factors, and to feel more ashamed of failure. Not only women themselves fall into this pattern of writing women's successes off to luck, but others do, too. In a study done at Purdue University,[8] researchers asked male and female subjects to take part in a test. The subject's job would be to evaluate how well a "partner" did on tasks that required identifying objects usually thought of as masculine or feminine—such as a tire jack or a double boiler. The subjects were supposed to pick the images of these objects out of a larger picture—something like a child's "find the hidden objects" game. The subjects heard, but did not see, a "partner" taking the test. The partner, however, was in fact a recorded male or female voice, so it was the researchers who determined precisely how well the "partner" actually did on the test. The subjects were asked to evaluate the partner's performance, and were reminded that the partner's score could depend on such things as luck or ability. They were asked to take these into account in their evaluation. The findings are described by the subtitle of the report on the experiment: What is skill for the male is luck for the female. Though the male and female voices on the tapes were carefully prepared so both did equally well on the tests, the subjects didn't see it that way. "As expected," said the researchers, "a male's successful performance on a masculine task is explained by invoking skill on the part of the performer, while the same performance by a female tends to be more attributed to luck." Interestingly enough, men who did well on the female tasks were not generally seen as lucky. So men were seen overall as more skillful than women. For students to see women who did well as "lucky" was not atypical. When a woman is successful, the word luck is often heard. When a male reporter interviewed Juanita Kreps, President Carter's secretary of commerce, he remarked that she had been lucky in her career. Kreps disagreed. "First of all," she said, "it was *not* luck." Unfortunately, many women are not as quick as Mrs. Kreps to recognize that luck wasn't the issue. The tendency to "write off" success seems to start early in many women and to persist throughout their lives. Kay Deaux, from the department of psychological sciences at Purdue, decided to study the attribution patterns of women in management, since affirmative action had opened up new opportunities for women in that field.[9] Not enough attention had been paid, she said, to the factors inside women themselves that might serve to hinder their advancement in the managerial field. She wondered if women in management had the same "write-off" pattern that showed up in other women.

She chose to study thirty male and twenty-five female executives from a California retail chain who were comparable in age, education and position. These executives were asked to evaluate themselves on a number of qualities, including initiative, ability and difficulty of assignments. The males saw themselves as having significantly more ability and as having significantly better overall performance than did the females. In addition, the men saw themselves as having much more difficult jobs than did the women. Yet the women held identical jobs, and according to their supervisors' ratings, there were few differences between the male and female executives.

There was also a difference, Deaux found, between the younger and older women managers. The younger, better-educated women had higher estimates of their abilities than did the older women, and they were less satisfied with their promotions and pay. "These data would suggest there is a new breed of woman developing," says Deaux, "for whom some of the earlier findings may not be applicable."

That piece of news is encouraging, but the tendency to discount success and to be cowed by failure is still a major stumbling block for many women. The inability to claim success, the tendency to see oneself as less talented, less intelligent, less able than one really is can be a major psychological crippler. That this tendency exists is well documented—but how does it come about? Who is the carrier of this lethal virus of self-effacement?

Developmental psychologists often tackle such problems by asking "when did it start?" Low expectancy seems to surface shortly after the child enters school, say Michigan psychologist Jacquelynne Parsons and her colleagues.[10] Younger children don't seem to link failures with subsequent attempts. They sometimes fail repeatedly at certain tasks but cheerfully stick with them as if they fully expect to succeed. By the time the child reaches school age, however, she may begin to incorporate sex-role stereotypes from the world around her. Parsons says, "If the incorporation of the feminine sex-role stereotype implies the lowering of one's feeling of competence, we should expect young girls to develop lower estimates of their abilities than young boys." The researchers did their own study of children from kindergarten through fifth grade and found that girls indeed perceived their ability on cognitive tasks as lower than the boys even though the girls actually outperformed the boys. So the problem starts as early as kindergarten.

If you believe you don't have much ability, and yet you do well, it must be luck. Thinking it's luck is not going to build your confidence for the next round; so starts the vicious cycle—low expectations, low achievement.

Girls also seem to have a different perspective on failure than boys do. A number of studies show that when girls get "failure feedback"—they are told they did not do very well—they take it to heart and next time tend to try less hard or avoid that task completely. Boys, on the other hand, faced with failure feedback, show improved performance and greater persistence.[11] They seem to respond to the challenge. Why the difference? Again, it may be due to the attribution process. Girls blame their lack of ability. Boys are more likely to claim they didn't work hard enough, or the test wasn't fair—factors that are either under their control or that might be different next time.

Noting these facts, psychologist Carol Dweck[12] of the University of Illinois decided to look at how teachers send messages to boys and girls in the classroom. Are teachers unconsciously sending out messages that tend to support the differences in the way boys and girls attribute success and failure? Dweck believes the answer is yes.

To begin her argument, Dweck points out that thanks to past research,

142

we know that feedback has to be fairly specific to have an impact on children's assessment of their own performances. "When feedback is used indiscriminately and for a wide spectrum of non-intellectual behavior, it comes to lose its meaning as an evaluation of the child's performance," Dweck writes. This is precisely what happens to boys in the classroom. Boys are always getting yelled at—to be quiet, to stop punching each other, to stop stuffing gum in each other's hair and for general rowdy conduct. One third-grade teacher, looking at his charges, muttered, "The girls are wonderful—they behave. But the boys . . ." and he rolled his eyes upward, appealing to heaven.

Boys get plenty of negative feedback—but much of it is not aimed directly at the quality of their work. When Dweck studied fourth- and fifth-grade classes, she found that the teachers gave negative evaluations about equally to boys and girls. For the boys, though, only *one-third* of the criticism had to do with the intellectual quality of their work. The rest had to do with conduct or other "intellectually irrelevant aspects of academic performance." For the girls, *two-thirds* of the criticism was specifically addressed to the intellectual quality of their work.

In addition, when the teachers did criticize, they explicitly attributed intellectual failures to lack of motivation *six times* as often to boys as to girls. In other words, the teachers were giving boys the message, "You can do it if you just try harder. You have the ability." Girls who do not get the message to try harder may assume they failed because they could not do the work. Research shows that girls often respond precisely as if that is what they are hearing.

Teachers may have a mind-set about boys and girls that makes them unconsciously give these disparate messages. Boys are expected to be rowdy and therefore inattentive about schoolwork. Girls are seen as well-behaved, dutiful and always exerting their best effort. So the boys are told "try harder," but the girls are just told they have done something incorrectly. The first message, to the boy, not only chalks up his failure to something other than his own ability—inattention—but it also gives him a strategy for succeeding. The girl is told she has failed, and often she thinks that is because she simply isn't good enough or smart enough to do the work. So she stops trying.

Studies also show that girls take the negative evaluations of adults more seriously than boys do. Perhaps because boys get hollered at so much in school, they tend to ignore much of the teacher's criticism. Girls are usually treated more gently by teachers—not disciplined as often, frequently praised. So the teacher's criticism has a powerful impact.

What does all this mean for later on? Carol Dweck thinks that the boys will take more risks, accept more challenges than girls. Teachers, she says, while trying to be helpful to girls, may be sending them messages which undermine their future achievement.

What the teachers can do when they criticize the work of girl students, Dweck suggests, is to be sure to give them a strategy for doing better. Girls should not be told simply, "You did it wrong," but should be given an explanation of how to do it right. Giving a girl a game plan for improving her skills lets her know she has the ability to perform the task. This is a good idea for all students, of course, but it seems to be crucial for girls, who may need special help to see the connection between their own efforts and a successful outcome. You don't give up—because you know you can do it. A failure then becomes a challenge, not a defeat.

Just as teachers may be sending unconscious messages to kids, so may parents. Jacquelynne Parsons and her colleagues suggest that parents could be conveying lower expectancies for girls "in a variety of subtle ways undetected both in laboratory experiments and field observations." So, "it appears that initial changes in this area must occur at the family level. Parents must make a concerted effort to prevent the emergence of the low expectancy pattern in their daughters and to keep themselves from reinforcing the cultural stereotype with their own behaviors. Parents and teachers must avoid the subtle cues which convey the lower expectancies for girls, such as excessive concern with their safety, reluctance to encourage high career aspirations, willingness to accept low ability attributions, and failure to urge continued effort in the face of defeat."

Most women who are adults today can probably recognize some of these attributional patterns in their own lives. But they are not doomed to repeat them over and over. Remember, one of the major points we have stressed is plasticity, the capacity for change throughout the life-span. One of Rosalind's clients gave us a heartening example of this sort of change.

This woman, single and in her early thirties, had been an elementary-school teacher. She had never thought of herself as particularly special, talented or competent. When she realized she was unhappy in the classroom, she decided to switch careers and go into educational administration. She was employed by a state-funded project in which she was part of a team that had to show teachers new curricula, new methods and set up workshops in various schools. The team also had to evaluate the project and compile a detailed report on its work. The woman did the lion's share of the fieldwork and the writing.

When she started this work, she felt very unsure of her ability to do well on the job. The workshops went well, however, and the school systems liked the new methods and she began to get positive feedback. Her confidence in her talents grew stronger. She began to think of herself as an able, competent person who could handle whatever assignment came her way. She came to recognize that her success was due to her own effort and ability.

But there was another step she needed to take. Many women get to the point where they can claim success privately, but not publicly. We have all seen the secretary who manages the office, but pretends the boss does; the woman scientist who, without thinking, lets the male member of the team get all the credit; the nurse who saves the resident from giving a patient the wrong medicine, and never is rewarded for her vigilance.

In the case of Rosalind's client, she was able to move from knowing she was good to wanting credit. When state officials did their own evaluation of the project, they said it was the best work they had seen in years. A number of parties and press conferences followed, and all the attention was focused on the director—a man. The woman watched him basking in the limelight, knowing that she deserved at least an equal share. She said to herself, I'm good, I can do the work and I want the glory. Next time, *I'm* going to be the director.

Nuts and Bolts

Many parents today are eager not to discourage their daughters' high ambitions, and would never think of saying "Girls can't be doctors," or "Girls shouldn't play sports." But it's harder to pick up some of the subtle clues girls give out that show they are starting, often at a fairly young age, to write off their successes. One thing we have noticed is that girls rarely seem to *brag* about their exploits the way boys do. If you listen to a couple of ten-year-old boys talking about their performance in the last Little League game, you'd think you'd just tuned in on a conversation between Ty Cobb and Joe DiMaggio. They tell of smashing hits and diving, one-handed catches. In reality, the smashing hit may just have dribbled by the pitcher, and the diving catch may have been a simple pop fly; but the boys aren't really lying. They are just using a little poetic license, and pretty soon they convince themselves that they are in fact as good as they say. Girls seem much more likely not to claim credit even for really outstanding feats. For example, one Little League team had a lone girl player. By the middle of the season, she had become one of the team's most reliable hitters. In a crucial game, she hit two home runs, one with the bases loaded, and it was her hitting that made the difference between victory and defeat. When a teammate congratulated her on those two hefty belts, she said, "I guess I was lucky." None of the boys *ever* said that about their hits. Even the youngest boys, who startled themselves and everyone else when they managed to connect with the ball, never talked about luck. Girls seemed concerned about "hurting" others by their achievements and then being hurt in return. Some worry that others will be jealous; some are concerned that being "special" will cause them to lose their friends. Others, unused to bragging, shy away from situations in which they will be the center of attention.

A few years ago, Grace studied fifth-grade girls' attitudes about achievement and success.[13] She asked them to complete a story about "Anne winning first prize in a science fair." Grace thought it sad to read stories like these:

> She was so happy, her friends were really mad. They also had a good exhibit but Anne won. On the way home from the Science Fair she was going to walk with someone but she had left so she went to walk with someone else but she ran away. Anne couldn't understand why.

> Sue and Mary Ellen got very jealous and started being very mean to Anne. They thought they should win because they took the courses for it and Anne didn't. The fair manager called and said that they had made a mistake and Anne won second prize. They made friends again even though Anne was disappointed.

When a girl belittles an achievement or seems not to want to talk about it, something more damaging than a lack of braggadocio may be at work. The girl may in fact be saying to herself—and believing—that what she did wasn't much.

These patterns—inability to build on success and claim it privately and publicly—are not traits that girls are born with. They are types of behavior that are learned—and can be unlearned. Contrary to the

146

opinion of some experts, it's never too late for girls or women to change these patterns, thanks to the lifelong "plasticity" we've mentioned.

Parents—as well as teachers—can keep an eye out for instances where girls are shying away from certain activities because of a supposed lack of ability. One little girl, for example, used to approach new challenges with an "I can't do it" attitude. At first she complained she couldn't do a cartwheel, but practiced until she could do a perfect one. Next she said she'd never learn to swim—then surprised herself by doing it. She stood at the edge of the skating rink for one season weeping because she said she couldn't skate. Then she tried it, and inside of a day, was gliding around. Each time it was pointed out to her that whenever she said she couldn't do something, she was wrong—she really could. When she started taking tennis lessons, her "I can't do it" attitude had disappeared. In fact, she started off by missing the ball by a good foot each time she swung at it, but didn't seem discouraged. Though she wasn't a natural at the game, she improved steadily and never once said she couldn't do it. Obviously, there had been a change in her attributional pattern—but only after it was made clear to her that she in fact could do a great many things but was assuming she couldn't.

It has been fashionable recently to talk about how much pressure to achieve parents are putting on children today, and how children are becoming more tense, and anxious. This is a legitimate concern, but it could lead to the adoption of the opposite extreme—no parental expectations or standards at all. Is it really healthy to say to a child, "I love you whatever you are, whatever you do, and I approve of you no matter what?" Parents who have too rigid or too high expectations for children can be destructive, but parents with no expectations at all—or those who are unwilling to voice any—may not be helping their children to become independent adults who can deal with the rest of the world. The world doesn't say to people, "You're terrific—no matter what." We've said before that in the outside world there are standards, tasks, tests—in short, there is competition—and feedback—and the child who gets no clues from parents about how to perform in that world may be in trouble. Girls are particularly vulnerable to this syndrome. If they expect to escape these facts of life because they are sweet, pretty or docile, they are in for a severe jolt. To say to a child, "I don't care what you are as long as you are happy" is to offer the child only a cognitive vacuum. A child has to be something besides "happy." That expression is probably used more often with girls than with boys—and it can communicate lowered expectations to a girl. Most parents realize that a boy has to be something besides "happy" or he won't be able to make a living. It's time to think about girls the same way.

We've seen, also, that girls may not only learn to discount success, but to take fewer chances, to venture less, and that this pattern can often be traced back to early childhood. If Lois Hoffman and others are right in saying that girls do not get the same training in independence that boys do, then it's important for parents to be aware of the dangers to girls in this area. We've talked before about the sense of mastery that is so important to independence, and the tendency of parents and others to "overhelp" girls. When parents become problem-solvers for the child, when little girls are given ready-made solutions too often, they never get the sense that they can control what happens to them. As adults, too many women feel out of control and rudderless, as if they cannot steer the craft that is their own life. Girls need to be given tasks that are not overly easy to accomplish, and to be asked and expected to complete those tasks. This process involves risk. The child who rides a bicycle is more exposed to danger than one who does not. But the bicycle also gives the child a sense of mastery and an ability to explore the environment.

Of course, parents must take reasonable safety precautions, but parents of girls also should be on the lookout for activities in their daily lives which can help girls enhance their sense of independence. Interestingly enough, that may be easier for families who live in the city than it is for those in the suburbs. Rosalind remembers growing up in New York City, and going off with her friends to museums on the subway when she was nine. Suburbs, designed to be good places for children to grow up in, may actually not be so great in one way; they are often sprawling areas with inadequate public transportation, which means that children have to be chauffeured everyplace. It's not so easy to send your daughter to the store on an errand when the store is a shopping mall five miles away. Suburban mothers can fall into the trap of doing too much for their daughters just because they themselves are available. If it's three o'clock, and a few drops of rain are falling, the urge to jump into the car and pick up a child at school is strong. In fact, a mother who doesn't do just that can feel like a "bad mommy." But little girls don't melt in the rain, and unless there are real safety reasons for the ride, or unless it's a downpour, it's probably better to let her walk home. Suburban parents may have to

148

be more creative than city parents in thinking up opportunities to help their daughters develop a sense of independence.

Mothers themselves may be "modeling" behavior for their daughters without realizing it. If a daughter sees that her mother is in fact not very independent, that she seldom ventures away from home, there's a message in that behavior. Some women rarely leave their homes for any substantial time unless they go with their husbands. Or they, in effect, ask for their husbands' permission to go out to a friend's house, to a movie or to take a course. It's interesting to note that mental illness in women often takes the form of some kind of phobia about venturing beyond one's own safe little environment—fear of the outside, fear of heights, elevators, cars and so on. These phobias are much more common among women than they are among men, leading us to wonder about the connection between these phobias and early restrictions on independence. Mothers should take care to let their daughters see them acting as adult human beings, who have a right to independent action, and who don't have to ask permission for the things they do in the outside world.

One theme that becomes increasingly important as women grow older is the need for the love and approval of others. This need is a universal human one, and a healthy one, unless it stems from fear and dependence, from a belief that one cannot act, or survive, alone. Lois Hoffman calls this "infantile fear of abandonment," the conviction that safety lies only in lifelines to others. This fear can interfere with girls' (and women's) achievements, decision-making and personal relations. When we talked about this issue among ourselves, all three of us came up with examples of times we had trouble saying—or doing—something that would make somebody else unhappy, even if only mildly so. We see this same sort of thing surfacing in young girls. Sometimes this concern can make them hesitant to accomplish something or claim success. One little girl, for example, gave up a part she wanted in a school play because a friend said she was unhappy because *she* didn't get it.

We have seen that girls develop a valuable sensitivity to others' feelings early in life, but that empathy can sometimes be overdone. There is a happy medium between being a self-centered boor and being a doormat. The girl who must always please others pays too high a price. You can't, after all, go through life failing just so your achievements won't make your friends feel bad. The sad fact of life is that some people are never going to love you, no matter what you do. And you may indeed pay a

149

price for achievement—it's possible that others will be jealous of you or not like you. In reality that's their problem, not yours. It's sometimes hard for girls to realize that. All of us, of course, want to be liked, but girls can fall into the habit of letting others' opinions shape their self-image. The knowledge "I am a good person" should come from within, not from others' perceptions. The girl or woman who is always eager to please makes life very complicated for herself. First of all, she probably exaggerates others' critical reactions. Rosalind remembers that once her husband made a dish which she thought was awful, but she ate every morsel of it. When she finally told him the truth, he wasn't upset. He just said that he guessed that he had combined the wrong ingredients. Caryl—who hates fish—always used to say, "I'm allergic to fish" when people suggested seafood restaurants. Now she simply says, "I hate fish," and nobody gets mad. Grace, who cherishes her rare opportunities for solitude, has learned to say no to friends and colleagues who suggest sharing a hotel room at out-of-town professional meetings. She finds that most of them understand—and even decide that they, too, should spend a bit more money in order to have that luxury. If every statement you make is a test of how well you are liked, you will be in a constant state of anxiety. In reality, you will probably not lose a friend by making a decision, stating a preference or disagreeing with that friend. If you do, it was probably not much of a friendship to begin with.

Parents who see their daughters falling into the trap of being overeager to please can get them to talk about what it is they really want. A girl should feel free to say, "I want this," without fear. She may not get what she wants, and others may in fact show annoyance, but she should feel that expressing her desires is legitimate.

This is another area where mothers send messages by their own behavior. If the mother is always eager to please her husband, if she hesitates to venture an opposite opinion, she may be denying her daughter permission to express her own desires. It's healthy for a child to see that her parents can disagree vigorously without either one withdrawing love from the other. She can also learn the important lesson that losing approval for a short time won't kill you. The girl or woman who can't venture a strong opinion or a definite statement doesn't get a chance to "reality-test" her own ideas about how people react. She may never find out that the consequences of such an action are less than lethal.

The woman who has to submit her actions and statements to a litmus test of what others may think adds a whole layer of anxiety to everyday life. She just has more factors to weigh before every action, every decision. Uncertain of herself, she may tend to distort or exaggerate the reactions of others, and make costly mistakes in her work life or personal life.

There will be times in the lives of girls and women when the sense of empathy will conflict with the need for achievement. The girl who gets the part in the play that her friend wanted will make her friend unhappy. That won't be comfortable. But why need she make the equally (or more) uncomfortable choice to give up the part and feel the pain of losing something quite valuable? Too often women do so because they feel they will not be loved if they don't.

Certainly there are many times in life when it is good—and appropriate—to put another's need before your own. But this decision should be made from strength, from considering oneself as sympathetically as one considers others. Girls can be helped to understand the difference between generosity and martyrdom.

8

ADOLESCENCE
To Hear a Different Drummer

Sometimes I try to put myself in another's place, and I am frightened to find that I am almost succeeding. How awful to be anyone but I. I know that I am too tall and have a fat nose, and yet how I pose and primp before the mirror, seeing more and more how lovely I am. I have erected in my mind an image of myself, idealistic and beautiful. Is not that image, free from blemish, the true self—the true perfection? Am I wrong when this image insinuates itself between me and the merciless mirror? Oh, even now I glance back on what I have just written, how foolish it sounds, how melodramatic. Never, never will I reach the perfection I long for with all my soul. My paintings, my poems, my stories, all poor, poor reflections . . .
—Sylvia Plath, writing in her diary as a teenager

Adolescence, Jean Piaget wrote, is the time of life when the child develops the ability to imagine herself as someone else. That is the cognitive border at the end of childhood. A young child cannot really imagine what it would be like to be somebody else, living some life other than the one she has known. On reaching adolescence, the child enters the foyer of adulthood, a crucial time, because now the future is so close. Before, it seemed lost in the mists of time. One could play at being a cowboy, a movie star, a tennis champion, a ballerina, and it would be little more than play. But adolescence is the time when real-life choices hover in the air. The roles taken on now can have some real connection to a future no longer obscured by distance.

It is the time, too, when the body matures from childhood to adulthood, bringing with it a succession of dizzying, puzzling changes. This time of physical and cognitive awakening has naturally drawn the scrutiny of the behavioral scientists. Unfortunately, in the case of women, the emphasis has been almost solely on the emotional and erotic development of the girl child. Can she transfer her love for her father to an acceptable "other male," with whom she can have a satisfactory heterosexual relationship? Can she accept her "feminine nature" without rebellion? Reading all this, one might assume that the girl child is possessed of a head that is filled with pink cotton candy where the gray matter should be. Studies of boys at this age often focus on cognitive development, skills, abilities—what they can *do*. Boys are seen through the eye of the motion picture—always active, doing; girls are caught by the lens of the still camera—at rest, simply *being*.

We are going to look at the adolescent girl through a new lens. We want to examine the crucial events in this time of a girl's life which may lead her down one of two paths—one that leads to self-actualization and a strong sense of self, to competence—and the other to a more passive, acquiescent role in life in which she is more acted upon than active. Adolescence is the time when the self, already given much of its shape by earlier experiences, takes on the form that will travel through adulthood. It is also the time when we witness a disturbing phenomenon: if life were a horse race, and kids were horses, the racers would be galloping along neck and neck until the arrival of puberty—and then, one by one, the girls would start dropping back.

In a recent and highly publicized study of male development, Yale psychologist Daniel Levinson[1] said he found in young males the formation of what he calls "The Dream," which is a sort of vision of self-in-the-adult-world. "A young man's growth depends a good deal on whether his early life structure is consonant with, and infused by—the dream—or is opposed to it. If The Dream remains unconnected to his life, it may simply die, and with it will die his sense of aliveness and purpose."

For young girls, it seems that The Dream—that sense of self-in-the-adult-world, may either fail to develop, or falter during adolescence. Boys aim high—they look at the stars. Girls seem to peer up to the lowest branch on a nearby tree. When girls think about the work they might do

153

in the adult world, they seem to focus more on the cultural stereotypes of what women can't do, rather than what they as individuals might do. In reviewing the research that has been done on girls' vocational choices,[2] here is the pattern we found:

1. Girls choose a more restricted, less varied range of occupations than do boys.
2. Occupational choices are highly stereotyped at an early age.
3. About one-half to two-thirds of girls aspire to be either a teacher, a nurse or a secretary, regardless of their social class or race.

Not only do the girls stay with their early choices, but there is evidence that they intentionally avoid high-prestige occupations. Rosalind gave 2500 boys and girls from ages nine to seventeen a list of fifteen occupations.[3] She asked them to choose those they would most like to enter and those they would least like to enter. When she compared the results, she found that for boys the prestige of an occupation was a positive influence in their decision to choose it. For the girls, however, the influence was negative. The higher the prestige of an occupation, the more they expressed an aversion to it.

This "dropping-back" effect is seen not only in the choices girls make, but in their performance as well. In one study of underachieving boys and girls done in the mid-sixties, the results showed that the boys who were not doing well in school had a history of low grades from early elementary school on. But the underachieving girls' grades dropped at the beginning of puberty.

To many young women, the idea of self-in-the-adult-world turns out to be that of second-class citizen. Jean Lipman-Blumen[4] of the National Institute of Education calls it "The Vicarious Achievement Ethic." Women, she says, tend to try to hitch their wagon to a star, then hang on and hope. In other words, they expect to experience achievement through the eminence of the man to whom they are married or with whom they are working. Looking at the jobs women and girls select, she notes that they are really extensions of woman's role in the family. The jobs involve helping others and are usually assistant roles, where women carry out tasks that are given them by others. These jobs are usually of lower status than the ones to which they are linked—the doctor-nurse combination, for example. By adolescence, Lipman-Blumen says, "girls in our culture traditionally are trained to experience vicariously certain key aspects of life, usually through the agency of significant others, usually males, in her life space." This pattern is found at all occupational levels. The wife of the Fuller Brush man writes his orders; the ambassador's wife entertains visiting dignitaries.

We have seen that girls are getting messages throughout their lives that women are limited people. Adolescence is when things really hit the fan, so to speak. This "dropping-back" phenomenon afflicts the brainy girl who gets all A's at least as much as the indifferent student. It is the time when precious human potential starts to get lost.

Elizabeth Janeway[5] was once asked to write an essay on the subject of "recognizing human potential," and she came up with this warning:

> Everybody is *for* realizing human potential. Who could consciously be against it? I can think of few people since Hitler who have openly advocated suppressing human potential. So I worry that it might be a little too easy to say, yes, yes, let us realize human potential, go right ahead, why don't you take yours around the corner or in the backyard and get busy realizing it—where you aren't going to bother anyone else. In fact, I am beginning to suspect that one of the problems women have today (and I don't confine this to women in my mind, but I am focusing there as I have agreed to do) is an excess of agreement, an excess if you will, of lip service . . . universal agreement that it's a fine thing has not resulted in every capable human being finding a spot to utilize his or her capabilities. Something intervenes, or more probably, someone intervenes, some enemies must be fought.

Some of those enemies turn out to be lodged inside the heads of girls and women. It might be appropriate to borrow Franklin Roosevelt's famous saying, "The only thing we have to fear is fear itself," and apply it to female development. For while boys may strive for achievement, and failure seems the worst thing that can happen, women often fear the polar opposite of failure. They are afraid to succeed, and this fear seems to have its first blossoming around the time of puberty.

Matina Horner, the psychologist who is now the president of Radcliffe College, did the initial work a decade ago on the syndrome that has come to be known as "fear of success."[6] She noticed that women seemed to become anxious when faced with the prospect of success because they thought they would pay a heavy price for it—the loss of femininity. They expected, as Horner put it, to be "unsexed by success." That notion should not come as a surprise to women who remember the "rules" of

155

their dating days: "Never let a man think you're too smart, never beat a man at anything, don't talk too much about yourself, listen to what *he* has to say."

Horner thought that ambivalence toward achievement would be more characteristic of women than men, and that it would hinder women's effectiveness in performing certain tasks, particularly when they had to compete with men. Bright women who could really outperform men would be particularly vulnerable.

To test her theory, Horner asked "able" college students to write stories about two students, "Anne" and "John," using this first sentence:

"At the end of her first-term finals, Anne (or John) finds herself at the top of her (or his) medical school class."

More than 65 percent of the females—but less than 10 percent of the males—wrote stories reflecting a fear of success—that is, if you do well, bad things can happen to you. For the women students, Horner found "unusual excellence in women was clearly associated for them with loss of femininity, social rejection, personal or societal rejection, or some combination of the above."

In the stories the young women wrote, poor Anne fared worse than the heroine of a long-running soap opera. She was described as unhappy and miserable at being single. She was called so ambitious as to use men, family and friends simply as tools for her own advancement. The "happy" endings the students wrote for Anne involved the sacrifice of her talents:

> "Anne has a boyfriend, Carl, in the same class, and they are quite serious. Anne met Carl at college and they started dating about their sophomore year in undergraduate school. Anne is rather upset and so is Carl. She wants him to be higher scholastically than she is. Anne will deliberately lower her academic standing the next term, while she does all she subtly can to help Carl. His grades soon come up and Anne drops out of med school. They marry and he goes on in school while she raises her family."

> "She is in a class of a great number of highly intelligent people, one of whom is her fiancé. Anne is ambitious and has more innate ability than does her boyfriend. Anne is fearful that this situation will have a detrimental effect on their relationship and later on in their marriage. Her superiority will mean that her eventual earning power will be greater. Although he would never let her know, her husband would

156

resent that. It is important that Anne marry this man because of their closeness. But Anne will never be entirely happy in their marriage because she must always hold back her mentality and vocational desires."

"Anne is talking to her counselor. The counselor says she will make a fine nurse. She will continue her med school courses. She will study hard and find that she can and will become a good nurse."

Perhaps the most important finding in the Horner studies was that women who feared success, as evidenced by the stories they wrote, performed more poorly on tasks in mixed-sex competition than they did alone. Women who did not show a fear of success, and most males, did better in mixed-sex competition.

So, Horner's study suggested that many able young women, for whom successful achievement was a realistic goal, expected negative consequences from success and managed to do less than their best when competing with men.

Horner's work aroused a great deal of interest, and other researchers set up the same kinds of studies to see if their results dovetailed with Horner's. The later studies failed to demonstrate that girls who hold back when competing with men write "fear of success" stories. Which isn't to say that fear of success in women doesn't exist—clearly, it does—only that you can't predict girls' behavior from the stories they write.

In fact, if you want to find out whether fear of success exists, you don't have to match up stories people write with their behavior. You simply have to find out how girls behave. Do they, in fact, pull back from their best efforts when they are competing, or think they are competing, with men? One 1978 study gives dramatic evidence that the answer is yes.

John C. Condry and Sharon L. Dyer of Cornell University set up a test involving sixty-one students from the fifth, seventh and ninth grades.[7] They were given what was described to them as an intelligence test, in which they had to unscramble a group of scrambled words. Boys and girls were seated opposite each other to take the test. When they had finished part one of the test, each boy and girl was taken aside and told privately that he or she had done better than the "partner" in the test. They were told: "By the way, I just finished grading the first scrambled word test, and you won. You scored five points better than (partner's name). At the end of the second scrambled word test, I'll tell you both how you did."

The students—knowing they had done well on the test—were then sent back to take another similar test. The researchers set up this situation deliberately. They predicted a "sudden onset" of fear of success among girls in mixed-sex competition at the time of puberty, when the idea of "sex-appropriate" behavior is deeply felt. They wanted to see if they were right.

The results of the second part of the test were striking. The fifth-grade students, both male and female, tended to increase their scores. They did better the second time around. But between the fifth and seventh grade a crucial event occurs: puberty. The seventh-grade students showed a radically different pattern than did the fifth graders. The boys still increased their scores the second time around, but the girls' scores took a nose dive. *Eighty percent* of the female students dropped their scores in the second test after they had been told they had bested a male partner. The fifth graders showed little evidence of behavioral fear of success—the tendency to pull back in mixed-sex work—but most of the seventh-grade girls and half of the ninth-grade girls retreated from competition.

The researchers asked the children about their performance, especially how they felt about competing intellectually with the opposite sex. Most of the boys were noncommittal on the subject, as were most of the fifth-grade boys and girls. With the seventh graders it was different. Almost every girl in the seventh grade said she didn't like to beat boys in a competitive game. Several said explicitly, "I'd rather be popular than have good grades or win a game against a boy." Among the ninth graders, most of the girls were saying the same thing. But of the ninth-grade girls who had a different idea—who said they always did their best no matter what the circumstances—not one dropped her score on the second test.

Of these ninth-grade girls, the ones who didn't retreat, the researchers said, "Perhaps they heard a different drummer, in a country which does not exist."

Anyone who is interested in developing competence in women will wonder about that different drummer and about how more young girls can be enabled to hear its cadence. Those seventh graders, the ones who denied their own talents rather than score five points better on a test than a boy, are settling into patterns which will not help them live a rich and satisfying life. First of all, they seem to be buying the idea that they must not do better than *any* man, at *any* place at *any* thing—unless it's a "safe" female activity. These were students from a middle-class university town, and as the researchers point out, the students were told that the task was a measure of intelligence, presumably a relatively important thing to students in such a town. This detail is a distressing one: here are students from a supposedly "enlightened" segment of the population, a place where you'd expect the grip of sex-role stereotypes to be loosening. But this wasn't the case.

If you are female, and you are uncomfortable about being better than any of the men you work with, then you have from the outset firmly entrenched yourself on the lower rungs of the vocational ladder. The facts of life in the modern world are that women work with men constantly in almost any job you can name. If women think they must defer to all men—the dullard and the genius alike, just because they are male—they will find this deference crippling their own abilities. They are fastening a set of shackles onto their intelligence, their talents and their creative power.

This sort of deference that sets in at puberty might seem on the surface to be a good thing for males. Perhaps it does cut down the competition, but at what price? The cultural ethic that girls must not be as good at things as boys has its logical corollary: Boys must be better at things than girls. During one mixed-sex ball game, a girl hit a home run, and one of the boys watching the game taunted the male players about her "blast," as if it were shameful to be bested by a girl in that way. But the facts of life are that we all have varied talents and abilities, that we're very good at some things and rotten at others. A young man who internalizes the idea that "I must always be better" is bound to take a lot of lumps in today's world, because time and time again, he won't be.

Condry and Dyer suggest, in the light of their study, that we look at the kinds of attitudes and beliefs youngsters of both sexes have about mixed-sex competition and how these relate to their behavior. Indeed, we should; we should not only look, but take some action. The beat of that different drummer needs to be amplified. Parents and teachers can be of help in that regard.

First of all, it would probably help if performance were stressed more than winning. If a girl thought of achievement as being "the best I can be" rather than being better than some boy, it would seem less threatening. But we can't pretend competition isn't a reality, especially in a society such as ours. Boys and girls need to be aware that the attitudes they are forming are products of cultural stereotypes. We should help both boys and girls understand that they are going to "beat" each other sometimes, to lose to each other sometimes, and that's natural. The pressures of competition are great enough without having to add the anxiety of "sex-appropriate" behavior.

In the past, we have let kids get their ideas about "sex-appropriate" behavior the same place they got their ideas about sex—in the streets. It's an issue that needs to be placed on the formal agenda in more homes and schools. One step in the right direction is a public television series called *Freestyle,* designed to show children that there are alternatives to the stereotyped ideas of the way boys and girls are supposed to behave. Girls will be seen in "male" jobs, boys will be seen as taking more nurturant roles in the family.

Another thing that girls need to know is that they are probably exaggerating the price they will pay in male disapproval for openly displaying their abilities. Do men really prefer the Dumb Dora who keeps saying, "You're wonderful"? Less often than girls would think, according to the evidence that does exist. In a series of studies done in the mid-sixties,[8] male subjects were asked to describe their "ideal woman." At the same time, female subjects were told to give their idea of what the men would say. The men consistently portrayed their ideal woman as more assertive than the women expected. The women assumed the men would want a clinging vine; the men rejected that notion.

In a study done in the mid-seventies[9] on whether being bright and ambitious was the kiss of death for women, researchers told subjects they were supposed to choose opposite sex partners for a team competition and for a social event. Men tended to prefer bright women for both, social mythology to the contrary.

Why do girls seem to be so hard hit by cultural stereotypes at adolescence? The answer is that it's an uncertain time—for boys as well as girls. They are moving away from their old identities as "somebody's child"—but what are they moving toward? They want clear and distinct guideposts: What is it to be a man? To be a woman? They are not happy with ambiguity. The stereotypes are rigid, easy to grasp. Teenagers need answers, and if the cultural stereotypes aren't the right ones, at least they seem to ease the confusion. Rosalind remembers going to the movies wearing jeans and short-cropped hair the year she was fourteen. At the

160

candy counter someone mistook her for a boy, and that was a dreadful event. It was terrible to be taken for a *boy!* She let her hair grow.

Adolescence is truly a time of passage. The adolescent is simultaneously discovering herself and at the same time losing the omniscient parents who have always played such a strong role in her life. She must move away from them to grow; at the same time, separation can be a painful and frightening process.

The focus of the adolescent's eye is inward, and to parents that can be exasperating. The cheerful, friendly child can suddenly turn into a stranger who broods in her room, spends hours combing her hair or ties up the telephone for interminable conversations with her best friend. Adolescence is a time of narcissistic self-infatuation; the teenager is not only discovering a unique, vulnerable self, but is looking for resources to shore up the developing ego. Sometimes the adolescent feels not only unique, but abandoned.

In *The Diary of a Young Girl*, Anne Frank wrote, "No one will believe that a girl of thirteen finds herself quite alone in the world. I can't refrain from telling you that lately I have begun to feel deserted. I am surrounded by too great a void . . . for in its innermost depths, youth is lonelier than old age. I read this saying in some book and found it to be true."

In adolescence, the mood often changes from exaltation and approval of the self to despair over imperfections and back again. Sylvia Plath wrote in her diary as a teenager: "Sometimes I try to put myself in another's place, and I am frightened to find that I am almost succeeding. How awful to be anyone but I. I know that I am too tall and have a fat nose, and yet how I pose and primp before the mirror, seeing more and more how lovely I am. I have erected in my mind an image of myself, idealistic and beautiful. Is not that image, free from blemish, the true self—the true perfection? Am I wrong when this image insinuates itself between me and the merciless mirror? Oh, even now I glance back on what I have just written, how foolish it sounds, how melodramatic. Never, never will I reach the perfection I long for with all my soul. My paintings, my poems, my stories, all poor, poor reflections . . ."

Sometimes the uniqueness, the specialness of the self seems ordained by unearthly powers. Simone de Beauvoir writes of herself as an adolescent in *Memoirs of a Dutiful Daughter*[10]:

"I became in my own eyes a character out of a novel. I invented all kinds of romantic intrigues that were full of obstacles for the heroine."

161

Once, playing croquet on the lawn with her sister and cousins, she thought to herself that while her girl relatives might be prettier and more popular, "something would happen that would exalt me beyond all personal preference; I did not know under what form or by whom I should be recognized for what I was. I imagined that already there was someone watching the croquet lawn and the four little girls in their beige pinafores; the gaze rested on me and a voice murmured: '*She* is not as other girls.'"

The adolescent is caught in a crosscurrent of emotions—the bodily changes, the need to complete the foundation of adult identity, the painful parting from the hegemony of parents. The latter is painful, but it must be made if the child is to grow into a healthy adult. The children who do not accomplish the separation remain hobbled in some way throughout life. Enmeshed in this difficult process, the adolescent is often caught between the tugs of independence and the siren song of childish dependency. When the confusions of the emerging self become too anguished, or too overwhelming, there is the temptation for the adolescent to lose herself in others, a temptation that must be resisted in the interests of the development of a healthy personality.

In our culture, as we have seen, the pressures on boys to achieve independence start early and don't relent. All along, girls are allowed much more passive, dependent behavior. That being so, we might expect that girls in adolescence have a more difficult time separating from parents, and this turns out to be the case.

Perhaps the most comprehensive study of adolescent behavior in the United States was the one carried out in the fifties by Elizabeth Douvan and Joseph Adelson of the University of Michigan.[11] They studied 3500 adolescents, both males and females, and they found striking differences between boys and girls in the throes of separating from parents.

Writing of girls, they say, "We imagined we would find evidence, however covert, of a struggle between parent and child as this process developed. But we find few signs of rebellion or conflict." Girls, it seems, accept rules with little protest. They are also compliant toward authority. "Girls look to their parents for guidance, yield to whatever demands are made by the family, and tend to identify with parental authority. Girls don't feel their parents want them to be independent or to take over the task of self-control, nor do the girls find within themselves any strong desire to do so."

162

The girls, Douvan and Adelson found, did not show much concern about achieving autonomy and self-direction. Only 13 percent said, when asked how they would like to change themselves, that they would like to be more self-reliant or self-controlled. Only one girl in ten mentioned these as desirable qualities in adults they admired.

What this adds up to, Douvan and Adelson believe, is that one major concept about the adolescent experience doesn't apply to girls: that of the teenager battling with both internal instincts and society's prohibitions and coming out of the battle with a set of internal controls that govern behavior. This model, the researchers say, is of little use in understanding the feminine experience. "Decorous, compliant, seeking love and support and guidance, they [girls] bend easily to parental regulation."

This pattern doesn't change much as girls get older, the researchers say. Younger girls don't go against parents' wishes because they feel they must obey, and older girls don't disobey for a fear of hurting their parents.

"To sum up, we may say that the line of moral development in girls moves from a rather passive, childlike acceptance of parental authority to an identification with the point of view of authority. As far as we can tell from our evidence, the transition is effected without an intervening phase in which the girl defiantly asserts her own values and controls before moving closer to those of her parents."

As a result, Douvan and Adelson say, the adolescent girl is less likely than the boy to act out of abstract principles of justice. "Which is not to say she isn't moral, but the question of moral behavior is less a matter of being good for an internalized set of principles, but of goodness for retaining the love of others. She will have her moments—pique, sullenness, aggressively provocative behavior towards her parents and so on." But this reflects, they say, a polarity between being willful, on the one hand, and seeking to restore the love tie on the other. "The boy is more willing to lean on his own controls and, in fact, may be eager to test and strengthen his own controls. The girl will continue to rely, and now even more urgently, on the support and control of her parents." Boys are much more willing to confront authority. In fact, the researchers say, when they asked one boy if he was willing to challenge teachers or parents, his reply was, "You kiddin', lady?"

If some women do identify internally with male authority, then they may stick with that identification even when it seems against their best interests—as in the case of woman suffrage and the Equal Rights Amendment. Both issues fly in the face of traditional, male-dominated authority.

The adolescent girl that Douvan and Adelson describe as typical seems docile, compliant, obedient. She is the sort of child teachers love, and about whom parents say thankfully, "She never gave us a moment's trouble!"

This may be fine for everybody who deals with the girl, but what about the girl herself? Will life for her be just one long, sunny plain of sweetness and light? The chances are that it will not. The conflicts and painful confrontations that she has avoided in adolescence may come crashing down on her when she is older—at twenty-five, or thirty-four, or forty-nine.

If the girl has not developed an inner set of controls, if she has simply bought her parents' values with no questions asked, the growth of her sense of self may be severely impaired. Douvan and Adelson tell the story of one young girl whose crisis hit as she was about to graduate from college. The young woman had been a model teenager, praised by her parents and her teachers for her energy and her devotion to her studies. She performed at a straight A level right through high school and college and had what appeared to be a normal social life. In her senior year, however, she was seized by panic, convinced that she was stupid, didn't really know anything, was a fake who would be found out by her teachers. She had delayed feelings of rebellion toward her mother.

Her fears about her competence were not groundless. As she reached the upper levels of college, she was called on to do original work, the sort that required her to think for herself, not just restate somebody else's ideas. "She found out that her devotion, her immaculate habits of work, were far less useful than they had been, and she was bright and honest enough to recognize it. She had been the dutiful student, adept at regurgitating back what was taught; but she had not really wrestled with ideas, never faced the conflicts involved with real achievement, and so her success had not been truly won. She had been a 'good girl,' and found out that wasn't really enough."

The girls who have not really separated from their parents often have particular problems in other relationships, particularly those with men. Rosalind finds in her clinical practice that many women are still locked into dependent ties with their parents. Many of their problems are bound to the fact that they are still trying to figure out what it means to be a "good daughter." That struggle interferes with the woman's personal growth and can also interfere with her relationship with her husband. Many husbands don't want to take care of a child wife. Many marriages flounder because a woman never established a separate identity as an adolescent and comes to that difficult process later in life. Since the women's movement brought the whole question of woman's identity out into the open, women have been making radical changes in their life-styles—joining consciousness-raising groups, returning to school, leaving marriages, starting new careers. In the days when the issue remained a hidden agenda, women seemed to take their delayed identity crisis and turn it inward—and wound up suffering from depression, alcoholism and drug dependence. Growing up when you are an adolescent is painful; it is much harder to do ten or twenty or thirty years later.

Parents of an adolescent girl can help with the vital separation process by encouraging her to develop and express freely her own set of ideas and values. It's a danger signal if a girl is too compliant; the girl who doesn't experience psychological adolescence at fourteen or fifteen or seventeen may be doomed to come to it at forty—when the options are much more limited.

It might help parents to understand, also, that part of the separation process involves a temporary "devaluing" of the parents—for girls, of the mother in particular. (The same thing happens with boys and their fathers. Mark Twain once said that when he was fourteen, his father was a fool, but by the time he reached twenty-one, it was amazing how much the old man had learned.) The "devaluing" process helps to make the loss of the omniscient parent less painful. Grace found the following example of this process in her analysis of Anne Frank's diary, a useful source for understanding adolescence.

"Mummy and her failings are something I find harder to bear than anything else. I can't always be drawing attention to her untidiness, her sarcasm, and her lack of sweetness. All this comes about because I have in my mind's eye an image of what a perfect mother and wife should be, and in her whom I must call mother I find no trace of the image . . ."

A need to compete with and be superior to her mother is evident in Anne's writings: "I face life with more courage than mummy; my feeling for justice is immovable, and truer than hers. I shall attain more than mummy ever had done, I shall not remain insignificant, I shall work in the world and for mankind."

This process is painful for the child, and can be equally so for the mother. It can be hard for a mother to let her daughter grow up. For one thing, the daughter's moving away can mean, quite literally, that the mother is out of a job. It is easy for the mother to get overinvested in her daughter's life, to relive her youth through her daughter. One woman remembers that when she was a teenager, the mothers of many of her friends seemed to focus their energies on their daughters' social lives. They spent hours with them shopping for the right dress, the right dyed-to-match shoes; adult conversation centered on which girl was going to which prom with which boy. When Betty Friedan was interviewing suburban housewives for her book *The Feminine Mystique*[12] she found a persistent pattern of mothers who lived through their children: "I noticed the same pattern in many of the women I interviewed, women who dominated their daughters, or bred them into passive dependence and conformity or unconsciously pushed them into sexual activities." She says that one of the most tragic women she interviewed was the mother of a thirteen-year-old girl. "A wealthy executive's wife whose life was filled with all the trappings, she lived the very image of suburban 'togetherness' except that it was only a shell. Her husband's real life was centered in his business, a life he could not, or would not, share with his wife. She had sought to recapture her sense of life by unconsciously pushing her thirteen-year-old daughter into promiscuity. She lived in her daughter's pseudo-sex life, which for the girl was so devoid of feeling that it became merely a 'thing.'"

For some women, an emerging adolescent daughter can be seen as "competition." One woman, a stunning beauty who had always been used to attention and admiring remarks because of her appearance, began to feel hostile to her beautiful daughter as the child moved into adolescence, because now the compliments were directed at the young girl. She began to feel that she was aging, losing her looks, despite the fact that she was a beautiful, mature woman, if not a young girl anymore.

Many mothers feel that if their daughters set out on what seems to be a separate path than the one they followed, they are being rejected by their daughters. We took part in one recent meeting in which mature women talked about their growing daughters. There was tremendous anxiety and bewilderment over the fact that many of the daughters had not married or were considering not marrying or not having children. The mothers seemed unable to understand such notions and were distressed by the idea that their own lives were being judged by their daughters and found wanting. They seemed unable to look at their daughters' life choices through anything but the lens of their own emotional reactions.

Symptoms of overinvestment and competition on the part of the mothers of adolescents can be a danger signal. A normal, healthy interest in a daughter's life is a good thing, but when a mother finds that the events of her daughter's life are the highlight of *her* life, or begins to feel competitive with her daughter, that's a sign she is too involved. At that point, the mother needs to move away and form a commitment to work or interests of her own, to build a separate base for her own life.

For fathers of daughters, adolescence can also be a troubling time. Some daughters will try to use their fathers to form an alliance against the mother. Simone de Beauvoir remembers, "My real rival was my mother. I dreamed of having a more intimate relationship with my father, but even on the rare occasions when we found ourselves alone together, we talked as if she was there with us. When there was an argument, if I had appealed to my father, he would have said, 'Do what your mother tells you.'"

Certainly, fathers don't want to get involved in a situation where they are allies in taking on "Mom." But many fathers, puzzled or disturbed by their daughter's emerging womanhood, simply withdraw from the field completely. Their daughters feel this withdrawal as a painful rejection.

What a father can be to his daughter is a bridge to the adult world. (A mother can do this, too, of course.) He should not assume that all the questions of her work and identity will be solved by some man who will define her life for her. As we have seen in the careers of achieving women, fathers have often been the inspiration for a daughter's life choice. Jane Howard remembers that from childhood on she "fell into the habit of retreating to whatever place smelled the most like Daddy's office. I went wherever I could find the urgent, pungent scent of newsprint, the heady excitement of fast-breaking news, free passes to conventions, free tickets to concerts . . . I never consciously planned to be like Daddy, but offices that smelled like newsprint, from grade school on, were a good place to find congenial people whose talk was not evasive."

Caryl remembers: "My lawyer-father and I used to talk a lot about the issues he confronted in his job as head of the Parole Board for the District of Columbia. He always treated my questions as serious ones, and since I planned to be a journalist we talked a lot about the practical side of relationships between government and the press. When I had

167

research to do in school, he helped me out—he once got me copies of Senate hearings on the control of narcotics traffic in the U.S., for example. We talked about his cases, how he handled less-than-competent staff members, how he dealt with the Congressmen on the Hill who reviewed his budget, the ways in which the prison system didn't work and how politics worked in the adult world. When I went to college I discovered I was much more sophisticated about these things than most of my classmates were. They often knew little of their fathers' work—it seemed distant and mysterious."

The messages fathers send to their adolescent daughters often give girls clues about the importance of the work they will do in life. Joseph P. Kennedy sent his sons to Harvard, where they could get the skills and make the connections to move up in the world. He sent his daughters to upper-crust Catholic schools where they could get a genteel education and make good marriages. The girl who is told directly or indirectly by her father that her vocational choice isn't all that important may have a hard time taking herself very seriously.

If relationships with parents are crucial to a girl's sense of competence at adolescence, her relationships to peers in the peer culture is also important, although it can drive parents slightly crazy. Well-mannered, well-brought-up young girls suddenly seem to metamorphose into members of some primitive cult, wearing bizarre outfits, talking in unintelligible patois, and listening constantly to an ear-shattering sound that resembles nothing more than an exquisite method of torture. This peer culture, however, may be a crucial support to the child who is separating from her parents. It is a refuge in the painful process of becoming a person separate and apart from her parents. Adolescent girls, Douvan and Adelson say, want friends who will be loyal and trustworthy, who won't gossip about them behind their backs or desert them in the face of an emotional crisis. Often, girls are using each other as a mirror to find themselves. "The girl is less interested in the other than she thinks. What she seeks in the other girl is some response to, and mirroring of, the self. She needs the presence of someone who is undergoing the same trials, discoveries and despairs." Later in adolescence, girls' friendships mature, they become less self-involved, and the girl becomes more aware of her friends' individual characteristics and qualities. She no longer needs a mirror.

Peer culture is important to the adolescent who is making the leap from parental control to autonomy. At times peer culture must appear all-consuming to the parent. "Peer opinion weighs heavily with the adolescent," write Douvan and Adelson, "so much so that the youngster often seems little more than a prisoner of peer norms, slavishly dependent on them for counsel on how to dress, what to say and do, and what to feel and believe." But she uses the peer culture to move away from the parents, and then she can begin to reject those parts of that culture that don't comply with her own personal norms and desires.

For young girls, the peer culture seems to glorify all the things many adults find to be the worst aspects of the female role in our culture: the exaggerated emphasis on beauty and appearance; a rampant materialism and the insistence on the "right" sort of sweater, jeans, hairstyle, automobile; a rigid insistence on dating and popularity. The whole notion of competence can seem to disappear in this gooey puddle, but teenagers can find peer groups in which their abilities are not submerged. Rosalind says that one woman she knows described how she survived the relentless emphasis on popularity by forming a smaller peer group which valued braininess and creativity. Members of this group used each other for support against the rather bland and fatuous peer culture around them. One high-school student who is a good athlete hangs around with a group of "jocks" who value each other's physical prowess. It may be important for girls at adolescence to be able to find a group that doesn't go along with the typical teenage norms so antithetical to the development of competence in girls. Parents visiting schools their teenage girls will attend should keep an eye on the social structure in the schools, to see if the possibility for this kind of bonding exists.

In their study of adolescents, researchers Douvan and Adelson found some intriguing sex differences in the development of friendships. Girls, they say, are socialized to place great emphasis on personal relations and cultivate such traits as sensitivity, warmth, tact and empathy. The boy, trained toward activity and achievement, seems to use friends as allies in efforts to break away from authority. The intimate friendship—which involves mutual trust, and sharing of private thoughts, and vulnerabilities—is not very common among boys. The researchers say they believe "There is among American males, an absolute inhibition of friendship which continues not only into late adolescence but into adulthood as well." There is little value placed on sensitivity or empathy in boys' friendships, they find. The boy wants, rather, a congenial pal.

The friendships and the capacity for intimacy that girls develop while growing up may serve them in later years as a bulwark against loneliness, failure and feelings of alienation. And these resources may be one of the great contributions of female socialization. Women in later life often find that this capacity for intimacy, which may have begun in the games of childhood, is a sustaining, life-giving force. One woman remarks, with some envy, about her mother's circle of friends. They met each other as young girls, maintained close friendships through the years when they married and raised families, were there to share joys and to help in time of grief. The women are in their sixties now, many of them widowed, but the friendships still sustain and nourish them. Many observers of American culture have noted how the intimate friendships permitted to women contrast with the rather sterile, business-related friendships of men that often go no deeper than shop talk or griping about the hometown baseball team.

The interpersonal skills girls develop from their early friendships have an obvious value in maintaining the quality of life in the home, but they may also be the source of sorely needed talents in the wider world as well. Most work situations today have little of the element of Lone-Man-Against-the-Elements in them. They tend to be group efforts requiring close cooperation and a ready understanding of the other person's point of view. The competitive mode probably doesn't work very well in such situations; at times it is destructive of productivity. In one large corporation several top executives were so insensitive to employees' feelings, so unable to read their signals, that the result was a wholesale revolt and an extended period of chaos. One executive uses the combative mode called "two scorpions in a bottle" in which he deliberately pits two employees against one another. The result is short-term high performance, but in the long run the results are devastating. The turnover is high, creative people burn out fast, morale is at a low ebb.

Just as women need to learn the sort of autonomy that society forces on men, so it would seem that men need to acquire the capacity for intimacy that girls come to when they are young. Many men do achieve empathy, and in other cultures men have close friendships in which they are allowed to be vulnerable. The capacity for empathy, and for nurture, is not in opposition to autonomy. They are not like the two ends of a seesaw—when one goes up, the other goes down. They should be seen as separate lines, unconnected; one can have a fair share of both. If men are not to be condemned to a life of sterile, casual personal relationships, perhaps at adolescence they should have some kind of "sensitivity

170

training"—in which they are encouraged to examine and evaluate for themselves the cultural stereotypes to which they will be expected to conform. They will then be equipped to start building their own model for their lives.

Looking today at the teenagers Douvan and Adelson studied in the fifties, it is easy to see that as adults, they have become, for the most part, what society expected them to be. As men, they are uncomfortable with intimacy; as women, they have problems with growing out of dependency. The adolescent casts a shadow of the adult that is to be. But what of today's adolescents? Are they just like the ones Douvan and Adelson studied some twenty years ago? In many ways they probably are, but there are some important differences. One of these involves the notion of work. The girls of the fifties talked of a future filled with suburban homes and station wagons. The girls of the seventies seem to see a different future. The University of Michigan's Institute for Social Research has been conducting an ongoing nationwide study of high-school seniors as part of its "Monitoring the Future" project.[13] A. Regula Herzog, a social scientist at Michigan, shared data with us collected from the classes of 1976 and 1977.

The most striking fact to emerge out of the study is that in the America of today, the work ethic is alive and well among teenaged girls.

Work—paid employment outside of the home—plays a strikingly large part in the vision today's teenager has of the future. In the Michigan study, students were asked: What do you think you will be doing thirty years from now?

Only 11 percent of the girls said they thought they would be full-time homemakers, 21 percent thought they would be in clerical or office jobs, 34 percent saw themselves in professional jobs that didn't require a Ph.D., and 10 percent saw themselves as professionals with a Ph.D. degree.

Work, most of the girls thought, was not going to be peripheral to their lives—not a hobby, not something to do for pin money; 72 percent of the girls said they expected work to be "central" to their lives (as did 76 percent of the boys). Fifty-six percent of the girls said it was important that their job be of high prestige, and 86 percent said that they wanted to earn a great deal of money.

But it wasn't just money that seemed to motivate these girls' ambitions. When they were asked if they would want to work even if they could live as comfortably as they liked without working for the rest of

171

their lives, 84 percent of the girls said they would want to work even under those circumstances (80 percent of the boys gave the same answer).

Most of the girls were optimistic about their future vocations. Sixty-two percent thought they were likely or certain to get the job they wanted, and 70 percent of them thought that job would be quite satisfying.

At the same time, the teenage girls weren't oblivious to reality. While most of them didn't think they would face discrimination in getting a college education, half thought they would face considerable discrimination in the work force. Thirty-three percent of the girls even thought that their sex would prevent them from getting the job they wanted.

Despite the importance of work in their plans, the girls did not reject the goals of marriage and family for themselves. Only 6 percent of the girls did not expect to marry, and a full 61 percent thought they would be mothers two years after their marriages. The survey showed that these adolescent girls, while considering work as very important to them, at the same time were voicing very traditional ideas about women's roles as wives and mothers as well. We'll explore these contradictions at some length in a later chapter, because these conflicting ideas could lead to severe conflict in later life.

9

ADOLESCENCE

Prince Charming Revisited

Mira knew that to choose a husband is to choose a life. She had not needed Jane Austen to teach her that. It is in a sense, a woman's first, last and only choice.

—Marilyn French in *The Women's Room*

I, for one, was not prepared for all the inexplicable things that were happening to the sturdy, uncomplicated little body I had come to know and love. Things bulged, sprouted, without my permission. It was very unsettling.

I was rather fond of the nice little pink-white V of skin I owned. To grow hair anyplace but where it properly belonged (i.e., on the head) was not quite decent. Pubic hair was something to keep hidden, like a wart or varicose veins or some other disfigurement. All the pictures I had ever seen of full grown ladies featured bare, pink patches of skin Down There. My bachelor uncle had a picture in his room in my grandmother's house of a naked Indian Lady standing on a rock in the middle of Niagara Falls, wearing a headdress and a grim expression. But maybe Indian ladies didn't grow hair there. Nature, alas, did not pass me by. My friend, Beano, who was two years younger and thus slower to fall victim to the ravages of puberty, did not hesitate to rub it in. I remember sitting on the beach one day and arguing with her about whether or not I had any. I kept my legs tightly pressed together during the argument.

BEANO: You do too have some. I saw it under your bathing suit. It sticks out.

ME: It does not, I don't have any.

BEANO: You do too.

ME: I do not.

BEANO: Yes you do.

ME: No I don't.

BEANO: I'll ask your mother.

ME: You do and you can't be in the Science Club (our neighborhood club of which I was president and membership Czar).

—Caryl remembers puberty—from *Aphrodite at Mid-century; Growing Up Female and Catholic in Postwar America*

Adolescence is the time when both boys and girls go through puzzling and disturbing physical changes. Puberty is not really easier on boys than it is on girls, but there is one major difference. Although boys may find the changes in their bodies as disorienting as girls do, they rarely see any incapacity or crippling effect in them. Quite the opposite. They are badges of manhood.

Girls, however, are confronted with menarche, the physical evidence of their womanhood. As they begin the menstrual cycle, they find themselves heir not simply to a physical function, but to a centuries-old tradition of taboo and superstition.

To primitive people, the menstrual cycle seemed magical—a woman bleeds with no injury. Primitive tribes ascribe magical powers or evil omens to women who menstruate. Paula Weideger, in her book *Menstruation and Menopause,*[1] says that in India there is a widespread belief that a woman who dies while menstruating will come back as a ghost and will lure others to their doom. Among the Dogon of West Africa a menstruating woman is believed to bring misfortune to everything she touches. She is segregated in a special hut, and if she is seen passing through the village a ceremony of purification must be held. The isolation of women is found in many cultures, along with the notion of special, evil happenings that might befall one who has contact with a woman at this time.

"The punishments meted out to men who break the rules attached to the menstrual taboo tend to support the idea that male castration anxiety plays a role in the genesis of the taboo. A common thread running through the taboos in many cultures is the belief that man will lose his potency if he comes into contact with the menstruating woman.

Reversing this logic, there is the belief that man will remain virile as long as he stays away from menstruating women."

We modern Americans may believe we are a long way from African tribes or Indian peasants, but the menstrual taboo operates in our society as it does elsewhere. It is still very much a subject that one does not discuss in polite society.

This silence exists, says Weideger, for two reasons: "women have been ashamed of menstruation and menopause, and menstruating women are taboo. When we are taught that something has to be hidden, we naturally believe that it contains an element that is not acceptable to other people. If menstruation were considered 'clean' and menopause 'decent' everyone would freely admit to their existence . . . we have been taught to hide all evidence of their existence and we have come to believe that there is something in those experiences that is 'wrong.'"

When women talk about their first experiences with menstruation, the elements that are intermingled are shame and dismay, mixed with pride.

Simone de Beauvoir writes in *Memoirs of a Dutiful Daughter*:

> I awoke horror-stricken one morning; I had spoiled my nightdress. I washed it and got dressed. Again I soiled my underclothes. I wondered what shameful malady I was suffering from. Worried, and feeling somehow guilty, I had to take my mother into my confidence. She explained to me that I had now become a big girl and bundled me up in a very inconvenient manner. I felt a strong sense of relief when I learned it had happened through no fault of my own; and as always when something important had happened to me, I even felt my heart swell with a sort of pride. I didn't mind too much when I heard my father whispering about it to his friends . . . but that evening, when we joined my father in the Rue de Rennes, he jokingly made reference to my condition. I was consumed with shame. I had imagined that the monstrous regiment of women kept its blemish a secret from the male fraternity. I thought of myself in relation to my father as a purely spiritual being. I was horrified at the thought that he suddenly considered me to be a mere organism. I felt as if I could never hold my head up again.

Caryl remembers that in the parochial school she attended in the fifties, "the girls who were more sophisticated—and the ones with older sisters—liked to tell horror stories about 'The Curse.' The stories were told with a fiendish relish, the way an older child might terrorize small siblings with Frankenstein. There were stories of girls carried moaning to hospitals with cramps; stories of girls bleeding to death before their stricken parents; stories of girls wearing white formals to proms and standing up to discover a large red stain on the back of a dress, A Fate Worse Than Death. . . . one girl told a story of walking with her boyfriend through a vacant lot on the way to the movies and coming across a soiled, discarded Kotex. We all sucked in our breath when the story was told, as if the cast-off Kotex had betrayed some shameful secret."

The women who responded to a questionnaire Paula Weideger sent out felt many of the same emotions:

"It would have helped if my mother hadn't treated the subject so squeamishly by telling me only the scientific causes and facts that were far removed from my reality. 'The shedding of the lining of the uterus' is a far cry from the reality that I was bleeding."

"I expected to turn into a beautiful fairy princess—felt ugly when I did not."

"I was very sensitive about my early development as compared to my friends. I was ashamed of my body—felt like a cow."

What does all this have to do with the subject we're interested in: female competence? A great deal, if at puberty a girl is not simply reaching physical maturity but also digesting a whole set of prepackaged ideas about woman's physical infirmity.

Despite evidence to the contrary, many people still believe that women inherit both mental and physical infirmities with menstruation. "The Curse"—as it has been popularly known—is hardly a cheerful nickname, or one that would reassure a young girl about to menstruate.

Our society is still suffering from outmoded ideas about the "ravages" of the menstrual cycle. It has been seriously argued, for example, that women should not be airline pilots because they are "unstable" at certain times of the month. A few years ago a medical doctor made headlines by saying that women should not serve in political office because of "raging hormonal imbalances." When his remark drew an angry retort from Congresswoman Patsy Mink of Hawaii, he cited the fact that she got angry as evidence of hormonal imbalances. Of course one can argue just as rationally that a man shouldn't fly airplanes, serve in Congress and certainly not be allowed anywhere near the trigger of a nuclear device with all that testosterone sloshing around inside. Who knows when he will be seized by an uncontrollable aggressive instinct? The game of "musical hormones" can easily be turned against either sex.

For most women, menstruation does not interfere with an active work life, or with leisure. Women who are menstruating play pro tennis matches, try legal cases, examine patients, drive taxis, teach courses and engage in all kinds of competitive sports every day. Some women at times experience menstrual cramping or predictable swings in mood about the time of the menstrual flow, but except for those with the most severe problems, these tend to be minor inconveniences.

The development of internal methods of collecting menstrual flow—the various brands of tampons—was a great step forward in erasing the inconvenience of "the period." It enabled women to swim or take part in any active physical sports without the bother of pads, pins and belts. But there are old wives' tales surrounding tampons, as well. Young girls are told they musn't wear tampons because it will damage their virginity or hurt them in some way. This is nonsense. A girl of any age can use tampons. If she has trouble with insertion, she can usually gently stretch the hymen so that the tampon will slip into place. The stories of injury or damage are simply a legacy of the idea that menstruation equals infirmity.

If some of the stories told by adult women about getting "The Curse" seem bizarre, artifacts of an earlier generation, today's girls may not be faring much better. Despite society's supposed openness about sexuality, one 1978 study shows the negative attitudes and expectations still associated with menstruation in the minds of young girls.

Anne E. Clarke and Diane Ruble of Princeton studied pre- and postmenarcheal girls as well as adolescent boys.[2] They found that "a girl enters menarche with a clear set of expectations, many of which are quite negative; and most of her peers, both male and female, hold similar expectations. Her experience of menstruation is, therefore, primed to be a self-fulfilling prophecy."

Most of the boys and girls believed that menstruation is accompanied by "physical discomfort, increased emotionality and mood changes, disruption of activities . . . and performance in school." Apparently the whole subject is still "taboo": Over 50 percent of the girls said they were worried that someone would know they were having their periods. Both boys and girls saw the whole phenomenon as one that had largely negative consequences for girls.

177

Clarke and Ruble say that a survey of educational materials on the subject of menstruation concluded that "the main message conveyed to adolescent girls is that menstruation is a hygienic crisis." They believe that this "crisis mentality" ought to change, and that emphasis on menstrual distress should be toned down. If girls are not to see menarche as a time of infirmity, weakness and shame, the ways girls are told about it need some overhauling.

Of course girls should be told the full facts about menstruation in a positive, encouraging way. They should specifically be told that it doesn't mean they are going to be weak, or "crazy" at certain times, or that they should take to their beds. Having a period doesn't mean you have to take "time out" from life. At the same time, simply being clinical and scientific ignores the emotional impact of the experience, denies the girl the opportunity to feel "special" because something important has happened.

One woman who answered Paula Weideger's questionnaire told about how she and her family handled her daughter's coming of age. "We have two daughters, twelve and seven. The twelve-year-old just had her first menstruation. Her father and sister and I were able to share her first menstruation. We drank wine and toasted her. Her father gave her a bunch of wild flowers. She seemed pleased and open. She seems to identify positively with her sex. Even though I was really unhappy and found my sex distasteful (for sixteen or seventeen years), my daughter appears relaxed and matter of fact with her sex and physical changes. It is a continual source of surprise and deep pleasure to me."

There is another load of emotional baggage that young women sometimes have to take on at puberty that is as damaging to the sense of self as the idea of being "unclean" or infirm. That is an exaggerated sense of the dangers of the world. With puberty, the girl child who has been allowed a fair amount of independence and free rein suddenly gets messages that her sexuality now makes her a potential victim. Certainly, parents and teachers should talk to girls about avoiding situations and places that could be fraught with danger. But this can be done without suggesting that women are natural victims, that the world of men is nothing but a jungle to be feared and it is best for a girl not to venture there.

The awakening of sexuality, with its symbolic and cultural history, seems to affect boys and girls differently. For a boy sexuality has something to do with what he does, not with what he is. Lord Byron expressed this idea in exaggerated form when he said, "Man's love is of man's life a thing apart, / 'Tis woman's whole existence." Here, Byron is giving a perfect statement of a cultural stereotype. The traditional idea has been that boys become men by *doing*; girls become women by finding a man.

Erik Erikson[3] sees the crucial task of adolescence as establishing an identity, as discovering "Who I am, where I belong." Edgar Z. Friedenberg, in his study of adolescents in America, *The Vanishing Adolescent*, says, "In a world as empirical as ours, a youngster who does not know what he is good at will not know what he is good for; he must know what he can do in order to know who he is."

That argument would be just as telling if the pronoun were "she" instead of "he." Unfortunately, society hasn't recognized that fact. Most girls at adolescence often perceive a shifting of values in the world around them. The girls who have gotten straight A's, the star athletes, now notice that these accomplishments seem to be less important than they once were. The major arena of concern shifts to their relationships with boys. Are they popular? Do they get asked to dances or out on dates? They now begin to see themselves valued in relation to how males perceive them. This shifting of the ground underneath them becomes a major problem in the development of their own sense of identity, making it a process over which they have little control. What can a girl do to make the captain of the football team choose her, other than do the best she can with her basic equipment—hair, body, eyes, clothes? There is no real guarantee her action will have results. She must wait to be chosen, and this waiting process can put the growth of her identity into a state of suspended animation. The Sleeping Beauty legend is thought to be a parable of sexual awakening; it might also be a fable about the suspension of the girl's ego growth.

This suspended development is not a myth. Douvan and Adelson, looking at the American teenage girl, found her spinning somewhere between the solid present and a future over which she had little control. "We have assumed," they say, "that adolescent adaptation directly depends on the ability to integrate the future to their present life and current self-concept." Boys seem to have a handle on the future; they are preoccupied with what they will do in the adult world of work. But the adolescent girl believes in a future that is "a romantic concept dominated by unconscious, uncontrollable forces. The distinctly American contribution to this myth is the competitive and conditional quality of love."

179

In other words, while the boys tend to compete for grades and glory, the girls too often compete mainly for the boys. And as Douvan and Adelson point out, "When a woman has only her wit and beauty to count on, when religion or social pressures or tradition do not support or bulwark marriages, then she must concentrate a great deal of energy on maintaining and enhancing her personal gifts."

And enhance them she does—with a vengeance. Adolescent boys have anxieties and uncertainties about their looks as well, but the boy knows they're not decisive. Good looks enhance a man's status and chances for success, but the homely football hero won't be a social outcast. There is something of a desperate quality to the female adolescent's quest for physical perfection. Caryl remembers it well: "Do you have gritty elbows? *Glamour* asked. (I looked. Oh God, yes, I had gritty elbows. They looked like cobblestone streets that hadn't been washed in years.) Use a pumice stone each night to keep them smooth.

"Do you have ugly feet? (I looked at them. Blaugh. Ugly feet. Not even a mother could love such feet.) Use skin oil daily and keep your toes well groomed and polished.

"Do you want shining hair? (YES YES YES.) Brush at least one hundred strokes a night.

"Are your eyes small and beady? Beauty advisor asked. (I peered in the mirror. Definitely small and beady. Like a myopic snake.) Apply three shades of eye shadow. Blue Coral, Misty Ash and Tahiti Green, white near the corner of the eye, liner three quarters of the way under the eye and use waterproof Roman Brown mascara.

"Is your skin caressable? (I slid an index finger down my arm. It felt more like burlap than velvet. Uncaressable.) Bathe in Sardo oil.

"Does your hair need sheen? Are your knees bumpy? Teeth stained? Hips big? Calves skinny? Do you have dandruff? Bad breath? Body odor? Psoriasis? Split ends?

"I read, sitting there on the glider, and I believed. I was perfectible. After all, had I not seen perfection emerge like a statue by Praxiteles out of human clay in *Glamour* Makeovers and *Ladies Home Journal* Beauty Biographies? It could be done.

"So I pumiced and I brushed and I sprayed and I bleached and I trimmed and I squirted and I slathered and I rubbed. I did all the things the magazines told me to do. And I discovered a terrifying fact. If I did all the things the magazines told me to do I would spend my entire life in the bathroom. I would be a shining, perfect creature, but the only people who would ever see me—briefly—were members of my own family and the occasional guest who wandered into the john."

In the fifties, you may remember, Douvan and Adelson found young girls not only consumed with the enhancement of appearance, but also looking forward to a future that seems to have come straight out of television situation comedies. When the girls were interviewed, most said they wanted a handsome husband with a good income, three or more children and a home in the suburbs. The researchers concluded that the typical young girl was "more concerned with living a series of roles, by adapting to a life pattern, than by becoming herself or acting and choosing out of an awareness of her unique qualities and desires." In other words, she was buying a prepackaged identity, just as she might buy the latest mix-and-match sportswear.

This willingness to accept a prepackaged identity seems to put dampers on a girl's fantasies of the future. Boys' fantasies, the researchers found, were directly tied to reality. A boy who dreamed of being a doctor, for example, might be looking at lists of schools that had premed courses. Girls' fantasies tended to be projections of childish wishes—being a ballerina, an actress, a model. More often than not these will remain hazy dreams. Few girls who dream of the glamorous life of a ballerina are suited to such a career, nor are they willing to spend the grueling hours of practice such a calling demands.

There were reasons for the differences in the boys' and girls' fantasies, the researchers said. The boy will make the dreams come true. "Mobility aspiration for the boy is no idle dream. It is rather the concrete expression of his faith in himself. The girl's mobility aspirations are less formed and fettered by reality. She need not test her desire against her talent and skill since these will not be the crucial determinants of her future status. Her access to status will come through marriage . . . the next steps for her have less to do with personal achievement than with being chosen as a mate by a suitable young man. Her identity is bound up not so much in what she is as in what her husband will be. Someone has spoken of marriage as a mutual mobility bet. We may add that for the girl it is also an identity bet." Girls have understood this to be so:

Mira, the heroine of Marilyn French's novel, *The Women's Room*, knew "that to choose a husband is to choose a life. She had not needed Jane Austen to teach her that. It is in a sense, a woman's first, last and only choice."

Alix Shulman writes in *Memoirs of an Ex-Prom Queen*: "In our own interminable adolescent discussions of whom to marry, no girl among us ever suggested that it would be better to marry poor, unless the alternative was not to marry at all. My mother was right. There was only one way for a girl to control her future. Choose her man."

At this point, hearing these voices with their familiar plaints, we might be tempted to say, "Look, that was twenty or thirty years ago. Things have changed. It isn't that way anymore." Although data from the "Monitoring the Future" project (described in chapter 8) show that girls are thinking more about careers, we suspect that the old pressures to define oneself through a man are still intense.

Support for our suspicion comes from the teenage girls who wrote letters to *Ms.* magazine in 1974 about what things were like in their homes and schools:

> One thing I think you should write more about is the problems of "homely" women, particularly teenaged women. I think people should realize that the prettier you are, the better you're treated. I am 15 and I have seen a guy tell a girl that she was "ugly" and then call her a lesbian because she didn't have a boyfriend. (Because of course she wasn't pretty.) So if you happen to be born ugly you live in a vicious, inescapable circle.

> The idea that I was the stereotyped blonde was something that people just couldn't divorce from me. Whenever I got the highest grade on a math test, the kids would accuse: Yeah, no wonder you've been wearing all those short skirts to school. If I had a problem in a technically oriented class, the teacher would say—well, blonde, what do you expect? . . . I'm hoping things will be better in college. However, recently a friend and I went to visit the college where I'd been accepted for next fall. After we'd arrived, my friend explained to a student there that I had been accepted—"early decision." The guy looked at me, winked and replied: "Oh I get it: the interviewer was a man." I'll never stop fighting, but I'm beginning to lose hope.

> I am 14 years old. Not too many other girls my age, if any, admit to being for women's liberation. I am the target for jokes, teasing and malicious comments from my family. They're always reminding me not to be too loudmouthed or pushy and remember that a boy likes a girl when she lets *him* be the intelligent one . . . I have an older brother, and while I do all the household chores he watches TV and pals around with my Dad. My dad has openly admitted his preference for him. "He's my son," he says.

I do not have a boyfriend. Neither does my friend Jane. It never used to bother us before, because we did have each other. However, as time progresses and we get older, our other "friends" start to get into society, where most teenagers fall into their traditional roles and stereotypes. It is starting to hurt us very much, because we have been scorned, mocked, laughed at and labeled outcast.

For many young American women, what we call the "Prince Charming" syndrome is alive and well. Many adolescent girls are still looking for an identity through a man, and if they are, what are the consequences of this pattern?

There is, first of all, that suspension of identity we spoke of. Douvan and Adelson say, "It is for this reason that the girl, unless she is one of the rare ones who remain committed to a work ideal, seems unrealistic and unromantic, often foolishly so, when asked to imagine a future for herself. She tends to retreat into stereotyped notions of the future . . . she seems more comfortable in the present. Her vision of the future is necessarily dim, and to this extent identity formation (in so far as it depends on anchorage to the future) is likely to remain incomplete."

With her vision of the future dimmed, the girl rarely makes any long-range plans for her life. It might have been fine for Snow White to sing about her Prince coming along, but most girls don't live in fairy tales. The girl who bets her identity on Prince Charming has made a bad wager. It's a course of action that, as the behavioral scientists would say, is "not adaptive" to today's world. In other words, it doesn't work. As we have seen, the notion that a woman will be taken care of for the rest of her life is not a very realistic one. So the woman who doesn't plan ahead, who has no concept of herself in the world of work, will be at a great disadvantage. She will inhabit the lower rungs of the marketplace, and she will be much later than her peers in developing work skills. She may never catch up.

Emotionally, the woman who binds her identity too closely with that of a man is often plagued with feelings of being out of control of her life. Candy, one of the young women in a book about a high school class ten years later, *What Really Happened to the Class of '65*,[4] remembers, "My state of consciousness when I was in high school was so incredibly low that I didn't have any aspirations. I was pretty happy with my life. I never thought about the future. I didn't fantasize about it at all. I can remember distinctly in the seventh grade looking at myself in the mirror

183

for a long time one day and wondering what I was going to look like. That was the extent of my thinking about the future. It was always assumed that I would get married as my mother had."

The woman who relinquishes control of her identity at an early age will have difficulty taking her life into her own hands. Rosalind sees women patients who seem never to grasp the idea that their life is in any way their own responsibility. They keep pinning their problems on the powerful figures in their lives. If their husband would only do so-and-so, things would be all right. If a lover could only be persuaded to stay, leave, be nice, stop drinking, whatever, life would run smoothly. These women cannot see that solutions to problems lie in their own actions or decisions.

The idea that a man is the answer to all of life's problems keeps some women in a state that might be called "drifting," going through life waiting for something to happen. Since the agent for change is put outside of oneself, waiting is seen as the only answer. From the class of '65, "The Beauty," working now as a cocktail waitress: "I'd really feel badly if I wasn't married some day, but I've never been that close to marriage. I've gotten some proposals but I knew they wouldn't work. Maybe I don't have the greatest life right now, but at least I have only myself to worry about. Later on I'd like to travel. I'd like to have an easy life. If I get married, I'd like it to be perfect, and that Prince Charming just hasn't come along yet. I'm sure things will change. And I cross my fingers."

Other women make attempts to take control of their lives, but they are very quick to abandon the struggle—lock, stock and barrel—whenever a man comes along. One woman, when her first marriage began to flounder, decided to continue her education. She had not been a particularly good student, but she felt that it was important to her sense of self to get her degree. With some negotiating, she finally convinced the admissions office of a good school to accept her. This period was a very good one for her. She did honors work in her field; she set out on a risky venture—for her—trying to write articles for a student publication. They were accepted, and for her it was the high point in a long process of developing self-esteem. She went on to get a master's degree. Then, along came Mr. Wonderful. She thought he was perfect. All her progress went out the window. She turned the keys of her self-esteem over to him. A good day was when he told her he loved her. On days when he was out of sorts, she was unsure, anxious, not certain of her

184

own worth. This kind of abdication of control is another version of the "identity drifting" pattern.

The negative consequences of this process can accrue to the man as well as to the woman involved in it. The man is literally forced to have a life that is fulfilling enough for two people—usually an impossible task. Often the wife becomes so heavily invested in the man's life and success that he has the sense that he is "carrying" her—which he is. One woman became emotionally ill after her executive husband suffered a series of reverses in the business world. A friend of the couple said sadly, "Mary is so involved with Bill's life that whenever he has a setback he feels he's caused her terrible suffering. It makes it twice as hard for him."

The Prince Charming syndrome does not afflict only those young women without ambitions and aspirations of their own. It can work its crippling effect on the best and the brightest of a generation's young women as well. A case in point is Sylvia Plath, a brilliant lyric poet, who took her own life one morning in her London flat by sticking her head in the oven and turning on the gas.

Sylvia Plath[5] was clearly not a "typical" young woman. But a number of the themes we've been dealing with here show up in her life, magnified by both her talent and her emotional problems.

Plath, a complex and driven woman, grew up in the fifties, a time when to find the right man was everything. Sylvia was conscious of the prejudice boys built up among themselves about "brainy" girls. Her mother writes, "By the time she was a senior in high school, she had learned to hide behind a facade of lighthearted wit when in a mixed group, and, after a triple date, was exultant as she reported to me, 'Rod asked me about grades I got. I said airily, "All A's, of course," "Yeah," he replied, grinning, as he led me to the dance floor, "you look like a greasy grind. Oh, mummy, they didn't believe me! They didn't believe me!'"

At seventeen, Sylvia wrote in her journal: "I want to be free—free to know people and their backgrounds—free to move to different parts of the world so that I may learn that there are other standards besides my own. I want, I think, to be omniscient . . . I think I would like to call myself, 'The Girl Who Wanted to be God.' Yet if I were not in this body, where would I be? . . . perhaps I am destined to be classified and qualified. But, Oh, I cry out against it. I am I. I am powerful—but to what extent? I am I."

But the girl who wanted to be God felt pangs of anxiety because the fact that she wrote poetry seemed to be a hindrance to her strategy of being popular. She wrote her mother from Smith College—at a point when she was between boyfriends, "I need rather desperately to feel physically desirable at all times and mentally desirable in cases where I admire a boy for his ideas." Once, after dating a young man who was a ski jump champion, she wrote, "I suddenly envied him so much for the life he leads. Boys live so much harder than girls and they know so much more about life. Learning the limitations of a woman's place is no fun at all."

Like most young women, Sylvia dated many boys, but for her, the temptations to find a powerful man in which she could lose herself may have been more compelling than for other girls. She had lost her father when she was a child, a loss that was to reverberate through her being, her poetry, her consciousness. She wrote to her mother about one young man, "I know, deep down, that I could never be married to him—physically I want a colossus. Mentally, I want a man who isn't jealous of my creativity in other fields than children." Her moods could swing to exuberance to despair and back again. Despite a trail of successes that would have inflated the egos of most college girls, Sylvia was a driven perfectionist who found it hard to believe in her own worthiness. When she returned from a guest editorship at *Mademoiselle* magazine, an honor most girls would have treasured, Sylvia worried her mother by her fatigue and her low spirits. "She finally began to talk to me, pouring out an endless stream of self-deprecation, self-accusation. She had no goal, she said. She couldn't read with comprehension anymore, much less write creatively, what was she going to do with her life? She had injured her friends, let down her sponsors—she went on and on." Her mother broke the news to her that she had not been admitted to a creative writing class she had her heart set on. In the weeks that followed, her depression deepened and culminated in a suicide attempt in which she took sleeping pills and crawled into a small space in the cellar. She was hospitalized, given shock treatments and spent time in a mental hospital. When she recovered, she returned to Smith, and at the time reminded her mother of "deep sea plants, the roots firmly grasping a rock, but the plant itself swaying in one direction, then another."

After graduation from college, Sylvia won a Fulbright scholarship to study in England. She found the people and the new experiences stimulating, but a thread of worry winds itself through her letters. She has not yet found the Prince Charming she sought, and time seemed to be running short.

"Don't worry that I am a career woman," she wrote her mother. "I sometimes think that I might get married in two years just to have children if I don't meet someone . . . Oh, I do hope someday to meet a stimulating, intelligent man with whom I can create a good life, because I am definitely not meant for the single life . . ."

Sylvia soon met and married Ted Hughes, the English poet, and stepped, willingly, it seems, into his shadow. "I can't for a minute think of him as someone other than the male counterpart of myself, always just that many steps ahead of me intellectually and creatively that I feel very feminine and admiring. I can appreciate the legend of Eve coming from Adam's rib as I never did before. The damn story's true . . . everything I do for and with Ted has a celestial radiance, be it only ironing or cooking." The Hugheses had two children, but the marriage faltered, a devastating experience for Sylvia, who, not long after her divorce, committed suicide. She was so invested in the relationship, she painted for herself such a perfect, matchless lover, grafted her own identity so firmly to his, that to lose him was a shattering experience. She struggled on without him, writing the poems that would one day make her famous, a fame she would never know. If Ted had not loomed so large in her eyes, if she could really have believed in the scope of her own gifts, Sylvia Plath might have made it through her dark night of the soul. Critic Elizabeth Hardwick writes, "If anything could have saved Sylvia Plath it would have been that she, in life, might have had the good fortune to know her own fulfillment, her hard, glittering achievement."[6]

Nuts and Bolts

Perhaps the most disturbing problem of adolescence for those concerned with the development of competence is the "dropping-back" virus that seems to hit girls at this stage. Adolescence thus becomes perhaps one of the most crucial times for parental expectations and standards to be maintained.

For if girls "drop back" at this time, parents, too, may also unconsciously move away from setting standards for daughters and letting them know they are expected to live up to their individual talents and abilities. Parents may not be thinking seriously about the occupational futures of their daughters and they may feel that being popular is more important than doing well in math.

We ought to make a distinction here between the "bad" sort of parental pressure and our notion of expectations. One hears a great deal today about kids who crack under what they feel as overwhelming pressure; college students who jump out of dormitory windows when they fail to get A's in courses. Caryl remembers one young woman student who sat in her office sobbing, "If I don't get an A in this course my father will kill me."

Much of this kind of pressure can be simply a parental ego-trip: fathers who want their sons to achieve the success that eluded them or mothers who have to have achieving children to validate their life's work. Douglas MacArthur's mother wrote this poem and sent it to her son when he was at West Point:

Like mother, like son, the saying is so true
The world will judge largely of mother by you
Be sure it will say, when its verdict you've won
She reaps as she sowed: "This man is her son!"[7]

The parent who pressures children by trying to stuff them into a mold of his or her own making is one thing: quite different is the parent who has expectations and tries to help the child define goals and use his or her own skills and talents to the fullest capacity. This process isn't always free of conflict, since the adolescent is feeling the pulls of other forces, including peer pressure. But parental expectations are a powerful force and may still hold sway beneath the surface when it seems that the adolescent has gone completely the other way.

One of the things that Douvan and Adelson noted in their study of adolescent girls was their "vagueness," their lack of connection with the realities of the adult world. The pressures of impending adulthood make boys at least somewhat realistic; they *have* to start looking at the future. Girls need more talk about what the future will *really* hold for them. As we've seen, they're often gripped by romanticized notions about "glamour" jobs that have little connection to reality. Rarely does anyone talk to girls about the cold, hard facts of money—about how much they will earn in the various jobs they might choose.

Girls have to be helped to develop internal, realistic goals rather than to follow parental prescriptions blindly: "If she doesn't get into an Ivy

188

League college it will be a disgrace to the family." Rosalind remembers that when she decided that she wanted to be a psychologist it was made clear to her that she had to get very good grades to get accepted into graduate school. She then developed the internal motivation that carried her through in a way that no external force could have done.

As difficult as it may be sometimes, girls at adolescence have to be forced to think about what their lives will be like at twenty-five, at thirty-five and at forty-five—even though they may think that forty-five is the outer edge of senility. This is a good time for parents to ask girls to verbalize their ambitions, their visions of the future, to help guide them toward an accurate look ahead. Parents ought to try to clear up the fog that clouds many girls' visions of their futures; the tendency not to look ahead, to let oneself be passively acted upon rather than controlling one's fate is evident in many adolescent girls. Girls need, at this age, to be introduced to the reality of economics and not be allowed to think that the things their parents own have dropped mysteriously out of the sky. How many parents think of sitting down with a teenage girl and saying, "This is what it costs to live the way we do?"

Girls need to be given information about the realities of the workplace, about what sort of environments certain jobs offer, what kind of hours you have to work, what kind of authority you have, what sorts of pay and prestige are offered. Young women often don't make these kinds of connections. For example, one of Rosalind's clients was hesitant to go back to school to finish her degree because she said she didn't like the idea of teachers telling her what to do. But at the same time she had a very menial girl-Friday kind of job where people constantly told her what to do. When she recognized that fact, she decided to go back to school.

Adolescence has advance billing as a very difficult time, and parents whose daughters seem to skim right through it with no problems may want to breathe a sigh of relief. As we've seen, though, that may be a sign that the girl hasn't worked through the separation process, hasn't begun the agonizing process of becoming an individual in her own right. Some people, of course, do make the transition smoothly. If a girl seems self-reliant, independent, able to make her own decisions and set out her own positions without alienating her parents, perhaps she is in for smooth sailing; but if the girl is too good, too docile, too willing to please, that isn't necessarily healthy. We've noted that it's a lot easier to come to psychological adolescence—the struggle to find a self—as a teenager than as a woman of thirty-five or forty-five.

Adolescent girls need models of women who are successful both in domestic areas (perhaps married mothers of children) and in the world outside the home. They need to see women in many different roles so they can develop a sense that there are options for them to choose. It's also important for girls to see older, single women who don't fit the "old maid" stereotype—who are clearly happy people, with rich, varied lives and some status in the community. If parents and teachers can understand this need they will expose girls to a variety of models.

The media are very little help in this regard. The most interesting women are presented as being single, divorced or widowed. There are very few images of women who are married, or in a stable relationship with a man, and doing interesting work at the same time.

The separation process that occurs at adolescence may be as difficult for mothers as it is for daughters. We've seen that it's easy for a mother to get overinvested in her daughter, and sometimes these anxieties surface over the issue of popularity. Girls are very peer conscious at this age; at perhaps no other time in life does the wish to be liked, the need for approval, burn any stronger. Mothers naturally want their daughters to have lots of friends—girls as well as boys. But a parent's anxiety is quickly sensed by a daughter. If Mom is upset when a girl doesn't get invited to a party, or isn't in the "in" crowd, the daughter will feel most keenly her own "failure" in popularity.

Parents can be helpful at this time by acting as a buffer against the pressures toward popularity. They can indicate to their daughters that staying home on a Saturday night isn't a terrible thing, that life isn't over if you're not the most sought-after girl in the freshman class. Adolescents tend to get very involved in the present—so much so that they assume that the future will be just like it. Parents can assure their daughters that just because no one has asked them to a dance—or a slumber party, or the "right" club—that doesn't mean those things will never happen.

Caryl remembers that when she was a teenager, gawky and cursed with braces, her mother very deliberately withdrew her from the intense competition for popularity that occurred with her peers. She told her daughter to wait, that dates and boys and parties and invitations to dances would come, and that they'd be more fun later on. The girls who dated and partied too early got bored too early. Thinking about that time in her life now, Caryl sees her mother's permission not to be popular as an invisible mantle that settled on her shoulders. It protected her from a great deal of uncertainty and pain, gave her time to explore her own unique interests and talents.

190

Rosalind remembers one particularly bad year in her adolescence, when her family moved to a new town, and she was lonely and miserable at a new school. Her parents suddenly were more available—they planned special outings on weekends, special events for Rosalind and her sister. Parents can, by making themselves more available to their children at these times, help combat some of the unrelenting pressure for popularity. It would probably help if adolescents themselves could talk about the pressures to conform, to be popular, to be just like everybody else. A high school in Newton, Massachusetts, staged a "peer pressure day" in which kids got together in groups and talked about these questions. At the very least, many adolescents probably realized for the first time that they weren't the only ones feeling these pressures, that all the other kids did, too.

For girls, adolescence brings with it physical maturity, especially in the form of the menarche, and this can be a disturbing time for parents and girls. First of all, we've seen that in this supposedly enlightened age girls still get largely negative information about menstruation and its consequences. And often, while the physical aspects of puberty and sex are explained and attended to, the emotional aspects are ignored. For example, the girl who is last among her peers to get her period is told, "Don't worry, you're just a little late." Such comments in no way address the intense anxiety she may be feeling. Girls who mature late often fear they are not really sexual beings, even worry about being abnormal, about homosexuality. Their self-esteem can suffer badly. Rosalind remembers one client who was very late in menstruating; the woman recalled that she felt very inadequate—"neuter" and "weird." (The emotional aspects of menstruation are examined with great understanding and humor by Judy Blume in her book for youngsters, *Are You There, God? It's Me, Margaret.*)

It is in adolescence, too, that girls are susceptible to what we've called the Prince Charming syndrome—the idea that a woman's life has to be merged with that of a man to give it meaning and direction. The syndrome is, alas, alive and well. Caryl's daughter brought home a magazine, aimed at teenagers, that she had won at a party. The publication carried a depressing series of articles with one theme: "How to be the girl that Shaun [Cassidy] loves"; "How to be the girl that Andy [Gibb] loves"; "How to be the girl that Parker [Stevenson] loves." The notion behind those headlines is, of course, that being loved by Andy, Shaun or Parker is so important that any girl would gladly transform her psyche in whatever ways were necessary. That same message is not beamed to young men. Young men are advised about techniques for attracting women, but it is not required of them that they make radical changes in themselves to gain love and approval.

The remedy for this syndrome begins not at adolescence but much earlier in a girl's life. The girl who has learned to be independent, who is not afraid of succeeding and who has learned to claim her successes will probably not be so fearful of life as a separate person that she abdicates her future to a Prince Charming. We must talk to girls about these issues, examine with them the dangers that lie in the purple prose about love and romance that adolescents are exposed to.

Too often, the message that girls absorb is that their existence is meaningless without the approval and love of a man. They can grow up to be women who are victims of a particularly debilitating kind of dependence. Psychoanalyst Jean Baker Miller describes this syndrome in her book, *Towards a New Psychology of Women.*[8] Women who fall victim to it, she says, are often not "dependent" in the usual sense of the word. They can care for themselves and others, but feel an inner vacuum. One woman was perfectly capable of nurturing her husband and children and her problem wasn't that she needed a man to do things for her. But her whole existence depended on her husband's approval. "Without his affirmation, she became immobilized, she felt like no one at all." The result, for this woman, was depression, because she was haunted by the idea that her husband didn't care enough—even though she admitted he was a good husband and father. In fact, no one could care "enough" to fill the void inside her, where a sense of her own worth should have been.

Active, successful women can fall prey to this syndrome. Miller recalls one woman who held a high academic appointment, yet struggled with an inner sense that nothing she did was worthwhile without a man to care for her.

Young women have to be given the message that they are important, useful, valuable people in their own right. Certainly their relationships with men can be rewarding, intimate, very important to their lives. But if they try to make these relationships the very core of their existence, they are bound to fail. No "prince," no matter how charming, can carry the weight of *two* souls.

10

SEXUALITY AND CONFLICT

One of the popular women's magazines of the fifties offered this advice to women on how to catch different types of men:

PLAYBOY: It hasn't occurred to him that life doesn't naturally begin at midnight. Strategy: Get twelve hours sleep the night before. Wear dancing slippers.

SOLID CITIZEN: He smokes a pipe and wears his frat or lodge pin in plain sight. Strategy; bring out the family album. Have dog-eared copies of civic league pamphlets inconspicuously conspicuous.

BUDDING GENIUS: He's writing the Great American Novel. Strategy: Show him how fast you can type.

─────────────────

"I'd rather have my daughter read pornography than 'Forever.' At least she'd know that was wrong, instead of having this book about a nice normal girl who has sex and then it ends and the book is over. Judy Blume had this beautiful opportunity to teach kids a lesson, if she'd just given an example of suffering or punishment. But the girl doesn't get pregnant or have a nervous breakdown."

For this mother of a thirteen-year-old daughter, a book by popular young adults' author Judy Blume[1] seemed as explosive as *plastique*. *Forever* has been causing a stir because of its theme: a nice, middle-class eighteen-year-old girl falls in love with a nice boy and they eventually have sexual relations. They part and life goes on—no hysterics, no unwanted pregnancy, no lacerations of guilt. Parents in such diverse places as Lenox, Massachusetts, and Austin, Texas, have tried, without success, to get *Forever* off the shelves of libraries. One Ohio mother told writer Joyce Maynard of *The New York Times* that she confiscated her daughter's copy, put it in a drawer and left a strand of hair across the pages so she would be able to tell if the book were disturbed. This is, she says, "the kind of trick you've got to know to keep on top of what's going on. You've got to keep your eyes open, all the time. You can't ever let your guard down, there are so many bad influences around."

Many parents of teenagers—especially of girls—have the sense today that they are under siege. So much has changed, so fast, with regard to sexual mores. Adolescence is the age at which sexuality *appears* to surface.

However, while a girl's sexuality appears to explode suddenly as a family issue at the time her body matures, it is not unconnected with the rest of her life—past as well as present. To many a parent, the adolescent girl may seem a total stranger—a completely different character from the child she once was—moody, even hostile, a far cry from the sunny, loving child of yesterday. These changes and the growth of sexual feelings, however, happen to a *person* who, although young, already has a unique set of experiences, attitudes, traits and ideas. Physical maturity may be new, but the way she handles it is intimately connected with her personal and family history.

Parents of young children often say, "I'm not looking forward to the teenage years—they're going to be rough." (We've said it often enough ourselves.) It helps to realize that what we say and do with four-year-olds or seven-year-olds affects, for better or worse, their future responses to sexuality. Most parents are aware, of course, that it's a mistake to tell young children that playing doctor is "dirty" or that the stork brings babies; many also realize that displays of affection between parents are healthy. But rarely do they see connections between a child's training in—and capacity for—achievement and independence and the issues of sexuality. Understanding these links, we believe, will be helpful to parents and daughters, as girls face—and have to deal with—the pressures associated with sexuality. We have already pointed to some of the disturbing patterns that emerge in the development of young girls. Girls often receive less support for independence than do boys, and as a consequence may tend to venture less, to cling to dependent ties to others. Thus they may be slow to develop an inner set of controls to guide their own decisions and behavior.

A mother who hides books about sex from her daughter, or who tries to police the life of her teenager, may be falling into the same trap as the mother of the nine-year-old who is so fearful for her daughter's safety

194

that she doesn't let her ride a bike. Both are depriving a girl of the experience of independent behavior, but there is one important difference. To the nine-year-old, the parent's word is law, however much she may grumble about it. The adolescent is hearing new voices—a chorus of them. She is developing new allegiances, new relationships, that may be deep and powerful. The parent's voice may no longer be the strongest gravitational pull in her life. To which voice should she listen? Perhaps the ideal answer is "her own." But how will she gain the ability to heed it, or even to recognize its legitimacy?

The girl who has experienced independence at an early age may have the best chance of doing so, but it is a difficult and ongoing struggle, one no young girl should be expected to handle alone. The power of peer pressure is tremendous. It is unrealistic to think that any child, no matter how well trained in independence (or morality, for that matter), can resist that pressure all the time.

One eleven-year-old girl tearfully confessed to her parents about a very unsettling experience in which she tried cigarettes. She knew it was wrong, and more important, she didn't even want to smoke, but she couldn't resist the pressure. She was tormented most by the knowledge that the same thing would almost surely happen to her again.

Although there are no magic ways to make such situations disappear, it helps if parents can understand how difficult such experiences are. Children need to know that even "good" people give in to pressure sometimes. The child who does so needs more than a lecture from her parents; she needs their support and understanding.

One often hears the phrase "children need rules"—and indeed they do. But rules are only temporary crutches to be leaned on until the girl can stand on her own. So teenagers need more than just a parental "No!" They need to be able to talk about their problems. Adolescents in particular are moving away from the world of childhood, when issues are black and white, and rules are well-defined. The girl who tried a cigarette and felt she had done wrong was much harder on herself than any parent could be. She didn't need to be told she had been bad. She needed to be helped to understand that life is difficult and confusing, and she needed reassurance so that she could try to do better next time. Similarly, a girl who has succumbed to pressure to get involved in sex too early needs to know she can discuss her feelings with her parents without fear that they will attack her as a tramp.

These issues are critical today, because the old social controls that were set up to contain female sexuality—and to protect young girls—are fast crumbling.

When the three of us were growing up, the double standard was securely in place. The rules were clear. "Nice girls don't." Nice girls did, of course, but usually kept quiet about it. Those young girls who were aware of sex and keenly interested—but not ready to try it—had a legitimate excuse. "I'm not *that* kind of girl," or "I won't go all the way until I'm married."

In one way these rules were very comforting. They provided a legitimate reason for making a decision that went along with the girl's own real feelings: interested, but not quite ready. Boyfriends might argue, cajole, display pique, but they, too, recognized the legitimacy of the rules. Social mores were a strong ally for parents worried that their daughters might begin sexual experiments too soon.

Today, however, we have to deal with a series of events and changes in attitude known as "The Sexual Revolution." The old Victorian, repressive notions about sexuality brought with them a host of problems. More permissive attitudes about sex don't eliminate problems, however; they simply substitute a new set for the old ones. In the sixties, many women (and men as well) plunged into sexual adventures, saying it was "all in fun." Many emerged with unexpected scars. If the old maxim of "Don't go all the way until you've got the ring" proved to be a disaster for women sexually, the new slogan of "Anything goes" has its own set of hazards. Yet it is this atmosphere that adolescents are faced with today. Teenagers can buy on the newsstands any day the sort of explicit sexual material that adolescents twenty years ago only spoke of in shocked whispers. One man who counsels teenagers says that eleven-year-olds tell stories of sexual involvements that he didn't experience until he was in his twenties. Young women are no longer expected to "protect" their virginity. Quite the opposite: the pressure on girls to have early sexual experiences can be intense.

In our society, however, we believe that serious sexual involvement is best avoided in early adolescence. We do not live in a simple culture like some remote South Pacific island, where the life-span is comparatively short, where all necessary skills can be learned in childhood and girls become mothers in their early teens. Western teenagers spend their adolescent years learning the complex skills needed to function in a modern, technological society, a process which early parenthood totally disrupts.

196

Young adolescents in Western society are still in the process of separating from their parents, and while they may be physically capable of heterosexual relationships, they are rarely ready emotionally. This is true for boys as well as girls. Judy Blume says, "It's not always the girls who get hurt. *I* set out to teach a very few things in my books, but I did set out, in *Forever,* to show that boys can love just as hard, feel just as much pain."

There are, however, special dangers for girls. We've seen that, from a very early age, girls are seriously invested in their relationships, so much so that researcher Janet Lever refers to girls' intense friendships with each other as minimarriages. It is unrealistic for a young girl to set out on a sexual adventure believing that her emotions won't be stirred. Such sexual involvement also tends to increase a girl's susceptibility to what we've called the Prince Charming syndrome. We have seen that young girls too often abdicate the search for self that is the true psychological adolescence in favor of the search for a man—and then experience an identity crisis later in life. Caryl remembers that a sense of peril tinged her yearning for adolescent romance when she was a girl:

> I had an ambivalent attitude towards every girl's dream of falling in love, which everybody around me seemed to be doing with alacrity. I wanted just as desperately as they to hear the violins, but at the same time I sensed in the music a tender cage, a misty mesh strong as any wire. My bright dreams of what I might be and do were merely little green shoots, and they could be cut down so easily. I wanted to soar, to test my wings. Only when I had flown on my own could I stand on the ground and be content. I dreamed of the faceless man who would love me forever and yearned for him as much as any girl. And yet, at times in my dreams he turned into giant scissors to clip my wings; castration in reverse. It was always said that men "lost their freedom" when they married, but I saw women hanging out the wash and dragging crying children down the aisles of supermarkets and I wondered whose freedom it was that really ended. So I dreamed, but fearfully. If only Mr. Right would just hold off for a while. But what if he never came at all? What if nobody wanted me?

That same fear—what if nobody wants me?—echoes through the letters that teenage girls send to syndicated advice columnists. When you look at these letters, you rarely see one from a girl who says, "I want to have sex, but my boyfriend doesn't." The question more likely to be asked is this one: "My boyfriend wants me to go all the way, but I'm not ready. I'm afraid of losing him. What should I do?"

One can see, in this question, a direct link to the issues of independence and assertiveness that arise early in a girl's life and that carry over into adulthood. *"I m afraid of losing him!"* That fear gives voice to the belief held by so many girls that value, worth and safety lie only in relationships with others, to the notion that if a girl makes a demand on her boyfriend to respect her feelings, she will be rejected. Too early, as we've seen, a girl comes to believe that others' wishes and desires must take precedence over her own, and this belief can cripple her ability to handle the issues involved with her sexuality. Combined with the intense peer pressure to "go along," such anxieties can be overwhelming even for a girl whose parents have tried to help her become her own person.

Her parents' values may prove to be the crucial ingredient in a girl's attitudes about sex—but she needs a strong sense of inner security to adhere to those values. For most young girls, saying, "I'm a nice girl" will not work. She has to do something much harder. She has to say, "No, *I* don't want to." She has to be assertive about her own desires and to understand that, in doing so, she may risk the loss of a boyfriend and perhaps of girlfriends who have behaved differently. It takes an enormous amount of self-esteem and strong family support to decide that *your* feelings are as valuable as a relationship. The girl who engages in sex according to her own inner timetable will probably not feel great guilt or regret when she does so. Whether the experience is wonderful, awkward or painful, she is probably ready to handle it.

Because there are no simple answers today about when—and with whom—a young woman should have a sexual experience, parents are extremely uneasy. They know the old rules don't work, but are unsure of any new ones. The result is a wall of silence. A study released in 1978 by the Harvard-based Project on Human Sexuality makes this crystal clear. Researcher Elizabeth Roberts and her colleagues,[2] in a two-year study of 1400 parents, found that fewer than 15 percent had ever discussed intercourse or masturbation with their children, and even fewer, less than 6 percent, had talked about contraception. Fewer than half the parents had talked about menstruation even with their older daughters. The parents wanted their children to have satisfying sexual lives, but were fearful that if girls came to associate sexuality with pleasure, they would run the risk of becoming pregnant or of losing their reputations

198

and becoming unmarriageable. So sex becomes a taboo topic in the family, more from anxiety about saying the right thing than out of the idea that sex is dirty. The study shows, as columnist Ellen Goodman writes; "Most of us prefer to present ourselves to our children as authorities rather than to share uncertainties. We prefer to give our children rules rather than informed choices. If we cannot devise a flawless set of guidelines we retreat, turning away their questions, allowing even more confusion and misinformation to percolate into their lives from friends, television—a host of other sources."

Choice may be the crucial word in this issue. Young girls today are being forced to make difficult choices. Parents may not like that idea, but the reality won't go away. So parents must talk to adolescents about sex, not as authorities but as people who recognize the anxieties and the shades of gray.

Mothers of daughters may have difficulty dealing with their own sexuality as well as that of their daughters. It would help daughters if mothers could communicate the fact that they, too, are sexual beings. For some women, it is only as they get older that they find themselves enjoying sex and losing their earlier fears and discomfort about sexuality. Open displays of affection between husband and wife can communicate the idea that sexuality is a good thing, a reflection of love between two people. Most adults do feel private about their sex lives, and that wish for privacy is legitimate. But it doesn't take any overtly sexual display to communicate physical affection—a touch of the hand, a hug between husband and wife—is sufficient. Mothers who do feel anxious about dealing with issues of sexuality can say honestly, "I was brought up not to talk about sex in public and I'm not comfortable with it. That's too bad, but it's how I feel. I hope you won't feel the same way." The whole subject is then no longer taboo, and the daughter can understand her mother's difficulty with it. Fathers can also talk to their daughters about men's feelings toward sexuality. Too often, the sexual urges and accompanying emotions of boys are a mystery to girls. Fathers can help "demystify" the whole question, make it more understandable. Many fathers totally avoid the whole question of sexuality, feeling that it's an issue they can't talk to their daughters about. Like a mother, a father who feels uncomfortable talking about sexuality can say so frankly to his daughter, rather than avoiding the whole subject as if it didn't exist, or as if it were "bad" or "dirty."

It is striking to see in the Harvard Project on Human Sexuality the

199

very small percentage of parents who had ever talked about masturbation with their children. Masturbation may be the first sexual activity in which most people engage. It is a normal, healthy practice, and the old wives' tales about it are nothing more than that. It does not cause insanity, sterility or any other ailment. But adolescent girls, in particular, can be heir to such outmoded ideas as the notion that genitals are dirty or "not for you." There is also the old idea that female sexual organs exist solely for male pleasure.

For most females, masturbation is a critical step toward healthy sexuality. Masturbation has several advantages over sex with a partner for the adolescent girl. It gives her a chance to discover her sexuality gradually, at an early age when she is not yet ready to handle the emotional complexities of a sexual relationship. She can relieve sexual tension and experience sexual pleasure free of worries about pregnancy. Girls in early adolescence certainly feel sexual urges. Often, in the past, girls were hurt because they engaged in sexual encounters at too young an age, simply because that was the only way they could find out anything at all about sexual pleasure.

The parents in the Harvard study seemed to worry about the consequences sexual pleasure could have for their daughters. Parents should feel free to discuss this worry openly, for if girls are ever to reach full emotional adulthood, they need to understand that sex, like other major actions, does have consequences. One problem girls often have in the sexual area, as well as in other areas, is that they cannot see beyond today. They may get involved in sexual activities as if pregnancy just couldn't happen to them. One of Rosalind's patients, a devout Catholic woman, never considered using contraception yet never expected to get pregnant, believing "God will take care of me." She nearly died from her fourth pregnancy, still wondering how things turned out the way they did.

The question most often asked "experts" today about adolescent sexuality goes like this: "What should a mother do when her fourteen-year-old daughter asks for birth control pills?" We believe that it is a trap for parents to get hung up over the issue of whether to answer yes or no. Rather, they should try to discover what the girl is asking.

The real issue may be something else—pressure from her boyfriend or peers, uncertainty about her own attractiveness or sexuality. Perhaps she is staging a rebellion against parental authority. So, instead of reacting to the contraceptive issue with panic, or feeling the need to respond

200

immediately to the specific question, a parent should recognize such questions as providing the opportunity to engage her daughter in a general discussion of sexual issues.

Mothers will have to realize that any such discussion must also include issues that at first glance appear unrelated to sex: anger and the management of conflict. Today's openness about sexuality means more decisions, sooner, for young people, and choice always involves some degree of tension and conflict. This is a notion that mothers may have a hard time dealing with. For if there is any issue that makes women even more uncomfortable than that of sexuality, it is the idea—and even more so the reality—of conflict.

The relationship between conflict and sexuality for women is one that has only recently been examined in any depth. As we will see, there is a link, an important one, between these two areas, both of which have in the past been declared taboo for women. If the open expression of sexuality by a woman was thought to be unseemly, the open expression of anger was perhaps even worse—unfeminine, unconventional, *unnatural*.

Female anger, pent-up, can take peculiar forms. Norman Mailer, writing of Marilyn Monroe in *Marilyn*,[3] describes the actress this way:

> The amount of animal rage in her by these years of her artistic prominence is almost impossible to control by human or chemical means. Yet she has to surmount such tension in order to present herself to the world as that figure of immaculate tenderness, utter bewilderment, and goofy dipsomaniacal sweetness which is Sugar Kane in *Some Like It Hot* . . . and what bile she must dispense, what poison to her tricks. On the set of *Some Like It Hot* she will drive fellow actors into horrors of repetition. Through forty-two takes, Tony Curtis has to nibble on forty-two chicken legs because Monroe keeps blowing her lines . . . she is also voiding her near to infinite anger at life, at men, and the movie-making world.

Marilyn Monroe was not alone in her inability to express anger directly and forcefully. Like many women, she felt she had to twist her outer self into a form society approved, and society very definitely does not approve of angry women. But anger is not an inert force. It boils and moves; like the churning steam in a teakettle, it has to get out somehow. Often it dribbles out, disguised. Marilyn's "poisonous" tricks were such fragments of anger, more devastating to the victim than an explosion would be. Women have become masters of the concealed cut, have learned to induce the kind of inner bleeding that is more painful than an open wound. In countless struggles between men and women, women have often taken the guerrilla role—retreat, hide, sulk, strike and vanish, inflict suffering *by* suffering—any stratagem is preferable to laying all the cards on the table and having it out.

These strategies have often given women some temporary victories— but at what cost? It's only recently that we have come to realize that the price women paid was in a seemingly unrelated area of their lives: sex. The common, often mysterious deficit in sexual pleasure that women experience often has its roots in chronic, unexpressed anger. The techniques of sexual functioning have been dealt with at length in many excellent books.[4] But it's our belief that this kind of technical information is useful only after a woman has come to grips with her own ability to handle conflict and to feel comfortable making legitimate demands on her own behalf. Some perversity in the nature of women is not what accounts for their difficulties in doing so, nor some immutable biologically determined trait. It has its origins in the centuries-old inequality of the power relationship that has existed between men and women.

The whole question of the flow of power in a love relationship is one that many people are uncomfortable with. The myth of romantic love dispenses starlight and tender emotions, and the intrusion of the notion of power seems callous and unfeeling. But the fact remains that in any relationship between two people there is a question of power, and the many ways in which that power can be distributed. It can be shared, or it can belong, in the main, to one partner. None of us is content to be totally powerless, and if we find ourselves in a social situation in which no power is assigned to us, we start figuring out a way to get some. If we can't reach for it openly, there are covert ways in which to get at least a piece of the action.

Psychoanalyst Jean Baker Miller examines this issue in her pioneering book, *Towards a New Psychology of Women*. Miller looks at the way societies operate and finds that often there are two categories of people, the "dominants" and the "subordinates," who behave in clearly different ways. The dominants are powerful, and they assign to themselves the tasks that are high in status and material rewards. The less valued functions are assigned to the subordinates, who are seen as not capable—

202

perhaps even incapable—of performing the valued functions. "It follows," writes Miller, "that subordinates are described in terms of, and encouraged to develop, personal psychological characteristics that are pleasing to the dominant group. These characteristics form a certain familiar cluster: submissiveness, passivity, docility, dependency, lack of initiative, inability to act, to decide, to think, and the like. In general, this cluster includes qualities more characteristic of children than adults—immaturity, weakness, and helplessness. If subordinates adopt these characteristics they are considered well adjusted."

Subordinates learn quickly that the display of these qualities can serve as protective cover. Blacks often had to learn the shuffle and the "Yassah, boss" posture to survive. Women used the "dumb blonde act" to get what they wanted. Too often, however, the subordinates internalize the traits the dominant group has selected for them. The shuffle becomes more than an act.

Subordinate groups, unable to make demands or reach for power openly, become experts at manipulation. Subordinates, Miller points out, know much more about the dominants than vice versa. They *have* to because their survival depends on it. "They become highly attuned to the dominants, able to predict reactions of pleasure and displeasure. Here, I think, is where the long story of 'feminine intuition' and 'feminine wiles' begins. It seems clear that these 'mysterious gifts' are in fact skills developed through long practice, in reading many signals both verbal and nonverbal."

Girls grow up learning how to read, understand and manipulate the emotions, egos and libidos of men. For example, one of the popular women's magazines of the fifties offered this advice to women on how to catch different types of men:

> PLAYBOY: It hasn't occurred to him that life doesn't naturally begin at midnight. Strategy: Get twelve hours sleep the night before. Wear dancing slippers.
> SOLID CITIZEN: He smokes a pipe and wears his frat or lodge pin in plain sight. Strategy: Bring out the family album. Have dog-eared copies of civic league pamphlets inconspicuously conspicuous.
> BUDDING GENIUS: He's writing the Great American Novel. Strategy: show him how fast you can type.

Reshaping oneself to fit a series of males may be a good strategy to catch a husband, but as we've seen, it is completely incompatible with developing a sense of one's own identity—the major cornerstone for a full life.

Most women who are adults today can remember the lore of catching a man, passed down by mothers, sisters and friends. All the advice was about how to please a man—never let him think you are smarter than he is, let him do the talking, gaze into his eyes and tell him he's wonderful. The reward would be male approval, and male approval was, quite literally, survival. Young girls who weren't engaged by the time they were old enough to vote often felt desperate, nagged by their parents and haunted by the possibility of becoming an old maid.

Girls often learn very early that openly expressed anger is not pleasing to a man and thus to be avoided. The angry woman draws some of the harshest male epithets: castrating bitch, ball breaker. Female anger, says psychologist Harriet Lerner[5] of the Menninger Clinic, can stir echoes in men of their childhood dependency on their mothers and arouse irrational fears of female authority, power and anger. "In the primitive mind of the infant and young child, mother is, indeed, far more than a person. She is an all-powerful and magical individual who possesses omnipotent powers for good and evil . . . Fairy tales, such as 'Hansel and Gretel,' about evil women who eat children capture the child's frightening experience of the omnipotent bad mother who destroys those who fall into her power. Witches, complete with magic spells and potions, still ride their broomsticks through the nightmares of children and remain lurking in the unconscious mind of grown men and women."

These irrational fears are not always held in check by adult logic and reason, Lerner says. "During the middle ages, thousands of innocent women were burned as witches by the same 'rational' adults who worshipped the Virgin Mary. And in more recent times, the dramatically high incidence of wife abuse reminds one of the irrational anger and rage a man may experience when his dependency on his wife reactivates feelings from an earlier dependency relationship on mother."

Trained to observe male moods carefully, warned of the danger of openly expressing anger, women become experts in the subtle arts of manipulation. The "Total Woman" phenomenon that has gained wide attention in the past few years offers a simple formula: learn to manipulate a man by pleasing him, and the rewards can be great. Marabel Morgan, high priestess of the cult, cannily explains that it's much easier to get your husband to buy the new washer you want by greeting him at the door dressed in Saran Wrap than it is by nagging him about it.

One of the appeals of the Total Woman movement—which is most popular among women in small towns in the Bible Belt—is that it legitimizes sex. Many of these women, raised with the hellfire and brimstone morality of fundamental Christianity, feel liberated by the message that sex is okay because Jesus says it's okay. But at base, Total Woman is a pessimistic assessment of woman's chances for gaining any real power. Its underlying credo is that men hold power and always will, and women must flatter them and prey upon their sexual appetites to get their way. Its view of men is both demeaning and patronizing (though not intentionally). Men are seen as being incapable of showing such traits as sensitivity or a sense of justice, but are viewed as rather simpleminded peacocks who can be controlled by sex. There is always an element of contempt in manipulation—what is so mocking as the laughter of servants? As Jean Baker Miller points out, subordinate groups have their own disguised ways of expressing defiance and contempt. The subordinates resort to disguised and indirect ways of acting. "While these actions are designed to accommodate and please the dominant group, they often, in fact, contain hidden defiance and put-ons. Folk tales, Black jokes, and women stories are often based on how the wily peasant and sharecropper outwitted the rich landowner, boss or husband."

Women have only recently recognized their inability to express anger as a legitimate problem rather than a virtue. "Assertiveness training" has been developed to help people move out of their subordinate position by learning to act more directly in their own self-interest.

The movement of women toward reclaiming anger can, understandably, make some men nervous. One male psychologist[6] writes that many women are living with frustration and anger which will be released when they understand their inferior position in society. But, he says, "acknowledgement of anger towards men almost invariably complicates women's relationships with men, and marital dissatisfaction is correlated with their increased anger. . . . One could argue that underlying rage is as bad as open rage. This may be true for the mental health of the woman, but it is not true for the stability of man-woman relationships."

In other words, men are better off with simmering volcanoes than with women who can express anger openly; the "stability" of the man-woman relationships depends on the ability of women to keep a cork on their anger. Is this true?

Not, it would seem, for any man who isn't a dedicated masochist. Women find ways to express their anger, to punish its object. Sometimes this whole process is unconscious. One of the most common by-products of repressed anger in women is a condition which is hardly a contributor to "stability" in man-woman relationships; that condition is female frigidity. Ann Birk, director of a direct sex therapy program in the Boston area, says that the major predictor of sexual dysfunction in women is chronic and underexpressed anger.

When women are angry with a husband or lover and that anger cannot vent itself, it can have a direct and crippling effect on sexuality. Repressed anger and loving abandon just don't seem to be able to exist side by side, in most cases. Birk recalls the case of one young woman who was very angry with her husband because he was rarely home. She could not bring herself to confront him with the fact of her anger and developed a vaginal condition which prevented her from having intercourse. As soon as she was able to confront him, to say, "I need you home more," the condition vanished almost immediately and she was able to function sexually.

Lillian Rubin, in *Worlds of Pain*,[7] her study of the working-class family, observes that sexual problems in working-class couples often surface with the first fight. "Regardless of what has gone before, at bedtime he's ready for sex, she's cold and aloof." One couple she interviewed explained what happens. The wife: "If we have a fight, I can't just turn it off. He has a hard time understanding that. I feel like that's all he wants sometimes." The husband: "I'll want to try to make up with her by making love, but she's as cold as the inside of a refrigerator. Sure I get mad when that happens. Why shouldn't I? Here I'm trying to make up and make love, and she's holding out for something—I don't know what."

Repressed anger is nothing new to women. In *Little Women*, Marmee tells Jo, "I am angry nearly every day of my life but I've learned not to show it; and I still hope to learn not to feel it, though it may take me another forty years to do so."

That anger may well have shown up behind the bedroom door; if it did, we can be sure she kept quiet about it. Women were expected to lie on their backs and think of England, as the Victorian saying went. But today, women are not content with stoic endurance. Bombarded by the media with the details of lovemaking and the fact of multiple orgasms, women are more likely to feel cheated if they cannot express their sexuality, and are more likely to seek help. In days past, men may have thought that female frigidity was the norm, although making love to a stoic, dutiful woman could not have been exactly the height of rapture.

It is nonsense to claim that recognition of the part that conflict and power play in sexuality will necessarily shatter male-female relationships. Honesty may indeed blow some relationships out of the water, but it will make others easier and more real. With these issues out in the open, sex may be used less often as a way for one party to get what it wants from the other. Women have long known the power of sex as one of their few real weapons. Men are often adept at using it, too. Lillian Rubin says, "There is plenty of evidence that the battle between the sexes is still being waged in the marriage bed." She reports that some of the sexual adjustment problems of the couples she studied "suggest that the struggle was not over sex, but over power and control." For example, one couple had intercourse like clockwork five or six times a week for years, with the woman unable to have orgasm. Then the wife began to read material about female sexuality, and one night, "The earth shook. I couldn't believe anything could be so great." Her husband immediately lost interest in sex.

"It would seem," Rubin says, "that as long as he could 'take what (he) needed' he could feel he was asserting some control over his wife and could remain sexually active and potent. When she unexpectedly became an assertive and active participant in the sex act, the only possibility for retaining control was to move from the active to the passive mode . . . His wife, now acutely aware of her sexual deprivation, is left torn between anger, frustration and the terrible fear that she is responsible for it."

This couple might indeed be called part of a "stable" relationship. They are not divorcing; neither party is running off to have an affair. But the price they pay is the great unhappiness of both parties and tension that must often be unbearable.

So anger in men and women will find a way to express itself, consciously or unconsciously. Harriet Lerner says that, "As a psycho-therapist I have noted that when patients are discussing situations in which they are mistreated, male patients typically say, 'I was angry' while female patients say, 'I was hurt.' This phrase, 'I was hurt' is a telling one. For when a legitimate anger cannot be acknowledged, recognized or expressed, women do indeed 'hurt.' Their hurt may take the form of headaches, fatigue, depression or sexual disinterest. Or it may even express itself in intellectual dullness, or a lack of capacity for creative and original work.

"Women may remain entirely unaware that their various symptoms or hurts stem from the suppression or denial of their anger. Indeed, they may not experience any conscious anger at all. Instead, women become hurt and reduced to tears when they are in a situation of wanting to vent their anger."

Women are often so unfamiliar with handling any kind of conflict that their automatic reaction in any tenuous situation is to take the blame themselves when anything goes wrong. Syndicated columnist Jane O'Reilly describes the time when she ran over the foot of a woman in a supermarket with her shopping cart, and the woman immediately apologized.

"'Why are you sorry?' I asked as she patted her ankle with her Kleenex. She said, 'I should have seen you coming. I shouldn't have been in the middle of the aisle. Oh, I'm terribly sorry. I usually carry a Band-Aid in my purse but I didn't today.' She limped off down the aisle muttering, 'I'm sorry, I'm sorry.'" O'Reilly then deliberately bumped into six other women, in the interests of science, and all of them apologized to her.

"When my dog trips me up in the hallways, I apologize to him. My sainted mother has not written me a letter in twenty years without apologizing for the weather, whatever it has been, wherever I have been. 'I'm so sorry it is so cold in New York,' she writes. I have never heard a man make a personal apology for the weather."

For women, the socialization that makes them the nurturers, the healers, the bearers of warmth, tenderness and care also can add to their problems in admitting to anger and dealing with conflict. Women often subscribe to an ideal of morality in which it is wrong to hurt anyone in any way.[8] Yet they often find it difficult to include themselves in the caring and compassion they extend to the rest of the world. Sometimes to avoid a minor injury (or an imagined one) to another, they will suffer severe consequences to themselves. This can lead them into a vicious cycle: Feeling it is their duty to put everyone's needs before their own, they wind up resentful because their own needs are not being met but they are unable to express that resentment directly. Their anger turns inward, often resulting in depression, phobias, anxiety, sexual dysfunction—hardly the hallmarks of a happy and fulfilled life.

The tendency automatically to put everyone else's needs before your own can leave women trapped in untenable situations. Sociologist Margaret Adams refers to this as "The Compassion Trap." She says that a metaphor based on the karate match might be appropriate. "Just as the karate player's strength is turned back against him, woman's supposed social strengths have been gradually turned to her disadvantage and now are used to blunt her protest and to bar her escape from the confining role that their exclusive exercise has forced upon her. Women in general have been restrained from any uncompromising or threatening action on their own behalf for fear of negative repercussions on other individuals towards whom they stand in a protective role." She points out that women, seeing themselves primarily as caretakers, often stay in untenable marriages because of the welfare of the children (although the children might indeed be better off in a serene, single-parent family than in a tension-ridden home with two parents).

Too often, giving, for women, is not a generous impulse born of strength but one that springs from anxiety and fear of disapproval and the loss of love. Believing that all others' claims on her have legitimacy over her own, expected to relinquish personhood itself at the demand of others, a woman can sometimes feel buffeted by demands that roll in like waves. The hunger for "a room of one's own," a place to be free of these demands, to exist for a time only for oneself, is a theme that women writers have seized on since Virginia Woolf first used that phrase. But sometimes a woman's life can shrink to the size of that room. "Death for women in literature is the ultimate room of one's own," says literary critic Carolyn Heilbrun in *Reinventing Womanhood*. In Doris Lessing's "To Room 19," a woman who seems to have everything takes a room in a shabby, run-down hotel, and finally kills herself there because "without the room I don't exist." Heilbrun points out that for this woman—as for many women in fiction—death becomes the only part of their lives that they can control. They can at least choose to die. A contemporary novel, *The Goat, the Wolf, and the Crab*, by Gillian Martin,[9] deals with the final two years in the life of a housewife who discovers she has operable cervical cancer, but chooses not to have surgery. She tells her doctor,

> "I am forty-two years old. My children are grown up. My husband is well employed. I have a marriage and a style of life that millions would envy. I have had my teeth looked at twice a year. I have had my eyes tested at suitable intervals, and, as you know, I have had cervical

smears taken as recommended. I have done my washing on Mondays, cleaned out my cupboards regularly, and lain dutifully on my back and thought of England. I have kept my figure reasonably well and paid passing attention to changes in fashion. I have done everything as and when it was expected of me, and in the doing I have abdicated myself entirely . . . In fact I have not done anything at all without someone else's interests being the prime factor. This is the last opportunity. I insist on doing this in my own way."

The inability to make demands, to be selfish at times, can lead women, in extremis, to desperate and pathetic gestures, although few women would choose to die in order to take control of their lives. Sometimes, however, they seize on what might seem to be an insignificant issue and flail away, to the puzzlement of their husbands, friends and relatives. They are seen as "making a mountain out of a molehill" or as being the victims of some sort of female neurosis. Unable to make demands, unused to even the possibility of conflict, women find that their attempts at assertion can trail away into ineffectiveness.

So for women, being in a subordinate position, believing that their identity derives from their relationship with men, learning to put others' needs first, all combine to create a way of life in which conflict becomes a highly charged issue. "It is practically impossible," says Jean Baker Miller, "to initiate open conflict when you are totally dependent on the other person or group for the basic material and psychological means of existence." So women resort to their guerrilla warfare, manipulating, wheedling, sulking, too rarely confronting a conflict with a man openly on the real issue. The conflict becomes a festering sore, not an opportunity for growth and greater understanding. All life involves conflict, says Miller, and it can be a healthy and normal part of human existence. Conflict does not have to be a frightening word, especially to women.

There is, Miller points out, good and bad conflict—conflict which is constructive as opposed to conflict which is destructive. A baby crawling around a room bumping into things comes into conflict with its environment, but through that process the baby learns and grows. In relationships between parent and child there will also be conflict, but out of that struggle the child will learn discipline, values and inner controls. The problem with our society's view of conflict, Miller says, is our assumption that if there's conflict, there's something wrong. We equate conflict with violence.

210

Jean Baker Miller sees violence as something that happens when we try to suppress conflict, when we don't accept it as a natural part of life. We find it hardest of all to accept the idea that conflict could be a necessary part of a loving relationship between a man and a woman. Everything is always supposed to be harmonious. Unfortunately there is only one way to achieve such harmony—for one party to abrogate all claim to individual needs, rights, wishes. Such self-denial is the essence of the traditional woman's role—the one who comforts, turns away wrath, makes sure that everyone's needs are attended to. But the fulfillment of this role requires a degree of self-abnegation achieved by only the rarest of saints. The woman who denies or suppresses her own needs in order to be at the beck and call of others will have to deal with a high degree of anger because of her unmet needs. If she can't express her anger openly it will find other, often destructive outlets, as we saw in the case of Marilyn Monroe. Other variations on this theme are the martyr syndrome, in which everyone else is made to feel guilty for the woman's sacrifice, and depression, which often results when women turn anger inward.

So, for their own emotional health, women have to learn to make demands and to tolerate the possibility of conflict. Often, however, they have great difficulty taking the first step, in saying, openly, "I want." Men don't usually have the same difficulty. In particular, they do not fear that someone will stop loving them if they make a demand. Why is this so? According to Jean Baker Miller:

"I think it basically stems from men feeling that they are the full-fledged people of society, the superiors. And having a sense that others are there to do for them willingly. So that they don't grow up with this fear that 'If I demand something, somebody's going to leave me' because they feel like they are doing the right thing in making demands. People don't leave you for doing the right thing."

It is doubly hard for women to initiate conflict by making demands, Miller says, first, because it's hard for a woman to recognize her right to make them, and second, because often she is in a highly unequal relationship. She is so dependent on the man that if the relationship were to be destroyed, her means of survival would be lost. Women, however, often exaggerate the ill effects of making demands. Like the little girl who fears that winning a prize in school will make her friends dislike her, the woman in a relationship with a man thinks that if she says, "I want this," he will no longer love her. In fact, Miller says, men are often relieved at being able to deal with direct demands from women:

it's easier than trying to be a mind reader, than dealing with sulking and wheedling. Initiating conflict can, of course, have real risks for women. Some men are simply not able to deal with conflict when it comes from an unexpected source—from the woman in his life.

From her vantage point as a psychotherapist, Jean Miller has seen a "tremendous change" in women's willingness to face their own needs and to make demands. How can young girls get the message that they aren't second-class people? Miller has an intriguing comment:

"This comes out with my patients. Many women say that they resent it terribly if they come from a home where the mother never got herself out of a bad situation, but just took it. So, in a way, the best thing a mother can do for her daughter is to initiate the kind of conflict that could be productive, not just sit back and take it."

In such situations, it was the father who had been unfair, abusive or condescending, but it was toward their mothers that the women felt the greatest anger. "They resent their fathers but it's amazing how much they resent their mothers. Now, of course, they understand what their mothers were up against. But many women have said, 'If I had seen my mother, just once, not just sit there and take it!'"

So women with daughters are not only ensuring their own emotional health by making demands and expressing legitimate anger, but they are giving their daughters permission to do the same. It's clear that young girls, too, should be allowed to take a stand and risk conflict at home, rather than feeling that they must preserve a facade of false harmony. That is not to say a child should be allowed to throw a tantrum or behave like a brat, but she can learn that verbalizing anger is a good thing to do. Of course, mothers who have trouble verbalizing their own anger may well have problems in getting this message across to their daughters. Mothers can remember that their behavior is a powerful model for their daughters.

It may not be possible, however, for some mothers suddenly to start dealing directly with conflict. Lonnie Garfield Barbach, a clinical psychologist at the Human Sexuality Program of the University of California Medical Center, has devised a method to help women learn to admit, and deal with, their own wishes and needs in order to realize their emotional and sexual potential.

For a woman to accept sexual pleasure, Barbach says, she has to feel that she deserves it, that she is an important person, as important as those she loves and cares for. She has to realize that it is as necessary to give to herself as it is to give to others. If she feels she always has to be the good,

212

strong, giving one, she can't help being angry at times about "getting the short end of the deal."

Barbach assures women that they have the right to refuse things they don't want and to ask for things they do want. She has worked out an exercise she calls Yes's and No's.

The "Yes" exercises require a woman to ask for—or allow herself—three things she normally would not have permitted herself. One woman asked her husband to make dinner one night when she was tired. Another bought a sweater she had admired for a long time but felt was too expensive for her. For the "No" exercise, a woman must say no to three things she didn't want to do anyway. One woman, for example, always hated collecting money for a certain charity but always said yes because she was afraid to refuse. She did refuse and felt a great sense of relief. Another woman always felt she had to go to bed with the man she was steadily dating, even if she didn't want to on a particular night. "She was afraid that if she refused she would lose them. She decided to take a risk and began telling her lovers, before she went out for the evening, that she did not want to have sex for a while and that she would tell them when she felt like it. To her amazement, her request was honored and respected. One lover did try to push her to make love, but she held firm." Not one man ended the relationship because she expressed her own feelings.

For this woman, the understanding that conflict did not necessarily mean personal disaster made it possible for her to feel comfortable with herself—and with the men in her life. Women have to learn that some conflict is not only inevitable but can be helpful as well. Conflict doesn't have to be like a football game where winning is everything.

As Jean Baker Miller says, "It isn't a zero-sum game where if I win you have to lose. Optimally, from conflict everyone should have grown in some way, seen something new, experienced another side of the thing. Certainly in human relationships there shouldn't be a winner and a loser."

Nuts and Bolts

There is no question that adolescent sexual behavior has changed in recent years. The rate of adolescent premarital intercourse has been on the rise since 1967. According to the Department of Health, Education, and Welfare, studies in various areas of the country showed that by 1973 about 35 percent of high-school seniors, both males and females, were nonvirgins. For college students as a group the figures were much higher: 85 percent of males and 60 to 70 percent of females had experienced sexual intercourse. Parents clearly face the likelihood that their adolescent children will begin sexual activity at an earlier age—and in an era of different mores—than they did, and the effect is concern and confusion. Jeanne Jacobs Speizer writes in the Boston Women's Health Book Collective, *Ourselves and Our Children*: "Watching our children develop sexually, we may be proud of their growth, anxious about their uncertainty and experimentation, sad at the reminder of our own 'lost youth,' jealous of their sexual blossoming—or some of each of these. Whatever we are feeling at any one moment, we are brought up against our own feelings about sexuality—for ourselves and for our children. Living with teenagers makes us confront every day our own sexual questions, practices, beliefs and values."[10]

To grapple with the question of their children's sexuality, parents must begin by thinking about their own. The Harvard-based study on human sexuality proved the existence of a Great Wall of Silence on the whole subject in many American families, a wall that must be breached. Most parents must venture into this difficult arena without benefit of easy answers, simple rules or the confidence of knowing precisely what they should do. Opening up a dialogue is vital, however, even if you are not sure of what happens next.

Parents often feel anxious because they think they are expected—by their children and by society—to do precisely the right thing, say precisely the right thing, all the time. Catherine Chilman,[11] author of a review of the research on adolescent sexuality sponsored by HEW, *Adolescent Sexuality in a Changing American Society*, has some comforting words on this issue.

> The anxiety of parents tends to be high concerning the sexual behavior of their teenagers. Many feel that the larger society will hold them responsible for whatever their youngsters do. This is less true than it once was. Although parents play an important part in the developmental outcomes of their sons and daughters, society takes a very large hand in childrearing from the moment children are born. By the time they reach adolescence, young people have been exposed to a veritable flood of societal influences. . . . Parents can be helped to realize that they are still responsible for their youngsters but not *totally* responsible; that both contemporary conditions as well as the youngster's developmental stage call for loving parental support and clear

214

guidance, but not parental overprotection and attempts to control or assume responsibility for all of the young person's behavior.

The setting of limits for teenagers, then, ought to be done in a setting of open communication and trust between parents and child but without unrealistic expectations of perfect agreement. Parents of teenagers may feel that they are in an endless series of debates, always negotiating, winning and losing points, always on the alert for a new offensive. Wearing as that may be, it helps the teenager move on to develop his or her own internal values and controls. Jeanne Speizer points out, "There are good reasons for setting limits, and yet there are limits to the limits we can set. We are in the odd position of having once (it seems like only yesterday) been the people who saved our toddlers from certain death at least once an hour, except when they were asleep. It is hard, even now—or perhaps especially now, when our children are doing things that are potentially dangerous to themselves and others—to give up the power of absolute protectiveness. We are getting close to the end of our function as limit-setter, and for some of us, letting go of that role is difficult."

Parents often wonder about the effectiveness of passing on to seemingly unreceptive teenagers the hard-earned wisdom they have gained just from being alive as long as they have. Yet even if teenagers appear to reject parental advice as hopelessly old-fashioned, much of it in fact sinks in and slowly takes root.

Because teenagers have an instinctive dislike of a rip-off, the "consumer" approach might be helpful. They can be made aware of the way sex is used as a commodity in our society, as a sales gimmick for everything from stereos to lipstick. They can be helped to understand that many aspects of the current sexual "freedom" are unfortunate and exaggerated reactions to the old repression. As Catherine Chilman points out, "In an effort to free people from the resulting 'hangups,' some proponents of the sexual revolution have seen any kind of limitation on sexual behaviors as an unwarranted restraint on human freedoms. Typically, revolutions push to extremes in order to bring about change. Resultant changes are often moderated, over time, by the majority who find that extremes fall considerably short of the proposed utopia." Parents can warn teenagers to take with many grains of salt the sexual gurus who offer the illusion that sex is simply another "fun" activity, like tennis or volleyball. Teenagers can certainly learn that compassion and concern for others—not just one's own hedonistic pleasure—must be part of all human relationships, including sexual ones. As Chilman says, "Advocacy of 'sex as play' in a consumer, leisure society seems to be a childish approach to a basically serious subject, although playful sex with one's committed partner is a different matter."

The sexuality of adolescent girls, as we've seen, may be a particularly charged issue for parents. While boys' sexual escapades have been generally viewed with tolerant indulgence by society, girls who engaged in premarital sex were often branded as "spoiled merchandise." The double standard may be fading away, but many of the old attitudes linger, even in the minds of people who consider themselves progressive. Anxiety for their daughter's reputation, for her physical health and emotional well-being, may lead parents to try to surround their girl child within a fortress of rules. But as we've seen, she is going to have to develop her own controls; the parents can't be in every back seat, in every darkened theater, at every party. The girl who has had parental encouragement to develop independence and assertiveness will probably be less likely to succumb to pressure from peers or boyfriends when she is unwilling or uncertain. It is unfortunately true that girls often do become sexually active for these reasons. Research on teenage sexuality, according to Chilman's review, shows that premarital intercourse is often associated for girls with low self-esteem, passive-dependent behavior and a desire for intimacy and affection.

Contraception is a difficult issue for teenagers and their parents alike. It requires, first of all, the parents' recognition of the girl's sexuality. However difficult, parents cannot ignore this topic. Studies consistently show that few sexually active adolescents manage contraception correctly. The great majority of sexually active adolescents have intercourse for at least a year before they seek information about contraception.

The idea of sex education makes some parents anxious; they reason, "If the kids learn more about it, won't they *do* more?" Given the statistics, it is clear that adolescents are not exactly sexually backward; their attitudes toward sexual encounters are controlled by forces other than a lecture on contraception. Personnel in family planning clinics, according to Chilman, report that many adolescent girls say they could not possibly talk to their parents about contraception. They feel freer to get involved in sex than to talk to their parents about it. "Conversely, parent educators often report parents' comments that they could not talk to their teenagers about contraceptives as this would seem to condone premarital intercourse." So, the silence continues, and both parents and children are the losers. Chilman's conclusion is that "Continuing effort appears to be necessary to make contraceptive education, counseling, and supplies available to adolescents where they are, such as in schools and recreation centers. . . . Condoms, foams, and jellies should be available to adolescents at the time of need, in public restrooms, gas stations and the like."

Such suggestions, many parents fear, will give approval and encouragement to early sexual activity. Yet many unwanted pregnancies result from teenagers' thinking that spontaneous sex is "okay," but planned contraception isn't. As the writer of the *Boston Globe* column "Ask Beth" says: "Teaching and preaching that sex is wrong simply hasn't worked. More and more people are involving themselves with sex at earlier and earlier ages. Keeping them in ignorance only promotes curiosity, experiment, bumbling, secretiveness and the tragic teenage pregnancy rate."

11

SCHOOL DAYS

The Pedagogical Harem

> I was always wondering whether it could really be true, as everyone thought, that boys were cleverer than girls. Indeed, I cared so much that I never dared to ask any grown-up person the direct question, not even my father or mother, because I feared to hear the reply . . . I can remember weeping over the account of Adam and Eve, because it seemed to me that the curse pronounced on Eve might imperil girls' going to college . . . I was terror struck lest I, and every other woman with me, were doomed to live as pathological invalids in a universe merciless to woman as a sex.
>
> —M. Carey Thomas, Bryn Mawr College president, 1907

> Education is greatly to be desired but it is better that the future matrons of the state should be without a university degree than that it should be produced at the fearful expense of ruined health.
>
> —The Regents of the University of Wisconsin (Quoted by historians Carroll Smith-Rosenberg and Charles Rosenberg.)

This dire prediction about what the rigors of a university education might do to women comes from the nineteenth century. But the same idea has been expressed throughout the history of modern education. If women were included in the idea of education at all, they were consigned to a narrow and limited niche. Jean Jacques Rousseau wrote in the eighteenth century about women: "To please, to be useful to us, to make us love and esteem them, to educate us when young, and take care of us when grown up, to advise, to console us, to render our lives easy and agreeable—these are the duties of women at all times, and what they should be taught in their infancy."[1]

Throughout much of the history of this country, what little education women received was in keeping with those sentiments. In the early nineteenth century, opportunities for girls to receive education even at the elementary level were very restricted.[2] In New London, Connecticut, for example, girls were allowed to attend the town school for the first time in 1805, but only in the summer: there would be no need for fuel and the boys would be busy in the fields.

As for higher education, since the opening of Harvard in 1636, universities wore an invisible but well-understood sign: No women need apply.[3] No American university admitted a woman from the date of the founding of Harvard until the creation of Oberlin College two hundred years later. As colleges gradually began to admit women, the reasons for doing so were less those of concern for women, more those of practical economics; sometimes a scarcity of male students, at other times a need for more teachers (willing to work for low pay) in the public schools. Even today, economics plays a large part in the interest of universities in attracting women students. The baby boom is over, and the colleges need warm bodies. One administrator at a large university spoke of all those housewives out there needing training to get back into the work force and the dollar bills danced in his eyes.

Between the years 1820 and 1920, admission to postsecondary schools was a revolution in the history of women's education, according to historian David Tyack,[4] accompanied by a gradual change in ideas about the intellectual capacity of women.

By the early nineteenth century, the conventional wisdom about women was still the one voiced earlier by Jean Jacques Rousseau: "A woman, who is naturally weak, and does not carry her ideas to any extent, knows how to judge and make a proper estimate of those movements with which she sets to work in order to aid her weakness; and those movements are the passions of men."

The emerging theories of medical "science" incorporated the myths of female weakness.[5] Medical texts of the nineteenth century declared that in males the intellectual faculties ruled, while in women the nervous system and emotions overruled intellect. In 1882, one Dr. Holbrook, author of a text on childbirth, declared, "The almighty in creating the female sex had taken the uterus and built a woman around it." The idea of woman as dominated by emotions was linked to the idea that any intellectual effort by young women would damage their developing reproductive organs; any strenuous course of study would be harmful to a woman's health. The brain and ovaries could not develop at the same time, it was believed.

We can only speculate about the degree to which this philosophy stunted the intellectual growth of women. M. Carey Thomas,[6] one of the pioneers of education for women and president of Bryn Mawr College, gave some sense of the impact of the ideas of the day on bright young women. She said in a speech in 1907, "I was always wondering whether it could really be true, as everyone thought, that boys were cleverer than girls. Indeed, I cared so much that I never dared ask any grown-up person the direct question, not even my father or mother, because I feared to hear the reply . . . I can remember weeping over the account of Adam and Eve, because it seemed to me that the curse pronounced on Eve might imperil girls' going to college . . . I was terror struck lest I, and every other woman with me, were doomed to live as pathological invalids in a universe merciless to woman as a sex."

Thomas describes how she paid a special visit to the one college woman she could find, trembling with fear that the woman would be some kind of freak, and heaving a great sigh of relief when she was not.

The idea of damage to women because of intellectual pursuits lingers on. In 1944, nearly half a century after M. Carey Thomas worried about the story of Adam and Eve, Helene Deutsch,[7] a disciple of Freud, wrote, "intellectuality is, to a large extent, paid for by the loss of valuable feminine qualities; it feeds on the sap of the affective life and results in impoverishment of this life either as a whole or in specific emotional qualities."

So it is not surprising that historically women have been second-class citizens in the whole educational process. Not only were they late entrants into the world of scholarship, but they were often ignored once they got through the doors. The studies done on underachievers in schools and on children who have trouble in reading are almost exclusively focused on males. Not until fairly recently has concern surfaced about how girls fare in schools, about what happens to them inside the classrooms. The Carnegie Commission on Higher Education, investigating the low enrollment of women in graduate schools, found a consistent pattern in American education: Girls achieve better grades

220

than boys at a young age, but the girls' grades decline with age until, by the graduate school level, the boys have surpassed them.

The schools cannot be solely blamed for this pattern. Children absorb sex-role stereotypes very early, as we've seen, and when they reach adolescence, girls fear that being too intellectual may interfere with their relationships with boys. But we can ask whether schools diminish or reinforce the sex-role stereotypes—particularly the ones that are harmful to a girl's sense of her own competence and talents. The answer seems to be that schools, like most of society's institutions, reflect the status quo: They tend to reinforce the behavior that conventional wisdom regards as appropriate at the time. There are a number of ways in which schools buttress the status quo; one of these is by the way the teachers interact with children.

Our society encourages boys to be active and independent, and girls to be dependent and passive. Do schools also reward the same virtues in each sex? There is evidence that they do.

One researcher, State University of New York's Lisa Serbin,[8] wanted to look at the ways teachers behave differently with boys and girls. She and a group of colleagues designed studies of two kinds of teacher behavior: how they dealt with children who were being aggressive, and whether or not they tended to reward dependent behavior in girls. The results of the studies were intriguing.

First of all, the teachers responded more often to aggressive behavior by boys than by girls; teachers responded to the boys' unruly behavior more than 80 percent of the time with a reprimand or some comment, but responded to the girls' aggressive behavior only 23 percent of the time. In other words, boys learn that acting unruly can be an effective attention-getting device. Girls who act up tend to be ignored.

Many studies of elementary-school teachers show a preference for what is considered "feminine" behavior in both sexes in young children—diligence, good behavior, not too much assertiveness. Teachers in elementary schools tend to be tougher on the boys, who are usually noisier and rowdier, and require attention just to keep order in the classroom. But to be less strict with the girls denies them standards to live up to. Some teachers show too much willingness to help a little girl with a problem she should work out by herself. Girls can easily fall into a pattern of learning not to try—of always asking for help without really making a concerted invididual effort to solve problems. This pattern can

221

be deadly to a child's sense of competence, because the child comes to believe she is incapable of performing on her own and incorporates that notion into her self-image.

In fact, Serbin and her colleagues found, teachers responded more often to boys than to girls, whether they were acting up or not. The only time girls got consistent attention from the teacher was when they were quite close to her. They report, "It does appear that all activities of boys, appropriate or inappropriate, are more likely to receive teacher attention. Girls are more likely to be ignored, except when directly beside the teacher." Girls got the teacher's attention by moving up close to her; boys were able to command the teacher's attention from any place in the room.

The researchers also noticed that the teachers used different teaching styles in working with the boys and the girls. The boys, they noted, tended to get detailed instructions in how to do things when they solicited the teacher's attention. Girls more often got praise, physical attention or had things done for them.

These differences, the researchers say, could affect the children's development. "Detailed direction, training in 'how to do something for yourself,' appears to encourage exploration and manipulation of the environment and simultaneously to provide a model for step-by-step problem solving. The existence of differences in the average amount of this sort of training given to boys might well be partially responsible for the sex differences in analytical and spatial reasoning reported in the primary grades and beyond."

This pattern could also make a girl feel ineffective in controlling her environment or make her hesitant to venture too far from the teacher, since the attention of the teacher, which is what she wants, is given only when she is in close range. One thoughtful preschool teacher says she has to remind herself to sit down and get involved with pairs of girls who are playing quietly rather than reserve her attention for the noisier boys.

If a girl's closeness to the teacher can encourage dependency and discourage her from independent work, it does seem to foster the development of verbal and other communication skills. Close interaction with an adult is a boon to these skills. Serbin and her colleagues speculate that boys may lag behind in skills learned by imitation and close relationship with an adult because they don't spend much time close to the teacher. They suggest that the increasing number of male teachers in elementary schools could change this pattern somewhat. In any event, girls would benefit if they were encouraged to spend more time away from the immediate vicinity of the teacher, and still be able to get her attention. What boys need, it seems, may be more opportunity to develop their communication skills through close interaction with an adult.

It's easy, too, for teachers not to notice when girls are timid—when they don't offer to read aloud, when they don't volunteer to lead a project, when they defer to others in an activity in which they might have to display their abilities. One fourth-grade teacher says, "I see that all the time—the girls holding back." Often, the overburdened and harried teacher just tries to get through the day, and the problem of such girls, being a quiet problem, is overlooked.

Teachers, like the rest of us, have grown up in a society where sex-role stereotypes are presumed to be the natural order of things. It's reasonable for them to be most comfortable when boys and girls act the way they are "supposed" to act. In one study of the kind of students elementary-school teachers preferred, the best-liked student was the girl who was dependent but also did well at her studies.[9] The least-liked student was the assertive, independent girl.

The picture changes at the high-school level. Girls are no longer the most preferred students. In a 1973 study of high-school teachers, these teachers said they preferred working with males, on the grounds that the boys were more active in exchanging ideas.[10] (This is the time, of course, when the "dropping-back" syndrome that afflicts girls at adolescence is in full sway.) The few teachers who preferred girls almost always referred to the ease in disciplining them.

These teachers also said they thought boys and girls *expected* to be treated differently, that boys expected teachers to be stricter with them. And, in practice, they usually are.

To the child, the school is a universe—and in the past, it was one brimming with sex-role stereotypes. There were books that showed only little boys having adventures, extensive athletic programs for boys while the girls got intramural volleyball, and limited career options offered to girls by guidance counselors. A great deal of attention has been paid to these issues in the past few years, and things are changing—but how much change is just on the surface?

The question of school textbooks is a case in point. In the early seventies, a task force of the National Organization for Women came out with a report on textbooks called, "Dick and Jane as Victims." They found that girls were portrayed less often than boys, tended to be minor characters or onlookers and showed fear and passivity much more often than independence or assertiveness. Pictures of mothers suggested that they were born wearing aprons, with babies affixed to their arms. The experiences and contributions of women were also found to be completely ignored in social studies curricula.

Women's groups put pressure on the schools and publishing companies to change all this. Today, many of the major publishers have come out with new series of books purporting to portray women in a better and more realistic light. But the question is, how well do they do the job? A research team at the Feminist Press in Old Westbury, New York, surveyed books published in the past five years.[11] Their conclusion: Among commercial publishers, tokenism has been masquerading as progress. The team selected books that were categorized as nonsexist, with particular emphasis on those with a girl as an active protagonist. Frequently in these books, the team said, the girl is placed in a "stereotyped environment where she exists as a 'freak' and must constantly prove herself. She is often loved in spite of, rather than because of, her individuality."

The team said that it was the rare book that showed independent adult women as well as the "nonconformist" young girl. "The message here is that you may manage to get away with unorthodox behavior as a child, but be prepared to give up your freedom when you grow up."

The researchers concluded that the prodding of the commercial houses by women's groups and others to get rid of stereotypes has had only limited success so far. "Our initial optimism about the appearance of a handful of very good books dissipated when we realized how few they were in relation to the approximately 2500 children's books published a year. At a recent conference on children's literature, a participant queried, 'When is this whole equality thing going to end? Hasn't it gone far enough?' If such a question is still being asked, then clearly we still have a lot more prodding to do."

Even when good books are available, the question is, how often and how widely are they used? In one Massachusetts school system, two teachers who had fought for the inclusion of new materials in the classroom and libraries reported that often the books were left to gather dust on the shelves, and that there was great resistance on the part of many teachers to using them.

Caryl's daughter, a third grader, brought home one of her school readers. It wasn't any different from the texts Caryl remembered from her school days. There were a number of stories about boys having wonderful adventures and being heroic. There were two stories about girls—in one, two girls bought the same dress at the store and didn't know it until they wore it to school. In another, a girl lost a bunny and a grown-up male found it for her. Caryl had this conversation about the book with her daughter, Alyssa:

"Do you have any stories about girls in the books you read?"

"Some."

"How about the stories of grown-up women? Do they do anything else but wear aprons and clean the house, like the ones in this book?"

"Nope. That's all they do. All the time."

"Is that what you think grown-up ladies do?"

"No, grown-ups don't just stay in the house and do housework all the time."

"How do you know that?"

"You go to work. So do Nancy and Sue. So does Trina's mother."

The books were obviously out of date about women's lives in today's world.

Another area where schools have tended to buttress the status quo in a manner that is not helpful to girls who will have to face the real world at graduation is in vocational choice and counseling. The material offered to girls about possible career choices still tends to be stereotyped into acceptable "male" and "female" jobs. In one study, guidance counselors were shown tapes of interviews with two girls who had made "deviant" (engineering) or "traditional" (home economics) career choices.[12] While the counselors reported that they liked both girls, the girl who had chosen home economics was seen as having made a better, more appropriate choice, while the girl who chose engineering was seen to be in need of vocational counseling.

For girls, the area of vocational choice may be another of those areas in which some change has occurred, but how much? Conservative columnist George Will wrote in *Newsweek*: "A mother in the school car pool swears she will strangle the next girl who announces an intention to be a lawyer. Suddenly the world seems infested with Napoleonic little girls who probably read Nietzsche and certainly burn with the desire to right wrongs and unchain the oppressed."

This may indeed be the case in Will's upper-middle-class Washington suburb, but it is definitely not the norm in a lower-middle-class town near Boston where the fifth-grade girls are talking about getting married and falling in love with the latest rock star idol.

(The adjective George Will applies to the little girls in his neighborhood who want to be lawyers is interesting: "Napoleonic." Boys of that social class who chose high-status careers are not seen as being possessed of overbearing ambition. They are expected to do so; in fact, in many of these neighborhoods, parents would have a seizure when confronted by a son who said he wanted to be an auto mechanic.)

Even in the upper-middle-class areas where it's chic for girls to talk about law school, how likely is it that they will actually be taking their bar exams some years hence? One guidance counselor in such a suburb has noticed the "lawyer" syndrome among young girls but wonders if it isn't simply the latest "glamour" ambition, replacing the wish to be a stewardess or a movie star. She notices that while junior-high-school girls may announce such intentions, they don't seem to do anything about them—just as the young girl who wishes she could be a ballerina doesn't practice her *plies*.

Even if a young female student is not being very realistic about becoming a lawyer, at least she has begun to think of her future career choice in nonstereotyped ways. Because of this, when she comes to making a serious choice, she may have a better chance of matching up her abilities with a career. Perhaps she won't fall into the trap of settling for a job just because it's something women are supposed to do. The young girl from a working-class family is often not so fortunate. She tends to see her future in much more limited terms, and unless someone opens a door for her, starts her thinking about what she might do with her talents in the job world, her options will be limited. San Francisco sociologist Lillian Rubin, in her study of the working-class family, *Worlds of Pain*, points out that girls in such families often find homelife very restrictive and yearn for a way out. Often they have to carry a heavy burden of work in the home, they are under heavier parental restriction than middle-class girls because "the culture dictates that 'nice' girls remain under the parental roof until a husband comes to take them away. For them, there is no other road to womanhood and independence."

These girls, as Rubin points out, rarely have a choice as to whether they will work or stay home. "Even those who wish least to work outside the home probably will do so sometime in their lives." This being the case, it is crucial for them to do as well as they can in the job market. If

226

they don't understand the importance of acquiring job skills, they will simply be fodder for what Lillian Rubin calls "the needs of the economy for a cheap supplemental labor pool that can be moved in and out of the labor force as the economy expands and contracts."

The person who deals with these questions at the high-school level is the guidance counselor, who is caught today in the conflicting currents that have traditionally been played out in the American public schools. One current moves in the direction of change. As historian David Tyack points out, schools have been chosen as the focal point for reforms in American society—racial integration being one of the latest and most dramatic examples. Educators are asked to be ahead of society at large, to be more free of prejudice, more enlightened in their views, in order to take the lead in undoing and remedying injustice. At the same time, the schools were also given the major job of "Americanizing" generations of children whose parents had come here from foreign shores. This meant that the schools had to put a premium on homogenization, on producing people who were more alike than different, who could function in American society as something other than strangers. This pull toward standardization, toward a lack of individualism, toward producing a student who would adjust to the society rather than vice versa, is a current that tends to support the status quo. Edgar Z. Friedenberg wrote in *The Vanishing Adolescent*, "In a school system whose historical function has been making Americans out of immigrants' children, students are likely to find they can only win esteem by how they look and behave, not for what they are. The effect of this is a severe form of alienation; they lose faith in their own right to an independent judgement of their own worth."

The school, particularly the high school, writes Friedenberg, is often primarily concerned with the adjustment of the student to societal norms. This pressure for adjustment to middle-class norms and values is harmful to working-class and poor students because it disparages their own experiences and values. His study, like most others, was concerned mainly with boys, and girls received little mention. But it's clear that the pressure for standardization that he observes can have an equally harmful effect on girls. Too often they are asked to adjust to a definition of themselves as docile, dependent, passive, and suited only to certain kinds of roles carefully labeled as sex-appropriate.

All throughout their school years—from kindergarten through high school—traditional definitions of the "good girl" hold true. Not only are girls expected to be this way, but they are rewarded for it—with good grades and teacher approval. On the surface, this kind of girl seems to be doing well in school. Psychologists Judith Bardwick and Elizabeth Douvan,[13] writing about the early years of grammar school, ask, "What do girls do especially well in? What are they being asked to master? Grammar, spelling, reading, arithmetic—tasks that depend a great deal upon memorization and demand little independence, assertiveness, analysis, innovativeness and creativity. The dependent, passive girl, cued into the affirming responses of teachers, succeeds and is significantly rewarded for her 'good' behavior and her competent memorizing skills."

Now, it's true that those memory skills are a crucial foundation for the rest of intellectual development. The child who doesn't learn to read will never do well in school. There is a point, however, at which the student has to pass beyond mere mastery of such skills to independent thought and analysis. For a number of students—male and female—that never happens. One university professor observes that by the time they reach college, many students are experts at regurgitation. They take notes on everything and think all that is required of them is to parrot back what the teachers or the textbooks say. So it's not exclusively a problem for girls. But it may be tougher for girls to cross the border between rote learning and creative thinking because girls receive more rewards for dependence and fewer for independence than boys do.

Part of this problem may be the nature of the environment in the schools. As Douvan and Bardwick point out: "Schools are generally feminine places, institutions where conformity is valued, taught largely by conforming women. The course content, the methods of assessing progress, and the personal conduct required create difficulties for boys, who must inhibit impulsivity, curb aggression, and restrain deviance. The reward structure of the school system perpetuates the pattern set by relationships with the parents—boys are further pressured to turn to their peers for acceptance and to develop internal criteria and objective achievements; girls are further urged to continue the nondeviant, noninnovative, conformist style of life."

"Feminine places" are the words Douvan and Bardwick use to describe the environment that is the school. Historian David Tyack refers to schools as "pedagogical harems"—the sultans, of course, being the principals and superintendents. Since children spend so much of their time in the schools, it's obvious that they learn much about the structure of society in that microcosm; they certainly learn some lessons about who are the Indians and who are the chiefs.

228

In American schools, women constitute 60 percent of all teachers and 80 percent of all elementary-school teachers; but 80 percent of all elementary-school principals and 98 percent of all high-school principals are men. Only about 1 percent of school superintendents are women. There is a vocational pyramid with men on the top and women on the bottom. The position of women today is worse than it was in the 1940s, when 41 percent of all elementary-school principals were women, although statistics from that era probably reflect the absence of men because of World War II.

What message is given to children—girls in particular—when most teachers are female and principals and superintendents are not, asks Harvard sociologist Sara Lightfoot[14]: "Does it seem confusing to children that the woman teacher dominates their world behind the classroom door while men (i.e., the principal, her husband) control the teacher in the outside world?"

It is probably not confusing for long. Children soon sort out the difference between being in charge of children and being in charge of the world. As the girl advances and enters college and graduate school, she sees, once again, that senior professors are mostly males, although women may be instructors, lecturers or laboratory assistants.

How and why did teaching—below the university level—get to be a largely female profession? Historically, we find a twofold cause: economics and the accepted ideas about the nature of women. During the fifty years from 1870 to 1920, public education expanded rapidly in an America that was changing from a rural nation to an urban one. Coupled with a growing school population was a labor-short economy; there was an urgent need for teachers who would put in long hours for little pay. Women, unmarried women in particular, were thought to be perfect candidates for the job—not only because women were thought to have a special understanding of children, but because women themselves were thought to possess certain childlike qualities. The woman teacher was expected to be able to deal with children, but at the same time she would be a submissive, easily managed employee. She was not expected—or encouraged—to have a voice in policy-making or management. In the 1860s the National Education Association did not permit full membership to women; they had to sit in the galleries at meetings and could not address the gathering.

The women teachers are out of the balconies now, but they do not seem to be advancing very far up the leadership ladder in the educational field. Male domination is the pattern of the upper echelons of education and there is often little concern about changing that pattern. In a 1975 analysis of school systems in the Boston area, writer Ruth Baden found little interest or concern among school administrators with the absence of women in their ranks.[15] Baden described the process of choosing principals and superintendents as nominally open and competitive, but in reality a fairly closed process: It begins with the advertising of positions but ends with the recommendations of male superintendents and staff. One personnel officer told her, "Actually we have a pretty good idea of who would make a good principal and we try to provide these people with leadership opportunities." There seemed to be no awareness that the resulting all-male structure should be any cause for concern. When Baden mentioned to an administrator the problem of women having no power, the administrator told her it was only her own small-minded view of power that was the problem: "This school system doesn't view principals and heads of departments as more powerful than teachers." The teachers would probably give a good horselaugh at that one. They know who can hire and fire and promote them, and if that isn't "power," what is?

It is true that until recently, administrators did not find many candidates even in the systems that were open to women. In the past, few women entered doctoral programs in educational administration, perhaps because to enroll required a self-image of oneself as a leader—of men as well as of women. When Baden asked one teacher if she had ever thought of becoming a principal, she said, "I couldn't expose myself like that—or balance a budget or do the things a principal has to do. I like to make waves, but when it comes to a confrontation, I hide behind the principal."

But for the women who did aspire to a leadership role, the doors were often barred. Administrative jobs in education are seen as "business" jobs—male arenas. Boards of education are like the boards of directors of any corporation—run by men. One survey of Oregon school superintendents done by researcher Patricia Schmuck[16] found that they preferred men as school board members, although some wanted the kind of women who "know when to keep their mouths shut."

These male-dominated boards want candidates who can fit into the old-boy network, who can attend Rotary meetings and get on well with male politicians, David Tyack points out. One woman administrator was told by a school board that although she was the best qualified candidate for superintendent, she was denied the job because hiring a woman would disturb conservative elements in the community.

230

When Patricia Schmuck interviewed administrators in the Oregon public school system, the men often cited their need to work closely with other administrators as a reason for their reluctance to hire women:

"It's easier to work without women. Principals and superintendents are a management team . . . We need each other for survival . . . I wonder if we could hang together so well if some of us were women. Could she protect my job as well as her own? I don't have that concern with a guy; he talks the same language."

A school superintendent in Utah told a reporter that aside from the woman who ran his lunch program, he was opposed to women administrators. Not only does no one want to work for a woman, he said, but "productivity in the school business is much better when males run the operation than when women do."

Is this true? Do things run better when men run the show? A national research study of elementary-school principals by social scientists Neal Gross and A. E. Trask found that students learned more and teachers performed better in schools with women principals.[17] What does this finding reflect? Not that women by nature make better principals, but that when a woman does get appointed, she is usually better qualified than most males. It may also reflect the fact that women who become principals have usually had extensive teaching experience, and thus understand teachers, students and their problems. Male administrators typically go right to a desk job without really knowing about the dynamics of the classroom or the system. The authors comment: "Women principals, perhaps because of the bias against them, were older and more experienced than the men; in fact, 34 percent of the male principals had *never* taught in the elementary schools compared with only 3 percent of the women."

As for the notion that no one wants to work for a woman, the researchers found that no differences in teacher morale were associated with the sex of the principals.

Their findings, Gross and Trask say, give the lie to the arguments generally used by school officials in defense of hiring primarily male elementary-school principals. In fact, one of the damaging consequences of this pattern, they say, has been that "the learning of pupils and the quality of performance of teachers has been adversely affected."

Clearly, the sexual division of labor in education will have to change if students are not going to expect the world to be like school where the women are in lower-paid positions with little authority. It seems important for both boys and girls that they see both men and women as classroom teachers, principals and superintendents.

Today, most teachers below the college level are women, and that fact could have a positive effect on education. They could constitute the critical mass necessary for a reform movement in education. Florence Howe, editor of the Carnegie Commission's *Women and the Power to Change*, writes, "Instead of bemoaning the fact that women numerically dominate the teaching, nursing, and social work professions, why not consider the fact strategically? Why encourage the most talented women to enter a physics laboratory rather than a school superintendent's office or a department of educational administration? Why is it more important to spread a thin tokendom of women throughout the non-traditional kingdoms than to attempt a transformation of those traditional ghettoes themselves—especially if one of those, the public school system, is responsible for the perpetuation of sex stereotyping and the low aspirations of women? . . ." In studies of education, Howe says:

> . . . women emerge as victims of both discrimination and socialization, but not as potential agents of their own change, much less agents of social change more generally. Since numbers are obviously useful for both building a base of support for change and for providing a wide pool of talent from which to draw leaders, I would concentrate major energies during the next decade on the female professions, especially public school teaching. If schools are the major social agency responsible for socialization of the young, and if these schools are populated mainly with women, themselves socialized to do the job, clearly it is essential to release those teachers from the treadmill. The process needed is one similar to that invented by teachers of women's studies: new teaching strategies and a curriculum that builds on the experiences of those teaching . . . Each year that I have traveled, I have met intrepid feminist teachers, leaving or in the process of leaving public education—whether for law school or a Ph.D. program, and often with a special interest in women's studies. Some of these women could have offered an alternative vision to traditional leadership, but to none of them had such a possibility occurred.

If the young girl attending school sees a "harem," when she gets to the university level, she is more likely to be confronted with something like a men's bar. While the lower grades are "feminine" in atmosphere, centers of higher education are overwhelmingly masculine, with women holding down a small percentage of the most valued academic jobs—full and associate professorships. Arlie Russell Hochschild writes in *Women and the Power to Change*, that for women students, the atmosphere is not welcoming. There are, for example, "the invisibility of women among the teachers and writers of the books one reads or among the faces framed on the walls of the faculty club; the paucity of women at the informal gathering over beer after the seminar. Then there are the pre-lecture jokes (to break the ice) that refer in some ways to pretty girls as a distraction or to getting into 'virginal' fields. There is also the continual, semiconscious work of sensing and avoiding professors who are known to dislike or discredit women or particular types of women."

A study sponsored by the U.S. Office of Education in 1971 found that "discrimination against women, in contrast to that against minorities, is overt and socially acceptable within the academic community."

The student at a university may find that not only does she not "fit in" in the seminar or the department, but she is not visible in the curriculum, either. Poet and professor Adrienne Rich[18] says, "What we have at present is a man-centered university, a breeding ground not of humanism but of masculine privilege. As women have gradually and reluctantly been admitted into the mainstream of higher education, they have been made participants in a system that prepares men to take up roles of power in a man-centered society, that asks questions and teaches 'facts' generated by a male intellectual tradition that both subtly and openly confirms men as the leaders and shapers of human destiny both within and outside academia."

In the context of a woman's education, Rich writes, "There is no discipline that does not obscure or devalue the history or experience of women as a group . . . Outside of women's studies, though liberal male professors may introduce material about women into their courses, we live with textbooks, scholarly sources, and lectures that treat women as a subspecies, only as peripheral to the history of men. In every discipline where we are considered, women are perceived as the objects rather than the originators of inquiry, primarily through male eyes, thus as a special category."

The absence of role models for women in higher education can be a stumbling block for a young woman who is looking for some image of herself in the future, some adult possibility. It is clear that girls need access to adult authority figures who are female and credible in the male world if they are to overcome the built-in tendency to devalue information when it comes from a female source. Sociologist Jessie Bernard[19] found, for example, that in a situation where a male and a female lecturer were trained to give the same lecture in the same manner, students perceived them differently. Students saw the male lecturer as presenting "facts," but thought the woman was merely presenting her "opinions." One 1975 study set out to examine interactions between professors and students.[20] It found that professors, whether male or female, responded as readily to male as female students when it came to answering their questions and encouraging discussion. Female students, however, were less likely to respond when professors asked questions and were less likely to volunteer comments than were males. These tendencies were lessened when the professor was female, the researchers said, perhaps because she was seen as less authoritarian and demanding. But the female students preferred the male teachers, tending to devalue members of their own sex despite the fact that they performed better with the female professors.

If the young women students take their male professors more seriously than female ones, the reverse is not the case: Male professors often do not take women students seriously. In a recent Carnegie Commission survey of 32,000 graduate students in sociology, 22 percent of the men and 50 percent of the women believed that the faculty did not take women graduate students seriously.

Of course, many male professors do take a genuine interest in the progress of their female students. As Adrienne Rich points out, "many intellectual women have been encouraged and trained by their gifted fathers or gifted male teachers. But it is the absence of the brilliant and creative mother, or woman teacher, that is of more importance than the presence of the brilliant and creative male . . . He may well be in a position to give her more, in terms of influence, training and emotional gratification, than any woman on the scene. If she succeeds, it is partly that she has succeeded in pleasing him, winning his masculine interest and attention."

The uglier side of the erotic aspect of the relationship between male professors and female students emerged into the public eye in 1977 when women students at Yale brought a suit claiming that sexual harassment of students by faculty members was common. When Adrienne Munich,[21] a fellow at the Center for Independent Study in New Haven, Connecticut, investigated sexual harassment on campuses, she was told by a professor at Yale Medical School, "The students call it put out or fail."

Not all the erotic encounters are under duress, of course. Many young women willingly get involved in such adventures without realizing the psychological forces at work in such relationships. Paul Schwaber, a Wesleyan University humanities professor, told Adrienne Munich that "By idealizing us, or falling in love with us, or with our styles of mind, students can enter our subject matters vitally, gain personal access to knowledge and mature thought. The danger is that they can relive needs of a much earlier dependency.

"For us, the danger is a Pygmalion fantasy. Those of us who teach college students deal with young people when they are most physically beautiful, most open to new thought and experience. All while we get older. It's quite a lure. We meet them vulnerably because we can see in them our past youth and thus an ideal and ghostly image of ourselves."

Schwaber believes the teacher is obliged to recognize these dangers and take them into account in dealing with students.

Adrienne Rich believes that the presence of more women as role models for female students, older women who could offer sympathy and support, would dilute the powerful image of the male as the source of wisdom. "Under such circumstances, it is likely that far less eroticism would glamourize the male teacher, and the woman student could use whatever he had to offer without needing to identify with him or adopt his perspective for her own."

The importance of female role models to the development of female competence should prompt us to take another look at a style of education which until fairly recently was thought to be going the way of the dodo: the single-sex school, which may offer young women some advantages that coeducation does not.

It has been part of the tradition of American progressive thought that all segregation is bad, whether of the sexes or the races. The underlying pressure for integration is the unequal status of the two groups involved. Usually there is a dominant group that is privileged, and an "underdog" group fighting to advance. Segregation is seen, often correctly, as an attempt to keep the less favored group in its place.

Segregation has been violently attacked because it runs contrary to liberal ideology. But there are two kinds of segregation—that which is imposed by others, from above, and voluntary segregation, in which the less-favored group separates in order to define its own goals, its own answers, its own style. This may be the case with single-sex education for women.

The data that we do have on the impact of single-sex education for women versus coeducation seem to show definite benefits attached to the single-sex school. A strikingly large percentage of successful women attended all-girls' colleges or high schools, where they may have received more encouragement from teachers who were not preoccupied with male students. The analogy to the daughter in a family that has no sons is clear—with no boys around, attention focuses on the girl. When Elizabeth Tidball[22] of George Washington University Medical School examined the records of fifteen hundred women in *Who's Who of American Women* in 1973, she found that a disproportionate percentage had attended all-female colleges. An analysis of her data indicated that the crucial difference seemed to be the large numbers of women faculty at the schools they attended. The number of men in the college environment related negatively to a woman's later achievement. The more men there were, the more the women seemed to slip behind.

Opponents of all-female institutions feel that women must learn early to deal with the real world, to compete with men and to test themselves against the whole range of talent available in society. The crucial question is—at what point in her life should the young girl do that? In a co-ed institution, is she vulnerable to the stereotyped ideas of women that society holds dear, as well as the ghettoization of female talent? In single-sex schools, women are the captains of the varsity teams, editors of the school paper and captains of the debating teams. In co-ed schools, these positions were held almost exclusively by men—most of them still are. The reluctance to compete against men that surfaces at adolescence may keep a woman student from stretching her talents and trying for high-level student positions. One intriguing study, done in 1974, measured "fear of success" in girls in co-ed and single-sex schools.[23] Girls in co-ed high schools were found to be significantly higher in fear of success than girls from all-girls schools. But none of the girls in a co-ed high school who had attended an all-girls elementary school showed evidence of this pattern. The researchers' interpretation was that early attendance at an all-girls school can provide some "immunity" from the forces that create ambivalence toward success. Perhaps nonstereotyped behavior becomes frequent, rewarding and thus habit-forming.

This immunity is something all girls can use, given the pervasiveness

236

of sex stereotypes. They are like mercury—slippery, always darting through our fingers. They are hard to fight because they are inside our heads. We reinforce them unconsciously, not out of malice but out of habit.

In the era when these stereotypes weren't seen as a problem—when it was thought to be perfectly fine that little girls didn't play baseball and little boys didn't cry—the single-sex school may have been one of the few places where girls could get some insulation against damaging stereotypes. Today, any school that is serious about developing students' full potential can start to counteract the viruses of underachievement, passivity and dependence. But the problem of stereotypes can easily be ignored; they are so pervasive as to be almost invisible, and school personnel must deal with what may appear to be more urgent problems—slow readers, emotionally disturbed children, budget constraints. Society asks more and more of its schools. Educators juggle so many problems, they must often feel as though they are tossing oranges in the air and hoping none lands on their heads.

Nuts and Bolts

The school is a large part of the child's world, where she spends nine months a year, five days a week, six hours a day. It's clear that what goes on in schools is vitally important in the lives of girls. Today, educators are beginning to recognize the problems girls have had in the past with achievement, independence and, of course, sex-role stereotypes. But too often, despite good intentions, efforts to remedy these problems are little more than token ones.

Although, unlike years past, good materials do exist now to help teachers deal with sex-role stereotypes, the best materials in the world won't make any difference at all if they aren't used—and if teachers in the classroom don't make strenuous efforts to understand how girls' talents and aspirations can be crippled by stereotypes. When teachers do start thinking and caring about these issues, good things happen. When we attended a faculty meeting at a junior high school, we were heartened by the lively interest teachers had in these topics, how eager they were to talk about these issues. When teachers jointly focus on them, questions get raised that might not otherwise surface. For example, one male teacher who taught biology said that when his class had to dissect a fish, he expected the boys to dive right in and the girls to be squeamish. It happened the other way around: the girls coolly sliced up the fish and the boys made faces. "Who says girls can't be surgeons?" he asked.

One of the women teachers chimed in, "But how did the girls code their behavior? I'll bet they weren't thinking 'surgeon.' They were thinking 'cooking.'" In other words, it might not occur to the girls that cutting up a fish was like what surgeons and scientists do, not just something their mothers do making dinner. If the teacher were to point out that the girls were good at this activity, and that surgeons and scientists have to be good at it also, the girls might make an important connection. Otherwise, the opportunity could well slip away.

As this example demonstrates, faculty dialogue can produce valuable insights into the problem of stereotypes. We recommend that such discussions be part of the *formal* agenda for school faculties. It would be helpful if people with special concern and knowledge in this area could act as catalysts for such sessions.

In many schools, resistance to the idea of combating sex-role stereotypes can be a real stumbling block to progress. Barbara Grizzuti Harrison, in *Unlearning the Lie: Sexism in Schools,*[24] found this to be true in one private, progressive school. The school took great pride in its success in combating racism, but pulled back when it came to sexism. There was anguished debate about whether children would experience "confusion" about their gender. There was more debate about whether it was proper to "impose" nonsexist values on children who were supposed to be learning to make their own moral judgments. (No one complained about "imposing" nonracist attitudes on the children.) Harrison described how the parents gradually came to realize the damage rigid sex roles did to their children. Only then did the school begin to change.

Sex-role stereotypes are tenacious and can't be eradicated by one-shot efforts—just as racist ideas don't disappear with a few nice words about black folks in a classroom. The power of stereotypes is illustrated by one study[25] in which first-, fourth- and seventh-grade classes were shown a videotape of a child's visit to his pediatrician, who was female. A male nurse greeted the boy. The names of each were repeated several times during the film: Dr. Mary Nancy and Nurse David Gregory. When the first graders were asked later about the film, *all but one* gave a male name to the doctor and a female name to the nurse. Results for the fourth graders were similar. Among seventh graders, however, only about 10 percent gave the wrong answer.

238

This study suggests that older children are more capable of accepting nontraditional sex-role behavior than younger ones are. Still, we shouldn't discourage attempts to tackle stereotypes at an early age. Even if children don't show much change right away, that doesn't mean there hasn't been or won't be change. There may be a "sleeper effect" operating, so that some time has to elapse before the change takes effect or becomes evident.

What can teachers and parents do with children on a day-to-day basis to help this process? First of all, they should remember that what adults do can have a powerful effect on children. Children imitate grown-ups they care about, and it is a vital process in their development. If an adult gets involved in an activity that crosses traditional sex lines, children, especially those of the same sex, may feel they have a green light to do the same. It also gives them permission to learn skills they otherwise wouldn't have mastered.

In one school a popular young teacher, himself an accomplished athlete, showed his fourth-grade boys how to jump rope and explained that fighters trained that way. Soon the boys were bringing their own jump ropes to school and jumping in the schoolyard. When boys from other grades started teasing them, the boys got together and counterattacked, saying the other boys were so dumb they didn't know this was how fighters trained. So, in effect, jumping rope was transformed from a sissy girl's game into an acceptable sport with a male image, and then the boys took part in it.

Another example of the power of modeling comes from Lisa Serbin and her colleagues who designed an intervention program at the nursery school level.[26] First, she gathered data about the children's play. Girls played much more frequently in the sandbox; boys played much more often with blocks. This was without the involvement of teachers, who were women. Serbin then instructed the teachers to engage in both those activities. When a teacher was building with blocks, many more girls joined in the activity. When the teacher went to the sandbox, the boys followed, too.

But what happened when the teacher stopped this kind of play? Did the children go right back to their old ways? In this case, they didn't. Girls still spent considerably more time with the blocks and boys spent somewhat more time in the sandbox. There was a long-term effect of the teachers' modeling, especially among the girls, because they had a model of the same sex to follow. Also, the block-building may have given the girls a chance for more imaginative play than the sandbox and more opportunity to use a variety of visual and spatial abilities.

If teachers' modeling can have a powerful effect on children's behavior, the jobs they assign to children in the classroom can be equally important, as the following anecdote illustrates.

In their book, *Women of Crisis*,[27] Jane Hallowell Coles and Robert Coles describe the feelings of a maid, a working-class woman, employed by an affluent family. When the daughter came home complaining that her teacher always asked boys to open the window, it stirred a powerful memory in the older woman.

> ". . . On my way home I had these memories. I was in the third grade, and the teacher, 'Miss Rotten,' we used to call her, had the boys, always the boys, open and close the windows. It was an old school building, and the windows were long and I can still see that pole she had leaning in the corner near her desk.
>
> "Once I came home and told my mother that I had one wish—that before the school year was over, I'd be able to take that window pole and open and close the windows. I remember the catch on each window, and how the boys raised their arms and got closer and closer to the catch with the pole.
>
> "It seems silly now, but to third grade children it was a big moment in the day. The teacher made it that way; she didn't say a word while the boy was at work. We had three or four big windows, and she'd wait until they were all the way she wanted them and that pole back in the corner, before she resumed her talking to us . . . I'll bet any girl could have opened and closed those windows with that stick. By the end of the year, she [the teacher] had us girls convinced we couldn't do it. And in the sixth grade we weren't allowed to be safety monitors, either. I remember the teacher choosing them—all boys. They wore those white belts, and seemed so big and powerful to us. I never wanted to be a boy as much as I did those few weeks of the sixth grade . . . I used to dream of stealing those belts but of course I never did."

Grace recently heard about a similar problem from her daughter Susannah's fourth-grade teacher. The teacher noted with regret that there were still occasional requests over the school loudspeaker such as, "I need four strong boys." This teacher simply included strong girls in any delegation she sent to the office.

240

Note here that we're putting a great deal of emphasis on what teachers can do for children, and on the unconscious ways in which teachers may have contributed to girls' problems with achievement. This is not meant to induce guilt in teachers. They are often well aware of these problems but need support and information. All of us have probably engaged in behavior that hasn't been helpful to girls—whether they are our students or our daughters. We are asking teachers to be several giant steps ahead of society in their attitudes and actions, and that isn't always easy.

One concrete thing that teachers can do is to give girls detailed instructions on how to improve their work. As we've seen, girls take teachers' criticisms more to heart than boys do, and need to be given specific strategies to succeed. If they aren't, there is a strong tendency for them simply to think, "I can't do it," and just give up. Teachers should also keep in mind that girls need standards to live up to, and that "permission to fail" can be lethal to self-esteem. This is particularly true in areas thought of as traditionally masculine. When a girl doesn't do so well in math, it's easy not to push her because girls aren't expected to be math whizzes anyhow. Physical education teachers can easily fall into the trap of letting a girl loaf or quit because they see her as "fragile"—which, of course, she really isn't. Seemingly trivial actions by teachers, such as asking students to open the windows or empty a trash can or move a table, can have a considerable impact. By only asking boys to do these things, girls often feel resentful and get powerful messages about who the competent people are.

One area where the school can be very helpful to girls is career counseling. Unfortunately, in many schools, the "guidance" department means one overburdened counselor, dealing with so many students he or she can't even remember their names. Moreover, school guidance counselors too often look at girls as a class, rather than as individuals. They tend simply to think, "nursing is a good career for girls," rather than match individual skills with career possibilities. Girls need hard facts about the economic realities of certain jobs. Is the field already overcrowded? For example, given the glut of teachers in the country today, combined with the falling birthrate, it seems that only the most motivated students should be steered toward a teaching career. Counselors who still think "teaching is a good career for a woman" could do real harm to a girl's economic future. One woman, trained as a dental hygienist because "it was a good job for a woman," found that when she looked for a job some years later, she could find nothing for a year and a half, and then had to take a job that paid less than her previous position. No one had warned her that that field was becoming crowded. The Department of Labor issues projections of the need for various jobs in the years ahead. Parents and counselors should make such information available to girls. Girls should also be cautioned about the "pink collar ghetto"—women's traditional jobs usually offer less pay and less status than do other jobs.

We have seen that girls tend to choose less prestigious occupations than boys do. Girls should be made aware of this tendency and of its consequences. They should be encouraged to think about how much money they might be earning in various fields at age thirty-five and about the challenge and opportunities for personal growth.

School guidance counselors can make a powerful difference in girls' lives by giving them realistic information about the world—but first, they themselves must start thinking of girls as lifelong workers. If they are still thinking that girls will only play around with work until they get married, or have children, they are seriously out of touch with current reality.

Counselors may be even more important to the working-class girl than to the middle-class girl. First of all, it's almost certain that the working-class girl will spend most of her life in the job market. And she probably has fewer connections to that market—particularly to the network relevant to high-prestige jobs—than does the middle-class girl. She is in real danger of slipping into the "ghetto"—of joining the mass of underskilled, underpaid, overworked women who inhabit the lower rungs of the American marketplace.

Parents can have an impact on their daughter's school experience by keeping an eye on what is happening in the school. What kind of material are girls reading? What kinds of experience are they offered—do they take cooking while boys take shop? Are they presented with useful career-related information and guidance? Parents should feel free to express their concerns to teachers, school librarians, physical education teachers, principals. Often these professionals will be open to such discussions and eager to help. Both teachers and administrators can get so bogged down by the sheer demands of their jobs that issues involving girls just get lost in the shuffle. Parents can get together in groups to help schools devise creative solutions for these issues. But first they—mothers in particular—have to understand that they have a right to voice their concerns and raise issues. It can be hard sometimes for mothers to do this—particularly when they have to deal with male authority figures, such as principals. One strategy might be to approach the principal in a group of three or four; it's hard for a busy administrator to dismiss such a group compared with one "complaining" mother.

Female teachers should remember that their own behavior gives messages to girls. If the female teacher always behaves with extreme deference to male teachers or male administrators, that deference is not lost on little girls. Caryl remembers that when she went to parochial school, many of the nuns were firm and independent—until a priest came into the room. Suddenly, the iron disciplinarians started bowing, scraping and fluttering. Somebody really important—a man—had come on the scene.

In most schools, female teachers outnumber men, but rarely, it seems, do these teachers perceive themselves as a group with special concerns, who can meet together to talk about their own issues—promotion, authority, and so forth—and about the special problems of female students.

All educators, especially school administrators, ought to be concerned about the power structure of the school system. Is the pedagogical harem the predominant pattern? If the girls see no women who have any real authority, they are getting a strong message about who runs the world. If they see that men have the really important jobs, it's not surprising that by the time they get to college they devalue their female professors and see male professors as more important and more authoritative. Often, when they look around them, they see that women are lecturers and men are full professors; that fact alone gives them negative messages about their own potential.

From the little girl who shies away from the block corner, to the twenty-year-old B+ student who thinks she won't be able to do Ph.D. work, to the forty-year-old woman panic-stricken at the thought of going back to school to finish a bachelor's degree—school, for women, has too often been a sorry experience. It has been a place where she learned her limits, not her potential; where she learned to accept defeat, learned not to try, instead of taking chances and learning to succeed.

It doesn't have to be this way. Americans have long looked to the schools as one of the builders of the national character. The goal of the schools, writes Columbia historian Diane Ravitch,[28] is "to mold characters, to instill patriotism, to develop civic responsibility, to provide occupational training . . . and to create equality."

It's time the schools lived up to those goals—for the millions of children in their care who happen to be female.

12

LIFE CHOICES

The Traditional Role

Many women go through what might be called "The Incredible Invisible Woman Syndrome." Caryl remembers going to a party with her husband one night, at a time when he was working in television news. She felt after a few minutes that there were footprints on her back from people who were marching over her to talk to her husband. A professor who was seated next to her at dinner took time out from his conversation with a man across the table to say, "And I guess you stay home and raise kiddies?"

Caryl said, "Yes, I have fourteen of them, fathered by Ho Chi Minh and the Secretary of the Black Panthers."

The professor, preoccupied, smiled and said, "That's nice," and turned back to his conversation.

"Que sera, sera," goes the title of the popular song.

It's a catchy tune, easy to hum, but unfortunately describes the attitude too many young women have about their futures. It is hard for them to look toward the horizon and see any clear shapes there. But they are not alone in their paucity of images of what it is like to be a grown woman. The behavioral sciences seem to have regarded the lives of adult women as a sort of Gobi Desert for research. At least, that's how it appears when you look at the record books. There is a vast amount of theory, data and conjecture on woman in her role as mother of the child, but what of the woman herself? We have only just begun to ask those questions.

There is, for example, no major theory of adult development in women comparable to those which have been formulated for men. As is often the case, theory is developed for, about, and by men, and the "woman question" is an afterthought. Behavioral scientists peer at her and try to figure out some way to try and fit her in—if, that is, they bother with adult women at all. Erik Erikson[1] is responsible for the best-known theory of human development through the life cycle. He sees life as a series of stages each person passes through. One of the most crucial stages, that of late adolescence and early adulthood, involves the task of identity formation. Each person must ask—and answer—the question, "Who am I?" Late adolescence and early adulthood is the time, according to Erikson, when one establishes a definition of oneself and discovers a place in the adult world. We find this model inadequate for an understanding of the lives of women.

For many a young woman, the periods of late adolescence and early adulthood have been devoted to finding a husband and raising young children. The identity issue does not become salient until the child-rearing period starts to wane in her late thirties or early forties. Erikson realized that his theories didn't quite "fit" women's lives. Instead of juggling the theory to try to fit the women, however, he tried to fit the women to the theory. If identity formation has to be crucial for males at a certain time in their young lives, it must be equally so for women. If women don't find out who they are by going out and wrestling with the world, how do they do it? The answer, according to Erikson, is that the resolution of the identity crisis hangs on the choice of a mate. In other words, the woman's identity awaits, cannot exist without, a man.

This is a chilling notion. What it suggests is that the woman who does not marry never establishes an identity; she is incomplete, unformed. What of the woman who marries at forty? Does she suddenly, magically, become a person? What of the woman whose husband dies? Does he take her identity along with him across the great divide, rendering her again formless? It seems obvious that if a person finds her "identity" only by attaching her psyche to that of another, she has not found an identity at all, but has become a sort of parasite being, feeding off the emotional life of another. It also leaves her vulnerable to the shifting winds of personal relations. If she is divorced, her whole identity as "John's wife" vanishes. If she remarries, she becomes "Leonard's wife"; is that a whole different person from "John's wife"? It's a process that seems guaranteed to induce, at the very least, mild schizophrenia. It is this sort of absurdity

245

that occurs when women are accorded only hand-me-down theories that fit as well as a cut-down man's morning suit might fit.

The recent work of Yale's Daniel Levinson and his colleagues on adult development is another example of theory based on the male life cycle. Levinson, too, sees life as a series of stages. The twenties are the time for entering marriage and the world of work, and the thirties are the time for getting established in the working world. Toward forty, his studies of men's lives indicate, there is a reevaluation of the choices one has made and an attempt to free oneself from the powerful figures who have helped in the climb, the "mentors," they are called. This transition has been labeled the "BOOM" phenomenon—Becoming One's Own Man.

It's hard to know how to think about women in terms of this pattern. A woman may not enter the world of work until her thirties, she has seldom had a mentor, and even women with lifelong career commitments are rarely in a position to reassess their lives at age forty—particularly if they have had to slow down the pace of a career due to family responsibilities.

To date, the theories that we do have about how women live and grow seem to be a pastiche of old myths, stereotypes and views of females as "satellite" people, existing only in the orbit of male lives. Helena Z. Lopata,[2] chairperson of the sociology department at Loyola University of Chicago, notes with dismay that most theories start off by accepting the cultural notion that what women do is less important than what men do, and then proceed to lock a woman into rigid stages of development.

> Her life is portrayed as a sequence of definite and irreversible stages. She is expected to move from birth and home-oriented childhood into school attendance for a time sufficient to find a husband, but not so long as to waste valuable youth on knowledge to be used for only a short time. The next appropriate stages are work before and after marriage, giving birth to a limited number of children, rearing children, caring for her retired husband, widowhood and death . . . The basic personality is supposed to be early developed, then continuously the same. The young girl is supposed to be boy-clothes-popularity focused. Motherhood brings maturity. The more educated the woman, the more dissatisfied she is expected to become in middle years. Even the labor-saving devices which the society has provided her are dysfunctional to the housewife, because they leave her with nothing to do . . . By past standards of virtue, she is defined as increasingly useless with each decrease in physical work. The expan-

246

sion of her time and energy has been equated with inevitable boredom and licentious behavior. (Women and the lower classes are not trusted to use leisure well, although a similar prediction of the dire consequences of lack of physical exhaustion does not seem to apply to the upper-class male.) The last stage of her life is pictured as even less functional, with travel funded by her late husband's estate as her main occupation. At the most extreme, the woman is seen as a parasite, passively taking economic goods from her husband and male offspring because of her own feeling of inferiority and wish to dominate.

Reading Lopata's dismal account reinforces our impulse to say that if this is the best social scientists can come up with for women, let's go back to the hand-me-downs. But, of course, that's not an answer. What we need are fresh examinations of women's lives—from which can be drawn new theories of how women can live and grow, not merely conform and decline.

In all the theories of adult male development, work plays a crucial role. A man's satisfaction with his life's work is seen as a major factor in his feelings about himself. For women, as far as the behavioral scientists have been concerned, work is peripheral, and given scant attention. Love and work, Freud said, are the twin pillars of a healthy life. But for women, one of those pillars bears all the weight. The focus of feminine development has been on the woman's erotic life, on her ability to find a satisfactory relationship with a man, as if the portico of her life were supported by a single pillar—Love.

But work has always been a major part of women's lives—with the exception of a small group of the very privileged. As we've seen, the concept of the man "at work" and the woman "at home" is a by-product of the Industrial Revolution, which separated the two. Before the rise of manufacture, work was done "at home"—in the manor house, on the farm, in the cottage industry. Men and women both did work that was recognized as necessary for economic survival. Today, much of what is called "women's work" is invisible. It is not even *called* work. The woman who is home caring for small children is said to be "not working." Her husband is said to be "supporting" her as if she were some inert blob of matter. The goods and services she delivers to her family are not counted in the gross national product.

In addition to ignoring the crucial role work plays in the life of any woman, our society generally relies on sentimentalized myths rather than on data to describe what brings fulfillment to a woman. The unmarried woman is still pitied, thought of as a "spinster" with her hair in a bun who owns a passel of cats. The woman without children is assumed to be in a perpetual state of misery. The woman with a nice house, husband and adorable children is presumed to have reached the apex of feminine happiness, despite the fact that many such women are going back to work, getting depressed or getting a divorce!

These ideas, of course, *are* changing—but probably not as fast as the media might have us believe. The old myths still have considerable power. Young women in their twenties today may talk about their careers a great deal, and college women wouldn't be caught dead saying they were out to get a "MRS." degree, but the anxieties underneath are very real. One young woman says it's okay to be serious about your work, but there has to be a guy around somewhere who at least *wants* to marry you. Unmarried career women in their thirties agonize over the fact that they might not have children. Sometimes it's not that they *want* children; they worry that their lives will be devoid of meaning if they don't have them. Under the surface of change many of the old stereotypes about female happiness are alive and well, ready to reappear.

How much do we really know about the ways different life patterns promote well-being and self-esteem for women—given that women are individuals and that one life-style won't fit everybody, just as one dress size won't. The answer is that we really don't know much about these issues because we haven't bothered to ask. We have tended to assume that all a woman needs is a man. We haven't looked at the other issues in a woman's life: How does she survive, economically? What does she *do* with the hours in her days? How does she feel about those hours?

One of the key ingredients for well-being in our society—in any society, in fact—is access to the means for economic survival. Without that, almost everything in your life comes crashing down around your head.

Women in what we call the "traditional" role have had access to economic resources only through men. We tend to think of that as natural, some sort of logical consequence of "Anatomy is destiny." In fact, it's a historically new phenomenon. Throughout most of human history, women have been economic providers. In the hunter-gatherer and agricultural societies that have made up 90 percent of human history, women have provided a substantial proportion of the economic base of their families' survival by food-gathering, farming and other

248

economically productive activities. The notion of the husband who "supports" his wife is quite new. So the massive movement of women into the work force in Western industrial societies is a return to an earlier pattern, not a brand-new one.

What happened to women in Western society when they moved away from their "old" role of economic provider, when the Industrial Revolution changed the face of the West? We might get an idea from what is happening today in the developing world. Anthropologist Beatrice Whiting[3] studies women in Kenya who grow crops on small plots, earn cash and provide food and clothing for their children. They do their work in the company of other adults, spending four or five hours a day away from their children, and their lives provide what Whiting sees as the critical components of human well-being: having a valued impact on one's environment, sufficient variety in stimulation and the assurance of comfort and support.

Urbanization, which is rapidly spreading across the developing world, is having an impact on these Kenyan women. As their husbands move into stable paid employment in urban settings, the women follow, leaving their family farms. Landless and jobless, they become economically dependent for the first time and must take sole, full-time responsibility for the care of their children in homes isolated from other adults. Boredom and irritability increase; well-being suffers. For these women to take low-paid factory jobs isn't the answer. That would result in insurmountable problems—lack of child care, fatigue—difficulties familiar to women in industrial societies. The supports and means of independence of the old rural society are gone, and no new ones have emerged in the urban setting. These social changes in Kenya that so trouble Beatrice Whiting are frighteningly familiar to our own "norm" for the American family—the man as sole provider, the woman jobless and in sole charge of children, often alone in her own home.

We as a society have been enamored of a Norman Rockwell image of the typical family—happy mom at home in her apron with her two shiny, scrubbed children, beaming in her spotless kitchen waiting for her husband to come home from work. We haven't stopped to consider that this all-American image is in fact an imported and distorted version of the ideal of the European upper-class woman of the Victorian era, who watched over home and family with the sweetness of an angel and the fragility of a porcelain doll.

In fact, Victorian upper-class ladies had servants to do the housework, nannies to care for the children and often had independent wealth in the form of trust funds left by well-to-do relatives. That's a far cry from the situation of the average middle-class American wife.

Today—and it's about time—some of the tint is rubbing off the proverbial rose-colored glasses. We are beginning to look at the consequences of economic dependence for women. These consequences have always been present, but they tended to be invisible. Girls brought up in the fifties expected to be supported by a husband for a lifetime. These women, now entering middle age, have been hard hit by calamities about which they had never been warned: They find themselves divorced, or married to men whose jobs were obliterated in an economic recession, or widowed—or unable to meet mounting expenses of a home and growing children, even with a working husband. Untold numbers of women in that age group find themselves trying to brush up on rusty typing skills, or working at jobs far below their intelligence and educational level. Older women find themselves in even more difficult straits. A lawyer who specializes in domestic relations says that women in their fifties and sixties have even worse problems. She suggests we look at who is serving us over the counters at drugstores or in shopping centers. Often, she says, it's the divorced or widowed older woman, once affluent, who now has to stand on her feet eight hours a day to keep body and soul together.

Unfortunately, the economic dependence of women becomes visible only when it becomes a social issue and involves taxpayers' money: when a woman goes on welfare, when a pregnant teenager has nowhere to go, when a poor elderly widow can't find a place to live, when a battered woman with children desperately seeks food and shelter. These situations are products of two factors that seem built in to the lives of many women: economic dependence and occupational "incompetence." Vast sums of public moneys are spent on women who are not able to support themselves, but the concern of the public only seems to emerge *after* the fact. It's a problem that parents, educators, public officials and mental health workers ought to address for girl children from the cradle on. Which brings us to the "housewife" question.

A great many housewives today feel they are under attack: they feel they have been maligned as "basically passive, unimaginative, uninterested in events outside their walls, chained to routine tasks and unable to understand the work their children do away from home." Those are

250

the words of Helena Lopata, who studied a thousand housewives in the Chicago area in a major research project.

Some women are angry with the feminist movement for what they see as attacks on their life's work and contribution to society. Some feminists have in fact made derogatory comments about housewives. But today the mainstream of the feminist movement is highly sympathetic to housewives and their problems. A housewife, Ellie Smeal, served as president of the National Organization for Women. There is no question, however, that the role of housewife is a socially devalued one in our society, and this is a condition that predates the latest upsurge of feminism in this country. Louise Kapp Howe makes that point forcefully in *Pink Collar Worker*. She points to the official Department of Labor rankings of jobs according to the complexity of skills required for the job. "Homemaker" gets the same ranking as "parking lot attendant"—but it is rated *lower* than "dog pound attendant" and "marine mammal handler."

We've talked about the social devaluation of the housewife role earlier, but it seems important to underscore the fact here, because so many women experience its consequences. Many women go through what might be called "The Incredible Invisible Woman Syndrome." Caryl remembers going to a party with her husband one night, at a time when he was working in television news. She felt after a few minutes that there were footprints on her back from people who were marching over her to talk to her husband. A professor who was seated next to her at dinner took time out from his conversation with a man across the table to say, "And I guess you stay home and raise kiddies?"

Caryl said, "Yes, I have fourteen of them, fathered by Ho Chi Minh and the Secretary of the Black Panthers."

The professor, preoccupied, smiled and said, "That's nice," and turned back to his conversation. Later in the dinner, when someone mentioned that Caryl was a writer, people started to turn and talk to her. She felt as if she had suddenly materialized from thin air, as if she had arrived by the matter transmitter on *Star Trek*.

Looking ahead, with so many women in the job market, the role of housewife seems unlikely to improve in the status ratings. There are groups that are fighting to change the negative "image" of the job, but it is an uphill battle all the way. For women who choose this role as their vocation, for all or part of their lives, this devaluation has sinister implications. It takes a strong ego and sense of identity to find self-esteem

251

in a job that others don't seem to value. That makes it all the more important that the woman who enters this life-style choose it because the job suits her, not because of societal pressures. Young women today have to take a clear-eyed look at the role of housewife, not as some sort of "natural" destiny, and not as the last reel in an MGM romantic comedy. To look realistically at the job of "housewife" and to examine its pros and cons is *not* to attack people who are and have been housewives. Women in that role have made tremendous contributions to society—even if those contributions often go unrecognized. However, no role is static, completely resistant to change, and no one role fits everybody. Times change, and so do social patterns and convention. A young woman looking ahead must ask herself whether or not the traditional role most women have adopted will provide her with fulfillment and self-esteem. For many, it will not.

At present, there is a heated debate about how satisfying the role of housewife is. In a recent review of the literature on the mental health of women, sociologist Jessie Bernard[4] said flatly that the mental health of housewives was "Public Health Problem Number One." In view of the evidence, she said, it seems that the traditional role of marriage and children and economic dependence constitutes a "health hazard" for women.

Some data on women and mental health support this view. Sociologists Walter R. Gove and Jeannette F. Tudor looked at the statistics on the mentally ill in Western societies.[5] They found that the highest rates of mental illness were to be found among married women. Marriage, Walter Gove says, seems to be a more difficult role for women than for men. He cites studies which show that women report more marital problems than men and are less happy with their marriages. Women are less likely than men to get satisfaction out of being a parent, and indicate they have more problems dealing with children. They also more frequently feel inadequate as parents. Wondering about why marriage in modern industrial society might produce the high incidence of symptoms among married women, he notes, "The married woman's structural base is more fragile than the man's. Women generally occupy only one major social role, that of housewife, whereas men occupy two major roles, household head and worker. Thus, a married man has two major sources of gratification, his family and his work, and a woman has only one, her family. If a male finds one of these roles unsatisfactory, he can frequently focus his interest and concern on the other role. In contrast, if a woman finds her family role unsatisfactory, she typically has no other major source of gratification."

Recently, Grace and Rosalind did a study comparing working women with women at home. All were middle-class mothers of preschool children. Although there were no overall differences in the level of self-esteem or satisfaction, the self-esteem of the working mothers seemed more firmly grounded. For the women at home, the only clear source of self-esteem was their husband's approval—actually their perceptions of his approval of their life pattern. In contrast, working women had two bases for their sense of well-being: they seemed to rely equally on satisfaction with work and family. These findings lend support to Gove and Tudor's speculations about the importance of the "two pillars" as crucial to a healthy life.

Gove believes that the lack of structure in the housewife role is also a problem. "It is possible for the housewife to put things off, to let things slide, in sum, to perform poorly. The lack of structure and visibility allows her to brood over her troubles,· and her distress may thus feed upon itself. Those who have an outside job, on the other hand, have a set of demands that have to be met—these demands not only keep them in touch with the world but also provide less time for brooding and anxiety."

If the housewife has fewer sources of gratification and more time for anxiety, Gove believes she also has another problem that contributes to distress: lack of control. He says that in past studies of women's attitudes toward their role, women have tended to perceive their role as reactive to what men do, while men see theirs in terms of their own needs and ambitions. "At the minimum," Gove says, "it is likely that women find their uncertainty and lack of control over their future to be frustrating."

Control may be a key issue in the high incidence of depression among women. Depression seems to be the "feminine" malady,[6] three times more common among women than among men. It is the most frequent complaint of women over eighteen who are admitted to psychiatric services in general hospitals across the United States. Why is depression so common among women? Many psychologists feel it is due to "learned helplessness." Most aspects of female socialization in our society— passivity, lack of assertiveness, the desperate need for approval—leave many women without the means to control their environment. Studies of laboratory animals demonstrate that a variety of species can learn helplessness by being placed in a cage where they cannot escape a painful stimulus. When later placed in a cage where they can escape, they remain passive, helpless, not even trying to get out.

"Uncontrollable" reward and punishment situations have been shown to result in the same kind of learning among humans—learning that one can do nothing to change what exists and thus learning not to try. Depression, some researchers believe, results from such learning.

Seen in this light, the housewife role—with its lack of control—has been called a "depressing life-style."

The importance of having control comes out in Lillian Rubin's study of the working-class family. The women who worked found the working world a satisfying place, at least when compared to the world of the housewife. "Like men, they take pride in doing a good job, in feeling competent. They are glad to get some relief from the routines of housewifery. They are pleased to earn some money, to feel more independent, more as if they had some ability to control their own lives . . . there is, perhaps, no greater testimony to the deadening and deadly quality of the tasks of the housewife than the fact that so many women find pleasure in working at jobs that by almost any definition would be called alienated labor—low status, low paying, dead-end work made up of dull, routine tasks; work that is often considered too menial for men who are less educated than these women."

Reviewing such studies, the reader might think that taking on a career as a housewife would be about as rewarding as serving time in Leavenworth. But there really is another side to this story. A number of well-designed, large-scale studies[7] show that housewives who prefer not to work, who enjoy their role, have at least as high a level of well-being as do employed women. So we're back to the theme we've stressed before—women who are where they want to be are happy. At the same time we've seen that too many women are at home not out of choice, but out of a sense of obligation.

Just as working women are not all alike, neither are housewives. Researchers are just beginning to build this awareness into their studies. In order to find out whether housewives are "happy," they have to find out first whether the women want to be in that role. If you don't know this, it's difficult to know what your findings mean. Perhaps the debate about who's more satisfied—the housewife or the working woman—is centered on a question that can only be answered by: "It all depends."

Satisfaction, after all, is a complex state of being. It seems to have several key determinants; one of those we've stressed is whether a person is where she wants to be. Another, equally important, is how well a role matches one's abilities and talents. One particular group of housewives seem to have special problems in this area—college-educated, intellectually able women. Able women are those with the most potential for moving beyond the boundaries of what has been called women's turf. If they decide not to do so, if instead they choose to focus their time and energies intensely on home and family, what happens?

One important large-scale national survey, *The Quality of American Life*,[8] published in 1976 by a team of social scientists at the University of Michigan, found generally similar levels of satisfaction among homemakers and employed women, with one striking exception. The college-educated housewives scored lower on satisfaction. "It is the highly educated housewife who does not have an outside job whose marriage seems mostly to be beset by disagreements, lack of understanding and companionship, doubts and dissatisfaction," the researchers conclude. In addition, these women score lower in general well-being than less-educated housewives and employed women.

"This decline in the level of well-being expressed by college-women housewives suggests that the role of homemaker is not as fulfilling to women at this level of education as it is to less educated wives." Among college women, this study found, those who were employed outside the home were more likely to see their lives as interesting and challenging than the homemakers.

The study of college-educated women done by psychologist Judith Birnbaum, described in some detail earlier, had similar findings. Married professionals, in the middle adult years, held themselves in higher regard than equally gifted nonemployed women. The homemakers had problems with self-esteem, anxiety and adjustment to the loss of their maternal role as their children grew older.

What's needed, Birnbaum says, is to give the gifted woman more space to grow and to use her abilities. "Given these striking findings, it seems we cannot in good conscience continue to raise girls to seek their *primary* personal fulfillment and identity within the family."

Among the homemakers that she studied, there was a disturbing note of self-sacrifice when they talked about their vocation. They often slipped into a defense of their life-style based not on individual choice, but on what women "should" be doing. As one virtuously put it, "Marriage is

255

not for the self-centered woman. It is a life of loving and giving in return for being wanted and needed and loved by her husband and later by her children."

Birnbaum comments: "One cannot help but read 'self-centered' pejoratively as a somewhat sneering dismissal of those selfish, un-feminine women who refuse to do their duty and sacrifice themselves on the altar of marriage. Such remarks might be less distressing if we did not have right at hand the self-esteem data on the homemaker. For given her low self-esteem score, her loneliness and pervasive sense of unrest, no matter how joyfully accepting she is of her 'feminine' lot in life, she pays a high price for the gift of love. Unfortunately, it seems to literally be true that she learns to think less of herself as an individual."

The homemakers—but not the professionals—talked of their children as giving purpose to their lives. Asked to write an essay about a woman whose youngest child is in school, the homemakers responded with stories about women who felt unloved, alone, in turmoil, desperate, aimless: "Time now to be creative, to contribute to the community, be an individual, but where to start, what to concentrate on? But the change was a turmoil. Lois went from one thing to another, never really accomplishing anything, rushing to be home when school·was out, ready to chauffeur to all sorts of extra-curricular activities . . . perhaps she had just gotten too deeply into the habit to get out of it or perhaps her sense of these needs to stay close to the children is realistic. She never felt she was cut out to be a mother and yet she couldn't turn her back on the needs of the children. They exerted a great pull on her . . . stronger than the pull of her own dreams."

Birnbaum found that among the traditional homemakers she studied, most had no clear internal standards of their competence and worth. "Despite faithful devotion to home, husband and family, and com-munity activities as central organizers of her life, she feels unattractive to men and not especially competent at anything . . . her husband and children are described as busy and successful and rewarding to her, yet personally she senses an inexplicable feeling of failure and disappoint-ment."

The note of duty and self-sacrifice—as if marriage and motherhood were a preparation for canonization instead of an enjoyable life-style—that Birnbaum found in her study is echoed in Helena Lopata's study of Chicago housewives. When asked about the "ideal" housewife, the women who answered rarely talked about the pleasure of the job. They said things like: "A mother has to give more than she gets in return"; "She must put herself on her children's level"; "One that keeps her family happy and content by doing the needed things"; "One whose family comes first above everything else"; "One who does her duty." Only rarely did Lopata find a woman who talked of personal qualities and enjoyment: "One who is a warm, efficient person who enjoys all phases of housework."

It's important to note here that not all housewives fall into the martyr category. There are many women who like the job for its benefits—being your own boss and setting your own timetable, having an opportunity for close involvement with young children and time for community activities. But clearly, too many women today view their jobs as housewives with some ill-defined sense of duty and sacrifice, hardly the best reasons for choosing a job. Probably the worst, in fact.

Where did that strain of martyrdom come from? The noted economist John Kenneth Galbraith has one intriguing point of view. He thinks it ties in neatly with the corporate, consumer-oriented society. Galbraith says that in any society, people are needed to "administer" personal goods and services. "In earlier times," he writes, "this administration was the function of a subordinate and menial servant class. Industrialization, to its great credit, forever liquidates this class. People never remain in appreciable numbers in such personal service if they have alternate employment. Industry supplies that employment. If consumption is to continue and to expand, it is imperative that substitute administrative talent be found. This, in modern industrial societies—the nonsocialist societies—is the vital function that women have now been persuaded to perform."

Galbraith sees the American housewife as the adjutant general in charge of consumption.[9] The more things that are consumed, the more products bought, the better for the economy. So women are urged to consume at a record level. The television ads for cleaning products are a good example of this. It is not enough that a woman keep her house tidy and the family's clothes decently clean. She must not have spots on the glasses or the neighbors will frown. If her kitchen has cooking odors a strange woman will come in and sniff around the sink with disdain. If her husband's collar has a ring around it, she gets disapproval (even though it's *his* dirt). A clean collar gets her a kiss. She is urged to keep her home more sterile than the operating room at Bellevue and her family wardrobe free of any hint of lint. In all the ads, the woman who does so is rewarded by love and approval.

This is an example of what Galbraith calls "The Convenient Social Virtue." Elite groups, he says, find ways of persuading other people to do the work they don't want to do. For example, young men can be persuaded to go out and get themselves perhaps maimed or killed in war because they are persuaded it is a noble or heroic thing to do. Women can be persuaded to manage consumption if they believe it is the right and virtuous thing for them to do.

"The family is both the justification and the disguise for the economic function of women. Their service in making possible the indefinite expansion, especially of affluent consumption and production, is justified, even sanctified, as a service to the family."

In Galbraith's view, the consumption-oriented society doesn't want a woman out working or getting seriously involved in community pursuits or creative endeavors. It wants her at home with her Mop & Glow, her Lysol, her Wisk, her Tide and Downy Fabric Softener. And a social ethic that makes her feel guilty when she strays too far from her role as manager of consumption suits the needs of the corporate state to a T.

The behavioral sciences have also helped to create in women the idea that their proper role in life is to be sacrificial to the point of self-immolation. A tour through the popular media of the fifties is enlightening. One psychologist, Clifford Adams, wrote for a popular women's magazine a column called "Making Marriage Work," in which he urged housewives to be more zealous in hunting down their sins than Trappist nuns are supposed to be. He suggested that if a wife was bored and restless at home, it was a sign of emotional immaturity. His solution was for her to give up outside activities that interfered with full-time devotion to home and family. "Marriage is a career in itself. A job does not relieve a wife of household responsibilities." Every marital problem, Dr. Adams believed, could be solved with a little improvement—on the part of the wife. To a woman who wrote in that her husband always teased her in a malicious and hurtful way, he said she didn't build his ego enough, and put together a little quiz for wives. "Do you:

Cheerfully adjust your wants to his earnings?

Kiss him because you want to?

Always have time to talk to him?

Find much to praise, little to criticize?"

258

If the wife gets a low score on ego building, she is advised to do better. "Both his personal happiness and his business progress are at stake."

If a husband is tired, it's his wife's fault. "Some husbands are chronically tired because their wives schedule too many activities for the weekend." The wife is advised to try to understand and make her plans around him. If a husband is fat, it's his wife's fault because she cooks too many fattening foods. If he is irritable, it's because she isn't sweet enough. Dr. Adams suggests that women keep a tape recorder going so they can hear the way they talk to their husband and children. The good wife is, above all, adaptable. "She conceals her disappointments. He is too tired for the movie she looked forward to, so she puts the big chair by the fire even though it spoils the effect she'd planned for the room.

"Adaptability means more than weakly giving in. Rather it means the ability to understand his needs, to see his point of view, and to identify with him so fully that his wishes are usually hers."

Millions of women were reading this sort of thing—and taking it seriously—for decades. Looking at it now, it's easy to see that such views are nothing more—or less—than a prescription for emotional genocide. Women were being told to obliterate their own egos and to destroy their individuality. The wonder is not that so many women survived that era with low self-esteem and a tendency toward depression, but that any at all came out whole.

Why did so many millions of women buy this idea? They can't all have been neurotic masochists. In fact, they were probably very much like women today, trying to understand just what it means to be a good wife or a good mother. The answers served up by "experts" like Dr. Adams gave women specific guidelines. The reward that a woman was supposed to get from self-denial was a sense of knowing that she was a good person who had done a good job. Maybe this image of the perfect wife and mother was hard to live up to, but at least it was clear-cut. Giving up those simple formulas means that women have to struggle—often painfully—to create new images and new rules. This process may lead to clashes—with husbands, children, parents, in-laws. There have been many casualties along the way—and there will be more—but there is no other route to being a fully independent adult.

If the media were constantly beaming the message of devoted wifehood to women, they were perhaps harping even more insistently on another theme: perfect motherhood. The idea was that a woman could find fulfillment only by becoming a mother. She would give of herself completely, and in return children would give her satisfaction, happiness and a sense of having achieved something important. If a woman wasn't constantly thrilled and happy with her children and her life, she felt something was terribly wrong with her. So children are supposed to make women "happy." But this myth doesn't always mesh with reality.

In *The Quality of American Life* study, the well-being of women with young children compares less favorably with women in most other situations. They have more disagreements with husbands, think of divorce more often and have significantly more worries about nervous breakdown. "We conclude," the authors say, "from these various pieces of evidence that the situation of young parenthood is a time of many dissatisfactions and psychological stresses . . . It is the young *mothers*, however, with their frequent thoughts of escaping from their marital roles and their fears of a nervous breakdown, who appear to feel this pressure most acutely."

A recent study done in the Chicago area confirms this notion. When sociologist Leonard Pearlin and his colleagues[10] studied 2300 people eighteen to sixty-five, they found that women at home with young children under six were especially vulnerable to depression. This vulnerability increases with the number of preschoolchildren. In the words of the psychologist Marcia Guttentag, who reviewed data on mental health from across the country, "There's nothing more depressing than a houseful of young children."

Helena Lopata, in her large study of housewives in Chicago, found that the birth of the first child was "the event causing the greatest discontinuity of personality in American middle-class women." In other words, it was an event that changed a woman's whole life and her view of the world. Rather than being a naturally and easily accepted change, it clearly offered the possibility for a great deal of stress.

The early child-rearing years are a difficult period for some women. For others, the rewards of the role and the demands it makes can lead to a feeling of usefulness and satisfaction. For them, it is later on that problems may set in. One not-so-young mother, Rosemarie Mitchell, put it poignantly in an article she wrote for the *Boston Globe*:

> There was a pain inside of me that wouldn't go away. Actually it was more of an ache, an ache that comes with being 38 years old, a mother, a housewife, a nobody.
> I told myself when all the children were in school, I'd do something,

go back to teaching or writing, be someone of value and importance. But in reality, I never believed that day would come. I would always be young and pretty, with a toddler running about, reminding me that I was, most of the time, happily tied down. It was true that I frequently envied Tom's freedom: out the door, briefcase in hand, a constantly changing world. But someday, I thought, they'll all be in school, and I'll be free.

This year I noticed that the lines around my eyes and my mouth no longer faded away when I stopped smiling. I remembered how I used to brag about being 30, a mysterious and alluring 30. But now, I swallowed quickly when I reluctantly revealed my age, and I waited, carefully gauging the reaction of those around me.

The parties we now went to had many younger women and the confidence and sparkle that was such a part of me seemed to have ebbed, replaced by a gnawing insecurity.

It wasn't that I dwelled on my age or my days at home, but there were situations, there were people who made comments, harmless remarks that affected me for days and week afterwards. There was the beautiful blonde whose eyes lit up when she spoke, who talked of her career, her husband and their decision to postpone having children for a few more years.

I listened serenely, the most intelligent-looking gaze fixed on my face, but inside I smoldered, jealous of her obvious charm. Finally she turned to me and politely asked, "What do you do?"

I froze. I searched for impressive words, but there were none. "I'm home. This is the first year the children are all in school." Hastily I added, "But I plan to work. At what? Well, I don't know yet . . ."

Like this woman, young women tend not to think about their middle years when they are making plans for their future. They tend to ignore those years, acting as if they would never come. One reason middle age is almost invisible to girls is that ours is a youth-oriented culture, even more aggressively so for women than for men, and nowhere so aggressively as in the media. Youth is presented as the only desirable condition for a woman. Clothes are modeled only by young and beautiful women, movie heroines (with a few notable exceptions) are also young and beautiful, and middle-aged women are never portrayed as drinking Coke, playing tennis, dancing or doing all the fun things on the TV set. The few times middle-aged women do appear they are baby-sitting or shopping for laxatives.

Research done in the past two decades indicates that a great many

261

women, perhaps a majority, suffer some ill consequences at some time in their lives from submerging themselves for long periods in the traditional feminine role—lack of self-esteem, episodes of depression, or feelings of being out of control. (We'll talk about the costs of nontraditional patterns in a later chapter.) Perhaps the most pressing problem, one that is built into the housewife role, is lack of economic viability. There was a time when all the forces in society came together to bolster even the most tenuous of marriages. A woman could expect that she would not be divorced by her husband, and if he took such action, he would be branded by society as a reprobate: His chances for advancement on the job would be marred, his family would disapprove of him and he could certainly never run for any public office. Such social pressures no longer exist. Divorce is becoming increasingly commonplace—40 percent of current American marriages are predicted to end in divorce. The young girl who is choosing her bridal dress today has a good chance of being an "ex-wife" at some time in the future. It's not something young girls want to think about—but they had better do so. Today, too many women face the possibility of divorce only when it is staring them in the face; the economic consequences for them can be disastrous. Other women endure miserable marriages because they see no way to support themselves on their own.

What, in fact, does happen to women who are separated and divorced? To find out, Boston psychologist Dorothy Burlage interviewed thirty such women in depth—women who had managed to avoid the welfare rolls.[11]

The most striking thing she found was the plunge in income the women experienced when their marriages dissolved. The average family income of the women she studied was $23,000 before the separation. After the separation the average family income for the women and children, including *all* sources of income, was $8000 per year. The women experienced a reduction of *two-thirds* in family income.

This drop was particularly devastating since the women had responsibility for the children and new, heavy expenses, particularly if they had to pay for child care. The ex-husband, on the other hand, experienced some loss of income through payments to his ex-wife, but his other expenses usually decreased.

Not only did the women face a precipitous loss of income, but they found themselves ill-prepared to be breadwinners for the family, even though many of them had held jobs before or during their marriages.

262

Even the women who had college degrees never really expected to carry the major financial burden.

"It was understood that you went to college, but you weren't really expected to be career oriented," said one. "You went to college because you were smart. You settled down afterwards and you had children and a family. You didn't really stay in a career or anything like that."

Because they hadn't developed what Burlage calls a "vocational identity" before the marital split, the women were confused and disoriented when they began the job hunt.

"You don't even know where to begin, you don't know what your job skills are . . . It's very hard to know what you want to do for work, where you can find it," one woman said. Not only did the women employ a hit-or-miss approach to getting a job—sometimes even going door to door in office buildings—they suffered from debilitating fears that they wouldn't be able to manage. Their fears were often realistic. Often they had to take the first job they could get, and experienced "downward mobility" in their work. One woman who had been a white-collar worker took a job washing bottles in a hospital. "Floundering," says Burlage, "is the only word that seems appropriately to describe how these mothers approached the problems of employment, occupational choice and careers. They had no information and no help with planning for the future."

The women didn't find themselves eagerly snapped up as newcomers to the labor force. Often they found themselves losing jobs to teenagers, because the youngsters would work for less and were more willing to take temporary jobs. When they did get jobs, they felt insecure as workers. They were hesitant to complain about bad working conditions and poor pay. One woman took the same job in a small factory as men did, and took on bookkeeping responsibilities in addition. But when the men received an increase of 25 cents an hour, she received only 10 cents. She was afraid to complain, fearing she might lose the job she so sorely needed as a single mother.

Most of the women Burlage studied found themselves having to provide most or all of the family income—a testament to the fact that a woman's "right to be supported" often turns out to be illusory. Even when the women did receive child support, it was not enough to keep the family solvent. Realistically, even if the ex-husband has the best intentions toward his ex-wife and children, unless he has an unusually high-paying job, his income won't stretch to cover two households.

Burlage found it startling that many of the women had to take two jobs to survive. One mother with four children, employed as a secretary full time, took a job as a salesclerk at night and did typing on the weekends to get her children through college.

Often, too, the women found that the traditional women's jobs that were available to them did not mix well with the demands of being a single parent. One woman who was trained as a nurse found that, to take a hospital job, she would have to work rotating shifts that were nearly impossible to combine with child care. She couldn't take on private-duty nursing because she would receive no health benefits, and she couldn't afford to purchase a health plan on her own. Another woman worked as a keypuncher, but found she had to work an all-night shift in order to make enough money to support her family.

For women with young children, child care was a constant hassle. One woman who had a master's degree had to settle for a low-paid clerical job at a university because the university had a child-care center. Most of the women suffered greatly from guilt about the time they had to spend away from their children—all the more so because they realized the children had suffered the loss of their father. One mother, wanting to be with her child during the day, took a night job and tried to stay up with the child during the day. She was able to get only four hours sleep each day. Finally she got sick and had to take a day shift.

Burlage found that almost all of the women she interviewed underwent a change in self-perception. In the past, they had not thought of themselves as breadwinners. After the separation, they looked on their jobs as the basis of their survival. Few talked of remarriage as a way of surviving.

"I feel I will have to work for the rest of my life," said one. Another said, "The whole experience of being on my own financially, having to take care of myself and my children, taught me that nobody is going to take care of me but me." They were deadly serious about their jobs. "I'm much more assertive, more competitive, more ambitious," said one woman. "And, on a social level, more masculine. It doesn't have to do with how I do my hair or how I walk, but more masculine in attitude, as far as 'This is my career and you're not going to take it away from me or I'll kill you.'"

Despite the difficulties these women found in the workplace, despite the wrenching change in their lives that forced them to become breadwinners, most of the women found satisfaction in their jobs. Their

264

jobs gave them a sense of independence, confidence and self-esteem. One woman said, "My job made me feel like a person."

In their isolated situations, their roles as mother gave them no such feelings. They reported getting a sense of value and importance to others *only* in regard to paid employment. For their jobs as mothers, they had no such network of positive feedback. Their mothering was done without the presence of other adults to say, in effect, "You're doing a good job." So they had to rely on their paid employment to give them a sense of value.

On the whole, the women experienced great stress in the process of separation and divorce. In this, they are typical of most divorced women. In fact, divorce seems to be a different experience for women than it is for men. In *The Quality of American Life* study researchers compared divorced men with other men and divorced women with other women. Divorced men didn't seem to differ very much from other men except in one area of their lives: their satisfaction with family life, which was not as high. But the divorced women viewed their whole lives much more negatively than other women, and more negatively than divorced men. For example, the majority of divorced men said they didn't worry about bills, but only a minority of the divorced women could make that statement. Divorced women experienced more stress than any other group of women. "Particularly striking is the high percentage of divorced women who fear they may have a nervous breakdown (25 percent) compared to the smaller proportion (8 percent) of divorced men. Divorce seems indeed to be a different entity for women that it is for men—for women it's much worse." This gloomy picture may change, of course, as more women develop the capacity to be breadwinners.

Nuts and Bolts

"Que sera, sera." It's a good description of how women have usually entered the traditional role as economically dependent wife and mother. We've just gone through a litany of the problems inherent in the role. They are real, they exist and they have to be faced—not by "taking sides" for and against, not by pitting women in different life-styles against each other. The role of homemaker is one that many women will continue to occupy for periods of their lives, but it may be a different sort of role than it was in the past.

First, all women, whatever life role they choose, *must* in the future avoid the pitfall of chronic economic dependence. Not to do so is to gamble recklessly with the future. The woman at home can take steps to ensure that she will not be devastated by circumstances the way the women in Dorothy Burlage's study were. One step is to keep her job skills fresh and to keep in touch with people in the working world, so that she can one day return there. Investing in part-time schooling while she is at home is a wise and reasonable insurance for her own economic viability, as is volunteer work that could lead to contacts that might result in a decently paid job. Whatever the method, the result should be a connection to economic independence that could be a lifeline in the event of divorce, widowhood or simply the termite-like action of inflation.

Second, women at home need not fall into the "feminine" traps of dependence and passivity. The women that Burlage studied found that these attitudes—plus little experience with any kind of assertive actions—made it hard for them to reenter the job world. Too many women, when they marry, abdicate all contact and responsibility for dealing with the adult world. It's much easier to let George do it—handle the finances, argue with the washer repairman and the Internal Revenue Service. This kind of retreat into the womb of home and family can be a crippling pattern for a woman, leaving her unable to cope with life's crises.

Women should realize that marrying and having a family are not some kind of natural female function that can be carried out as easily as breathing. Women at home with young children should understand that stress, isolation and anxiety are typical of women in their situation, and that taking steps to alleviate those problems is right and necessary for their well-being. In the past, many women who felt alone, trapped or overburdened turned their feelings inward, creating personal guilt: "If this is a woman's highest fulfillment, what's wrong with me?" This kind of thinking heightened their isolation, made them think they weren't entitled to ask for any help—from their husbands, neighbors or community.

Women at home have a vested interest in joining with other housewives to form networks that can offer them respites from the unrelenting demands of child care. These networks can act as pressure groups to make community organizations responsive to their needs: places to meet other adults where child care is provided. Some churches, schools and YWCAs have begun to provide child care during activities in

266

which mothers participate. There's no reason why museums, libraries and shopping malls couldn't do the same.

In the future, one hopes, the woman who is at home will be there because she has chosen a role she enjoys, not just one that society prescribed for her. She will have thought about the future—about what her life will be when the children are grown, about plans for her middle and later years—instead of blindly colliding with tomorrow. Her life will be purposeful and planned, not accidental. She will have chosen, rather than just accepted, her life. For today's girls, who will be tomorrow's women, "Que sera, sera" should be nothing more than a forgotten melody.

13

LIFE CHOICES

Women at Work

From our findings comes a very practical implication for lowering women's symptomatology, namely encouraging and enabling them to find jobs, especially of higher status.
—Frederick Ilfeld, in a summary of a survey
on psychiatric symptomatology

Who are the successful women in the world of work? First of all, the number of women who have achieved that status in our society has been small. Data from the 1970 census reflect the fact that women are still vastly underrepresented in most high-status occupations; for example, only 9.2 percent of physicians, 1.6 percent of engineers and 28.7 percent of college and university teachers are women. Even when a woman does make it into one of these prestige jobs, it's questionable how high she will climb. Most women in these fields tend to be clustered near the bottom in terms of professional status and financial reward. In 1974, only 5 percent of persons earning at least $15,000 were women. The reasons for these dismal statistics have been analyzed fairly thoroughly in the past few years. Blatant discrimination has kept women in large numbers out of such training grounds as law and medical schools. Women who entered traditionally male professions found that they had no access to the old-boy network of friendships that led to advancement, no "mentors" to help them climb the ladder. Social mythology has also stood in the way of success: the notion that women are too emotional to make decisions, that women make unstable employees because they will run off to get married or that men will never work for a woman boss. In spite of these barriers, however, some women have been successful in the workplace. Do they have any particular traits or family patterns in common? Studies suggest that they often do.

The characteristics common in the backgrounds of successful women are[1]: being foreign-born, having immigrant parents; coming from an affluent family; having one or both parents with high occupational or educational status; being an eldest or only child; and perhaps the most intriguing factor—having no brothers.

It's certainly not hard to see why women who achieve success tend to come from affluent families. After all, these are the families with the means to give daughters a good education, and often to introduce them to people influential in their chosen fields.

One study found that among women mathematicians considered especially creative, a high percentage was foreign-born or had at least one parent born outside the United States.[2] Why should being foreign-born—or having a parent who was—be so important in determining success?

The foreign-born women, it seems, come from societies where women of the upper classes are not expected to do domestic work. The housework and most of the child care are done by hired help. One successful female architect,[3] born into a wealthy Argentinian family, said that large numbers of women of her class entered what are considered in the United States to be traditionally male professions. It was only when she came to settle in this country as a young adult that she realized there was anything innovative about her career choice: "From a mundane architect, I was transformed into a pioneer!"

The experience of girls from poorer immigrant families is quite different. The parents often feel great pressure to better themselves in this new society and consequently they urge their children to succeed. Isabelle Karle, a physical scientist (crystallographer), remembers that her Polish-born parents taught her reading and arithmetic before she entered school. They urged both Isabelle and her brother to get good educations and to enter professions of high prestige. Though Isabelle Karle's mother was a seamstress, certainly not a high-status job, she, like other immigrant mothers, served as a competence model for her daughters. Such women were admired for their ability to earn a living and make their way in a new culture.

269

A girl child who is the only or elder child in the family, studies show, has a greater chance of achieving success. Even more striking in "group portraits" of achieving women is the lack of a brother. For example, in Margaret Hennig's study[4] of twenty-five top female executives, not one had a brother and all were firstborn or only children. It seems that when achievement-oriented parents have no sons, a girl, usually the eldest, is selected as the surrogate "son"—the vehicle for the family ambitions.

By recounting the patterns that seem to crop up again and again in the lives of successful women, we don't by any means intend to suggest that these elements are *necessary* for success. Girls don't have to go out and advertise for foreign-born parents to replace their American ones, or put out a contract on their brothers. Running through the patterns found in the backgrounds of successful women is some element different enough from the "usual" situation to protect these women from social pressures that discourage achievement. Their families were atypical in a particularly important way—they did not steer their daughters away from high ambitions. Clearly, parents don't have to be foreign-born or without sons to encourage daughters to achieve; they must simply be willing to do so.

We've noted in earlier chapters that the encouragement of fathers often seems to play a strong role in the lives of successful women. Many of these women identified with their fathers, but did not suffer any loss of feminine identity and had good relations with their mothers as well. The role of mothers in promoting achievement among daughters is less well-defined. Though successful women may have good relationships with their mothers, the pattern of successful women who have chosen mothers as role models is thus far quite rare. There are some notable exceptions to this, of course.

Margaret Mead[5] accompanied her mother on travels necessary to her work, and her mother's career had a strong impact on her. Mead said, "My earliest field trip was with my mother when she was doing graduate research on Italian-Americans . . . Years later I did my master's thesis in psychology at Columbia on the children of the families she studied."

In general, the reason for the conspicuous absence of the mother as role model for achievement is obvious—few women have been free to achieve in our society. That role has been reserved largely for males. Times are changing, however, and we can predict with some confidence that in the future many more women will be role models for their daughters in the world of work. In the study that Grace and Rosalind did

270

of mothers of preschool girls, all the mothers were sensitive to the importance of their daughter's career choice. The working women often said they hoped their daughter's work would be as satisfying to them as their own—if not more so. The nonworking mothers seemed equally concerned about their daughter's future career. Many of them felt they had married too young and had children too soon. They hoped their daughters would think more seriously about a career choice, marry later in life than they themselves had done and postpone childbearing. So it seems that in the future, the father—while certainly important to his daughter—may lose his status as the primary "window" on the world of achievement and success. Some indication that this is already happening comes from a study of two hundred college graduates done by psychologist Sandra Schwartz Tangri,[6] now with the U.S. Commission on Civil Rights.

Tangri selected young women she called "role innovators"—college women who had aspirations to enter and succeed in areas that were formerly identified as all-male preserves. The typical role innovator woman did not identify with her father. "In fact," says Tangri, "more educated working mothers, particularly those who are in male-dominated occupations, are taken as role models by their daughters."

Tangri's role innovators seemed headed for success. But what about their emotional well-being? What kind of people are they? Emotionally healthy ones, according to Tangri. They are individualistic, able to make decisions on their own, to choose a vocation for personal satisfactions rather than for security in the event of divorce or widowhood. They did not reject the female roles of wife and mother—most expected to marry and have children, though they planned to marry later and have fewer children than did more traditional women. They did not think of themselves as masculine, and had as many relationships with men as did traditional women. Interestingly enough, a supportive—or at least tolerant—boyfriend often provided them with a needed sense of support. They did seem to show more self-doubt and questioned their ability to succeed more than traditional young women did—probably, Tangri says, because they had set out on a more difficult course.

Both Tangri's role innovators and successful women studied by others generally disprove the widely held notions about "career women." They don't come from unhappy families, don't reject men and femininity, don't seem destined for miserable marriages. As usual, though, social mythology manages blithely to ignore reality. It has a staying power of its

271

own. For example, in one 1968 book,[7] *Developing Woman's Potential*, Edwin C. Lewis says, "The girl who aims for a career is likely to be frustrated and dissatisfied with herself as a person . . . she is less well-adjusted than those who are content and become housewives. Not only is she likely to have a poor self-concept, but she probably lacks a close relationship with her family." Lewis suggests that "There is the possibility that career orientation among girls grows out of personal dissatisfaction, so that the career becomes a frustration outlet." Lewis cites a number of studies to support these statements. But remember, *interpretations* of scientific data are often opinions, not facts, and can be just as vulnerable to error as any other opinions.

Ravenna Helson of the University of California, Berkeley, illustrated this in reexamining some of the studies that led Lewis to his conclusions. One of these was a well-known study of Vassar graduates of the mid-fifties, which said, according to Lewis, that the best-adjusted women were the underachievers who didn't prepare themselves for an "unrealistic" future by concentrating too much on academics. Instead, they were oriented more toward the traditional feminine role. But, Helson says, the researchers may have been relying more on their own perceptions of what women should be than on objective data. Members of the all-male team made such comments about the underachievers as, "Is personally charming"; "Arouses liking and acceptance"; and "Is adequate in sexual role." Those remarks don't sound much like objective science, and Helson doesn't think they are. "They did not take sufficient care, it seems to me, to protect themselves against hedonistic male bias in their evaluation of women."

In another study, a researcher waxed poetic about a "warm reaching for people," when he was describing the needs of homemakers. Helson notes, somewhat wryly, that "warm reaching for people" would probably be called dependence if the women were being compared with men.

Not only did the interpretations of the studies bend to fit the prevailing ideas, Helson notes, but studies in which career women looked good tended to be ignored. For example, researcher Herbert Spohn,[8] studying women at Sarah Lawrence in the 1950s, found that the college women who did not have vocational aspirations—as compared to those who did—were superficial, immature and tended to be on bad terms with their families. Helson says, "I have never seen a reference to this finding. It would be interesting to know how many studies reporting favorable characteristics of career-oriented women were never published at all because they seemed unconvincing or against the hunches of the reviewer about the true state of affairs."

If young women are to make realistic decisions about the part work will play in their lives, the old scare stories about unhappiness and loss of femininity must be jettisoned, and replaced with information about real women and how they cope with the rewards and hazards of the working world.

The three of us have a special interest in these issues because we have been employed for most of our adult lives. Caryl has always felt that her work has been very important to her sense of identity, but it is only now, as she enters her forties, that she is really beginning to understand the implications of that. She is entering mid-life, a time when the prime of physical beauty is past, when the role of mother diminishes in importance—but she is doing so with a sense of anticipation. She feels that she is just beginning to come into her own in her work—having finally lived long enough to know a few things about how the world operates. She knows her skills, her ambitions—and her limits. She has worked hard at her craft and has seen some of the rewards—despite a nagging suspicion that she is at heart someone who would, given the chance, sit around eating bonbons and reading movie magazines. She and Grace and Rosalind are the same age as what one psychologist calls "the command generation"—people in their thirties and forties who run the world. We have no illusions about running the world, but the word command has a nice ring to it. And we do feel in command—or at least in control—of our lives. We do not have the sense that we are drifting along with some unseen current.

For Caryl, work is a passport to the adventures she dreamed of as a child. She always wanted to see other places, to step, however briefly, into the lives of other people. In the past few years, she has had a chance to travel on the women's professional tennis circuit and to spend time backstage with a Broadway show. Her work also gives her a chance to comment on the foibles and follies of society and to have those opinions appear in journals of some reputation.

For Rosalind, research and writing are intellectually challenging— "like solving a puzzle." She enjoys the collegiality of working with other behavioral scientists, of sharing her knowledge with them. In her clinical practice, she gets tremendous satisfaction—sometimes even exhilaration—from sharing experiences with her patients and seeing them work out creative solutions to the problems they face in their personal lives.

273

Grace finds that research and writing give her an opportunity to do what she likes and is good at. She often hears women of her age say with resignation, "It's all downhill from here." She doesn't feel that way; she sees an exciting future ahead.

All three of us find that our work offers us freshness, challenge, new possibilities—the sorts of things that make the loss of first youth seem, if not insignificant, at least not central to our lives. We have all struggled to maintain a balance in our lives—the Love and Work that Freud wrote about. It's not always easy, but it's worth the effort. We see so many women our age who are floundering—bright, talented women who have been hit by the approach of mid-life as if it were a huge wave. When Caryl talks with old friends she knew in high school, she hears too many horror stories: divorces, separations, depression, bouts with the bottle, a settling into the "my-life-is-over" frame of mind. Not that a commitment to work insulates you from personal disaster—but the women we know who have emerged, if not unscarred, at least with the capacity to heal fast, were those who were invested in their work lives. Work seemed to act as a rudder for keeping their lives on course.

The three of us came to career decisions in different ways. Caryl decided while still in high school that she wanted to be a journalist and never seriously entertained the idea of any other career. Her heroine was Maggie Higgins, the *Herald Tribune* reporter who was the first woman to cover the war in Korea. Rosalind was influenced by a high-school mathematics teacher, and entered college planning to follow in her footsteps. It was only by chance that she enrolled in a psychology course and found that she was excited by it. Grace, when she graduated from college, decided against the idea of getting a Ph.D. because she thought that spending so much time in graduate school would be a "grubby and unfeminine" thing to do. She started training in social work but hated it and dropped out. She then switched to education, hoping to become a guidance counselor, but finally realized that only the commitment to the hard work of getting the advanced degree would give her the opportunity to do the sort of academic study and writing she really wanted to do.

Like many professional women, we have had what might be termed "patchwork careers." We've worked part-time, juggled our hours to meet family needs, often worked in several different areas instead of sticking to a career ladder at one place. As a result, we find ourselves in different places than do men our age. As Rosalind notes, men in her field have made sure to get onto a tenure track, have invested a great deal of time and energy in making the contacts that will ensure them positions where they will have both a good income and the freedom to do what they want. Fewer women than men have been able to do that.

One problem we have all had is the lack of role models. Even now we don't know many women who are ten or twenty years older than we are and doing what we would like to be doing at their age. We must, in a very real way, "invent" our roles as we go along.

We are far from being superwomen, and the conflicting demands of our roles as wives, mothers and workers can sometimes leave us feeling overburdened, but we do like our work and get great satisfaction from it.

We have been hearing too much lately of what we've called the "rotten pie" argument, to wit: Work in America is nothing but a dog-eat-dog struggle to get ahead and make money, and the whole pie is rotten, so why should women want a piece of it? The fact is, the whole pie isn't rotten, just parts of it. The man who bought into the work-is-everything syndrome, whose major goal was to climb one more rung on the ladder, may have awakened one day at fifty with a life that seemed meaningless. Women, it is argued, will be in the same boat—alone and ulcerated. But nobody says women have to buy the whole system, just because they want to be a part of the world of work. Not all men have done so, and more and more men today are trying to balance their work lives with their personal lives. The rewards of achievement and hard work are real, they are internal as well as external, but like anything else, they can be overdone. Perhaps Aristotle had the best suggestion centuries ago when he proposed the notion of the "Golden Mean" between the extremes, of a life that had a proper balance. "All work and no play makes Jack a dull boy," goes the rhyme. But the second line, less familiar, reads like this: "All play and no work makes Jack a mere toy."

It reads just as well—and as truly—with "Jane."

We've started off this chapter on women and work with the good news—portraits of successful women and the comments of people who enjoy their work. (Not that life is problem-free for these women, as we'll see later.) But the really bad news can be summed up by facts from the Department of Health, Education, and Welfare about the jobs most women hold. These jobs offer mainly low pay, little status, low skill requirements and little chance for advancement. A whopping 78 percent of all working women are employed in four occupations: clerical workers, service workers, factory workers, sales clerks. This distribution is so lopsided that some social scientists and economists have called it "occupational segregation." It's almost as separate as the "white" and "colored" designated areas of the old South.

Currently, about 50 percent of the women in America work outside the home. Forty-four percent of these women are married. The average time in the labor force for women today is twenty-five years—even accounting for time out for raising children. Yet women earn, on the average, only three-fifths as much as men.

Statistics of this kind have been around for years, but people tend to shrug them off by saying that women only work for "pin money" anyhow. That is patently untrue. An HEW survey in March of 1973 showed that of the nearly thirty-four million women in the labor force, nearly half were working because of severe economic need. They were either single, divorced, widowed or separated or had husbands whose incomes were between $3000 and $7000 per year. Clearly, these women's salaries were more like "bread money" than "pin money."

As we've seen, the idea that women do not or should not have to work—in the same sense that a man does—is fairly new, a by-product of the Industrial Revolution. Society's ideas about women as pampered darlings applied only to an affluent, elite class and were never extended to working-class women. As Linda Gordon and Susan Heverby point out in *America's Working Women*, the females of the working class were a handy source of cheap, expendable labor. "Not only could women be forced to absorb unemployment and seasonal work, and to perform the most tedious jobs, but their availability to do so was used to keep men's wages and resistance down."

Many middle-class women today are finding themselves in the situation that working-class women have grown accustomed to. Trying to find jobs after their children are grown—or facing divorce, like the women Dorothy Burlage studied—they find themselves working at jobs far below their capabilities. Often, both working-class women and middle-class women are ill prepared to survive in the workplace, as the statistics so painfully show.

So what do we do about this? We should look at the present and future as they really are, and tell young women about it. First of all, the odds are high—and getting higher all the time—that women will be in the workplace for a good percentage of their lives. Whether we are delighted with that idea or hate it, it's a fact too omnipresent to be ignored. A report prepared for HEW by the Center for Vocational Education at Ohio State puts it quite bluntly: "We must not lead our daughters to

276

believe they will not have to work after marriage (assuming they *will* marry). We must help our sons to see that their 'masculinity' is in no way threatened if their wives work—because, like it or not, their wives probably will work. And unless we want our daughters to spend about 25 years of their lives working for little pay in dead-end jobs, we'd better make sure that they prepare for occupations that best reflect their interests and capabilities. In short, we must define what's best for our children to include career planning for both our daughters and sons."

Some parents will wince at those blunt words; we're reminded of one man who, though sympathetic with the aspirations of women, sighed and said rather wistfully, "But I'd hate to see us get into a situation where women feel they have to *work.*"

Many misconceptions are floating around in that statement: for example, the idea that a woman bending over a toilet rinsing out dirty diapers is not "working." And, given the statistics about the social and psychological costs of the traditional role for women, it might be more appropriate for him to worry when his daughter says all she wants to do is get married and raise a houseful of kids. But myths die hard, and as critic Elizabeth Janeway points out, society more often acts on the basis of myths than on the basis of social reality.

The truth about the future is so important to women's lives that not to help them to face it amounts to criminal negligence. The information is of vital importance to women of all classes, not just the affluent. It's easy to see why a middle-class woman with brains and the chance at a good education would rather be a lawyer than a typist. But for women who are not part of "elite" groups, serious attention to their work lives may be even more important. Louise Kapp Howe, who studied workers in traditional "women's jobs," notes that as more college-trained women come into the job market, "workers with less than a college education, particularly women, will have less of a chance of advancing in professions than they did in the past, particularly in such professions as accounting. They will have less opportunity for promotions in sales, managerial and some clerical and service occupations . . . the availability of more college-educated workers will limit workers with fewer years of schooling." In other words, the competition is going to be tough.

If the disinclination of women to plan their life long work continues, it will be akin to fastening a set of hobbles on their feet. Many able women who might move up into high-prestige jobs will not do so; for others, it may mean the difference between a good job and a rotten one.

This shortsightedness means that it is often hard to unionize women workers. The Texas Instruments Company in Austin is a good example: The United Auto Workers and the International Association of Machinists have spent a reported $3 million over the past twenty-five years trying to unionize this industrial giant, with little success. Beth Nissen, a *Wall Street Journal* reporter who worked on the assembly line at Texas Instruments, says that despite employee complaints of low pay and compulsory Saturday work, none of the women wanted anything to do with unions. They were frightened of company reprisals, and many of the workers were young women barely out of their teens who considered themselves lucky to have a job. They tended to be happy with the present, and not worry about the future.

Of course, the record of unions in battling for women workers is hardly a shining one. Louise Kapp Howe says, "Even in those unions where women form the bulk of the membership, the overriding pattern of labor has been first and foremost to protect the white male members and that surely remains the predominant pattern today. Historically women's place in the labor force has been as restricted by unions—organized white male workers—as it has by management."

The availability of a large, floating pool of cheap female labor is useful to industry—and it will not vanish unless women perceive their problems at work not just as individual ones, but as a part of the structure of society, and begin to organize. A few token females in prestigious positions won't change reality for the majority of women.

If women are not going to end up in dead-end, low-paying jobs, realistic information about the working world has to be available to them at an early age. We've seen that girls tend to choose less prestigious occupations than boys do as they get older, and that guidance counselors in schools tend to steer female students toward the traditional "female jobs" where pay and advancement are lower. A great deal of myth and misinformation need to be jettisoned. Consider the belief that nursing is an ideal career for a woman who wants a family. As several of the divorced women Dorothy Burlage studied found out, nursing shifts are ever-changing and often involve odd hours, and private-duty nursing doesn't provide many of the benefits families need, such as medical coverage. Medicine, however, could in fact be an ideal career for a woman with a family. A woman doctor can choose a specialty that allows great flexibility in hours and produces enough income for the woman to hire competent household help. But girls are rarely helped to think in those terms, and we keep on seeing human potential going to waste. For example, in one well-known thirty-five-year study by psychologist Lewis Terman of more than 1300 men and women whose IQs averaged a near-genius 151, 86 percent of the gifted men had become prominent professionals and managers. Of the women who were employed, 37 percent were nurses, librarians, social workers and noncollege teachers. Twenty percent were secretaries, stenographers, bookkeepers and office workers. Only 11 percent achieved the sort of successful career advancement the men achieved. But of all the women, 61 percent were full-time homemakers at the age of forty-four, well after their children were in school.

If a girl has to learn about the realities of the working world in terms of what it will mean to her economic future, she also ought to know about the effect it will have on the quality of her "interior" life. We've discussed the current debate in the social sciences about whether the housewife or the employed woman is more satisfied with her life. Several national surveys have shown that, in general, employed women are at least as satisfied as women at home. And we've said the answers don't mean much unless you know other things about the women, such as whether they prefer to work. Not too long ago, it was believed that women who worked did so because their marriages were unhappy, and that "career women" were an unhappy, masculinized breed of female— the kind that Joan Crawford used to play in the movies, with her hair in an upsweep and her eyes cold and steely. That image is the stuff of myth, not reality. There is a growing body of evidence today that paid employment can be a boon to the emotional health of women. We don't, unfortunately, know as much as we should about women and work, because social scientists have been obsessed with the idea that children and homemaking were central to the well-being of women. Another problem with the data is that working women are often lumped together in studies as if they were a homogeneous group. Clearly, an overworked, ill-paid woman who has inadequate arrangements for child care is going to feel much differently about her work than a highly paid executive who can afford a housekeeper—and her work will probably have a less favorable impact on her well-being. Work is not the same experience for all women, and shouldn't be treated as if it were.

Despite the imperfections in the research, we are beginning to understand that work can protect women from some of the emotional problems they have been vulnerable to in our culture. We've already

279

discussed studies suggesting that working women are less susceptible than women at home to such symptoms as depression because they have more sources of support and involvement. A more recent, major study by Frederick W. Ilfeld,[9] a professor of psychiatry at the University of California Medical School (Davis), confirms this notion. He surveyed 2299 households in Chicago in 1977, focusing on symptoms of stress and psychiatric disorder. He found that the percentage of women who have "high symptomatology"—a lot of problems—was twice that of men. Men's symptoms only rose to the general level of women's when they were in certain situations—including being widowed, single, poor (a family income of under $10,000), or black. The only group of women who had symptom rates as low as men were employed women whose occupational status was high. In other words, they had very good jobs. Ilfeld concluded, "From our findings comes a very practical implication for lowering women's symptomatology, namely, encouraging and enabling them to find jobs, especially of higher status."

A high-status job seems to be a boon to both men and women—not exactly surprising in our upwardly mobile, achievement-oriented society. When Judith Birnbaum studied married professionals, these women seemed to be doing very well. They were pleased with themselves, had high self-esteem and they hardly ever felt lonely. Indeed they felt personally competent and worthwhile. They felt attractive to men, and while they sometimes worried about whether or not they spent enough time with their children, they believed themselves to be good mothers. To read Birnbaum's description, they seem fairly glowing with good emotional health. They show few signs of the malady that such women are supposed to fall victim to: "role strain."

What is role strain? It sounds like some new form of hernia, but it is actually a useful term to describe three different sources of strain that working mothers are supposed to be burdened with.

First, there are the demands on people who function simultaneously in a variety of roles. Each separate life role brings a separate set of relationships and "rights and duties" to other people. For example, the college student living in a dormitory only has to worry about relating to teachers and peers. When she goes home, she is a daughter to her parents and has to deal with their expectations—and maybe their worries as well. If she works part time, she has a boss to relate to, and perhaps co-workers or customers to deal with. The more roles you are involved in, the more complicated life becomes.

The second source of role strain is the internal consequences of crossing sex-role boundaries—as when mothers become wage earners. They are supposed to be suffering from guilt and ambivalence about "unfeminine" behavior, and feeling confused by the overwhelming demands of living in both the "assertive" male culture and the more gentle, loving female one.

The third aspect of role strain is just plain overload: having only a twenty-four-hour day to cope with the workplace, and the home, the kids, the dirty dishes and the laundry.

No one—male or female—entirely escapes role strain. Birnbaum's married professionals sometimes felt burdened by their dual work load, and wished they had more time, but for the most part they felt a sense of freshness and pleasure from the variety of shifting back and forth between jobs of wife and mother to worker.

Of course, one can see that class and money are relevant here. These professionals obviously had the resources to hire help, making house-keeping less onerous, and seemed to have the support of their husbands. But what of a woman like "Linda," a beautician who was one of the women Louise Kapp Howe studied in *Pink Collar Workers?* Linda not only stood on her feet all day at a very difficult job, but she also had to bear the full burden at home. She told Howe that she not only did all the housework, but wanted it that way. "I don't believe in women's lib. And I don't believe in all that crap—making a husband do half the work . . . My mother taught me it was the responsibility of the woman to clean the home and cook and clean the clothes and everything. And my mother is that way and I'm going to stay the way my mother is. Because I don't believe in all that garbage and my husband thinks it's a lot of garbage too."

Linda, who was not happy with having to work anyway, is clearly vulnerable to experience a heavy dose of "role strain." It is not working per se that creates this kind of strain for a woman, but the conditions of her work, her attitudes and the attitudes of her family about it.

Psychologist Abigail Stewart[10] of Boston University found this to be so when she looked at the life satisfaction of ninety women, ten years after their college graduation. She discovered that high role combination—defined as being a wife, mother and worker—wasn't a source of psychological distress. On the contrary, personal fulfillment seemed to be associated with high role combination. Interestingly enough, both the working mothers and the at-home mothers expressed satisfaction with their lives—but the women at home were eager for "radical change" in their lives, and the working mothers were not. The problem for the at-home mothers, Stewart suggests, is "underload"—boredom and lack of challenge. The two groups tended to react to stress in different ways—the mothers at home with depression, and the working mothers with physical symptoms.

The whole question of role strain might be answered with common sense: a woman who is hassled—with family disapproval, too much housework and worries over child care—will naturally show strain. Satisfaction, self-esteem, well-being and the like do not depend simply on whether one is or isn't working. It's a whole package. In general, high role combination—being involved in a variety of activities—is good for psychological health; it helps eliminate boredom, gives one a sense of purpose and zest for life. When Rosalind and Grace studied 142 white, married middle-class women who were mothers of preschoolers, they found that a strong work commitment had a positive impact on the well-being of the employed mothers. The idea that a woman who has several roles will run into inevitable strain damaging her sense of well-being just isn't so.

Work turns out to be a valuable source of self-esteem and satisfaction for women—for those who like their work and who don't feel overloaded with anxiety about child care, family disapproval or overwork. This is true for women who have young children—and it may be even more important for women beyond the child-raising years.

Overall, work looks like a good prescription for mental health for women. But work isn't a magic answer to every woman's problems.

When Jessica Segrè[11] of Boston University and the Somerville Mental Health Clinic studied a group of middle-aged, middle-class women, she asked whether there were any differences in self-concept or depression in full-time housewives, part-time workers and full-time employed women. She found no differences in overall satisfaction among the groups, though she did pick up a few important variations. The homemakers said most often that the reason they weren't working was that mothers *should* be home with their children. They seemed to need, Segrè says, not only to prove to the interviewers that they were happy and fulfilled, but also to insinuate that women who were working must not be.

The full-time workers, on the other hand, possessed one characteristic as a group—they had less happy marriages than the other women. Was this because they were working? Yes, but not because of work per se, but because of their attitudes about it. These women had been socialized in the traditional pattern, and their resentments surfaced in the interviews. One woman summed up the feelings of the group with the comment, "I should not have had to have worked now." They seemed to feel that women should only have to work after all their maternal duties had been performed, and many of them still had children at home. Most of them were working because the family—despite its upper-middle-class status—needed the money. They felt forced into the workplace ahead of schedule, and they felt their husbands had therefore failed them.

Clearly, for these women, a job was a source of anger and resentment toward their husbands, even if it otherwise gave them satisfaction. The traditional idea that a husband must support his wife created real problems when their husbands couldn't live up to it. The same thing happened with Linda, the beautician, when her idea that a wife ought to do all the housework ran smack into the physical reality that she couldn't carry the entire burden of the home and a full-time job as well. Given the statistics about the number of women who are working today—and projecting that trend into the future—we may be creating great problems for people by keeping these old ideas alive. Is it fair to men—or to the women they will marry—if they are taught it is unmanly to wipe a dish or a kid's runny nose? We will be setting them up for inevitable conflict in the future. Is it fair to let a woman expect to be supported—and leave her open to the anger and shock of discovering that is not true? (In the next chapter we return to this crucial issue.)

The Segrè study was atypical in finding marital problems among married working women. Repeatedly, national surveys have found no difference in marital satisfaction between working and nonworking women—whether they asked the husband, the wife, or both. When James Wright of the University of Massachusetts reviewed these surveys, he found that "Among middle-class women, especially, there is simply no difference in marital and familial satisfactions between housewives and working women." Nor are working women more prone to have problems with their children. "The popular notion that families with a working mother would produce more 'problem children' is not confirmed in this data. The proportion reporting problems with their children is the same whether the woman works outside the home or not . . . working women may well face special strains in managing their marriages and family lives, but such strains as do exist do not, it appears, create greater dissatisfactions in these areas."

Segrè's women obviously were a special group—they were affluent, mostly middle-class suburban women, apparently raised to believe they should not and would not have to work. These difficulties reflect what happens to women who are socialized for a future that doesn't exist. Let's not make the same mistakes with our children. Today's protected girls are tomorrow's resentful women.

14

ALTERNATE PATTERNS

Staking Out New Territory

Unmarried women all share in not realizing that they have traits which are unlovable, or in having failed to acquire traits that are lovable. It takes most unmarrieds about a year to face up to this fact, and to be able to bring themselves to the point where they will work at achieving lovability.

—Director, American Institute of Family Relations'
Marriage Readiness course

The fountains mingle with the river
And the rivers with the ocean,
The winds of heaven mix forever
With a sweet emotion;
Nothing in the world is single;
All things by a law divine
In one spirit meet and mingle.
Why not I with thine?

—Percy Bysshe Shelley

It is a woman's business to get married as soon as possible, and a man's to keep unmarried as long as he can.

—George Bernard Shaw, *Man and Superman*

Being single—unwed and by inference unwanted—seems so wrong that romantic poets like Shelley cried out that it was contrary to nature; a more cynical observer like Shaw saw the whole mating process as a chase, with the male the quarry and the female in hot pursuit. In any event, being single isn't an approved situation for anyone, though the carefree bachelor certainly comes off as a more appealing character than the spinster or the old maid. Today one can, of course, be a "swinging single" of either sex, but the phrase has a tawdry ring to it—one thinks of psychedelic lights, loud music, tight pants and see-through blouses, apartments with mirrors on the ceilings and a sort of wham-bam, thank you, ma'am (or sir) approach to personal relationships, hardly substantial enough to build a life around. All in all, the single state suffers from, at the very least, a bad press.

For women, the state of singlehood has usually been seen as nothing less than personal disaster. The behavioral sciences, with their insistence that only husband and family could fulfill a woman, added the weight of science to that notion. Sometimes, in fact, psychologists decided it was their job to play matchmaker to the unmarried women of America, to deliver them from spinsterhood to the arms of some willing man. In the mid-fifties, for example, the American Institute of Family Relations devised a Marriage Readiness course to wrestle with the problems of single women. Single women did have problems, of course. The director of the institute, a psychologist, decreed, "Unmarried women all share in not realizing that they have traits which are unlovable, or in having failed to acquire traits that are lovable. It takes most unmarrieds about a year to face up to this fact, and to be able to bring themselves to the point where they will work at achieving lovability."

The unmarried women of America—some of them at least—trooped to the institute to learn to be lovable. The story of "Marcia Carter" was the case history of a success. Here's how she described it:

"I squeezed the orange juice, popped hot toast onto plates, splashed scalding coffee into the cups and called through the hall door: 'Eggs will be done in thirty seconds, dear!' A few minutes later we said morning grace and I was eating breakfast across from the man I love most in the world.

"It still seems incredible to me—that I have so much. I still catch myself sitting cross-legged on the couch, naively surveying our domain with abandoned delight. Everything as I had hoped for: blue and yellow provincial print on the wing-back lounge, braided oval rug on the floor, maple rocker and cobbler's bench, bookcases loaded with our favorites, a golden splash of sunshine coming through the curtain. Four years ago I had tried to quell what seemed to be the hopeless desire for these very experiences of happiness. I asked myself, 'If I am not going to live them, why do they keep torturing me?"

So Marcia Carter took action. She went to the Marriage Readiness course. She rooted in her family tree to find out if "unlovableness" might be due to a bad gene: "On the surface everything for an early happy marriage seemed to be in my favor. There were no bad examples around me. My parents and my brother were happily married." She took a battery of personality tests to see how she rated on such qualities as Nervous, Aggressive, Submissive, Cordial, Hard-boiled, Sympathetic, Quiet. She dutifully went to work on her rough edges—she was a bit too shy, a bit too proud, a little too demanding and not really a "fun" person. She worked very hard, and finally her file was closed. Marcia Carter, spinster, twenty-nine, became Mrs. John Doe, married lady.

If Marcia Carter seems obsessive about the furniture and somewhat vague about the man, no matter. She was married and thus, de facto, happy.

Conversely, the single woman is expected to be unhappy—and personally flawed to boot; if she weren't, why would she still be single? Social work consultant Margaret Adams, author of *Single Blessedness*,[1] contends that the greatest frustration for single women in contemporary society is the fact that people think they have not married for psychological reasons—all of them bad. She says that psychology has been "put to the unworthy end of helping to diminish the social structure of single individuals."

If single people say they *like* being single, Adams says, they are told they are rationalizing—"Making the best of a bad job." If they persist in saying that being single suits them fine, they are accused of overcompensation. "Overcompensation, interpreted by the psychiatrically sophisticated, means that in reality we single people are unhappy, but being unable to face this unpalatable situation, firmly stifle the realization by harping obstinately on the positive aspects of our lives."

What in fact, is the reality? Are single women destined to be lonely, unhappy creatures? One would certainly expect that the single woman in our society would be fighting an uphill battle for fulfillment, given the prevailing social mythology and given, too, the syndrome that Rosalind sees often among women in therapy: "I am nothing without a man."

The Quality of American Life study, which we've referred to several times before, found that, in general, both unmarried men and women over thirty describe their lives in negative terms. The women, however, are better off than the men—more satisfied with their education and their jobs, less vulnerable to psychological disorders such as mental breakdown. Half the women surveyed in this category were over fifty-five, and one wonders whether their reported dissatisfaction reflects real unhappiness in their daily lives or a sense of failure to live up to the societal norms they grew up with. The researchers Campbell, Converse and Rodgers, suspect the latter. "In 1971, being single was not a favorable condition of life for either women or men; if prevailing folkways regarding marriage change as dramatically as some observers think they may, the fact of being single or married may lose much of the significance it now has for the quality of life."

Large-scale surveys are limited, of course, in that they can't probe issues deeply, and all kinds of "singles" are lumped together, from the woman in her fifties in a low-paying job who feels personally defeated, to the thirty-year-old executive whose work brings her many economic and personal rewards. The single state is not the same for all women. Psychologist Judith Birnbaum, whose studies of homemakers and married professionals we've cited earlier, looked at single professionals and found them to be highly satisfied with their lives, in contrast to the women in *The Quality of American Life* study.

The typical single professional, Birnbaum reports, is a bright woman from a lower-class background. Growing up in conditions that were not affluent, she may have developed a somewhat jaundiced view of men as "providers." Often, in childhood, she was a tomboy, felt herself shy, awkward and estranged from the typical girls' games and pursuits. She did well in school and hit on achievement as the avenue to make her way in the world without having to charm a man. Later, as an adult, she proves to be very work-oriented, depending on work for both personal satisfaction and economic independence. Often, she sees herself channeling her "feminine" qualities of nurture into the world of work. One woman told Birnbaum that she has broadened her capacity for "mothering" to include many others, "really caring about other people, whether and how they hurt. It adds a quality of humanity to the professional world which helps to combat some of the sterility characteristic of that world." The single professional often sees marriage as incompatible with her life-style, which is independent and career-oriented. The lack of children can seem an empty space in her life, one she fills with friends, students, co-workers. But she sees herself as happy, and she feels

288

competent and productive. She may have her regrets, but as Birnbaum describes her, she is far from the miserable spinster of legend. She experiences herself as a successful adult, and, as Birnbaum writes of one woman, "she recognized with a sense of pleasure and comfort she is no longer a 'black sheep' (the feeling she had as a child) but at home in the larger university family, productive and recognized, although not procreative in the narrowest sense."

A sense of loss about not having children seems common to these single professionals. That doesn't necessarily mean that they would make a different life choice if they had to do it over again. To many, childlessness may be seen as the price to be paid for a life that seems overall quite satisfying.

For many parents, the prospect that a daughter might not get married is frightening. These concerns often get translated into pressures on daughters to date more often, go to co-ed schools or opt out of career training that might interfere with their social lives. Daughters have their own anxieties on this score, and it would be helpful to them to be able to talk to their parents about the subject without feeling that their parents' reaction will be panic—"You'll be an old maid," or, "You're throwing away your chances for happiness for that Ph.D."

The only image most parents have of singlehood for women is the shriveled old maid. Who would want that for a daughter? But these images may be changing. In the future, one suspects, the onus of singlehood for women may be reduced by a number of factors, a major one being the sheer numbers of people who are remaining—or becoming single. There are presently some fifty-two million single people in the United States. *Newsweek* magazine in 1978 reported that one securities firm has projected that people who live alone may account for 25 percent of the households in the United States by 1985. Arthur Norton, chief of the marriage and family statistics branch of the Bureau of the Census says, that "more and more people will find themselves single at some time. Proportionally, more and more will be living independently, and more and more will be breaking up their marriages."

Not only are more people single today, but more of them have positive ideas about their status. Some are choosing the single state for its economic and social benefits—fewer expenses, more mobility, intense involvement in careers that marriage might interrupt. *Newsweek* cites sociologist Arlene Skolnick, of the University of California, Berkeley, saying that singles are "losing the image of being life's lonely losers."

289

For women, new opportunities in high-level jobs such as management, and decreased emphasis on marriage and motherhood as woman's only fulfillment, will mean that the single state will more and more become an attractive option. The relaxation of rigid sexual mores also makes a difference. Not too long ago, a woman who had sexual relations outside of marriage was regarded as a fallen woman. Chastity was the only course for the respectable unmarried woman. Today, many single people, both male and female, have intimate relationships with members of the opposite sex and few eyebrows are raised. Being single need not mean forgoing intimacy or sexuality. It could mean that a career will be more important for a woman in determining how satisfied she is with her life. If her time and energy are focused on her job—rather than on home and children—an exciting, well-paying job can be a major source of self-esteem and satisfaction.

If the single life-style is becoming more and more socially acceptable, there is another alternative to traditional family life that is on the increase. Many married couples today are making deliberate decisions not to have children. This is in stark contrast to the usual pattern, which is, as the children's chant puts it: "First comes love, then comes marriage, then comes (fill in the name) pushing a baby carriage." A fair number of women today are deciding against that last step. There are some who think they are unnatural for doing so.

The childless woman is, in popular mythology, a sorry figure, and the words chosen to describe her ring with the imagery of desolation. "Barren" brings to mind fields laid waste, streets emptied of people, a wasteland. The woman who cannot have children is pitied, thought to be shorn of the chance for happiness. The woman who chooses not to have children receives a harsher verdict. She is *unnatural*.

Failure to procreate, especially by a woman, represents a failure of normal development, so the theory goes. Some theorists don't mince words in making this point. In her 1971 book *Psychology of Women*,[2] Judith Bardwick states: "In the reality of current socialization and expectations, I regard women who are not motivated to achieve the affiliative role with husband and children as not normal." She calls marriage and children the most important of all feminine needs and says, "When these are absent, denied or defended against, my clinical observation is that there is evidence for pathological levels of anxiety, a distorted sex identity and a neurotic solution."

If this is indeed the case, then women who have chosen to remain childless shouldn't be a very happy group. Judith Guss Teicholz,[3] a psychologist at Massachusetts General Hospital, suggests a picture of what these women should be like. They should, she says, be more anxious and neurotic than other women, less feminine in their identification and less well socialized—that is, adjusted to the expectations of society. Teicholz set out to study married women who had remained childless, comparing them with a similar group of married women who did wish to have children but had not yet started families. She called her groups the nonmothers and the future mothers.

The nonmothers ranged in age from twenty-three to thirty-eight. They were women in stable marriages who had made a fully voluntary decision to remain childless and regarded that decision as permanent. Both groups were on the upper end of the socioeconomic scale and had attained "an unusually high educational level"; the two groups of women were very much the same except for one important difference: the decision about children.

The women were given a battery of psychological tests, and the scores of the groups were then compared. Was there the huge gap that might be expected between these groups of women—the one group "abnormal" and the other "normal"? Were the childless women anxious, neurotic and poorly adjusted?

In fact, they were not. There were no significant differences between the two groups on the measures of socialization, neurotic symptoms or feminine identification. The only measure on which the two groups did differ significantly was on a test which assessed their "male" and "female" personality traits. The nonmothers were more likely than the future mothers to be "androgynous"—that is, to possess a high level of both "male" and "female" characteristics. In other words, the nonmothers tended to see themselves as less limited by sex-role stereotypes.

Teicholz says that the results of her study do not confirm the bleak picture of the childless woman often painted by behavioral scientists. Quite the contrary. The nonmothers, she says, were a highly educated and achievement-oriented group of women who scored higher than the national norms on tests of social maturity, flexibility and achievement. Their anxiety level was no greater than that of the women in the study who did plan to have children. The nonmothers were no less identified with female values and interests than were the other women. On a test of unconscious sexual identity, the scores of the nonmothers were as "feminine" as those of the comparison group. They were also equally satisfied with their marriages.

"We must conclude from these findings," says Teicholz, "that the decision to remain childless is not necessarily associated with social maladjustment or immaturity, nor with neurotic adjustment, nor with poor feminine identification." For the group of women she studied, Teicholz says, "the choice against motherhood does not appear to distinguish these women from other women of similar age and background."

Teicholz's conclusion is backed up by several other studies described at the 1978 meeting of the American Psychological Association. In general, childless couples have not been looked at with much favor by the mental health professions. Such couples have often been described as selfish, immature, sexually incompetent and maladjusted. Robert A. Brown, a University of Maryland psychologist, and his colleague R. Magarick did a study comparing forty-four married, childless men with fifty-one fathers, and found no differences in their overall psychological adjustment.[4] The two groups did not differ in regard to psychiatric symptoms. Their data, they say, strongly support the idea that childless men are at least as healthy emotionally as men who have children.

These childless men were hardly a grim lot; there were no more divorces in their families than in the families of the men who were fathers, and they weren't any different than the men who had children in estimating the happiness of their parents' marriages—or their own happiness as children. However, the childless men seemed to be more flexible and independent than did the men with children. Brown and Magarick concluded that their study, along with a small but growing body of literature, suggests that "childlessness is not determined by or associated with social or personal pathology and may be considered a viable, healthy lifestyle."

Another researcher, Sharon K. Houseknecht[5] of Ohio State University, studied the motivation of women who decided not to have children. One-third of this group, she said, decided quite early not to have children. They felt intense pressure for achievement from their parents and came from families where the atmosphere was emotionally cool. These women might be said to have negative reasons for remaining childless. Two-thirds of the childless women, however, were quite different. They were encouraged by their parents to be independent and to make their own decisions. They decided not to have children only after being involved in careers in which they had a strong interest, and which they did not wish to interrupt for child rearing.

Remaining single, or marrying and not having children, are not the only alternatives to the "traditional" life-style that women are choosing today—and will choose in greater numbers in the future. For many couples, the terrain of marriage itself, along with parental roles, is changing. A new kind of marriage, the two-career couple, is gaining more acceptance, particularly among young, educated, urban dwellers. This isn't surprising when you look at the attitudes of young women who are attending college now, or have graduated fairly recently. The College Research Bureau (affiliated with the Educational Testing Service of Princeton, New Jersey) has been studying the attitudes of college women over the past ten years. The findings indicate that young women today want smaller families, are more serious about careers and have a more liberal view about women's role in society than students did in the past. For example, in 1965, 45 percent of female freshmen said they wanted four children. But in 1973, 65 percent of the freshmen women (and 50 percent of the men) wanted only two children. In 1965, 37 percent of these women expected a life centered on home and family. But by 1971, less than one in five expected to be a housewife in fifteen years. A majority, 53 percent, projected a combination óf career and marriage, with or without children.

These facts are going to upset some tidy little models that social scientists have used to explain the way families ought to behave. For a long time, the "lens" for looking at marriages, and deciding whether they were or were not working was the theory of Talcott Parsons, a "functional sociologist."[6] (That is the technical name for a person who looks at different social systems and figures out how they work.) According to Parsons' mode, marriage called for a clear-cut division of labor between husband and wife. The husband serves as the family's link to the world of work; he is the breadwinner, and the status and prestige of the family are determined by *his* status and prestige. The woman is in charge of the "expressive" side of family life—she nurtures others, eases emotional crises and takes care of the family's social life. This model, Parsons suggested, offered the maximum opportunity for a conflict-free relationship, since each partner had his or her own sphere and there was little chance of competition between the two. If the situation were altered—particularly if the wife started to compete in the male sphere of

293

work and prestige, then trouble could very well be expected. Social scientists have accepted this model, often without question, for years. Women who work have been warned that they were running a severe risk of causing marital maladjustment and disrupting the family.

One should be careful, however, to keep in mind what functional sociologists do—and don't do. They look at systems and describe how they work—but that doesn't mean that those systems are the best ones possible for the human beings in them, nor that better ones couldn't be devised. For example, a functional sociologist might have looked at the agricultural society of the old South and decreed—quite rightly—that that system could not exist without slavery. But that didn't mean that slavery was right, or that the region might not fare much better under a different kind of system.

One problem with the Parsons model of marriage is that it doesn't allow for individual differences. It assumes that every woman—and every man—is just the same, and all will be happy with the same rigid assignment of roles. The people who stuck to the Parsons model as something akin to Sacred Writ didn't deal with the fact that the woman's role was the socially devalued one, or that her assigned area was much more constricted than the man's, one that gave her little opportunity to be involved with the affairs of society at large.

The specter of the Parsonian model still hovers over the behavioral sciences today. Or perhaps specter is the wrong word, because the traditional model still has plenty of meat on its bones. Three social scientists who have studied dual-career families—Lynn Simonsen Walker, Barbara Strudler Wallston and Howard M. Sandler[7] of George Peabody College in Nashville, say that some of their colleagues may be part of the problem, not part of the solution. "Researchers," they say, "by continuing to rely on [this] model as a framework for their research, have contributed to the maintenance of constraints on changing marital roles. Empirical research, for example, has not generally been directed towards discovering conditions that allow couples to be successful in deviating from traditional roles."

Two Maryland therapists who are working with couples to help them achieve more egalitarian and more satisfying marriages have found this sort of resistance in the hierarchy of social service agencies. Naomi Dagen Bloom and Ronald L. Bloom[8] found that couples who came to traditional marriage workshops were "involved in more dysfunctional relationships than we expected and we needed to develop our skills in

294

order to accommodate them. It was this that led us both to begin group work training in Washington, D.C., in group counseling and psychotherapy."

The Blooms found, however, social service agencies resistant to their ideas. "There seems to be more willingness to provide preventative services to single parents and to teenagers but not to married couples struggling with the burdens of the nuclear family . . . Perhaps the reluctance is tied up with something nobody really wants to face. Our experiences have been that the people in positions to make decisions . . . all have something in common. Whether they are mental health professionals or not they share an uneasiness; they are not quite sure about how they feel about marriage—both their own and marriage in general. They are even less sure that they approve of the idea of several couples meeting to talk openly about their relationships. And a great deal of their uneasiness comes from their own sexist attitudes. They know where women belong, but they are afraid women may have other ideas."

This reluctance to look beyond the Parsons model of marriage has resulted in a great deal of skewed research about family and marital adjustment. Remember, we said earlier that there is good science and bad science; the latter often results when mythology gets in the way of research. The marital adjustment literature locks people into Parsonian categories with men having the instrumental (doing) role and women the expressive (feeling) one. So, much of the research has been focused on finding out what awful things happen when women step out of that role and into the "male" one. The Nashville researchers say, "The result has been research that examines the women's work role for its threat to marriage and family welfare, and overlooks or misinterprets findings that do not fit [this] model."

By now, common sense should tell us that the rigid Parsonian model just doesn't fit many people in today's world. Men are not emotionless doers; women are not inert blobs of feeling. This model has something of the assembly line mentality to it—each person does her or his own little job and doesn't interfere with the other. Now we've discovered that the assembly line is driving workers crazy, and companies are finding that one way to make workers happier is to have them working on teams where each member does many different jobs, interacting with others.

The Parsonian model assumes that if men and women do not stay in their separate spheres, the result will be competition, then tension and ultimately chaos. But few people bothered to question whether that assumption was in fact true, and perhaps even fewer looked at the drawbacks. These drawbacks are illustrated by the data on the dissatisfaction of the bright, college-educated housewife. When one partner in the marriage is bored, restless, asking about life, "Is this all there is?" tension and chaos can also result. The assumption has been that marriage is like the original Model T Ford—which, if you remember, came in one model and one color (black)—and you had to take it or leave it.

But as we've seen, having a valued instrumental role in the outside world often enhances women's happiness in the marriage. The Nashville researchers point out that instrumental roles for women are not only legitimate but also are a potential asset for the family. "The need for research with a new orientation is becoming more apparent, given the growing social recognition of a new kind of marital relationship—the 'dual-career' couple." In such marriages, the researchers say, both parties have a significant link to the world of work, and this usually leads to a shuffling around of roles and duties at home. "Because of the relative lack of role models, dual-career couples are forced into stressful personal negotiations in working out an individualized marriage contract. They attempt to reallocate both instrumental and expressive roles, defining their marital relationship in a manner that is at odds with the common social definition shared by the society in general."

In other words, if you can't do what Mom and Dad did, and if you bring a whole truckload of emotional baggage to nightly negotiations about who does the dishes, that's trouble.

How do couples actually navigate these tricky new waters? One crucial element seems to be necessary to success: clear-cut agreement on who should, and who will, do what. Studies have shown that agreement on marital roles is important for the stability of the marriage. Some theorists view each marriage as a little world, in which the two partners create their own image of reality, one which both come to share. In traditional marriages, the occupants of that world were handed a ready-made set of blueprints. The dual-career couple may have to draw up their own plans, from scratch. Serious marital strain is created when spouses can't understand and accept each other's views.

The Nashville researchers, in their study, looked at fifty-seven couples who were classified into three groups: traditional, nontraditional and mixed. In the first group, the couples agreed that the man's job would take precedence particularly in deciding where to live. The nontraditional couples were those in which both the wives' and the husbands' jobs would be given equal weight in such a decision, or in which the wives' jobs would take precedence. The mixed group was composed of couples who did not agree on what should be done in such a situation. The fact that both spouses were engaged in careers did not automatically mean that marital roles were nontraditional. There are many families in which the partners stick quite closely to traditional roles despite the fact that the wife works.

The researchers compared the two groups on marital satisfaction. They found that there were *no* significant differences between the traditional and the nontraditional couples. Both groups of couples agreed on their roles, though what they agreed about was different in each group. But the mixed group, which had not reached such agreement, was significantly lower in marital satisfaction.

The researchers conclude: "This study provides evidence that agreement on roles is related to marital satisfaction in dual-career couples. In fact, agreement appears to be more important than the actual content of the roles; couples were equally satisfied with their marriages regardless of whether they agreed on traditional or non-traditional roles. Placing equal or greater importance on the woman's link to the occupational system does not seem to threaten the marital relationship as long as both partners agree to this non-traditional role for the woman. A satisfactory marriage thus appears not to be dependent upon the traditional functional division of roles, but rather upon shared perceptions and expectations regarding each other's role."

In other words, what people feel about what they should or shouldn't do in marriage is more important than what they actually do. So it's crucial to look at people's attitudes when you are thinking about whether or not nontraditional patterns will present major problems to couples.

One nationwide survey, *The New York Times*–CBS poll, reported in 1977 that "Americans are more likely to believe that marriages in which the partners share the task of breadwinner and homemaker are a more satisfying way of life than they are to prefer the traditional marriage in which the husband is the provider and the wife exclusively a wife and mother." The poll showed wide disparities between young and old on attitudes about marriage, with the young people being more liberal, a sign, *Times* reporter Richard Meislin noted, "that more liberal positions are likely to become more prominent over time."

Of those interviewed, 48 percent said they preferred the idea of more liberal roles in marriage and 43 percent favored traditional roles. In the oldest group, those over forty-five, 44 percent chose traditional marriage. In the youngest, eighteen to twenty-nine, only 27 percent approved that option.

The image of working mothers has improved in the eyes of the general populace, the poll revealed. In a 1970 poll, 48 percent of those sampled said that they thought working women were worse mothers than those at home. In the 1977 survey, only 40 percent gave that answer. So a substantial proportion approved of working mothers.

It's important to note that men's attitudes about family life are also changing. For example, the *Times*–CBS poll asked whether a woman should work "even if she has a husband capable of supporting her." Twenty years ago that question would no doubt have brought a thunderous no, given the social mores of the time. However, in 1977, 54 percent of those interviewed said yes, including 58 percent of the women and 50 percent of the men. In the youngest age group, fully three-quarters of the *men* said a woman should work.

Attitudes clearly are changing, but social scientists sometimes don't keep up with the changes. We've seen how they sometimes make generalizations from inadequate data. For example, the author of one book on the father's role in child development states that although he believes feminists' demands for equality to be just, he also believes they will lead to great human cost in tension between men and women.[9] It's the Draconian grip of the Parsons theory: If you deviate from that one "right model," chaos is come again. What "evidence" does he cite for this opinion? First, a single 1955 study suggesting that marital deterioration is likely to occur when conjugal roles are not rigidly defined by society. As we've seen, however, several more recent studies show that agreement on roles seems to be the crucial issue, not the content of those roles. The only other piece of evidence for his opinion is an experiment conducted in 1971 by two college women at the University of California at Davis. These students decided to reverse the usual rules of dating, so they not only asked men out, but they opened the door for them, lit their cigarettes, drove the car, paid the bills and initiated good-night kisses. The young women reported that the typical college male was uncomfortable in that situation, and didn't try to arrange another date.

This experiment, the researcher says, "clearly" shows that men are threatened by women who behave in a manner that is in opposition to expectation. In fact, the only thing this bizarre and unscientific "experiment" clearly shows is that college men get flustered when a young woman starts acting like a fraternity stud. This situation is so far from the ordinary behavior of most young women that to say it proves anything about the consequences of more equitable sex roles is nonsensical.

This is not to say, of course, that changing roles, behavior and expectations for the sexes never involve tension and conflict. There are a great many emotional depth charges planted in these issues, whether they involve men and women, or parents and children. In the latter case, we've seen that many mothers see their daughters as "rejecting" them if they choose different life-styles, marrying late or not at all, remaining childless. Sometimes the whole subject gets so charged that it becomes "taboo," robbing mothers of communication with their daughters, and robbing daughters of support they may need very much. One woman found that her phone calls from her mother were reduced to questions about her studies, the weather—anything but the real issue—social life. During one call, the woman's mother had asked about all the trivia she could think of and was finally reduced to asking, "How's your car?"

"Not seeing anybody special," replied the daughter.

For young women, the pressure of being "deviant" among one's peers can be severe. If everyone around you is getting an engagement ring or having a baby, and you're grinding away at a paper for law school, you can't help feeling like a social outcast. Many of the accepted "timetables" for adult life don't really fit in with a woman's serious involvement with a job. Women are urged to have their children young, because "it's wonderful to be young with your children." For many women, it isn't wonderful at all. They are frustrated because they find they have to put so much time and energy into the difficult and often lonely job of raising children at an age when they feel they haven't really done anything in the outside world, haven't really lived. They plan to go into the job market when the children are school age, but discover that they are years behind the women who either didn't have children or postponed their childbearing. For a woman who is seriously committed to her work, a better strategy might be to use the early years for advancement in her career, and then have children. An experienced and valuable employee often has more flexibility with employers than someone new on the job. It's easier to arrange such things as flexible hours or a part-time schedule when you already have a good track record. The chances are also better that at that time you will be earning enough money to afford child-care help—the sort of expense few young women at entry-level jobs can afford.

Women often need the support of family, friends—and husbands, when they have them—to get over that period when they feel "different" from everybody else. It's not easy for all concerned. Even the most understanding of parents will sometimes let their concern sneak out. Caryl remembers that her mother, a professional woman who didn't have her first child until she was thirty, rarely brought up the subject of children to Caryl and her husband. One day, however, the three of them went together to the gymnasium at the school where Caryl had attended high school ten years earlier. The members of the championship basketball team of a decade past were scheduled to play the current varsity, and Caryl's husband and mother had come along to cheer on the aging warriors. All the other women passed around color pictures of their kids—with the exception of one woman who was playing in full nun's habit. Caryl's mother sat in silence and watched as the veterans huffed and puffed their way down the court. Finally she turned and said to her son-in-law: "Do you realize that the only ones on that court who don't have children are Caryl and the nun?"

If lack of communication is one of the major roadblocks between parents and children on these sensitive issues, it's also a problem in relationships between men and women. Many married couples find themselves embroiled in major conflicts about subjects that they had never talked about before marriage. The myths of romantic love can interfere with such discussions. One is supposed to be swept away, walking on air, flying to the moon; it's a magical happening that isn't supposed to be messed up by such mundane things as negotiations about how both parties can get what they really want out of life. How many couples before marching to the altar have seriously thought about such items as, "How old will I be when I have my first child?" or "Who is going to do the dishes since we're both working?" and "Who stays home when the baby is sick?" Couples at best only stumble onto solutions for these problems when they arise. Too often they find out that they really don't agree on the answers, and then conflict is inevitable. If *he* dreamed of the wife who would greet him at the door each night with a cold beer and a sympathetic word about his hard day, he is going to have trouble dealing with the fact that she gets out of work later than he does. If *she* thinks her work is as important as his, but whenever the first grader is

300

home from school with a cold, he won't think of rearranging his schedule, she is bound to get angry. The relationship where both parties are heavily involved in outside pursuits takes much more thought and negotiating than the one in which the husband and wife step automatically into traditional roles. So it's crucial that both parties understand what each wants, and how each feels about it.

We've noted that attitudes about marriage, and about men's and women's roles in society are changing, and there can often be a good deal of confusion at such a time. Often, the old ideas and the new ideas get all tangled up in people's heads, and it's not easy to sort them out. This may be the case with a good many young people today. You may remember that when we talked about the data from "Monitoring the Future," a study of contemporary high-school students, we said that the young women were very work-oriented. But at the same time, they also held onto many traditional ideas; that inconsistency is undoubtedly going to give them some sticky problems to wrestle with in the years ahead.

The young women expressed a strong commitment to work outside the home. Seventy-six percent of them thought such work should be central to their lives. They also said they wanted good jobs—often demanding, high-prestige jobs—with good salaries. But at the same time, most of the young women expected to be married within five years of graduation and to start a family within two years of marriage. Thus, most of them expect to be having children in their early or middle twenties—which is exactly the time that anyone who wants a high-prestige job should be in training for that job. Law students usually don't start working until their mid-twenties—young people in business careers are just getting to know the ropes. It seems that two expectations of these young women—for high-level jobs and early childbearing—are bound to collide.

There also seems to be some confusion about who is supposed to do what in caring for children. A large majority of the young men and women said that if the wife was working, a husband should have a greater role in child care and housework. But 63 percent of the girls, and a similar percentage of the boys, said that the wife should do most of the child care. Here's the potential for another conflict. A woman who has a demanding job, but at the same time feels she has to assume most of the child care and can't ask her husband to share the responsibility, is a sure candidate for "overload." She may, like "Linda," the beautician we mentioned in an earlier chapter, wind up trying to do everything and living with barely suppressed anger. Rarely do people point out these contradictions to young women, or to young men, and encourage them to think seriously about these issues.

The three of us have said before that we enjoy working and find it brings a freshness and challenge to our lives. But there are costs, too, especially when one is involved in raising children as well as a "two-career" marriage. Those costs showed up very clearly during the many meetings we had while writing this book. One time Rosalind got a call from day camp—her son Jonathan had hurt his hand. She had to decide whether to rush there and disrupt a crucial writing session (we had an urgent deadline) or let him wait a couple of hours. No one could tell her if the injury was minor or major.

At another session Caryl could hardly stay awake, much less be creative—she had just come from "sleeping" on the ground as a leader for a Brownie overnight.

Grace usually had to call a time-out period (always at the worst moment) so she could drive her daughter Susannah to her after-school program.

Not only did we never get away together for the weekend writing retreat we craved, but at this writing we have yet to find time for the leisurely nonwriting lunch we promised ourselves a year ago.

Social life suffers, too—one night Caryl and her husband, Alan, were sitting watching the fifth-grade Christmas-Hanukkah play, and she turned to him and said, "Do you realize that this is our only evening at the theater this year?"

Logistics can be a major problem when you are trying to manage two careers in one household. Caryl and Alan juggle two children, a Victorian house and a neurotic dog. Their daily schedules can get as complicated as the plans for the D-day invasion. Who will pick up Alyssa at gymnastics? Who will get to freeze his (or her) bottom at the midget hockey game? They have worked out a division of labor that is haphazard, but goes something like this: She usually does the cooking, keeps the children's clothes in order and vacuums. He does the food shopping, bedmaking and much hauling of children to and fro. Both do laundry—both, in fact, can do anything at any given time, like good utility infielders. The Parsonian division of labor would clearly be a disaster here. In looking at job opportunities, both Caryl and Alan put a high priority on jobs that offer them flexibility, rather than a rigid nine-to-five (or longer) schedule. They have both been willing to sacrifice some money and some prestige to do so. Neither accepts assignments requiring lengthy travel. Both realize that there are areas right now in which they can't compete with the people who work sixteen hours a day, but think that what they gain as a family is worth it. Franklin and Grace, who are both in academia, have worked out a similar arrangement. We met often at Grace's house, and Franklin and Susannah—off to the dentist or coming home from the library—were a familiar sight. Rosalind and her husband, Norman, an investment counselor, have less flexibility in their schedules, a fact that kept us in touch with the problems many people face. They find it takes constant planning to keep things running smoothly.

Logistics will continue to be a problem to all of us as long as we have young children at home, and we have to face that fact realistically. Like many other couples in our situation, we have to improvise. We usually can't learn from parents about how to work these problems out, because their marital patterns were so different from ours. More and more couples will be facing these issues as women enter the labor market and come to realize they can't handle the workplace and the complete management of the home as well. "Superwoman"—the executive who is a whiz from nine to five and dashes home to whip up a marvelous soufflé and read fairy tales to the kids—is not the role model most of us ought to try to emulate. That kind of life-style is only made possible by more energy than most people possess, or by enough money to hire full-time household help (a luxury few people can afford)—or by martyrdom.

Difficult as the problem of logistics may be, however, it can be worked out if both parties can agree to share goals and responsibilities. As we've seen, the important thing is that both parties *agree* on marital roles. This isn't always easy, especially given the sex-role stereotypes so deeply rooted in our culture and our consciousness. There are hundreds of little time bombs hidden in the small chores we do each day, chores divided up into "his" or "her" jobs. The "her" jobs usually include the grubby or most menial, and doing them is part of being a "good" wife, mother, homemaker. This equation of menial work and female virtue runs deep. Consider the Wisk commercial on television: the wife who doesn't get hubby's collar clean is a bad wife.

This layer of emotional values and social approval that has been slathered over such grungy—and not inherently sex-related—jobs as cleaning a collar or washing a floor makes renegotiating of job duties a tricky thing. A woman simply does not say, "I don't want to wash the floor" if she was raised to believe that washing the floor is a labor of love.

She may be suffering pangs of guilt because somewhere deep down inside she feels she is betraying some universal female instinct. And her husband may not be hearing, "I don't want to wash the floor." Having been schooled in the same social values as she, he may be hearing, "I don't love you," or he may feel demeaned by having to do a chore identified in his head as irrevocably female.

In fact, one emotion that seems to surface in many couples who are trying to change marital roles today is a sense that they have been somehow "betrayed," that things aren't supposed to be like this! The women in Jessica Segrè's study who went back to work because of family finances were clearly suffering from such feelings. They felt they were "supposed" to be taken care of. A man putting a load of laundry into the dryer—if his father never did such a thing and if he believes this to be women's work—can be in for a heavy dose of feelings of betrayal.

Change is never easy, and it may be particularly hard for a man who finds himself taking on household responsibilities. The truth is that washing dishes, doing laundry and housework is not fun—it's drudgery. The man who has always had these services performed for him can hardly be expected to leap with joy when he has to do some of them himself. The costs of the change to him are immediate and obvious. The benefits—more economic security, his wife's feelings of usefulness and challenge, less tension and resentment on her part—are more subtle and long range. Even people who are earnestly trying to change their marital patterns to achieve a more equitable share of responsibilities often find that the emotional weight of old roles burdens them with feelings and resentments they really want no part of. They also may find that their separate perceptions about how much they each *do* are at odds. In a questionnaire filled in by readers of *Psychology Today*, husbands tended to overestimate the percentage of the housework they performed compared to their wives' estimates of what they did. One man who has custody of his three children says, "When I was married I thought I was doing fifty percent of the work. Now that I have to do it all I realize I was doing only about thirty percent."

It's clear that changing marital roles requires sympathy, understanding and a clear channel of communication between the man and woman involved. The couple that has lived in a traditional pattern faces perhaps the most difficult task of all when the wife returns to work. One major problem may be that women don't have much experience in negotiating, in coming right out and asking for things. Sometimes women project their own socialization and reactions onto their husbands. A woman who has been in a caring role at home develops sensitive antennae toward the needs of her husband and children. She often senses their worries, their problems, before they ask. Like the wives in the TV ads who come running with the cold tablets the first time their husband sneezes, they are there when they are needed. It's easy for a woman to expect her husband to do the same for her once she's out in the job market helping to support the family. Why doesn't he *offer* to do the dishes; can't he see she's tired? Why doesn't he pick up the junk in the hallway instead of letting her do it? Rather than saying, "I'm tired, it's your turn to do the dishes," she may go ahead and do them, seething all the while. She may have a hard time even feeling *entitled* to ask; like Linda, the beautician who thought she had to do everything at home despite the fact that she stands on her feet eight hours a day, she may be left with a great deal of unresolved anger.

If housework is a major stumbling block in the path to egalitarian marriage, the real crunch often comes over the issue of child care. Care of children has been a female domain in our society—as in most societies—and women have been given little support when they looked for help.

The hassle of trying to find good child care so that both husband and wife can lead independent lives can put a real strain on a relationship. Caryl remembers a period when she was working part-time and doing a constant search for baby-sitters. It drained much of her energy, and there were many times she resented the fact that her husband could sail out the door leaving all the planning to her.

Later on, at another period, things were partly reversed: he was writing a book, and her teaching salary and writing jobs paid the freight. He was home every morning to take care of their daughter, give her lunch and drive the car pool to kindergarten at noon. Caryl noticed after that time that a gleam of sympathy would appear in his eyes when anyone talked about the problems of women who feel trapped at home.

Is this the wave of the future? Only time will tell. In the past, man's work was supposed to come first; and if he provided economically for his family, his duty was done. When Dwight Eisenhower married Mamie, he told her point-blank, "You will always be second. My country comes first." Priorities are not so clear-cut today for most people.

With two careers and children in a family, priorities simply have to change. To make a nontraditional marriage work, both parents have to recognize the career sacrifices necessary. It's not that you have to give up ambitions or chances for advancement, but you achieve them more slowly. You have to learn to pace yourself with the family timetable. You have to accept a child's illness, a school holiday or the need to leave the office to go home to fix dinner as necessary disruptions of the routine— but you have to maintain a work routine, nonetheless. Working women have always known this, some men are beginning to learn it, too.

The working world is usually not attuned to this private rhythm. Work schedules are still geared to the man in the traditional marriage, the one who can leave the cracked water main or the kid with the flu to the care of a full-time wife.

The traditional pattern of marriage is not without its benefits to men. It's nice to be the "star" of the family, the one whose life is the center of gravity, around which everything else revolves. The Parsonian model does indeed offer to many people a harmonious life—though one suspects it's more harmonious for men than it is for women. The costs may be more subtle than the benefits, but it's pretty obvious that the center of gravity, the man, has to keep holding and holding and holding for traditional marriage to work. Not only does he often have to live a life exciting and fulfilling enough for two, but he is not allowed to falter in his role as breadwinner. That can mean very little flexibility in one's life—a feeling of no leeway for taking chances, changing directions, even getting sick.

Many men seem to have that feeling. In *Sexual Suicide*, George Gilder argues that a man must have the obligation to protect and support his family to make him feel like a man. Supporting a family *is* a heavy load, but taking it on should make you feel not like a man but like a parent. Today sending a couple of kids through college can land you in the poorhouse. We see many men trying to do this alone, trapped in jobs they hate, unable to leave. When a woman shares the economic load, the man can get out from under the full weight. He also has more flexibility—an important consideration if, like most people, you have a less than totally fulfilling job. Caryl's husband could spend two years writing a book because she could carry the economic burden for that period of time. He doesn't have a servant—but having to put his own wash in the laundry was not a bad trade-off for those two years. Caryl doesn't have somebody who will keep her in mink, but she does have somebody who respects her work and who can carry the load if she wants two years to write.

306

The utility ballplayer analogy used before applies again. In an egalitarian marriage you have to be able to be competent in many roles. A major problem with the old sex-role division in marriage was that it often left women crippled as far as economic self-sufficiency was concerned. But it also left men crippled in the skills of caring for themselves. How many men go to pieces when their wives die? They find they can't turn on the gas range, operate the washer, fix a simple meal. One divorced man describes how he handled the laundry after his wife was gone:

At first he would buy new clothes when the old ones got dirty, but he knew that couldn't go on. Finally he worked up the nerve to go to the Laundromat. He was very nervous when he walked in, but he kept telling himself, "I'm a successful businessman, I can do a simple thing like this." He carefully watched women working the machines until he thought he had the hang of it. He loaded the machine—it was a front loader—and read the instructions. "Put the detergent in when the yellow light flashes." He waited. The yellow light flashed. He opened the front door of the machine and water and clothes poured out all over him, all over the floor. He did not know the detergent went in at the top.

In many families, even when couples do a lot of dividing of chores, the sense of primary responsibility often rests with the wife—thinking ahead about finding a music teacher, remembering to buy the birthday present for the child next door, meeting with teachers. If a woman feels she must be the major "psychological" parent, that burden can put her under a lot of stress. If both parents can share responsibility—as well as just chores—the stress can be considerably reduced. Grace and Franklin find that they have made real inroads in this area, and despite the conflicts involved in working things out, they both believe they are happier trying to approximate a just division of leisure and labor. A major turning point, they realize, came when Susannah planned to bring a friend home from school on a day her father was home and her mother was not. Susannah's bed was left unmade that morning. Franklin, noticing the unmade bed, felt for the first time that house-wifely reaction: I need this room to look better—it reflects badly on the family. So he made the bed and straightened up the room, a bit more weighted down with duties, guilt, role conflict, and so forth—but a bit more fully a parent and empathetic spouse.

Ironically, new marriage patterns may be causing problems for women who have been content in the traditional pattern. Suddenly, their husbands, who had wanted them at home, are starting to grouse about the fact that they aren't out making money like the wives of some of their peers. Both Grace and Rosalind have had men say to them how lucky their husbands are because they are working. At a dinner party one man said to Grace—in front of his wife—"I want her to be doing something interesting, like you." Men who have been happy to have a wife at home solving all the domestic problems, dealing with the children, managing the house, suddenly want a woman who is more "interesting," more "involved." Would these men have shared the housework and helped with the children so that their wives could have completed a college degree, or have taken a job with a future? Probably not, but now, faced with economic pressures and children who are growing older, they suddenly want to rewrite the script for their wives. The women, who have been assured all along that they have been doing what both of them wanted, can feel threatened, attacked, betrayed.

While the woman may be the catalyst for an egalitarian marriage, the man is often the key to its success or failure. Many men are struggling honestly, but the going isn't easy. Sometimes women struggle through a long process of change and then expect the men in their lives to become overnight converts. Men need time to change as well. If every battle over the dishes or the checkbook becomes a feminist issue, the tension gets as thick as fog. People sometimes respond better to personal arguments than to political ones. It's more effective to say to a partner, "This is what I need to live and grow" than to cite chapter and verse of a feminist manifesto, no matter how right that manifesto might be.

It's obvious that marriages—like people—are different and no one model will fit everyone. But it seems clear that the Parsonian model of a rigid division of roles and jobs will be of decreasing usefulness in the future, given present trends. We've seen the problems women can encounter when they are not prepared to be economically independent. But men may be equally victimized if they are raised to believe that there will always be a woman available to tend to their domestic needs. If young men don't learn some of the skills involved in running a house and caring for children—or if they are taught men must avoid such jobs to be "masculine"—they are being set up for future problems. Like the divorced man who tangled with the washing machine, they are going to have a hard time managing their daily lives. The boy who learns it is "unmanly" to wash a dish or change a diaper may be programmed for conflict when he grows up and marries. The chances are good that his wife will be working for a good part of her adult life. If he is physically or emotionally unable to share management of the home, he will have to face her open (or even worse, suppressed) anger. It is no favor to young men to lead them to expect a future that probably will not exist.

As feminists, and as veterans of marriage, we look with encouragement on the countless experiments that are today's marriages. The goal of feminism is to transform society at all levels, to infuse its institutions including, perhaps especially, the family, with a humane and caring quality that has too often been the private trust of women. The family is the crucible of identity. From it, we learn more than we care to recognize about the world and our place in it.

The family is not "foreign" territory for feminists—quite the contrary. The well-being of women—and men—will be enhanced by a family structure that offers them the opportunity for both emotional support and individual growth.

Our daughters and sons can reap the benefits of the struggles many of us are involved in. We may fall short of working out ideal solutions in our own lives. We may even feel, at times, a bit like Moses wandering in the desert: We may not see the promised land, but like Moses, we can take comfort in the thought that our sons and daughters may get there one day.

NOTES

Chapter One:
INTRODUCTION
Growing Up Competent

1. An excellent account of these trends can be found in K. E. Taeuber and J. A. Sweet, "Family and Work: The Social Life Cycle of Women," in *Women and the American Economy: A Look to the 1980s,* ed. J. M. Kreps (Englewood Cliffs, N.J.: Prentice-Hall, 1976).
2. Colette Dowling, "Confessions of a Dependent Woman," *New York,* August 8, 1977.
3. This quote comes from a chapter by Kevin Connolly and Jerome Bruner, entitled "Competence: Its Nature and Nurture," in a volume they edited: *The Growth of Competence* (London: Academic Press, 1974).
4. M. Wolfenstein, "Trends in Infant Care," *American Journal of Orthopsychiatry* 23 (1953): 120-30.
5. B. L. White, *The First Three Years of Life* (Englewood Cliffs, N.J.: Prentice-Hall, 1975).
6. Their study is reported in detail in R. R. Sears, E. E. Maccoby, and H. Levin, *Patterns of Child Rearing* (Evanston, Ill.: Row, Peterson, 1957).
7. D. C. McClelland, C. A. Constantian, D. Regalado, and C. Stone, "Making It to Maturity," *Psychology Today* 12 (1978): 42 ff.
8. The seminal work in this field is that of J. Piaget and B. Inhelder, *The Psychology of the Child* (New York: Basic Books, 1969).
9. B. B. Whiting, "Changing Life Styles in Kenya," *Daedalus* 106 (1977): 211-25
10. N. Weisstein, "Psychology Constructs the Female," in *Woman in Sexist Society,* eds. V. Gornick and B. Moran (New York: Basic Books, 1971).

Chapter Two:
FATHERS AND DAUGHTERS:
Out of the Shadow

1. The quotations are taken from Brazelton's article, "What Makes a Good Father?" *Redbook,* June 1970.
2. Elizabeth Janeway, *Man's World, Woman's Place* (New York: Dell, 1971).
3. Robert L. Trivers, "Parental Investment and Sexual Selection," in *Sexual*

Selection and the Descent of Man, ed. B. Campbell (Chicago: Aldine, 1972).

4. David Gutmann, "Men, Women and the Parental Imperative," *Commentary* 56 (1973): 59-64.
5. Lionel Tiger and Robin Fox, *The Imperial Animal* (New York: Dell, 1972).
6. For a critique of these studies, see J. B. Lancaster, "Sex Roles in Primate Societies," in *Sex Differences: Social and Biological Perspectives*, ed. M. S. Teitelbaum (New York: Anchor, 1976).
7. William K. Redican, "Adult Male-Infant Interactions in Nonhuman Primates," in *The Role of the Father in Child Development*, ed. Michael E. Lamb (New York: Wiley, 1976).
8. Henry Biller and Dennis Meredith, *Father Power* (New York: David McKay, 1974).
9. Mary Maxwell West and Melvin J. Konner, "The Role of the Father: An Anthropological Perspective," in *The Role of the Father in Child Development*, ed. Michael E. Lamb (New York: Wiley, 1976).
10. An excellent review of the studies can be found in E. Herzog and C. Sudia, "Children in Fatherless Families," in *Review of Child Development Research*, vol. 3, eds. B. M. Caldwell and H. N. Ricciuti (Chicago: University of Chicago Press, 1974).
11. The following references will provide the reader with a good introduction to this new work: Henry Biller, *Paternal Deprivation* (Lexington, Mass.: D. C. Heath, 1974); Henry Biller and Dennis Meredith, *Father Power* (New York: David McKay, 1974); Robert A. Fein, "Men's Experiences in the Weeks Before and After the Birth of Their First Child" (Paper presented at meeting of the Massachusetts Psychological Association, October 1973); Milton Kotelchuck, "The Nature of the Child's Tie to His Father" (Ph.D. diss., Harvard University, 1972); David B. Lynn, *The Father: His Role in Child Development* (Belmont, Calif.: Brooks/Cole, 1974).
12. This collection also contains a chapter in which Lamb reports his own research on infants: Michael E. Lamb, ed., *The Role of the Father in Child Development* (New York: Wiley, 1976).
13. Milton Kotelchuck, "The Infant's Relationship to the Father: Experimental Evidence," in *The Role of the Father in Child Development*, ed. Michael E. Lamb (New York: Wiley, 1976).
14. M. Lester, M. Kotelchuck, E. Spelke, M. J. Sellers, and R. E. Klein, "Separation Protest in Guatemalan Infants: Cross-cultural and Cognitive Findings," *Developmental Psychology* 10 (1974): 79-85.
15. Martin Greenberg and Norman Norris, "Engrossment: The Newborn's Impact Upon the Father," *American Journal of Orthopsychiatry* 44 (1974): 520-31.
16. Robert A. Fein, "Men's Experiences in the Weeks Before and After the

311

Birth of Their First Child" (Paper presented at meeting of the Massachusetts Psychological Association, October 1973).

Chapter Three:
FATHERS AND DAUGHTERS:
The Magic White Knight (and Others)

1. Jeffrey Z. Rubin, Frank J. Provenzano, and Zella Luria, "The Eye of the Beholder: Parents' Views on Sex of Newborns," *American Journal of Orthopsychiatry* 44 (1974): 512-19.
2. The studies drawn upon for this section include D. F. Aberle and K. D. Naegele, "Middle-Class Fathers' Occupational Role and Attitudes Toward Children," *American Journal of Orthopsychiatry* 22 (1952): 336-78; R. J. Tasch, "The Role of the Father in the Family," *Journal of Experimental Education* 20 (1952): 319-61.
3. See, for example, S. Dinitz, R. Dynes, and A. Clarke, "Preference for Male or Female Children: Traditional or Affectional," *Marriage and Family Living* 16 (1954): 128-30.
4. F. A. Pedersen, "Beyond Father Absence: Conceptualizations of Father Effects" (Paper presented at meeting of the Society for Research in Child Development, Denver, 1975).
5. E. W. Goodenough, "Interest in Persons as an Aspect of Sex Differences in the Early Years," *Genetic Psychology Monographs* 55 (1957): 287-323.
6. Talcott Parsons, "Family Structure and the Socialization of the Child," in *Family, Socialization and Interaction Process,* eds. T. Parsons and R. F. Bales (Glencoe, Ill.: Free Press, 1955).
7. Elizabeth Janeway, *Man's World, Woman's Place* (New York: Dell, 1971).
8. Barbara Grizzuti Harrison, "How Fathers Shape Their Daughters' Lives," *McCalls,* August 1976.
9. Joseph P. Lash, *Eleanor and Franklin* (New York: W. W. Norton, 1971).
10. This quote appears in Germaine Greer, *The Female Eunuch* (New York: McGraw-Hill, 1970).
11. Sally Kempton, "Cutting Loose," *Esquire,* July 1970.
12. Barbara Howar, *Laughing All the Way* (New York: Fawcett World, Crest, 1974).
13. Barbara Grizzuti Harrison, "Liza Talks," *McCalls,* May 1975.
14. Marjorie R. Leonard, "Fathers and Daughters," *International Journal of Psychoanalysis* 47 (1966): 325-34.
15. Much of this material is reviewed in our article, Grace K. Baruch and Rosalind C. Barnett, "Implications and Applications of Recent Research on Feminine Development," *Psychiatry* 38 (1975): 318-27. Original sources

drawn upon in this section include: J. H. Block, "Assessing Sex Differences: Issues, Problems, and Pitfalls," *Merrill-Palmer Quarterly* 22 (1976): 283-308; D. M. Connell and J. E. Johnson, "Relationship Between Sex-Role Identification and Self-esteem in Early Adolescents," *Developmental Psychology* 3 (1970): 199-201; A. Heilbrun, "Sex-Role Identity in Adolescent Females: A Theoretical Paradox," *Adolescence* 3 (1968): 79-88; M. Lozoff, "Changing Life Style and Role Perceptions of Men and Women Students" (Paper presented at the Radcliffe Institute Conference: Women: Resource for a Changing World, Cambridge, Mass., 1972).

16. David F. Aberle and Kaspar D. Naegele, "Middle-Class Fathers' Occupational Role and Attitudes Toward Children," *American Journal of Orthopsychiatry* 22 (1952): 366-78.

17. Margaret Hennig, "Career Development for Women Executives" (Ph.D. diss., Graduate School of Business Administration, Harvard University, 1970).

Chapter Four:
MOTHERS AND DAUGHTERS:
How Will My Life Affect My Daughter's?

1. Charles F. Osgood, George J. Suci, and Percy H. Tannenbaum, *The Measurement of Meaning* (Chicago: University of Illinois Press, 1957).

2. J. J. Jenkins and W. A. Russell, "An Atlas of Semantic Profiles for 360 Words," *American Journal of Psychology* 71 (1958): 688-99.

3. Jerome Kagan and Judith Lemkin, "The Child's Differential Perception of Parental Attributes," *Journal of Abnormal and Social Psychology* 61 (1960): 440-47.

4. Lawrence Kohlberg, "A Cognitive-Developmental Analysis of Children's Sex-Role Concepts and Attitudes," in *The Development of Sex Differences,* ed. Eleanor Maccoby (Stanford, Calif.: Stanford University Press, 1966).

5. Ruth Hartley and A. Klein, "Sex-Role Concepts Among Elementary School-age Girls," *Marriage and Family Living* 21 (1959): 59-64.

6. For a review of several of these theories, see Jerome Kagan, "Acquisition and Significance of Sex-Typing and Sex-Role Identification," in *Review of Child Development Research,* vol. 1, eds. M. L. Hoffman and L. W. Hoffman (New York: Russell Sage, 1964).

7. S. Smith, "Age and Sex Differences in Children's Opinions Concerning Sex Differences," *Journal of Genetic Psychology* 54 (1939): 17-25.

8. Shirley Maclaine, *Don't Fall Off the Mountain* (New York: W. W. Norton, 1970).

9. Claudia Dreifus, *Woman's Fate* (New York: Bantam, 1973).

10. Joan Marans Dim, *Recollections of a Rotten Kid* (Indianapolis: Bobbs-Merrill, 1974).
11. Jane Howard, *A Different Woman* (New York: Avon, 1974).
12. Betty Friedan, *The Feminine Mystique* (New York: W. W. Norton, 1963).
13. Major among these studies are: Grace K. Baruch, "Feminine Self-Esteem, Self-Ratings of Competence, and Maternal Career-Commitment," *Journal of Counseling Psychology* 20 (1973): 487–88; D. M. Connell and J. E. Johnson, "Relationships Between Sex-Role Identification and Self-Esteem in Early Adolescents," *Developmental Psychology* 3 (1970): 199-201; J. T. Spence, R. Helmreich, and J. Stapp, "Ratings of Self and Peers on Sex-Role Attributes and Their Relation to Self-Esteem and Conceptions of Masculinity and Femininity," *Journal of Personality and Social Psychology* 32 (1975): 29-39.
14. For an introduction to these studies, the reader is referred to: A. Freud and D. Burlingham, *Infants Without Families* (New York: International University Press, 1944); R. A. Spitz, "Hospitalism: An Inquiry into the Genesis of Psychiatric Conditions in Early Childhood," *Psychoanalytic Study of the Child* 1 (1945): 53-74.
15. Barbara Wallston and Michelle Citron, "The Myth of the Working Mother" (Unpublished paper).
16. J. Kagan, R. B. Kearsley, and P. R. Zelago, "The Effects of Infant Day Care on Psychological Development" (Paper presented at meeting of the American Association for the Advancement of Science, Boston, 1976).
17. B. M. Caldwell, "The Effects of Infant Care," in *Review of Child Development Research*, vol. 1, eds. M. L. Hoffman and L. W. Hoffman (New York: Russell Sage, 1964).
18. These studies include: Lois W. Hoffman, "The Effects of Maternal Employment on the Child: A Review of the Research," *Developmental Psychology* 10 (1974): 204-28; and Barbara Wallston, "The Effects of Maternal Employment on Children," *Journal of Child Psychology and Psychiatry* 14 (1973): 81-95.
19. Lois Hoffman has herself written extensively in this field. She and her students have produced a number of major studies. The following two review articles include much of their material: Lois W. Hoffman, "The Professional Woman as Mother," in *Women and Success*, ed. R. Kundsin (New York: Morrow, 1974); Lois W. Hoffman, "The Effects of Maternal Employment on the Child: A Review of the Research," *Developmental Psychology* 10 (1974): 204-28.
20. F. I. Nye and L. W. Hoffman, eds., *The Employed Mother in America* (Chicago: Rand McNally, 1963); S. R. Vogel, I. Broverman, D. Broverman, F. Clarkson, and P. Rosenkrantz, "Maternal Employment and

314

Perceptions of Sex-Role Stereotypes," *Developmental Psychology* 3 (1970): 384-91.

21. See, for example: Grace K. Baruch, "Maternal Influences upon College Women's Attitudes Toward Women and Work," *Developmental Psychology* 6 (1972): 32-37; and S. R. Vogel, I. Broverman, D. Broverman, F. Clarkson, and P. Rosenkrantz, "Maternal Employment and Perceptions of Sex-Role Stereotypes," *Developmental Psychology* 3 (1970): 384-91.

22. Elizabeth Douvan, "Employment and the Adolescent," in *The Employed Mother in America*, eds. F. I. Nye and L. W. Hoffman (Chicago: Rand McNally, 1963).

23. M. R. Yarrow, J. D. Campbell, and R. V. Burton, *Child Rearing* (San Francisco: Jossey-Bass, 1968).

24. Judith A. Birnbaum, "Life Patterns and Self-Esteem in Gifted Family-Oriented and Career-Committed Women," in *Women and Achievement: Social and Motivational Analysis*, eds. M. Mednick, S. Tangri, and L. W. Hoffman (New York: Hemisphere-Halsted, 1975).

Chapter Five:
GAMES:
The Playing Fields of Childhood

1. Eleanor E. Maccoby and Carol Nagy Jacklin, *The Psychology of Sex Differences* (Stanford, Calif.: Stanford University Press, 1974).

2. Jeanne H. Block, "Assessing Sex Differences: Issues, Problems, and Pitfalls," *Merrill-Palmer Quarterly* 22 (1976): 283-308.

3. Beverly I. Fagot, "Sex Determined Parental Reinforcing Contingencies in Toddler Children" (Paper presented at meeting of the Society for Research in Child Development, New Orleans, March 1977).

4. Richard Bell, "Reinterpretation of the Direction of Effects in Studies of Socialization," *Psychological Review* 75 (1968): 81-95.

5. Harriet L. Rheingold and Kaye V. Cook, "The Content of Boys' and Girls' Rooms as an Index of Parents' Behavior," *Child Development* 46 (1975): 459-63.

6. Jane M. Connor, M. Schochman, and Lisa Serbin, "Sex-Related Differences in Response to Practice on a Visual-Spatial Test and Generalization to a Related Test," *Child Development* 49 (1978): 24-29.

7. Janet Lever, "Sex Differences in the Games Children Play," *Social Problems* 23 (1976): 478-87.

Chapter Six:
THE SPORTING LIFE:
The Second Baseperson Is Here to Stay

1. Eve Babitz, "The Way We Were," *WomenSports*, August 1977.
2. J. S. Hyde, B. G. Rosenberg, and J. Behrman, "Tomboyism: Implications for Theories of Female Development" (Paper read at meeting of the Western Psychological Association, San Francisco, 1974).
3. Their review has been referred to earlier; it addresses the issues raised in the preceding pages. Eleanor E. Maccoby and Carol Nagy Jacklin, *The Psychology of Sex Differences* (Stanford, Calif.: Stanford University Press, 1974).
4. Helen Harris Solomons, "Sex-Role-Mediated Achievement Behaviours and Inter-Personal Dynamics of Fifth-Grade Coeducational Physical Education Classes" (Ph.D. diss., Bryn Mawr, 1976).
5. Dr. Torg's comments were cited in Jack H. Wilmore, "The Complete Athlete," *Medical World News*, May 24, 1974.
6. John Marshall, "The Weaker Sex? Hah!" *Time*, June 1978.
7. Jack H. Wilmore, "The Complete Athlete," *Medical World News*, May 24, 1974.
8. Margaret Hennig and Anne Jardim, *The Managerial Woman* (New York: Anchor/Doubleday, 1977).
9. Talcott Parsons, "Family Structure and the Socialization of the Child," in *Family, Socialization and Interaction Process*, eds. T. Parsons and R. F. Bales (Glencoe, Ill.: Free Press, 1955).
10. Sandra Bem, "Probing the Promise of Androgyny," in *Beyond Sex-Role Stereotypes*, eds. A. G. Kaplan and J. P. Bean (Boston: Little, Brown, 1976).

Chapter Seven:
ACHIEVEMENT:
Stamping Out Smother Love

1. Lois W. Hoffman, "Early Childhood Experiences and Women's Achievement Motives," *Journal of Social Issues* 28 (1972): 129-56.
2. Nancy Chodorow, "Family Structure and Feminine Personality," in *Woman, Culture and Society*, eds. M. Z. Rosaldo and L. Lamphere (Stanford, Calif.: Stanford University Press, 1973).
3. E. D. Collard, "Achievement Motive in the Four-Year-Old Child and Its Relationship to Achievement Expectancies of the Mother" (Ph.D. diss., University of Michigan, 1964).

4. J. Kagan and H. A. Moss, *Birth to Maturity* (New York: Wiley, 1962).
5. Among Diana Baumrind's studies are: "Patterns of Parental Authority," *Developmental Psychology Monographs* 4 (1971); "From Each According to Her Ability," *School Review* 80 (1972): 161-98; and with A. E. Black, "Socialization Practices Associated with Dimensions of Competence in Pre-School Boys and Girls," *Child Development* 38 (1967): 291-327.
6. For an excellent introduction to this field of research, see: I. H. Frieze, "Women's Expectations for and Causal Attributions of Success and Failure," in *Women and Achievement: Social and Motivational Analysis*, eds. M. Mednick, S. Tangri, and L. W. Hoffman (New York: Hemisphere-Halsted, 1975); B. Weiner, I. Frieze, A. Kukla, L. Reed, S. Rest, and R. Rosenbaum, *Perceiving the Causes of Success and Failure* (New York: General Learning, 1971).
7. References for the original study and the follow-up are: L. Baird, *The Graduates* (Princeton, N.J.: Educational Testing Service, 1973); and L. Baird, "Entrance of Women to Graduate and Professional Education" (Paper presented at meeting of the American Psychological Association, Washington, D.C., 1976).
8. K. Deaux and T. Emswiller, "Explanations of Successful Performance on Sex-Linked Tasks: What's Skill for the Male Is Luck for the Female," *Journal of Personality and Social Psychology* 27 (1974): 80-85.
9. K. Deaux, "Women in Management: Causal Explanations of Performance" (Paper presented at meeting of the American Psychological Association, New Orleans, 1974).
10. J. E. Parsons, D. N. Ruble, K. L. Hodges, and A. W. Small, "Cognitive-Development Factors in Emerging Sex Differences in Achievement-Related Expectancies," *Journal of Social Issues* 32 (1976): 47-61.
11. Carol Dweck, "Sex Differences in the Meaning of Negative Evaluation in Achievement Situations: Determinants and Consequences" (Paper presented at meeting of the Society for Research in Child Development, Denver, 1975).
12. Among Carol Dweck's studies are: "The Role of Expectations and Attributions in the Alleviation of Learned Helplessness," *Journal of Personality and Social Psychology* 31 (1975): 674-85; with E. S. Bush, "Sex Differences in Learned Helplessness: (1) Differential Debilitation with Peer and Adult Evaluators," *Developmental Psychology*, in press; with D. Gilliard, "Expectancy Statements as Determinants of Reactions to Failure: Sex Differences in Persistence and Expectancy Change," *Journal of Personality and Social Psychology* 32 (1975): 1077-84.
13. Grace K. Baruch, "Sex-Role Attitudes of Fifth-Grade Girls," in *And Jill Came Tumbling After: Sexism in American Education*, eds. J. Stacey, S. Bereaud, and J. Daniels (New York: Dell, 1974).

Chapter Eight:
ADOLESCENCE:
To Hear a Different Drummer

1. Daniel Levinson et al., *Seasons of a Man's Life* (New York: Knopf, 1978).
2. Rosalind C. Barnett and Grace K. Baruch, "Empirical Literature on Occupational and Educational Aspirations and Expectations: A Review," Journal Supplement Abstract Service, *Catalog of Selected Documents in Psychology* 6 (1976): 49.
3. Rosalind C. Barnett, "Sex Differences and Age Trends in Occupational Preference and Occupational Prestige," *Journal of Counseling Psychology* 22 (1975): 35-38.
4. Jean Lipman-Blumen, "The Vicarious Achievement Ethic and Non-Traditional Roles for Women" (Paper presented at Eastern Sociological Society meeting, New York, 1973).
5. Elizabeth Janeway, *Between Myth and Morning: Women Awakening* (New York: Morrow, 1974).
6. Matina Horner, "Toward an Understanding of Achievement-Related Conflicts in Women," in *Women and Achievement: Social and Motivational Analysis*, eds. M. Mednick, S. Tangri, and L. W. Hoffman (New York: Hemisphere-Halsted, 1975).
7. John C. Condry and Sharon L. Dyer, "Behavioral and Fantasy Measures of Fear of Success in Children," *Child Development* 48 (1977): 1417-25.
8. For a report of these studies, see A. Steinmann and D. Fox, "Male-Female Perceptions of the Female Role in the United States," *Journal of Psychology* 64 (1966): 265-76.
9. L. S. Davis and M. D. Spiegler, "Bright and Ambitious: Kiss of Death for Women?" (Paper presented at meeting of the American Psychological Association, New Orleans, 1974).
10. Simone de Beauvoir, *Memoirs of a Dutiful Daughter* (New York: Harper & Row, 1974).
11. Elizabeth Douvan and Joseph Adelson, *The Adolescent Experience* (New York: Wiley, 1966).
12. Betty Friedan, *The Feminine Mystique* (New York: W. W. Norton, 1963).
13. Dr. A. Regula Herzog kindly facilitated our early access to these important data. For reports by project staff see: J. G. Bachman, L. D. Johnston, and P. M. O'Malley, *Monitoring the Future: Questionnaire Responses from the Nation's High School Seniors, 1976*; and L. D. Johnston, J. G. Bachman, and P. M. O'Malley, *Monitoring the Future: Questionnaire Responses from the Nation's High School Seniors, 1977*. Both reports are 1979 publications of the Institute for Social Research, Ann Arbor, Michigan.

Chapter Nine:
ADOLESCENCE:
Prince Charming Revisited

1. Paula Weideger, *Menstruation and Menopause* (New York: Knopf, 1976).
2. Anne E. Clarke and Diane Ruble, "Young Adolescents' Beliefs Concerning Menstruation," *Child Development* 49 (1978): 231-34.
3. Erik Erikson, "Identity and the Life Cycle," *Psychological Issues*, no. 1, 1959.
4. Michael Medved and David Wallechinsky, *What Really Happened to the Class of 65* (New York: Random House, 1976).
5. Sylvia Plath, *Letters Home* (New York: Harper & Row, 1975).
6. Elizabeth Hardwick, *Seduction and Betrayal* (New York: Random House, 1970).
7. Cited by William Manchester in *American Caesar* (Boston: Little, Brown, 1978).
8. Jean Baker Miller, *Towards a New Psychology of Women* (Boston: Beacon Press, 1976).

Chapter Ten:
SEXUALITY AND CONFLICT

1. Judy Blume, *Forever* (Scarsdale, N.Y.: Bradbury, 1975).
2. E. Roberts, D. Kline, and J. Gagnon, *Final Report: Family Life and Sexual Learning* (Project on Human Sexual Development, Population Education Inc., 1978).
3. Norman Mailer, *Marilyn* (New York: Grosset & Dunlap, 1973).
4. See Helen Singer Kaplan, *The New Sex Therapy* (New York: Brunner/ Mazel, 1974), and Lonnie Garfield Barbach, *For Yourself: The Fulfillment of Female Sexuality* (New York: Doubleday, 1975).
5. Harriet Lerner, "The Taboo Against Female Anger," *Menninger Perspective*, Winter 1977.
6. David B. Lynn, *The Father: His Role in Child Development* (Belmont, Calif.: Brooks/Cole, 1974).
7. Lillian Rubin, *Worlds of Pain* (New York: Basic Books, 1976).
8. For an excellent analysis of this issue, see Carol Gilligan's "In a Different Voice: Women's Conceptions of Self and Morality," *Harvard Educational Review* 47 (1977): 481-517.
9. Gillian Martin, *The Goat, the Wolf, and the Crab* (New York: Scribner's, 1977).

10. The Boston Women's Health Book Collective, *Ourselves and Our Children* (New York: Random House, 1978).
11. Catherine Chilman, *Adolescent Sexuality in a Changing American Society* (Washington, D.C.: U.S. Department of Health, Education and Welfare, 1979).

Chapter Eleven:
SCHOOL DAYS:
The Pedagogical Harem

1. Cited by Florence Howe in Florence Howe, ed., *Women and the Power to Change* (New York: McGraw-Hill, 1975).
2. K. K. Sklar, "The Founding of Mt. Holyoke Female Seminary: A Study in the History of Female Education in New England, 1790–1837" (Paper presented at Mount Holyoke College and South Hadley, Massachusetts, Bicentennial Celebration, 1976).
3. We draw here on the research of historian Patricia Graham, especially her "Women in Academe," *Science* 169 (1970): 1284-90, and "So Much to Do: Guides for Historical Research on Women in Higher Education," *Teachers College Record* 76 (1975): 422-29.
4. David Tyack, *The One Best System* (Cambridge, Mass.: Harvard University Press, 1974), and David Tyack, "Some Approaches to the History of the Education of Women" (Unpublished paper, Stanford University, 1975).
5. We have relied here on: Carroll Smith-Rosenberg and Charles Rosenberg, "The Female Animal," *Journal of American History* 2 (1973): 332-56.
6. M. Carey Thomas, "Present Tendencies in Women's College and University Education," in *And Jill Came Tumbling After: Sexism in American Education*, eds. J. Stacey, S. Bereaud, and J. Daniels (New York: Dell, 1974).
7. Helene Deutsch, *The Psychology of Women* (New York: Grune and Stratton, 1944).
8. See L. Serbin, K. O'Leary, R. Kent, and I. Tonick, "A Comparison of Teacher Response to the Preacademic and Problem Behavior of Boys and Girls," *Child Development* 44 (1973): 796-804.
9. T. E. Levitin and J. D. Chananie, "White Middle-Class Suburban Teacher Liking," *Child Development* 43 (1972): 1309-16.
10. F. A. Ricks and S. W. Pyke, "Teacher Perceptions and Attitudes That Foster or Maintain Sex Role Differences," *Interchange* 4 (1973): 26-33.
11. In: "Any Change in Sexist Texts?" Women's Studies *Newsletter* 2, no. 3 (1974).

12. A. H. Thomas and N. R. Steward, "Counselor Response to Female Clients with Deviate and Conforming Career Goals," *Journal of Counseling Psychology* 18 (1971): 352-57.
13. Judith Bardwick and Elizabeth Douvan, "Ambivalence: The Socialization of Women," in *Woman in Sexist Society*, eds. V. Gornick and B. Moran (New York: Basic Books, 1971).
14. Sara L. Lightfoot, "Sociology of Education: Perspectives on Women," in *Another Voice*, eds. M. Millman and R. M. Kanter (Garden City, N.Y.: Anchor Press, 1975).
15. Ruth K. Baden, "No Room at the Top," *Boston Sunday Globe Magazine*, October 19, 1975.
16. Patricia A. Schmuck, "Deterrents to Women's Careers in School Management," *Sex Roles* 1 (1975): 339-54.
17. Neal Gross and A. E. Trask, *The Sex Factor and the Management of Schools* (New York: Wiley, 1976).
18. Adrienne Rich, "Toward a Woman-Centered University," in *Women and the Power to Change*, ed. F. Howe (New York: McGraw-Hill, 1975).
19. Jessie Bernard, *Academic Women* (Cleveland: World, 1966).
20. S. H. Sternglanz and S. Lyberger-Ficek, "Sex Differences in Student-Teacher Interactions in the College Classroom," *Sex Roles* 3 (1977): 345-52.
21. Adrienne Munich, "Seduction in Academe," *Psychology Today*, February 1978.
22. Elizabeth Tidball, "Perspective on Academic Women and Affirmative Action," *Educational Record* 54 (1973): 130-35.
23. R. Winchell, D. Fenner, and P. Shaver, "Impact of Coeducation on 'Fear of Success' Imagery Expressed by Male and Female High School Students," *Journal of Educational Psychology* 66 (1974): 726-30.
24. Barbara Grizzuti Harrison, *Unlearning the Lie: Sexism in Schools* (New York: Liveright, 1973).
25. R. S. Drabman, D. Hammer, and G. J. Jarvie, "Children's Perception of Media-Portrayed Sex Roles Across Age" (Unpublished manuscript, University of Mississippi Medical Center).
26. Lisa Serbin, "Sex Stereotyped Play Behavior in the Preschool Classroom: Effects of Teacher Presence and Modeling" (Paper presented at meeting of the Society for Research in Child Development, New Orleans, March, 1977).
27. Robert Coles and Jane Hallowell Coles, *Women of Crisis* (New York: Delacorte, 1978).
28. Diane Ravitch, "The Public School's Tasks and How They Grew," *The New York Times*, November 17, 1975.

Chapter Twelve:
LIFE CHOICES
The Traditional Role

1. Erik Erikson, "Identity and the Life Cycle," *Psychological Issues*, no. 1, 1959.
2. Helena Z. Lopata, *Occupation Housewife* (New York: Oxford University Press, 1971).
3. See Beatrice Whiting, "Problems of American Middle-Class Women in Their Middle Years—A Comparative Approach" (Unpublished paper, Harvard University, 1978).
4. Jessie Bernard, *The Future of Marriage* (New York: World-Times, 1972).
5. See Walter R. Gove and Jeannette F. Tudor, "Adult Sex Roles and Mental Illness," *American Journal of Sociology* 78 (1973): 812-35; and Walter R. Gove, "The Relationship Between Sex Roles, Marital Status, and Mental Illness, *Social Forces* 51 (1972): 34-44.
6. See: M. Guttentag, "Women, Men and Mental Health," in *Women and Men: Changing Roles*, eds. L. Cater, A. Scott, and W. Martyna (Palo Alto, Calif.: Aspen Institute for Humanistic Studies, 1975); L. Radloff, "Sex Differences in Depression: The Effects of Occupation and Marital Status," *Sex Roles* 1 (1975): 249-65; M. Seligman, "Depression and Learned Helplessness," in *The Psychology of Depression*, eds. R. J. Friedman and N. Katz (Washington, D.C.: Winston, 1974).
7. See: L. S. Fidell, "Employment Status, Role Dissatisfaction and the Housework Syndrome" (Unpublished paper, California State University, Northridge, Calif.), and J. Wright, "Are Working Women Really More Satisfied? Evidence from Several National Surveys," *Journal of Marriage and The Family* 40 (1978): 301-14.
8. A. Campbell, P. E. Converse, and W. L. Rodgers, *The Quality of American Life* (New York: Russell Sage, 1976). See especially chap. 12, "The Situation of Women."
9. John Kenneth Galbraith, "How the Economy Hangs on Her Apron Strings," *Ms.*, September 1974.
10. L. I. Pearlin and J. S. Johnson, "Marital Status, Life Strains and Depression," *American Sociological Review* 42 (1977): 704-15.
11. Dorothy Burlage, "Divorced and Separated Mothers: Combining the Responsibilities of Breadwinning and Child-Rearing" (Ph.D. diss., Harvard University, 1978).

Chapter Thirteen:
LIFE CHOICES
Women at Work

1. Helen S. Astin, *The Woman Doctorate in America* (New York: Russell Sage, 1969).
2. R. Helson, "Women Mathematicians and the Creative Personality," *Journal of Consulting and Clinical Psychology* 36 (1971): 59-64.
3. In this section we draw heavily upon the volume *Women and Success*, ed. Ruth Kundsin (New York: Morrow, 1974).
4. Margaret Hennig, "Career Development for Women Executives" (Ph.D. diss., Graduate School of Business Administration, Harvard University, 1970).
5. See T. G. Harris, "A Conversation with Margaret Mead," *Psychology Today*, July 1970.
6. Sandra Schwartz Tangri, "Determinants of Occupational Role Innovation Among College Women," *Journal of Social Issues* 28 (1972): 177-99.
7. Cited by Ravenna Helson in Ravenna Helson, "The Changing Image of the Career Woman," *Journal of Social Issues* 28 (1972): 33-46.
8. Herbert Spohn, "Vocational Orientation and Growth," in *Achievement in the College Years*, eds. L. B. Murphy and E. Raushenbush (New York: Harper, 1960).
9. Frederick W. Ilfeld, Jr., "Sex Differences in Psychiatric Symptomatology" (Paper presented at meeting of The American Psychological Association, San Francisco, 1977).
10. Abigail Stewart, "Role Combination and Psychological Health in Women" (Paper presented at meeting of The Eastern Psychological Association, Washington, D.C., 1978).
11. Jessica Segrè, "Self-Concept and Depression: Mothers Returning to Work or Remaining at Home" (Ph.D. diss., Boston University, 1977).

Chapter Fourteen:
ALTERNATE PATTERNS:
Staking Out New Territory

1. Margaret Adams, *Single Blessedness* (New York: Basic Books, 1976).
2. Judith Bardwick, *Psychology of Women: A Study of Biosocial Conflicts* (New York: Harper & Row, 1971).
3. Judith Guss Teicholz, "Psychological Correlates of Voluntary Childlessness in Married Women" (Paper presented at meeting of The Eastern Psychological Association, March 1978).

4. Robert A. Brown and R. Magarick, "Social and Emotional Aspects of Voluntary Childlessness" (Paper presented at meeting of The American Psychological Association, August 1978).
5. Sharon K. Houseknecht, "Timing and the Decision to Remain Voluntarily Childless" (Paper presented at meeting of The American Psychological Association, August 1978).
6. Talcott Parsons, "Family Structure and the Socialization of the Child," in *Family, Socialization and Interaction Process*, eds. T. Parsons and R. F. Bales (Glencoe, Ill.: Free Press, 1955).
7. See Lynn Simonsen Walker, Barbara Strudler Wallston, and Howard M. Sandler, "Dual Career Couples: Job Seeking Strategy and Marital Satisfaction" (Unpublished paper).
8. Naomi Dagen Bloom and Ronald L. Bloom, "Couple Assertiveness" (Presented at Annual Forum, Maryland chapter of The National Association of Social Workers, May 1978).
9. David B. Lynn, *The Father: His Role in Child Development* (Belmont, Calif.: Brooks/Cole, 1974).

INDEX

Aberle, David F., 58
Achievement, 132–51
    attribution theory and, 138–40
    independence and, 132–37
    low expectations for, 140–44
    vicarious, 154–55
Adams, Clifford, 258–59
Adams, Margaret, 209, 287
Adelson, Joseph, 162–64, 169, 171,
        179–81, 188
Adolescence, 152–92
    establishment of identity in, 179–87
    fathers and, 167–68
    fear of success in, 157–60
    feelings of uniqueness in, 161–62
    friendships in, 169–70
    independence in, 162–65
    moral development in, 163–64
    mothers and, 165–67
    myths about menstruation and, 174–78
    peer culture in, 168–69
    sexuality in, 193–201
    vicarious achievement in, 154–55
    vocational plans in, 171–72
*Adolescent Sexuality in a Changing
        American Society* (Chilman),
        214
Adult development, theories of, 245–47
Aggression, 34
    response of teachers to, 221
    sex differences in, 113–14
America's Working Women (Gordon and
        Heverby), 276
Amniocentesis, 47
Androgynous behavior, studies of,
        122–26
Anger, expression of, 201–13
*Aphrodite at Mid-century: Growing
        Female and Catholic in Postwar
        America* (Rivers), 174
Appearance, adolescent concern with,
        180–81
Are You There, God? It's Me, Margaret
        (Blume), 191
Aristotle, 275
Assertiveness training, 205
Association for Intercollegiate Athletics
        for Women, 114
Athletics, *see* Sports
Attribution theory, 138–40
Authority, identification with, 163–64
Autonomy, identification with father and,
        57–58

Babitz, Eve, 109–10
Baden, Ruth, 230
Barbach, Lonnie Garfield, 212–13
Bardwick, Judith, 228, 290
Baumrind, Diana, 137
Bean, Joan P., 126
Beauvoir, Simone de, 25, 51, 163–64,
        167, 175
Behrman, J., 112–13

Bell, Richard, 102
Bem, Sandra, 122–26
Bernard, Jessie, 252
Beyond Sex-Role Stereotypes (Kaplan and
    Bean), 126
Big Daddy style of fathering, 52–54
Biller, Henry, 31
Birk, Ann, 206
Birnbaum, Judith, 88–89, 255–56, 280,
    288–89
Block, Jeanne H., 100
Bloom, Naomi Dagen, 294–95
Bloom, Ronald L., 294–95
Blume, Judy, 191, 193
Bolton, Sarah K., 62
Bonheur, Rosa, 62
Boring, Phyllis, 115, 116
Boston Women's Health Book Collective,
    214
Bowlby, John, 38, 82
Brazelton, T. Berry, 29
Brown, Robert A., 292
Bruner, Jerome, 17
Burlage, Dorothy, 262–64, 266, 276, 278
Burton, Richard, 46–47
Bushmen, 33
Butler, Samuel, 70
Byron, Lord, 178–79

Campbell, A., 288
Carnegie Commission, 220, 232, 234
Child-rearing theories and techniques,
    19–24
Childless women, 290–92
Chilman, Catherine, 214–17
Chodorow, Nancy, 134–36
Citron, Michelle, 83
Clarke, Anne E., 177–78
Cognitive development, 23
Coles, Jane Hallowell, 240
Coles, Robert, 240
College Research Bureau, 293
Communication skills, sex differences in,
    222–23

Competence, 15–27
    in adolescence, 168
    masculine and feminine traits and,
        80–81
    social values and, 17–18
Competition
    mixed-sex, 158–60
    between mothers and adolescent
        daughters, 166–67
Condry, John C., 157, 159
"Confessions of a Dependent Woman"
    (Dowling), 15, 17
Conflict, sexuality and, 201–13
Connolly, Kevin, 17
Connor, Jane, 103
Consumer-oriented society, 257–58
Contraception, 200, 216–17
Converse, P. E., 288
Cook, Kaye V., 102, 103
Cross-cultural studies
    of father-child relationships, 33–35
    of mother-child relationships, 83

Day-care, 83–84
Deaux, Kay, 141
Delinquency, 84–85
Demands, inability to make, 208–13
Depression, 253, 260
Deschryver, Adrian, 31–32
Deutsch, Helene, 220
Devaluing of parents, 165
Diary of a Young Girl, The (Frank), 161
Different Woman, A (Howard), 77
Dim, Joan Marans, 76–77
Divorce, 16, 262–65
Dodson, Fitzhugh, 44
Dogon tribe, 174
Doll's House, A (Ibsen), 25
Don't Fall Off the Mountain
    (MacLaine), 70, 75
Double standard, 196
Douvan, Elizabeth, 87, 163–64, 169,
    171, 179–81, 188, 228
Dowling, Colette, 15–17

326

Dreifus, Claudia, 76
Drinkwater, Barbara, 119
Dweck, Carol, 142–44
Dyer, Sharon L., 157, 159

Economic dependence, 248–50
Education, 219–43
  in elementary schools, 221–23
    expectations for achievement in,
      142–44
  environment for, 228
  in high schools, 223
  higher
    absence of female role models in,
      232–35
    sexually segregated, 235–26
  sexual division of labor in, 229–32
  textbooks and, 223–25
  vocational choice and, 225–27
Education Amendment Act (1972), 117
Eisenhower, Dwight D., 305
Elementary schools, 221–23
  expectations for achievement in,
    142–44
  textbooks used in, 224–25
"Empty nest" syndrome, 69
Engrossment, 39–41
Environment
  educational, 228
  of young children, 102–4
Erikson, Erik, 121, 179, 245
Executives, women
  family backgrounds of, 270
  fathers of, 62–63
  self-evaluation of, 141
  sports and, 120

Fagot, Beverly, 101–2, 126, 135, 136
Fantasies, adolescent, 181
Father Power (Meredith and Biller), 31
Fathers, 28–69
  of adolescents, 167–68
    sexuality and, 199
  attachment of infants to, 36–38

encouragement of caretaking by, 41–43
identification of daughters with, 56–64
impact of newborns on, 39–41
nurturing behavior of
  cultural variations in, 33–35
  primate studies of, 30–33
plasticity of role of, 35
preference for male babies of, 46–48
roles adopted by, 50–56
  Big Daddy, 52–54
  Invisible Man, 56
  Patriarch, 55–56
  Pygmalion, 54–55
  White Knight, 50–52
sex-role stereotyping by, 45
of successful women, 270
teaching of sex-role differentiation by,
  49–50
Fear of success, 157–60
Fein, Robert, 41–43, 48
Feminine Mystique, The (Friedan), 80,
  166
Femininity, old definitions of, 18
Feminist Press, 224
Ford, Susan, 52
Foreign-born women, career success
  among, 269
Forever (Blume), 193, 197
Fox, Robin, 30
Frank, Anne, 161, 165
Freestyle (television series), 160
French, Marilyn, 173, 181
Freud, Sigmund, 26
Friday, Nancy, 78, 89
Friedan, Betty, 80, 166
Friedenberg, Edgar Z., 179, 227
Friendships, adolescent, 169–70
Frigidity, 206–7
Fuller, Margaret, 62
Fuller, Timothy, 62

Galbraith, John Kenneth, 257–58
Games, sex-differences in, 97–108
Gender identity, 115–16
Gilder, George, 306
Girls Who Became Famous (Bolton), 62

Glamour (magazine), 180
Goat, the Wolf and the Crab, The
    (Martin), 209
Goodman, Ellen, 112
Goodman, Katie, 112
Gordon, Linda, 276
Gove, Walter R., 252–53
Graduate school, achievement in, 140
Greenberg, Martin, 39–41
Gross, Neal, 231
Guidance counselors, vocational choice
    and, 225–27
Gutman, David, 30
Guttentag, Marcia, 260

Hardwick, Elizabeth, 187
Harrison, Barbara Grizzuti, 50, 53, 64,
    238
Hartley, Ruth, 73, 85, 92
Harvard Project on Human Sexuality,
    198–99
Heilbrun, Carolyn, 209
Helplessness, learned, 253
Helson, Ravenna, 272
Hennig, Margaret, 62–63, 74, 120, 270
Herald Tribune, 274
Herzog, A. Regula, 171
Heverby, Susan, 276
Higgins, Maggie, 274
High schools, 223
    vocational counseling in, 225, 227
Higher education, 218–20
    absence of female role models in,
        232–35
    expectations for achievement in, 140
    sexual segregation in, 235–36
Hochschild, Arlie Russell, 233
Hoffman, Lois, 85, 87, 89, 133, 135–37,
    148
Holbrook, Dr., 219
Hormones, 113–14
Horner, Matina, 155–57
Hosmer, Harriet, 62
Houseknecht, Sharon K., 292

Housewives, *see* Traditional role
How to Father (Dodson), 44
Howar, Barbara, 55–56, 77
Howard, Jane, 77
Howe, Florence, 232
Howe, Louise Kapp, 251, 277, 278, 281
Hughes, Ted, 187
Hyde, Janet S., 112–13

Ibsen, Henrik, 25
Identification
    with authority, 163–64
    with father, 56–64
    with mother, 74–81
Identity
    in adolescence, 179–87
    traditional role and, 245
Ilfeld, Frederick W., 268, 280
Immigrant women, competence of, 269
Imperial Animal, The (Tiger and Fox), 30
Independence
    in adolescence, 162–65
    sexuality and, 194–95
    encouragement of, 132–37
India, superstitions about menstruation
    in, 174
Industrial Reolution, 247, 249, 276
Infants
    day-care for, 83–84
    fathering behavior toward, 30–42
        attachment, 36–38
        cross-cultural studies, 33–35
        encouragement of, 41–42
        engrossment, 39–41
        primate studies, 30–33
    sex differences in socialization of, 102
    sex-role stereotyping of, 45
Institutionalized children, studies of, 82
Intellectual growth, myths about, 219–20
Intercollegiate sports, 114
International Association of Machinists,
    278
Invisible Man style of fathering, 56

Jacklin, Carol Nagy, 98–101, 113–14

Janeway, Elizabeth, 29–30, 50, 155, 277
Jardim, Anne, 120
Johnson, Samuel, 70
Juvenile delinquency, 84–85

Kagan, Jerome, 71–74
Kaplan, Alexandra, 126
Karle, Isabelle, 269
Kempton, Sally, 54–55
Kennedy, Joseph P., 54, 168
Kenya
   market women in, 25
   social change in, 249
Kinney, Deborah, 116–17
Kohlberg, Lawrence, 72, 106–7
Konner, Melvin J., 33–35, 57
Korean war, 21, 274
Kotelchuck, Milton, 37–38
Kreps, Juanita, 141

Ladies Home Journal, 180
Lamb, Michael, 36–37, 49
Lash, Joseph, 52
Laughing All the Way (Howar), 55
Learned helplessness, 253
Lemkin, Judith, 71–73
Leonard, Marjorie R., 57
Lerner, Harriet, 204, 207
Lessing, Doris, 209
Lever, Janet, 97, 104–8, 129, 197
Levinson, Daniel, 153, 246
Lewis, Edwin C., 272
Life cycle, theories based on, 245–47
Lightfoot, Sara, 229
Lipman-Blumen, Jean, 154
Little League, 114–16, 130, 145–46
Little Women (Alcott), 206
Logistics in dual-career marriages, 302–3
Lopata, Helena Z., 246–47, 251,
     256–57, 260
Lozoff, Marjorie, 57–58
Luria, Zella, 45

MacArthur, Douglas, 188

McClelland, David, 22
Maccoby, Eleanor Emmons, 98–101,
   113–14
MacLaine, Shirley, 70, 75–76
Mademoiselle (magazine), 186
Magarick, R., 292
Mailer, Norman, 201
Man and Superman (Shaw), 285
Managerial Woman, The (Hennig and
   Jardim), 120
Man's World, Woman's Place (Janeway),
   29
Marilyn (Mailer), 201
Marriage
   dual-career, 293–309
     child rearing in, 301–2
     logistics of, 302–3
   See also Traditional role
Marriage Readiness course, 286–87
Marshall, John, 119
Martin, Gillian, 209
Masturbation, 200
Maternal Care and Mental Health
   (Bowlby), 38
"Maternal deprivation," 20, 35
   working mothers and, 81–83
Maynard, Joyce, 193
Mead, George Herbert, 104
Mead, Margaret, 83, 270
Meislin, Richard, 297
Melanesians, 33
Memoirs of a Dutiful Daughter
   (Beauvoir), 161, 175
Memoirs of an Ex-Prom Queen
   (Shulman), 181
Menstruation, 174–78
   sports and, 119
Menstruation and Menopause
   (Weideger), 174
Mental health
   of childless women, 290–92
   of housewives, 252–54
   of single women, 287–88
   of working women, 271–72, 279–84
Meredith, Dennis, 31

Miller, Jean Baker, 192, 202–3, 205, 210–13
Mink, Patsy, 176
Minnelli, Liza, 56
Minnelli, Vincente, 56
Mitchell, Maria, 62
Mitchell, Rosemarie, 260–61
Money, John, 115
Monogamy, fathering behavior and, 33
Monroe, Marilyn, 54, 201
Moral development
in adolescence, 163–64
games and, 104, 106–7
Morgan, Marabel, 204
Moss, Howard, 102
Mothers, 70–96
of adolescents, 165–67
sexuality and, 199
children's perceptions of, 71–74
dependence encouraged by, 133–37
expression of anger by, 212
identification with, 74–81
overinvestment by, 77
of successful women, 270–71
working, 16, 81–89
changing image of, 298
day-care and, 83–84
divorced, 262–65
juvenile delinquency and, 84–85
"maternal deprivation" and, 81–83
role strain among, 280–82
social myths about, 20
See also Traditional role
Ms. magazine, 182–83
Munich, Adrienne, 234, 235
My Mother My Self (Friday), 78
"Myth of the Working Mother, The" (Wallston and Citron), 83

Naegele, Kaspar D., 60
National Education Association, 229
National Organization for Women (NOW), 223, 251

New York Times-CBS poll, 297–98
Newborns, see Infants
Nightingale, Florence, 62
Nissen, Beth, 278
Norris, Norman, 39–41
Norton, Arthur, 289

Oberlin College, 219
O'Reilly, Jane, 208
Osgood, Charles, 71
Ourselves and Our Children (Boston Women's Health Book Collective), 214
Overinvestment, maternal, 77
adolescents and, 166–67

Parr, Carol, 117
Parsons, Jacquelynne, 142, 144
Parsons, Talcott, 49, 121, 293–94, 298
Patriarch, father as, 55–56
Patriarchal cultures, fathering behavior in, 33, 34
Pearlin, Leonard, 260
Peer culture, adolescent, 168–69
pressure of, 195
Physical education classes, 117–18
Piaget, Jean, 104, 106, 152
Pink Collar Worker (Howe), 251, 281
Plasticity, 21–23
of fathering, 34, 35
in primates, 31
Plath, Sylvia, 152, 161, 185–87
Play, sex differences in, 97–108
Polygamy, fathering behavior and, 34
Power
division of, 50
in love relationships, 202–3
Pregnancy, 200
Primate studies, 30–33
Protective fathers, 52–54
Provenzano, Frank J., 45

Psychoanalysis, 25
  theory of identification in, 74
Psychological sex differences, 98–100
Psychology of Sex Differences, The
    (Maccoby and Jacklin), 98
Psychology of Women (Bardwick), 290
Puberty, 173–78
Pygmalion style of fathering, 54–55

Quality of American Life, The
    (Campbell, Converse and
    Rogers), 255, 260, 265, 287–88

Ravitch, Diane, 243
Recollections of a Rotten Kid (Dim), 76
Redican, William, 28, 31, 32
Reinventing Womanhood (Heilbrun), 209
Rheingold, Harriet L., 102, 103
Rich, Adrienne, 233, 235
Riesman, David, 108
Rivers, Helen, 90–92
Roberts, Elizabeth, 198
Rodgers, W. L., 288
Role innovators, 271
Roosevelt, Eleanor, 44, 51, 52
Roosevelt, Elliott, 51, 52
Roosevelt, Franklin, 155
Rosenberg, Benjamin G., 112–13
Rosenberg, Charles, 218
Rousseau, Jean Jacques, 218, 219
Rubin, Jeffrey, 45
Rubin, Lillian, 206, 207, 226–27, 254
Ruble, Diane, 177–78
Rwala Bedouin, 33

Sandler, Howard M., 294
Sarah Lawrence study, 272
Schmuck, Patricia, 230–31
Schools, *see* Education
Schwaber, Paul, 235

Science, 21
Segrè, Jessica, 282–84
Self-sacrifice, 255–59
Serbin, Lisa, 103, 221–22, 239
"Sex Differences in the Games Children
    Play" (Lever), 97
Sex education, 216
"Sexual Revolution," 196
Sexual Suicide (Gilder), 306
Sexuality, 193–217
  adolescent, 193–201
  conflict and, 201–13
    frigidity, 206–7
    inability to make demands, 208–13
    power relationships, 202–3
Shaw, George Bernard, 285, 286
Shelley, Percy Bysshe, 285
Shulman, Alix, 110, 183–84
Single Blessedness (Adams), 287
Single parents, 262–65
Single women, *see* Unmarried women
Skolnick, Arlene, 289
Smeal, Ellic, 251
Smoth-Rosenberg, Carroll, 218
Social class differences
  in role strain, 281
  in vocational choice, 225–27
Social myths, 18–20
Socialization, 16
  for competence, 17–19
  sex differences in, 100–4
Solomons, Cyril, 118
Solomons, Helen Harris, 117–18, 120,
    131
Some Like It Hot (film), 201
Speizer, Jeanne Jacobs, 214, 215
Spohn, Herbert, 272
Sports, 109–31
  fathers' encouragement of interest in,
    64
  gender identity and, 115–16
  hormones and, 113–14
  integrated, 117–18
  menstruation and, 119
  tomboys and, 109–112

Springfield College, 116
Stewart Abigail, 281–82
Success, fear of, 157–60
Suci, George, 71

Tangri, Sandra Schwartz, 271
Tannenbaum, Percy, 71
Teaching as female profession, 229
Teicholz, Judith Goss, 291–92
Terman, Lewis, 279
Texas Instrument Company, 278
Textbooks, 223–25
Thomas, M. Carey, 218, 220
Thonga tribe, 33–34
Tidball, Elizabeth, 236
Tiger, Lionel, 30
Time magazine, 114, 116
Tomboys, 109–12
Torg, Joseph S., 118
Total Woman movement, 204–5
Towards a New Psychology of Women
        (Miller), 192, 202
Toys, 103
Traditional role, 244–67
    adult development theories and,
        245–47
    devaluation of, 251–52
    divorce and, 262–65
    economic survival and, 248–50
    mental health and, 252–54
    in middle age, 261–62
    satisfaction in, 254–55
    self-sacrifice in, 255–59
Trask, A. E., 231
Trivers, Robert L., 30
Tudor, Jeannette F., 252–53
Twain, Mark, 165
Two-career couples, 293–309
Tyack, David, 219, 227, 228, 230

Underachievement, 154
Unionization, 278
United Auto Workers, 278
U.S. Children's Bureau, 20
U.S. Department of Health, Education
        and Welfare (HEW), 83–84,
        117, 213, 275–76
U.S. Department of Labor, 242, 251
U.S. Office of Education, 233
University of Georgia, 117
Unlearning the Lie: Sexism in Schools
        (Harrison), 238
Unmarried women, 285–90
Urbanization, 249

Vanishing Adolescent, The (Friedenberg),
        179, 227
Vassar, study of graduates of, 272
Vicarious achievement, 154–55
Violence, suppression of conflict and,
        210–11
Vocational choices, 154
    education and, 225–27

Walker, Lynn Simonsen, 294
Wallston, Barbara Strudler, 83, 294
Weideger, Paula, 174–76, 178
Weisstein, Naomi, 25–26
West, Mary Maxwell, 33–35, 57
What Really Happened to the Class of
        '65? (Medved and Wal-
        lechinsky), 183
White Knight style of fathering, 50–52
Whiting, Beatrice, 249
Who's Who of American Women, 236
Widowhood, 16
Will, George, 225–26
Wilmore, Jack H., 119
Woman's Fate (Dreifus), 76
Women of Crisis (Coles and Coles), 240
Women and the Power to Change
        (Carnegie Commission), 232,
        233
Women's Equity Action League, 117
Women's Room, The (French), 173, 181
WomenSports (magazine), 111
Woolf, Virginia, 209
Work, adolescent views on, 171–72

332

Working women, 16, 268–84
  jobs available to, 275–78
  mental health of, 271–72, 279–84
  single, 288–90
  successful, 268–70
  See also Mothers, working

Worlds of Pain (Rubin), 206
Wright, James, 283
Wylie, Philip, 21

Zilbach, Joan, 115